Praise for *Reasonable People*

"*Reasonable People* is the story of a passionate family and their journey with and of their adoptive son DJ as he dances with the shadows of post-traumatic stress disorder whilst trying to tame the wildness of mind and emotion which won't listen fluently to each other and the blessing and curse of a dramatically divided identity.

Struggling to develop comprehensible interpretive language until late childhood, and often simultaneously being emotionally and behaviorally 'feral,' I can deeply relate to DJ's struggles. As someone for whom typing gave me my own first look at an intelligent, deep, and caring person which testing and observation hadn't found, I stand by and stand up for the celebration of typing which allowed DJ to channel his own functionally nonverbal chaos into a ray of hope that is typed language. Here, he could demonstrate a wholeness of self, a passionate and compassionate self and artistic self, which could progressively allow him to work through the labyrinth of divided identity, deal with his abusive and traumatic past, his transition into adoption, and the foreignness of a caring and committed family and beyond to the goal of an empowered and empowering life as a young adult.

Ralph Savarese's book is only one story of trauma, adoption, and of autism, each of which will have many faces, many manifestations. But it is an important one as a contribution to the diversity of literature on the combination of these three and maintains an open-minded, humanistic, and holistic view throughout. DJ's final chapter is a wonderful contribution to the growing genre of works by those with autism whose typing is as valid and equal a form of communication as signing is to many in the deaf community."

—Donna Williams, Dip Ed, BA Hons,
Autistic author of nine books including
Nobody Nowhere and *Somebody Somewhere*

Turn page for more praise for *Reasonable People*

"This is the crucial book, a gem of clarity and hope for anyone who wishes to understand the experience of subjectivity in autism. As the father writes about his son's traumatic history in this very book, his son is listening. We are shown how an entry into language, which finally gives DJ his own story, also imposes traumatic memories, nightmares, and anguished fears. Mr. Savarese shows us the place where language itself is traumatizing, breaking into the logic of the body's responses and imposing another, intergenerational logic. As DJ learns a world of words through his mother's steely dedication to provide him an education, he tunes into his father's signifiers, emerging from his isolation in a way that most would predict would be impossible."

—Annie Rogers, Ph.D., author of
The Unsayable: The Hidden Language of Conflict

"Engaging...enriches our understanding of autism . . . *Reasonable People* may do for autism what Michael Bèrubè's *Life As We Know It* did for Down syndrome. Together these parental memoirs encourage the inclusion in public schools and public life of children who were once thought not to belong there. The value of such books is immeasurable, and to write a good one requires a combination of narrative and descriptive skill, good judgment, compassion, and ruthless self-analysis. *Reasonable People* has all the necessary features. It is a remarkable achievement."

—G. Thomas Couser, author of
*Recovering Bodies: Illness, Disability,
and Life Writing*

"In this comprehensive, charming book about the author's adopted autistic child, DJ, Savarese covers a wide swath of literary, sociocultural, educational, and psychological influences on the rearing of a challenging, often unruly, mute young child. . . . An inspiring, informative read."

—Karen Zelan, Ph.D., author of
*Between Their World and Ours:
Breakthroughs with Autistic Children*

REASONABLE PEOPLE

a MEMOIR *of*
AUTISM & ADOPTION

Ralph James Savarese

*On the Meaning of Family and
the Politics of Neurological Difference*

Other Press • New York

Permission to reprint excerpts from the following is gratefully acknowledged:
—"Altruism," from *Cornucopia: New and Selected Poems* by Molly Peacock. Copyright ©
2002 by Molly Peacock. Used by permission of W.W. Norton & Company, Inc.
—"Easter Sunday," copyright © 1987 from *Bertolt Brecht: Poems 1913–1956* by Bertolt
Brecht, edited by John Willet and Ralph Manheim. Reproduced by permission of
Routledge/Taylor & Francis Group, LLC.
—"Moving," from *The Complete Poems* by Randall Jarrell. Copyright © 1969, renewed
1997 by Mary von S. Jarrell. Reprinted by permission of Farrar, Straus and Giroux, LLC.
—*Oh, The Places You'll Go!* by Dr. Seuss, copyright TM & copyright © by Dr. Seuss
Enterprises L.P. 1990. Used by permission of Random House Children's Books, a divi-
sion of Random House, Inc.

Production Editor: Robert D. Hack
Text designer: Jeremy Diamond
This book was set in Janson Text by Alpha Graphics of Pittsfield, New Hampshire.

10 9 8 7 6 5 4 3 2 1

Library of Congress Cataloging-in-Publication Data

Savarese, Ralph James.
    Reasonable people : a memoir of autism and adoption / by Ralph James Savarese.
    p. cm.
  ISBN-13: 978-1-59051-129-9
  ISBN-10: 1-59051-129-8
  1. Autistic children–Biography. 2. Parents of autistic children–Biography.
  3. Autistic children–Care. 4. Special needs adoption–United States–Case studies.
  5. Adopted children–United States–Biography. 6. Adoptive parents–United
  States–Biography. I. Title.
  RJ506.A9S38 2007
  616.85'8820092–dc22
  [B]
                                                        2006018901

With DJ and Emily by my side
(and often at the keys),
for all of the many people who helped
us to make this difference.

What should I care about what matters only to me?
—ANDRÉ MALRAUX, *Anti-Memoirs*

———————

Perhaps those of us fascinated by the autistic phenomenon
get carried away by our prized conjectures.
—KAREN ZELAN, *Between Their World and Ours*

———————

"i eant [want] you bto be poriudf [proud] of me
iu dfeam offv [of] that becasuse in the fdtercare [fostercare]
i had no one"
—DJ SAVARESE

CONTENTS

CONTENTS

Some Get Eaten

In July of 2004, the physicist Stephen Hawking officially conceded a bet to his Cal-Tech colleague John Preskill. For thirty years, Hawking had been arguing that particles emitted from black holes reveal nothing about the goings on inside of these paradoxical entities or how they occur in the first place. "Information swallowed by a black hole is forever hidden and can never be revealed," Hawking had stated. But now the physicist, who has Lou Gehrig's disease, said that the particles do reveal something. As the headline from the Technology and Science page of the MSNBC Web site put it, "Hawking changes his mind on black holes: Galactic traps may actually allow information to escape." At the 17th International Conference on General Relativity and Gravitation in Dublin, Ireland, Hawking presented Preskill with a book: *Total Baseball, The Ultimate Baseball Encyclopedia*. In doing so, the world's most famous physicist mocked his own theory with an object from which, in the words of one reporter, "information is easily retrieved."

Why preface a memoir of autism and adoption with a debate about black holes and an anecdote about a scientist's good-natured retraction? A scientist, no less, who communicates with a computer by moving his eyes and who might otherwise be mistaken for mindless? To many experts, the nonspeaking Autist resembles the old version of a black hole: swallowing everything, emitting nothing; forever hidden, never to be revealed. The anecdote about Hawking thus suggests, with special significance, the need for a similar retraction in the field of cognitive disability. Either the experts have "classical" autism all wrong, or there's some subset of those labeled "classically" (i.e., severely) autistic that differs from the majority. With the emergence of thinking, feeling, and communicating Autists such as Tito Mukhopadhyay, Sue Rubin, Lucy Blackman, Larry Bissonnette, Sharisa Kochmeister, Alberto Frugone, Richard Attfield, Jamie Burke, and many others (including my son DJ), the current paradigm has begun to falter.

Yet still, the experts cling to accepted notions. In *The Structure of Scientific Revolutions*, Thomas Kuhn reminds us of

> what scientists never do when confronted by even severe and prolonged anomalies. Though they may begin to lose faith and then to consider alternatives, they do not renounce the paradigm that has led them into crisis. They do not, that is, treat anomalies as counter-instances, though in the vocabulary of science that is what they are.

Subjecting science's vaunted objectivity to the pressure of a professional narrative, Kuhn exposes the complicated status of received wisdom. He understands scientific revolution as the gradual, if tumultuous, achievement of a discipline disinclined to overturn what it knows.

In the case of autism, the reigning view speaks relentlessly and narrowly of deficits, and it loves to generalize, catching "all autistic individuals" in its bottom trawling nets. Oliver Sacks offers a summary of this view in his famous profile of Temple Grandin, "An Anthropologist on Mars." It is a view that has more or less prevailed since the 1970s. Sacks writes,

> It was not until the 1970s that Beate Hermelin and Neil O'Connor and their colleagues in London, trained in the new discipline of cognitive psychology, focused on the

mental structure of autism in a more systematic way. Their work (and that of Lorna Wing, in particular) suggests that in all autistic individuals there is a core problem, a consistent triad of impairments: impairment of social interaction with others, impairment of verbal and nonverbal communication, and impairment of play and imaginative activities. The appearance of these three together, they feel, is not fortuitous; all are expressive of a single, fundamental developmental disturbance. Autistic people, they suggest, have no true concept of, or feeling for, other minds, or even their own; they have, in the jargon of cognitive psychology, no "theory of mind."

The American Psychiatric Association's current definition of autism in the *DSM-IV* lists "qualitative impairment in social interaction," "qualitative impairments in communication," and "restricted, repetitive and stereotyped patterns of behavior, interests, and activities" as symptoms of autism, and it isn't difficult to see how this definition derives from the portrait that Wing and others have sketched—over and over, I might add, as if themselves autistic. In short, the reigning view posits a devastating global disorder that robs people with autism of their very humanity. Moreover, it offers little hope of treatment but for modest behavior modification. No wonder parents of autistic children panic when receiving a diagnosis.

Complicating this basic understanding of autism has been the idea of a spectrum. On one end, there is "classical autism"; on the other, Asperger's syndrome. The former, Sacks tells us, "summon[s] up a picture of a profoundly disabled child, with stereotyped movements, perhaps head-banging; rudimentary language; almost inaccessible: a creature for whom very little future lies in store." The latter allows for children who "may go on to develop fair language, a modicum of social skills, and even high intellectual achievements; they may develop into autonomous human beings, capable of a life that may appear full and normal—even though, beneath it, there may remain a persistent, and even profound, autistic singularity." The ultimate difference is that

people with Asperger's syndrome can tell us of their experiences, their inner feelings and states, whereas those with
classical autism cannot. With classical autism, there is no
window, and we can only infer. With Asperger's syndrome
there is self-consciousness and at least some power to in-
trospect and report.

This book stands in direct opposition to the begrudging appreciation of autistic accomplishment and, even more important, to the notion of "classical autism" as not affording "a window" on an Autist's
interior. Indeed, it demonstrates just how dynamic and human that interior can be, and it demands that we rethink the "creature for whom
very little future lies in store."

Still in its infancy, the new view of autism begins by acknowledging
anomalies, and then it tries to account for them. In accounting for them,
it "elicit[s the] perspectives of people classified as autistic," and it "place[s]
the perspectives of labeled people in the foreground." As James Charlton,
an historian of the global disability rights movement, would say, "Nothing about us without us." These so-called anomalies indicate something
very different from the devastating global disorder of the self that the
proponents of the "theory of mind" hypothesis advance. I'm thinking,
for instance, of Tito Mukhopadhyay, who has appeared on "Sixty Minutes" and authored a stunning book of poetry and reflection called *The
Mind Tree*. And I'm thinking of Sue Rubin, who wrote the screenplay
for, and starred in, the 2004 Academy Award finalist for short documentaries, *Autism Is A World*. The cases of Tito and Sue are especially in-
structive, and so I take the time to talk about them here.

How to convey the affront to expectation that these two people with
"classical" autism represent? Crudely put, both *look* about as disabled as
they could. And yet, like Hawking, Mukhopadhyay and Rubin demonstrate the lack of a correlation between physical appearance and cognitive competence. (Hawking's mind moves even if his body doesn't;
Rubin's and Mukhopadhyay's words sing even if their arms flap or they
perseverate.) Further, they demonstrate the lack of a correlation between
speech and intelligence. Just as it would be inaccurate to bandy about

the phrase "deaf and dumb" with respect to the hearing impaired, so it would be inaccurate to bandy about the phrase "profoundly retarded" with respect to these two (and other) "classical" Autists.

One of the theories that has emerged to account for the conflict between appearance and ability centers around a notion of dyspraxia: "difficulty in initiating and carrying out voluntary actions that cannot be explained by an obvious physical disability such as cerebral palsy." As a movement and/or activation disorder, "classical" autism would thus allow for the possibility of an intact mind trapped inside of an uncooperative body, a mind that through cumulative isolation and the absence of reciprocal sociality would seem to confirm the idea of innate social and emotional impairment just as the absence of communication might seem to confirm an innate lack of intelligence. Listen to what Sue Rubin has to say about the problem of response: "When someone asks me to do something, sometimes I can and other times I can't. I understand the request but I can't follow it. I absolutely will eventually be able to do it, but no one waits long enough." Referring to her automatic movements and limited, echolalic speech, Rubin adds, "I certainly understand why I was assumed to be retarded. All my very awkward movements and all my nonsense sounds made me appear retarded."

Or consider what Tito has to say about his body challenges—in particular, the act of drawing. (Tito mischievously renders his autobiography in the third person, as if to underscore his capacity for self-reflection—over and against the experts' understanding of "classical" autism.) Tito writes, "Mother had to hold his hands and make him draw the figures, as the boy was slowly beginning to understand 'how' to do it. I repeat 'how' to do it and not what to do. My readers must not have the impression that he did not know what to do, but it was 'how' to do. In fact, every problem that he faced was due to this 'how.'" In a chapter called "Obeying Self Commands," Tito is even more explicit about his body challenges:

> Sometimes I felt that my body was made of just my head while sometimes I felt that it was made of just my legs. It was very difficult to feel the complete body when I was not

doing anything. Sometimes I had to knock my head or slap it to feel it. Of course from my knowledge of biology I knew that I had voluntary muscles and involuntary muscles. I also knew that my hands and legs were made of voluntary muscles. But I experimented with myself that when I ordered my hand to pick up a pencil I could not do it. I remember long back when I had ordered my lips to move I could not do it.

For all of Tito's difficulties with voluntary movements, involuntary movements come too easily and, as with Rubin, constitute a source of embarrassment. Only through laborious training and practice have Sue and Tito managed to master activities like drawing, writing, and typing.

At the heart of the new view of autism lies a commitment to hope and a respect for the person with this condition. By "hope" I do not mean a cure, but, rather, a practice of full inclusion that might lead to enhanced participation and communication. I mean an ethic of humane discovery, not dire presumption and prognostication. I mean, finally, an appreciation of diversity in all of it forms, including what Sacks, in one of his better moments, calls the "brain's remarkable plasticity, its capacity for the most striking adaptations" or, more simply, the "creative potential" of disease.

Recently, in the *New York Times*, after a long series of articles bemoaning autism, an article appeared that reflects the kind of perspective I'm advocating. Entitled "How About Not Curing Us, Some Autistics Are Pleading," the article spoke of a "growing number of autistics [who] are staging what they say amounts to an ad hoc human rights movement. They sell Autistic Liberation Front buttons and circulate petitions on Web sites like neurodiversity.com to 'defend the dignity of autistic citizens.'" It mentioned Joe Mele, 36, "who staged a protest at Jones Beach, on Long Island, while 10,000 people marched to raise money for autism research recently." "'We need acceptance about who we are and the way we are . . . That means you have to get out of the cure mindset,'" Mele said. No matter how hyperbolic it might seem—and to the parents of some children with autism it seems outrageous—this perspective allows the Autist to feel good about him- or herself. When parents objected to the disease-as-identity framework, claiming that people with the most severe form of autism can't afford such a precious politics,

> the three owners of autistics.org, a major Web hub of autistic advocacy, issued a statement listing their various impairments. None of them are fully toilet-trained, one of them cannot spcak, and they all have injured themselves on multiple occasions. They wrote, "We flap, finger-flick, rock, twist, rub, clap, bounce, squeal, hum, scream, hiss and tic."

The Canadian writer and blogger Estee Klar-Wolfond, founder of the Autism Acceptance Project, even speaks of the "joy of autism," and her Web site begins with this lyrical mantra: "Because finding joy doesn't come without struggle; because the point is to find it; because if an autistic person calls autism a way of being, not an illness, then it is; because every human has value and is a joy; because despite inhumane acts, I believe in humanity; but most of all, because of my son Adam." Shocking this celebration of dis-ability and staunch refusal to apologize for autistic "behaviors" (the very thing that a major form of therapy seeks to eradicate). Now, though you might not want your child to be diagnosed with autism and though you might work assiduously to ameliorate its impact, you'd certainly want, if faced with a diagnosis, for your child to feel good about himself. As the father of an Autist, I can tell you that feeling good about oneself is a big problem for people with autism. What do you say to an eleven-year-old who so understands the world's intolerance of difference that he starts announcing on his computer at night, "freak is ready for bed"? Like other people with disabilities, some with autism have found that identity politics offer a vehicle for fighting discrimination *and* improving self-esteem. It locates the problem with difference where it should be: outside of the self, in a world of ignorance and fear.

And yet, for all of the recent progress in how we conceive of autism, a dire medicalized view continues to prevail. Even when a particular individual manages to triumph over a diagnosis of mental retardation, there's always some expert ready to discount him or her—if only by calling the individual an exception, not someone from whom we might learn something revolutionary. Here's Lorna Wing in the foreword to Tito's book *The Mind Tree* (subtitled *A Miraculous Child Breaks the Silence of Autism*):

> It is important to emphasize that Tito showed, very early on, clear signs of good cognitive ability through his recognition of and ability to match numbers, letters and shapes. This encouraged his mother to work with him, using her truly remarkable intelligence, ingenuity and dedication, with the results we have seen. Children who do not exhibit any signs of good cognitive ability are very unlikely indeed to develop skills through any method of teaching, including facilitated communication. The fact that Tito began to write for himself at the age of six is corroboration of the fact that the ideas he expresses are his own.

As my wife, Emily, an inclusion expert, has put it, "What, exactly, is Wing trying to achieve with this statement and what good does it do anyone to listen to it? What might hope endanger?" The answer to this final question: Wing's very paradigm, her professional expertise. Of "counter-instances" Kuhn writes, "By themselves they cannot and will not falsify . . . [a] philosophical theory, for its defenders will do what we have already seen scientists doing when confronted by anomaly. They will devise numerous articulations and *ad hoc* modifications of their theory in order to eliminate any apparent conflict." At the age of six, when my son came to live with us, he was still in diapers and showed few if any signs of cognitive ability. But why should the prior demonstration of ability constitute the prerequisite for effort and training? Does an infant exhibit the skill, say, to write a poem? It is only our faith that she might one day be capable of doing so, our faith and our effort, hour after hour after hour, that make it happen. In sum, why not discover the limits of hope, if hope has limits, rather than predicting them pessimistically.

If you think I'm being too hard on Wing, consider the conclusion to her foreword, where she tries to preserve a central component of her theory-of-mind hypothesis: the self-absorption of people with autism:

> Tito's writings are characteristic of someone with an autistic disorder in that they basically revolve around himself and his personal experiences. When one considers the physical and psychological disabilities he has to overcome, this self-absorption is perhaps not so surprising. Despite this, his writing provides a vivid description of what it is like to be autistic and his thoughts about the meaning of life. . . . Individuals with autistic disorders are endlessly fascinating. Those like Tito, with remarkable skills in contrast to their general level of disability, arouse feelings of wonder, astonishment and intellectual curiosity, which are among the many rewards experienced by those working in this field.

Self-absorption? Wing is speaking about the genre of autobiography, after all! By this reasoning, any life-writer would be autistic, really any American. Moreover, it is Wing who comes across as self-absorbed. Observe how quickly she turns her attention to herself and her profession. She's more interested in a freak-show mentality—all of that "wonder, astonishment and . . . curiosity"—than in what Tito actually has to say, what he teaches us. Perhaps "autistic" ought be reserved as a modifier for narrow-minded scientists, if not for any neurotypical person empathetically challenged. Indeed, in the book I suggest that most Americans have "no true concept of, or feeling for, other minds," and might, thus, themselves be labeled "autistic." As DJ reminds us, this great country abandons the poor and disabled alike.

Even Sacks, who has been deeply influenced by Wing's work, understands that something is changing. On the back of Tito's book he proclaims, "The book is indeed amazing, shocking too, for it has usually been assumed that deeply autistic people are scarcely capable of introspection or deep thought, let alone of poetic or metaphoric leaps of imagination—or if they are, that they are incapable of communicating these thoughts to us. Tito gives the lie to all these assumptions, and forces us to reconsider the condition of the deeply autistic." Of course, eight years earlier in *An Anthropologist on Mars* Sacks wrote, "When I first read [Temple Grandin's] book, I could not help being suspicious of it: the autistic mind, it was supposed at the time, was incapable of self-understanding and understanding others and therefore of authentic introspection and retrospection. How *could* an autistic person write an autobiography?" The similarity of these two responses suggests how entrenched the theory-of-mind hypothesis is; though the Tito blurb indicates a desire to move beyond the present understanding, it almost seems stuck in the syntax of surprise. Along with Amanda Baggs, a critic of the marketing of Tito's "miraculous" book, we might ask, "How many times must the experts be forced to reconsider before they consider?" Tito is most certainly not the first nonspeaking Autist to manifest "authentic introspection," as Baggs points out, despite the book's "miraculous" claim. Shouldn't Sacks be more aware of the many exceptions to the rule? Baggs asks, "What planet have these 'experts' been living on since 1985? Have they been studiously ignoring David Eastham? Sharisa Kochmeister? Lucy Blackman? Sue Rubin? All the others like them?"

I'd like to add my son's name to that list, eschewing claims of autistic exceptionality. I'd only propose that DJ's early life experiences—poverty, abandonment, separation from his sister, foster care, physical and sexual abuse—mark him as especially challenged. If DJ, a "classic" case of hopelessness, can achieve, how many other kids might as well? I don't know the answer to this question, except to say that more than we think—but only if we work to make this occur. Can I argue for a paradigm shift if I'm uncertain of how prevalent these "counter-instances" are? Perhaps there's just a subset of people with "classical" autism who can communicate, but let's find this out after we've adopted different assumptions and devoted ourselves to the task of developing potential. Even this more modest possibility would mean that scores of people could be leading very different lives from the ones they are presently leading. At least then, the experts would have to stop speaking of "classical" autism generally—as one "disorder" with one grim prognosis.

* * * * *

When Wing writes of the unlikelihood of any kind of intervention having a positive effect on the vast majority of those with "classical" autism, she mentions the technique of facilitated communication explicitly. That technique is the primary means by which my son and most of the Autists I've cited communicate. The subject of much controversy in the early 1990s, FC, in Rosemary Crossley's words, is "simply a way to help improve someone's ability to point." Citing problems in Autists with "finger isolation," "tremor," "radial ulnar instability" ("the wrist bends and the person veers to the left or right, depending on whether left or right handed, when pointing"), "perseveration" ("repeating the same action multiple times"), "initiation difficulty," "proximal instability" ("difficulty separating movement of limbs from the trunk"), and "proprioceptive awareness" ("awareness of location of body parts in space"), Crossley proposed providing hand, wrist, or arm support so that nonspeaking people might be able physically to communicate. When many of these people began to type sentences, thereby freeing themselves from labels of profound mental retardation, the world cried, "Hurrah!" and, then, soon after, "Hoax!"

Unfortunately, the phenomenon became entangled in the sex abuse hysteria of the same period, with children typing allegations against their parents and caregivers, and in unsympathetic authentication procedures that revealed questionable authorship. It became too easy to suspect a method that often had, at least at the outset, a facilitator's hand entwined in the Autist's, as the latter marveled people with flights of sentient fancy. In addition to genuine concerns about fraudulent communication, of which there was plenty, there were, it must be said, careers to protect, ideas of autism to be enforced. How could an Autist express himself if he had no theory of mind? He had no theory of mind; therefore, *he* couldn't be expressing himself. The end result: the phenomenon was dismissed outright.

Very quickly, scientists and education specialists refused to associate themselves with FC, for fear of having the accusation of quackery rub off on them. The technique, however, didn't disappear completely; rather, it went underground. Doug Biklen, the man who brought the technique to America from Australia, and his colleagues at Syracuse University remained outspoken—a bit like scholars under house arrest, free to do their work but not to circulate. In the last three years, I've met all sorts of people who told me that their daughter or nephew uses facilitated communication when I admitted that my wife and I use it with DJ, but it's all very hush-hush. I've even met doctors who swear by the practice but who won't recommend it to their patients. A lot is at stake in this debate, and FC's opponents have been vicious. Biklen was lampooned and sued for thirty million dollars. Recently, he was subjected to an on-line "statement of disapproval of the research and teacher education communities in special education," a statement signed by scores of professionals in the field, after Syracuse appointed him Dean of its School of Education. The statement accuses Syracuse of "selecting someone whose record constitutes an argument against rigorous science in research involving individuals with disabilities."

And yet, even as some FC users have accomplished the goal of independent typing, thereby doing away with the question of authorship altogether, the scientific community has refused to reconsider its blanket repudiation. To this day, the American Psychological Association refers to facilitated communication as an unproven technique, though now, more than ten years after the initial controversy, there exist nearly as many studies offering support for the technique as debunking it. A book called *A Passion to Believe: Autism and the Facilitated Communication Phenomenon* would have us understand FC as an example of the most desperate sort of wishful thinking. And yet, if anything, I have detected a passion to *disbelieve* in purportedly objective discussions of the technique.

In response to the recent Academy Award–nominated documentary about Sue Rubin, *Autism Is A World*, Gina Green, former president of the Association for Behavior Analysis, insisted that Sue's independent typing is a sham: "Very subtle influence can affect people's behavior. It doesn't even have to be touch. It can be the slightest sound, the slightest visual cue." Green further implied that the film, which CNN coproduced, might have been edited to facilitate the illusion. "You can edit videotape to show whatever you want. They'll show you a close-up of the finger moving across the keyboard . . . but you're not getting what else is going on," Green claimed. Playing the psychologist and cynical economist, she concluded that because FC proponents were so "invested emotionally, and even financially, in a very public way, they find it hard to back off."

Sid Bedingfield, Senior Vice-President of CNN Productions, re-sponded to the *Washington Post* article in which Green's comments ap-peared by noting that neither Green nor the reporter had bothered to interview Sue "before raising such a serious allegation." "A *Newsweek* reporter," he writes, "spent two days with Sue and came away impressed." Why *didn't* Gina Green ask to see Sue before calling her a fraud? Why doesn't she want to see her now? Why doesn't Fred Volkmar, director of autism research at Yale and primary author of the autism chapter in the *DSM-IV*, who, the *Post* article says, "personally has never seen a case of validated FC"? You'd think if he were interested in "classical" autism, he'd be banging on the door of Sue's small house, where she lives, with assistance, independently. You'd think other experts would as well. And not just Sue's door, but Tito's, Lucy's, Larry's, Sharisa's, Alberto's, Richard's, Jamie's and a host of other people's as well.

As I write this introduction, the tide is beginning to turn. A recent *People Magazine* article featured a story on Jamie Burke, who types inde-pendently and has learned how to speak while typing and/or reading something that he has typed. A fascinating development if ever there was one. A million questions come to mind. Why only something that he has *typed*? What was it about the physical act of typing that allowed him to acquire speech? Again, you'd think that the experts would be travel-ing to Syracuse, where Jamie lives, to interview this "classical" Autist. Another news source featured a story about Sean Sokler, a twenty-four year-old senior at George Mason University, who uses FC to commu-nicate. Graduating with a degree in psychology, Sokler, the article re-lates, can translate as many as ten languages: an ability that must have come in handy when battling the skeptics. All you'd need is a facilitator who doesn't speak Russian, who doesn't even know the Cyrillic alpha-bet, say, and you could test Sean's authorship. The article quotes Asso-ciate Professor of Astronomy Rita Sambruna, who says that he was "one of the best students [she] ever had."

I write of independent typing as if it were a self-evident phenomenon. It's not. Some FC users require a facilitator to stand behind them while they hunt and peck or to hold an arm a few feet above their composing hand. Some need the intermittent touch of a finger on their shoulder or leg. All began with massive amounts of facilitation at the hand, but gradually over time their facilitators withdrew support—from the hand to the wrist to the arm to the shoulder. Jamie Burke was five when he started typing; Sue, thirteen, and Larry Bissonette, nearly thirty. Biklen has made videos of various independent typists (including these three), but the videos have, until recently, received little attention. Independent typing, it must be pointed out, can take years to accomplish, and no one knows exactly why some accomplish it and others do not. No one knows why some need that regular tapping on the shoulder or leg. No one knows, for that matter, what role psychology plays in this phenomenon, especially when the Autist wants his facilitator to stand behind him—though the locution, in its idiomatic inflection, probably tells us some of what we need to know.

Undoubtedly, there *were* instances of fraudulent communication back in the early 1990s, plenty of them, as I've already stated. Some of these instances had far from innocuous consequences, and I share the concern of experts who want to be certain that the writing of FC users is legitimate, particularly when something as serious as a charge of sexual abuse emerges. I'm with Margaret Baumann, a neurologist at Harvard who appears in *Autism Is A World* and who is quoted in the *Washington Post* article as saying that FC was "oversold in the beginning" and then, like the proverbial baby, "thrown out with the bath water." But one would want to ask about even those cases of fraudulent communication: under what circumstances did the Autist fail to convince and, even more important, how long had he or she been using facilitated communication? This latter question, of course, pertains to the facilitator with equal urgency. "Rigorous science in research" is crucial, but such "rigor" must involve more than citing the infamous *Frontline* documentary and subsequent studies that discredited FC. It must account for different studies and basic, message-passing protocols that have supported it. It must account for those who now type independently or very nearly independently (finger on the shoulder, tapping on the ankle, etc.).

I want to make two points: 1) there's so much that we don't know about why FC does and doesn't work and 2) before coming to a definitive conclusion about its efficacy, people ought to give the technique a sustained try. Now that it has been proven unequivocally successful with some Autists, it could prove successful with others. If the "severity" of a given case of "classical" autism isn't a function of appearance—the "competent" and "incompetent" Autist look the same—then how can one know in advance who might profit from the technique? I'm not hawking FC as a miracle cure, nor am I overlooking the host of other therapies presently available, therapies my wife and I have utilized with DJ. I'm simply advocating the importance of giving someone a communication system, and this particular system, despite its checkered past, has rescued people otherwise discarded by the medical and educational professions.

In the book, I present a twist on the conventional FC narrative of discovered ability and, in doing so, offer additional justification for its use: modeling literacy. Indeed, I contend that the presumption of literacy skills in nonspeaking Autists may have been what got the FC movement into trouble in the 1990s. Though no doubt some Autists teach themselves how to read, most need innovative instruction. The presumption of potential competence is crucial, but I would distinguish that from the presumption of ready-made ability. While teaching DJ how to read over the course of several years, my wife Emily and I used hand-over-hand typing as but another means of accustoming him to print. The keyboard, we thought, would stabilize and standardize the letters, and the act of pointing at and typing the solutions to fill-in-the-blanks and then placing them in the appropriate spaces on worksheets would drill the desired skill sets in a meaningful way. At the beginning, we knew that DJ was neither coming up with the answers nor typing them on his own, but gradually, after much, much practice, he sprang to literate life: pointing correctly on his own and then moving his facilitators' hands. It wasn't long before he was composing sentences. The moral of this literacy tale? Exceptional measures for exceptional children.

Where is DJ on the path to independent typing? While still requiring support at the wrist for most of his communication, he can type individual words and phrases entirely on his own. I have gotten him to type sentences by facilitating at the bicep, but as you move farther from the hand, you sacrifice accuracy. Recently, at an FC conference, Rosemary

Crossley had DJ typing at the elbow without any errors at all. In his case, the issue of independence has been complicated by profound anxiety about losing us as parents should he no longer require facilitation. (He heard the phrase "typing on my own" and thought it meant a return to foster care.) Unlike a majority of FC users who have only one or two facilitators, DJ has multiple facilitators: eight, to be exact. (Altogether he has had fifteen.) This fact helps to dispel the incredulity that customarily engulfs the technique, because a group of people can vouch for its legitimacy. With only one facilitator, especially if, as is often the case, it is the Autist's parent, the user can't help but be on the defensive.

Though we didn't set out to establish competence before trying facilitated communication—we didn't think we were using FC, or at least didn't call it FC until DJ was becoming literate—that DJ did so with number and word recognition and accurate pointing only made his emergence into full-blown communication more believable. That he passed several informal message-passing protocols further testified to his abilities. The teachers and administrators at DJ's school in Grinnell have been unfailingly open-minded and supportive. We've also received support from DJ's psychiatrist, his therapists, and a host of other people in the Grinnell community. As a result, I've felt emboldened to go public with my son's story before he has achieved complete independence.

The final two-thirds of the book contains countless conversations with DJ and a final chapter composed entirely by him. Because from the beginning DJ typed on a computer (and sometimes a labeler), Emily and I have an enormous archive of nearly everything DJ has said, from his first words to his most recent. I'm talking about thousands of pages. Whatever appears in this book I've taken exactly from the archive, typos and all—with a couple of exceptions. Sometimes, DJ wrote someone a letter on the labeler, which doesn't have significant storage, and I have had to reproduce the letter from memory (without his characteristic typos and lack of punctuation). Certain school assignments were also composed on the labeler (the labeler is lighter and more compact and doesn't have to boot up), and the originals have gotten lost. With school assignments, we have increasingly pushed DJ to respect the rules of grammar, punctuation, and spelling, so you will see more polished work: the result of multiple revisions. By "revisions" I mean simply asking DJ to clarify or correct something he has written; not once has Emily or I added a word of our own. When just conversing at home, we have, as with any neurotypical child, simply let him speak—that is, type—as he will.

The archive as a whole affords a glimpse at the formation of a self in language—and an adopted self at that. Imagine having nearly every word your child has ever said. Now imagine your child has been silent for nine years and suddenly explodes into communicative exchange. Besides the enormous personal boon, the record of that explosion would reveal a look at all sorts of things, including the process by which children are socialized—especially if your child, in addition to being unable to speak, couldn't previously understand what was said to him. "As I began to type, my mind began to wake up," Sue Rubin says in *Autism Is A World*. How to describe the subjectivity of someone, in Rubin's metaphor, who has been "asleep" (in her case for thirteen years)? If, like Rubin, my son couldn't decode spoken language until he read and typed, then how much more difficult is it to conceptualize this state of silent exclusion, let alone this shock of emergence? With respect to the brain and the never-ending Broadway show we call the self, we clearly don't have all of the answers, and many of the answers we do have are wrong.

Before concluding the introduction, I wish to say a few words about the book's chosen form: memoir. Though often narcissistic, memoir allows for the evocation of lived life. The pieties I spout—about adoption, about neurological difference, about social commitment—need to be tested against the messiness of experience. The most rewarding thing I've ever done, adopting DJ has also been the most challenging and exhausting. For this book, this plea, to be credible, the reader needs to see just how challenging and exhausting it has been. The reader also needs to see that Emily and I are not saints. An idealized portrait that glosses over the agonizing difficulties of the experience or the inadequacies of my character (I'll let Emily speak for herself) would actually undermine the message, for it wouldn't be faithful to the site of conflict and imperfection where any dream of a better world must play itself out. Real life. Real setbacks. Real progress. Presenting each of us in our fullness corrects for the easy sentimentalization of hope and the grossly oppressive view of "classical" autism that has triumphed for the last thirty years. Writing a memoir also allows me the chance to try to evoke DJ's emergence into social selfhood—to re-create it in all of its remarkable intensity. I'm a writer, after all, not a scientist, though I have, as a friend once put it, "done some reading."

What of the obvious legal difficulties in publishing such a book? The book is as accurate as I could make it based on my own recollection of events as confirmed by as many records or corroborative sources as I could locate. I have removed the personal identification of certain people I write about, especially my son's birth parents, to avoid any unnecessary harm. I have omitted the city in Florida where DJ's birth mother used to live and where the first part of the book takes place. I have also omitted the city in the Northeast where my son's birth father and sister reside, a city to which we travel in the course of the story. Though my son wanted his sister's name to remain, I have changed it to protect her privacy. Additionally, I have changed the names of my son's foster parents and certain caseworkers, judges, DCF administrators, doctors, therapists, and school personnel who appear in the book. At times, one or two people go by their real names. They either refused a name change or the lawyers who vetted the manuscript believed that my remarks about these people were sufficiently flattering as not to require a change. I have not changed the names of friends and family. Disguising familial identities would have been pointless in this age of Google, and doing without an account of my own family experience would have marred the narrative of alternative family-making I seek to present.

In general, I have adopted the following rule: disguise identities whenever something unsympathetic gets said. The solution to competing legal and literary obligations, such a rule allows me to tell the story as I wish. My aim was not to injure anyone needlessly, though there is much that is unsympathetic in the book. Although I insist on the legitimacy of my opinions and social critique (what happened to my son is unforgivable), I try to foreground the *problem* of opinion, again exploiting what I take to be the paradoxical virtue of memoir as a genre: its radical subjectivity. A big part of that subjectivity is, of course, the element of feeling, which, as scientists increasingly tell us, constitutes the basis for ethical decision making (even as it just as often gives rise to insoluble conflict). Playing off the title, I would ask, are there any strictly rational or objective memoirists? Would we want to read them if there were?

My argument for greater social engagement leans heavily on Freud's notion of "feeling our way into others," and that process is always imperfect and incomplete, not to mention turbulent. Dramatizing the plight of a thoroughly situated and human narrator, I thus strive for what might be called a pragmatics of feeling. I try to be reasonable, you might say, about being subjective. And so this solution to the predicament of reporting from the scene of life: my facts are accurate, and my dialogue is as faithful as memory will allow. (I follow the age-old convention of remembered speech in literary nonfiction for everyone but DJ, whose "speech," I repeat, is taken verbatim from the archive, and for Emily and me when we, too, were using the computer to communicate.) At the same time, the identities of most of the people in the book are generously disguised.

But a key question remains. Having taken such precautions with strangers, is it reasonable to invade my son's privacy without changing his name and, thus, obviously my own and Emily's as well? I've agonized over this question, believing in the end that the story of DJ's emergence ultimately outweighs these concerns and, as well, that writing under a pseudonym would both undermine what is irrefutably factual—namely, his emergence—and inhibit the work of activism I wish this book and its author to perform, however modestly. DJ himself has said that he wants to help kids with autism, and, anyway, I gave him veto power with respect to the book's publication. He chose to let me publish it.

Moreover, as it became clear that DJ could represent himself, the form of the book changed, to the extent that it now contains a final chapter composed entirely by him, a chapter in which he takes me to task on any number of things. I'm thrilled that he challenges me, for, in the process, he takes possession of the story. *He represents himself.* There is no perfect solution to the quandary of protecting his privacy—he may well resent this book's existence when he's older—just as there is no perfect solution to the quandary of his sister discovering the book now that their visits have resumed. I certainly don't want her parents to forbid future visits, but at the same time we've reached a point in the relationship where the truth of what happened to DJ ought to come out and, indeed, where it has already begun to do so.

I celebrate the reasonable—defined in one sense as not expecting or demanding more than is possible to achieve (though that definition smacks, I think, of too much resignation). Although I do wish to be viewed as reasonable in my conception of human nature and authorial responsibility, I don't mind being viewed as unreasonable in calling for a better life for America's poor and disabled. I strive to engage the other half of the dialectic that animates our democracy: a commitment to noble ideals. Amidst the rancor and standstill of competing views on all manner of problems, the Constitution articulates a standard against which we must constantly measure ourselves. To put it simply, one can be pragmatic *while* looking up at the stars. In this way, I revere the concept of "reasonable accommodation" at the heart of the ADA (Americans with Disabilities Act) exactly as I oppose the courts' excessively restrictive readings of it. Analogously, I concede the unworkability of grand historical alternatives to capitalism exactly as I insist on more equitable economic policies.

Let me conclude this lengthy introduction with a poem. In the fall of fifth grade, DJ wrote an acrostic about prairie dogs as part of a language arts assignment. An acrostic is a form in which the poet spells something vertically by using letters from the customary horizontal words of the poem. DJ spelled the word "prairie dog" down the left-hand margin. His class had just finished a unit on prairie dogs in science, and so the assignment asked that the students make use of what they had learned. While most of the kids focused on innocuous details, DJ focused on the trapping and marking of prairie dogs and the prairie dogs' grim habit of eating each other's young. I would point out that his treatment of these details differs greatly from the textbook's, which, in the voice of a child, adopts an upbeat tone. A couple of examples: 1) "Studying prairie dogs is fun, but the part I like best is catching the babies in 'live traps' so we can mark them"; 2) "One day we caught a female that had been in another female's burrow. I noticed something strange stuck in her fur. It turned out to be the leg of a newborn prairie dog. We realized then that she had killed and eaten the other mother's babies!"

Such innocent enthusiasm acquires a sadistic edge when remobilized by DJ. All of that trapping and tracking seems a bit too much like the activities of the child welfare system. "What's the poem about?" I asked gingerly after he was through. "its personal," DJ replied. Only when I pushed him did he type, "about fotercare." And, of course, being about foster care, it's also about disability, for it was DJ's autism—or, rather, the reigning view of this "disorder"—that allowed his birth father to imagine it was perfectly acceptable to take his sister but not him when the State removed the two kids from the custody of their mother. As you read the poem and consider the brutal economy of the final line (the phrasing throughout is entirely DJ's), tell me that this Autist doesn't have a theory of mind or an impressive analogical flare or a keen understanding of contemporary social relations.

PRAIRIE DOGS

Prairie dogs live in burrows,
Race out of their holes.
A lot of people like to catch them
In cages,
Rolling the little ones in paint,
Identifying them in the wild.
Everyone is trying to catch one.

Dogs fight in springtime.
Other females in need of meat
Get their babies from others' nests.
Some get eaten.

—DJ SAVARESE

PART I

I have studied the science of saying goodbye.
—OSIP MANDELSTAM

CHAPTER 1

Severe and Profound

With great difficulty Ellie pulled DJ uphill. At six, her birth brother, whom she hadn't seen in nearly three years, understood rollerblading to be a matter exclusively of somebody else's exertion. While you labored, he'd stand with his legs a bit too close together, his chest a bit too rigidly upright, and his eyes more than a bit too captivated by whatever birds were darting overhead or leaves were rustling in the wind. Picture a bespectacled two-by-four being wheeled around a park or rink—he was that stiff, that skinny. If the person who was pulling him jerked suddenly or, worse, went down, disaster ensued and DJ would be angry, indeed extraordinarily upset, so the person pulling would have to stand guard as strenuously as he or she would have to skate.

It's not that DJ was lazy or spoiled or even demanding in any conventional sort of way. At this point in his rollerblading career, we had only managed to teach him the basic art of balance. He simply *had* to hold someone's hand if he expected to move. Of course, he seemed to *like* holding someone's hand (especially Emily's or mine or preferably both of ours at the same time), though to use the word "like" is to suggest a more familiar mode of feeling and, in particular, response to the pain of past abuse, neglect, and abandonment. DJ's emotions were all

3

there; they just seemed to be distorted by the autism, like sound, say, by water. Or, to extend the analogy in a manner that doesn't press a normative judgment, DJ was like a dolphin out of water: an exquisite listening device compelled to function in an alien medium.

He loved going fast, which meant the person pulling him would have to work that much harder, but not without compensation. DJ's smile would broaden at the prospect of significant speed, and he'd appear considerably less distracted, as if he, too, understood the greater risk of tangled arms and legs and, thus, the need to concentrate on what he was doing. The true reward, however, was what Emily would call "joint attention." DJ was having fun *with* you. His eye contact would increase, and you'd get a sense of a truly shared activity—albeit a perilous one. It would be an experience of giddy, if wordless, interaction. And yet, exactly as I speak of "joint attention," I must concede that DJ never completely jettisoned his distractedness. Even as he'd be looking at you, you could tell that he was simultaneously lost in the sensation of air moving across his cheek.

It was precisely this "here and not here" phenomenon that his birth sister appreciated in a way that most adults cannot. At seven, she remembered that to be with DJ was to be with him on *his* terms without demanding more. You could gently ask for more, as we have made a practice of doing, but he needed—still needs—to feel comfortable. He needed to sense that you were also trying to communicate somehow in his medium. Too much pushing and he'd withdraw.

With amazement, we watched the girl effortlessly reassume the role of facilitator as she directed DJ around the park, like some tiny tugboat on the river. Already smaller than DJ, she refused to be frustrated by his failure to aid in their ascent up an especially daunting hill. Even more significant, she refused to be saddened by what her brother couldn't give her after their long separation—what he couldn't say or do. But then he *had* given her something. In fact he'd stunned her, stunned all of us, when just before we were to meet in the city, he'd spotted his sister a full block away, run up to her, and, like a character in a French movie, placed his hands on her shoulders and kissed her on both cheeks. We'd never seen him do this before; we've never seen him do it since. The girl seemed to ride the gesture right into the afternoon, as if it were pulling her.

Yes, there was plenty of sadness, great paved and unpaved mounds of it, but the sadness had nothing to do with DJ. It had to do with the fact that his sister, despite being a very young child herself, had taken care of him when their mother was drunk or high, which was a good deal of the time. Indeed, it was she who'd regularly piloted him through the back alleys of town in search of food, she who'd tucked him into bed at night. But then the process had commenced that had cleaved her from her brother, placing him in the hands of perfect or, rather, quite imperfect strangers.

For months Ellie had sobbed herself to sleep, insisting that her father go rescue DJ. Again and again, the man and his wife had explained to her what foster care was, why DJ was better off with a family that knew how to treat his disability. Though she wasn't aware of the inadequacies of foster care generally or of the beating DJ suffered there specifically, she must have sensed, in a way that children always seem to know when grownups are lying, that there was something fishy about her parents' explanations.

Now, another bunch of strangers, or at least relative strangers, was taking care of him. The girl feared that we couldn't do it properly, drilling us with questions about his eating habits, his favorite activities, and his peculiar penchant for getting into any make-up that might be lying around. "He especially likes lipstick," she reported, "and he'll draw all over your bathroom mirror. He still does this, right?" She feared that we didn't understand her brother, and yet, in truth, part of what saddened her—the part that also vexingly relieved her—was exactly how much we *did* understand him and how attached to us he seemed. This same girl had sent us a card upon DJ's arrival at our house. "Thank you for letting DJ stay with you. We love him very much," it said in sprawling children's script. *Stay* with us? we'd wondered.

Can a smile ward off the always approaching, always overtaking, demon Loss? Ellie seemed to think so. She'd figured out a way of keeping her balance while taking longer, more powerful strides, and now she was really moving. Not once had she and DJ fallen or come unhitched. Her look of accomplishment at having reached a down-slope suggested each time, if not the possibility of retrieving those absent years, then that of barreling into the future together—away, far away, from the cruel and unabashedly self-serving decisions of adults.

* * * * *

We'd been planning a trip to the Northeast for some time—from the very moment, in fact, that DJ and his garbage bags full of clothing had appeared on our doorstep. We'd wanted to introduce this curly-haired marvel to our extended families but thought we should wait until the six-month adoption trial period had elapsed and the adoption had become final. It was important to give DJ as much time as possible to adjust to his new home. Though he was presently faring well, we knew just how up and down the process of adjustment could be. No doubt there would be more anxiety, more insecurity—especially in a child who couldn't speak. After all, ours was his fourth home in five years. When, at last, the 21st of December had arrived and the adoption papers were signed, we decided to celebrate DJ's new status by booking flights in early spring.

At this time, we set out to arrange a visit with his birth sister as well. We knew that his sister lived a mere six blocks from my aunt's apartment, where we would be staying; it would be crazy not to try to arrange a visit. DJ, it was clear, longed to see his sister. Included in the card she sent when he came to live with us was her school photograph. We attached this photo to the refrigerator, and DJ would point to it each morning at breakfast, his chair always positioned so that he was facing her, as if they were somehow eating together. "Yes, that's Ellie, your sister. You miss her," we would say.

Emily and I wanted to preserve this birth tie. After all of the pain and loss that DJ had experienced, it was important for him to have a connection to his past, especially this connection. Not every twig or leaf should be swept downstream in some muddy, rain-engorged creek. Adoption needn't constitute a second storm. We understood that in order to preserve this tie we would have to preserve others, if only to a lesser degree. In choosing to adopt DJ, we had vowed to ourselves that we wouldn't behave like the kind of adoptive parents who sever all birth ties in an act of compensating for their child's lamentably unnatural arrival. We, especially I, harbored notions of reconfiguring family, of making it less like the genetic version of a gated community than a shelter of shared intimacy and support, open to the needs of the world outside.

Within limits, of course. We had no intention of doing away with traditional family roles altogether or of confusing our son by maintaining a close relationship with his birth father, but neither did we want to pretend that his birth parents didn't exist or that they were entirely uninterested in his welfare. We were pretty sure that DJ didn't really remember his birth father, as the man had left his birth mother well before DJ had turned two. In the photographs he sent, not once did DJ point to him—only to his sister, over and over again.

Of course, we recognized that our lofty ideas about adoption would be difficult to achieve in the lower realm people call "real life." We knew what his birth mother was like—we'd spent months trying to help her— and we'd already had enough interaction with his birth father to sense what trouble lay ahead. The point is, we couldn't imagine decreeing it best for DJ to forget his birth family. Adoptees often spend a good part of their adulthoods trying to undo what had been thought best for them. Anyway, we knew that in order for DJ to see his sister, we would have to indulge his birth father's not uncomplicated desire to see his son, even as we planned subtly to remind the man that the purpose of the visit was for the two kids to see each other.

I set aside a Saturday afternoon in early January to ring the man up. When I got Dan on the phone, he continued in exactly the same vein as when I'd spoken to him a year earlier about terminating his parental rights. He felt a need to confess. He felt a need to convince the person who'd come to his rescue, who *wanted* to do what he'd failed to—namely, parent his disabled son—that he was a decent person. But I could offer only the thorniest of absolution: a wordless resentment that drove him ever forward. He hadn't known how to care for a child with a severe disability, he explained. Moreover, hard as he had tried, he simply hadn't been able to persuade his new wife to take his son—he'd begged her, but she'd refused. Finally, how could he not have thought of the welfare of his daughter, who had so much to gain from coming to the Northeast and living, as he put it, a life of opportunity?

Having conceded he'd very much like for his daughter to be able to see her brother, he launched into a description of Ellie's initial reaction to the estrangement. She couldn't sleep. The darkness petrified her. In it she imagined DJ banging his head against an unfamiliar wall, crying out for her, wanting her to crawl into his bed as she had on nights he didn't want to sleep. How could there be no one there for him? How could *she* not be there for him? How, alas, could she be safe, could she be happy, while he was in some stranger's home? The man was nearly frantic. He seemed to recount the story of his daughter's pain to make clear that at least someone in his household had wanted to take DJ or, rather, to ask that his daughter be considered its more honorable representative and that he be allowed to pose, say, for a photograph beneath her banner. He said nothing of the fact that he hadn't bothered to visit DJ in the hospital—hadn't bothered to visit him but once in the previous four years.

I found his contortions of guilt excruciating. I wanted to puncture the man's self-serving rationalizations, but I'd promised Emily I'd keep quiet in order not to jeopardize DJ's future contact with his sister. At this point I couldn't determine if he was simply demonizing his wife, seeking refuge in her refusal, or if he was indeed as powerless as he claimed. In a sense it didn't matter. A decision had been made that had affected DJ terribly, a decision that his wife had certainly not resisted and that neither of them had tried at all to mitigate. However controlling or dictatorial she was, the man's account had the distinct ring of convenience.

In the weeks leading up to the visit, Dan took to checking in with us about our travel plans, plans we'd already reviewed with him several times before. And he took to telling us other intimate details about himself. The impending visit was dredging up a range of unresolved feelings. He also kept repeating that he wanted to buy DJ a gift. "What does he need?" he'd ask. "Come on, he must need something." Each time, we'd discourage him with a lighthearted rejoinder: "That's very nice of you, but you don't need to do that."

Then, three days before we were to leave for the Northeast, he let slip he hadn't yet told his wife, Pat, about the visit. When he'd mentioned the idea previously, she'd opposed it, insisting such an occasion would be harmful to *their* daughter. Why make her agitated again, she'd said. Why go through another good-bye? The woman must have envisioned something preposterously self-destructive, like a backhoe operator turning on himself, undermining the ground his own massive supports rested on. Dan said he'd inform his wife of the visit the morning we were to arrive—an uncharacteristically bold gesture on his part and a measure of how much he wanted the visit to occur.

It was during that final, pre-visit phone call that I'd heard how eager Pat had been to have Ellie and, as well, the frankly incredible story of how she and her husband had met in the first place. DJ's caseworkers had divulged many of the same details about the family when we first considered adopting DJ (as had DJ's maternal birth aunt with whom we had some contact). The woman descended from an affluent family. She lived in a large apartment that was filled with expensive antiques. She worked in advertising and vacationed all over the world. For years she'd wanted to be a mother, but having contracted HIV through an unprotected sexual encounter, she'd believed painfully that marriage and children were unavailable to her. Then, at an HIV support group she'd met an unemployed former drug user (the man's description of himself), and an improbable marriage had ensued.

Dan's daughter had unexpectedly completed the picture—not in the way the woman had always imagined, but close enough to pass as something like her fantasy. Of course, the girl had needed work; she'd been living with her alcoholic welfare mother and, like her father, knew nothing of upper-middle-class life. She'd had to be tutored before she could enroll at a private school; they couldn't just put her in a uniform, wind her up, and let her go. She'd had to learn how to speak properly; she'd had to learn how to carry herself. She'd had to—well, the list was endless. If one wanted to capture the gist of the woman's development project it would be this: the girl had had to forget every last detail of her former life. In a sense, she'd entered a kind of witness protection program, except what was required of her was that she *erase* what she had seen, refuse to testify: things her father had been only too happy to do.

The woman's theory of adoption was diametrically opposed to ours. She'd gotten out her earth-moving equipment and buried the past as quickly as she could, covering it with grassy swales and beautiful flowering gardens—the kind of project where you cart in mature plants and trees to make it look like the whole thing has been there for years. One moment piles of dirt, the next a luxury life ready for immediate occupancy. No doubt the urgency of the project was a reflection of the woman's uncertain medical prognosis, but knowing this only complicated my feelings toward her.

The flights to the Northeast were even more difficult than we had feared. DJ had never been on a plane before, and he didn't take well to the confinement, or to the feeling of pressure in his ears, which made him scream. We'd brought with us a collection of new toys and small mechanical gadgets, the kind whose effects could be repeated obsessively, to try to distract him. And we'd brought lots of food as well. But right from the beginning, Luck was a no-show, abandoning her seat to some standby passenger. On our first flight from Jacksonville to Atlanta, we sat on the runway for nearly an hour, using up our precious allotment of acceptable behavior. We weren't watching an hourglass; we were inside one, falling with the final grains of sand.

Barely at our cruising altitude, DJ began kicking the row in front of him and giving us the "all done" sign, one of a handful of signs he'd learned since coming to live with us. It meant that he was through with the peculiar activity his parents had imposed on him. He wanted to go; he wanted to go right now. But where? I remember trying to point him to the window to make clear that "going" was out of the question, but he simply repeated his request with his hands, adding a kind of frustrated flourish. There was no telling what he made of the fluffy shapes now strangely *below* us. Did he honestly think we could open the door and step outside? Did he think his father could land the plane? Did he understand we were flying?

We tried to walk a bit in the aisle; we tried to go to the bathroom. We resorted shamefacedly to giving him candy, our final weapon in the war of distraction. Whenever he raised his voice excessively—and I mean excessively—we gave him another piece. I guess I should say *I* gave him another piece: by this point Emily and I were arguing about everything. I don't think DJ understood that he was holding us hostage; he was simply delighted and somehow frantic to discover the new limit to his requests. At home, one piece of candy had been the limit.

The truth is, he was anxious about leaving. Although he appeared to know he was going to visit his sister, he might have thought he was leaving us. In fact, he'd become agitated when I pulled out the suitcases and started to pack. Emily had put together a picture schedule to show DJ the sequence of the trip: a photo of our house, a photo of our car, a photo of a plane, a photo of the city, a photo of my aunt, a photo of Ellie, a photo of Emily's brother and his family, a photo of a plane, and a photo of our house again. The picture schedule seemed to work but it had to compete with the deep associations of loss that the suitcases unearthed.

By the time the pilot announced we were making our initial descent into Atlanta, never mind the city of our final destination, I was having to keep DJ in his seat with his seatbelt fastened, using both of my arms and a knee to do so, as he was sobbing, screaming, and fighting me every stomach-turning dip of the way. Much as we wanted to, we simply couldn't assume that because he longed to see his sister, he would behave. It wasn't a question of behavior; it was a question of too much unfamiliarity, too much sensation, too much instinctive panic.

At last, we arrived. As we headed in a cab for my aunt's apartment, we were all immeasurably stressed. DJ was stimming at passing cars, making a low humming noise and lightly pulling his hair—a clear sign of his anxiety. I was barking something about never doing this again, never getting on a plane with him. (Emily wisely resisted reminding me of our impending flights home.) Part of what had so disturbed me was having DJ confirm people's prejudicial view of cognitive disability, having him elicit looks of annoyance and, worse, pity. One woman, across the aisle from us, said to her six-year-old, "I'm very proud of the way *you* conducted yourself today." I wanted everyone we came in contact with to see what DJ could do. In the nine months he'd been with us, he'd come a great distance: in the first two weeks, he'd learned to use the toilet, thus making it possible to do away with those awful big-kid diapers.

Over the summer, DJ, in fact, had learned how to do all sorts of things the special ed people thought he'd never do, such as ride a bike with training wheels and swim and sit placidly at a restaurant. In the fall he'd begun attending a regular school, where he made friends, learned how to communicate and, in general, became more engaged with the world around him. Looking back on it, I think we were hilariously ambitious, but it was precisely such ambition that allowed for a whole string of marvels from this boy who'd otherwise have languished under the moniker "severe and profound disability." We were committed to DJ being in public, and so it was crushing to see him experience such a meltdown, even as we understood how stressful the trip was for him. I knew he'd eventually master air travel, but in the short term there would be much pain for everyone.

Also contributing to our stress was a medical problem that had developed over the winter, a problem whose complications nearly made us cancel the trip. DJ started having partial-complex seizures, and the medication he was put on began to irritate his liver just two days before we were to leave. A known and very dangerous side effect of the medication, this complication had our developmental pediatrician leaving us messages all over town—anywhere she thought we might be—saying, "Do not give DJ his next Depakote. Call immediately." We thus had to remove DJ from the Depakote all at once, itself a somewhat dangerous proposition.

We had several lengthy discussions with the pediatrician about whether or not we should postpone the trip, whether or not there would be enough Depakote in his system to prevent a seizure from breaking through. She didn't want to start him on a new anticonvulsant while we were away and thought we could probably make it back to Florida without anything happening—after all, we'd only be gone for four days. She nicely gave us her beeper number and told us to go to the hospital the second we spotted anything out of the ordinary. A woman with a huge heart, the one medical professional we'd met who didn't pathologize disability, she understood the import of the visit. We didn't want to disappoint the two kids unless it was absolutely necessary. The visit already seemed tenuous at best; a postponement might mean they'd never be able to see each other.

What we didn't discuss was the role of the visit itself—having to say good-bye again to his sister and having to endure those taxing plane rides—in the production of a seizure. Such stress certainly didn't minimize the chances of producing one. In retrospect, we probably shouldn't have gone, but like everything else in this story, there was no uncomplicated choice. It was like being taught, again and again, the meaning of a dilemma. After the umpteenth example, you feel like shouting from the back of the classroom, "And the point of recognizing a dilemma is? How about helping us to make a decision."

Ellie's school let out at 3:15, and her father had hoped to pick her up and take her straight to our meeting point. We would then walk back down to the park near the river, where the kids could rollerblade. This park was a mere stone's throw from my aunt's apartment. The next day, if the visit was going well, we'd spend the afternoon in a park closer to where they lived.

We had no idea if Dan's wife would be with him or if she hadn't already managed to cancel the visit. We should have known that, short of nixing the visit, she'd be there to police it. The first thing Pat did, after introducing herself, was to ask if we had coached DJ to run up and kiss his sister—a question that couldn't conceal its agenda. Almost immediately it became apparent that she and her husband needed to prove something to Ellie, and DJ wouldn't help them. *We* wouldn't help them. Rather, we'd contradict them; in fact we'd already contradicted them simply by wanting to parent DJ, by loving him, by admiring his willingness to move out into the world despite all that had happened. To us there was no such thing as sufficiently or catastrophically disabled, no such thing as unbridgeably distant. For the adults this conflict remained largely invisible: it moved like the subway beneath the streets. You could

REASONABLE PEOPLE

feel it; you could see steam rising from vents; you could see people descending into its labyrinthine stations. Or it was like the George Washington Bridge that I remember crossing as a boy I don't know how many times—a giant sign instructing drivers: LOWER LEVEL HERE.

Ellie was dressed in her school uniform: a plaid skirt with a white blouse and dark knee socks. Her hair was longer than in any of the pictures, neatly pulled back. She had with her an overstuffed backpack and a pair of gym shoes. Her father was carrying her rollerblades and a windbreaker in case it rained. Like his wife, he was dressed to the nines, as if meeting a dignitary. The two of them seemed shocked to discover that Emily and I were in jeans. "We're going to the park!" I wanted to shout, suddenly defensive about a presumed class distinction. Dan had tried to give DJ a hug when we met up, but DJ had pulled away—not meanly, gently, as if to say, "I've seen you in a photograph, but I do not know you." This, I must confess, was a relief. Dan kept saying, "He looks so much like my brother. Check out those curls."

Dan was tall and, in today's body-loving lingo, buff—a good six- foot-two and two hundred pounds, apparently all of it muscle. I remember thinking it was hard to believe he'd once progressed to the point of full-blown AIDS. He wore his clothes and his Rolex watch like someone who hadn't yet become them, someone who still took too much pleasure in their transformative powers. What really gave him away, though, were his bad teeth and the heavily accented words that sometimes leapt from his mouth, like overbearing actors onto a stage. (The man had grown up in Boston.) Walking down to the park, I could sense the woman's embarrassment or, rather, the way that she'd learned, for the most part, to repress her embarrassment whenever he spoke in this manner. And yet, whenever he did speak like this—to tell us, for example, of his enthusiasm for pumping iron—she clearly registered his faulty impersonation.

Pat was also tall—around five-foot eight. She was slightly less robust than her husband but in no way sickly. She wore an elegant blue pants suit with a pretty pin. Her hair was cut very short and was fashionably spiked. From the outset, she assumed the role of official spokesperson, beginning

14

each sentence conspicuously in the first-person plural: "We often rent a movie on Friday nights . . . We sometimes go to the ballet . . . We're learning French in school . . . isn't that right, Ellie?" When DJ made the sign for gum and I asked Ellie if she wanted a piece, Pat remarked, "We normally don't allow gum chewing; it's vulgar. But perhaps just this one time, as it is a special occasion."

While her parents were trying to make conversation, Ellie seemed afraid to speak, as if in doing so she might awaken from her dream. Her father had only told her of the visit some fifteen minutes earlier, fearing, I suppose, that she might say something before he got around to informing his wife. It had never occurred to us that he would be surprising his daughter as well. I tried to imagine bounding out of school and learning that today, an ordinary Thursday in March, I would get to see my brother. Nearly a thousand other days had passed without so much as acknowledging her, and now here, without warning, one had stopped to grant her wish.

Slowly but surely, the girl inched forward into speech, like someone familiarizing herself with a high diving board. She couldn't get over how big DJ was. She asked about his glasses, which made him look, she said, "intellectual." "Where did you learn that word?" Emily teased.

"School," Ellie said, for the first time taking in the fact that I was holding DJ's hand. "I've learned all sorts of things—like, did you know that crayfish are related to barnacles and wood lice—both are invertebrates."

"No I did not," Emily replied. I told her about DJ's eye problem, how it had been difficult at first to get him to wear his glasses, so accustomed was he to relying on his sense of touch and smell.

"He broke the first three pairs we gave him," I reported.

"Really?" she said. I told her he still prefers to identify people by smelling them.

"I remember that. He used to smell my mother's boyfriends whenever they came over," she said, pausing slightly. "But he clearly saw me just a few minutes ago. The glasses must be working."

We were nearly at the entrance of the park—I could see the river in the distance—when she asked, "Where does DJ go to school?"

"A regular school, just like yours," Emily responded. "He has an aide who helps him."

"It's not a school for people with autism?" the girl inquired. "No," Emily said, aware of the delicate ice we were venturing out on and yet refusing to lie.

"Are the kids nice to him?" Ellie asked.

"Yes, they are," Emily told her. "He has lots of friends. At lunch, if you've studied hard, you're allowed to eat outside with a classmate. The kids in DJ's class all line up to see which one of them he will choose."

"Who's his favorite?" Ellie asked.

"A boy named Austin," I said. "You like Austin, don't you, DJ?" DJ seemed to smile upon hearing Austin's name. "He also likes a girl named Teresa."

"So, he can learn," his sister interjected, apropos of nothing but the spurious information she'd been given by her parents and the clanging reverberations of that subway just beneath our tongues. "*I* want to have lunch with DJ," she said. "I study hard."

At this point, Ellie's stepmother, who'd been silent during the exchange, attempted to redirect us. We'd reached the basketball court, and she proposed that the kids put on their rollerblades. Dan produced a helmet and a pad for what seemed like every one of his daughter's innumerable joints; we watched uncomfortably as it took her nearly fifteen minutes to suit up. Dan then tried to help DJ with his rollerblades, but DJ rebuffed him, this time less casually. When the stepmother realized that DJ had neither a helmet nor pads, she proceeded to lecture us on proper parenting. Emily said something about DJ being unwilling to wear a helmet, as he was particularly hypersensitive when it came to his head. "Then he shouldn't be allowed to skate," Pat said curtly. I informed her we usually skate in a rink where no one wears a helmet. "It doesn't matter," she maintained. "Safety first."

Rather than allow myself to be provoked, I decided to show Ellie how she might skate with DJ. I took the two of them out to the center of the court and told her to take hold of her brother's hand. "You're going to have to pull him," I said. "He's only learned how to remain upright."

"I can do that," Ellie replied eagerly.

"And you're going to have to make sure your skates never come in contact. He really doesn't like to fall."

"He won't fall," she boasted. "I'm pretty good at rollerblading." And she was. Soon, she was making turns, picking up speed, and looking back to see if her brother was having fun. At first a little bit wary, DJ quickly grew comfortable with his new pilot, began to flap his free arm (his signature stereotypy when watching anything in motion), and produced a broad, if somewhat distant, grin. This grin he occasionally punctuated with a gleeful, high-pitched shriek, scaring Ellie the first time he did so. But after this first time, she started to enjoy these shrieks, laughing whenever one escaped from his mouth, even as I was telling DJ not to be so loud.

I wanted the two siblings to have some time alone, so I drifted back to the bench where the adults were sitting. I caught the tail end of a familiar anecdote about one of DJ's classmates. Apparently, Dan now wanted to pursue the topic of his birth son's schooling. Emily told him how the classmate had said to her that DJ was just like a boy on his soccer team. "What do you mean?" Emily had asked. "Well," the classmate had replied, "my friend speaks two languages just like DJ." "What languages are those?" Emily had asked. "English and Spanish," the boy had said. "And what are DJ's two languages?" Emily had inquired. The classmate looked at her as if she'd lost her mind. "Sign language and pictures," he'd said. "Don't you remember coming in to teach us these languages?" Emily was telling the anecdote in order to underscore how naturally children can accommodate disability, in fact not even understanding it as *dis*-ability.

"But what does he *do* at school?" Dan wondered. "I mean, he can't possibly do the work the other kids are doing, right?" Something about his tone had changed; he seemed to be going on the offensive. "Does he take their tests? What's the point of this inclusion stuff, to make the parents feel better about having a retard for a son?"

The man had actually used the word "retard." I don't know if he'd discerned that he was in trouble with his daughter, having exaggerated

DJ's disability, or whether he suddenly felt that he was in trouble with himself. I don't know if he had been hurt by DJ's coolness toward him—it did seem to have left him a bit like a child on a bike with a flat tire in the middle of nowhere. I don't know if he was merely like so many other people who know nothing about disability and advance a case of prejudice. It was probably all three. In any event, I thought it contemptible of him to express his frustration and despair, as well as his anger at us for being truthful to Ellie, by demeaning DJ, and I was angry. How could the boy be disabled enough to be demeaned but not disabled enough to have provoked his birth father's guilt about abandoning him?

Emily tried to explain what an adapted curriculum is and how the aide helps DJ to stay on task. She highlighted a whole host of things that DJ had learned to do—things as simple as walk in line or eat his lunch unsupervised in the cafeteria. It was as if she'd decided to teach right through a tornado, fastening herself to the blackboard and clinging to her lesson plan. "He's just beginning to learn his letters," Emily told the man firmly.

"But does he flap his arms like that in class?" Dan asked. (As DJ turned beneath one of several basketball hoops, he flapped his free arm wildly.) "Does he always scream?"

"He's happy," I snipped. By this point Pat had started moving to the other side of the basketball court, closer to where the kids were skating. Was she uncomfortable with the conversation or simply confident that her protégé would strike a decisive blow?

"To be honest with you," Dan said, "I'm not sure I'd want some handicapped kid in Ellie's class; he'd be a nuisance. He'd probably hold the other kids back."

Should I have been stunned? An objection I'd heard a thousand times—from school administrators and teachers, from the odd parents of a classmate, from politicians—now managed to wound me, coming as it did from DJ's own birth father. The entire visit seemed to have been heading fatalistically toward such irony, as in Zola's *La Bête Humaine*. Had this subway conductor fallen asleep? Would his train crash? Should I let mine crash as well or, better yet, burst through the macadam of our conversation like that subway-turned-missile at the end of the movie *Speed*? "This is YOUR fucking child we're talking about," I thought to myself.

Was he aware of what he was doing—arguing against inclusion as a way of justifying splitting up his kids? I tried to pretend the man was any of a number of familiar opponents. I told him about the research suggesting classrooms with cognitively disabled children actually perform better on standardized tests than classrooms without such children. But Dan pressed on, needing to emphasize what DJ couldn't do. "How much help will he have to have when he's older?" he asked.

"It's not clear," Emily replied. "Some, but we don't know where he'll be by then. He's only now really getting a chance to develop."

"Looks to me like he'll need a lot," Dan insisted.

"Perhaps, but he keeps surprising us," I said, controlling my annoyance. "When we first took him rollerblading, for example, he couldn't even stand up. And when we first tried to include him in story time at school, he couldn't sit for five minutes; now he can make it all the way through."

I'd done it. I'd fallen completely into advocacy mode, armed with anecdotes and an obdurate optimism and using a tone reserved for the instruction of the most incorrigible pupils. I just kept focusing on our long-term goal: the restoration of the sibling relationship. Of course, I was not unaware of the effect my tone was having on DJ's birth father, who flailed against my passive aggression.

"Can you really blame them for not wanting a boy with autism? Don't they have enough medical problems themselves?" a friend of mine had countered when I told him about DJ's birth father and his new wife. Standing there in the park, I found myself restaging arguments I'd staged countless times before. How could they parent a child who'd need assistance well into adulthood when their own futures were in question? Wasn't this what Dan was getting at, at least in part, when he belabored DJ's lack of future self-sufficiency? Moreover, even if they'd been willing to take DJ, how could anyone ask of them the day-to-day effort required to raise a child with a neurological disability when all they really wanted was a second, temporary shot at normalcy? Had I no sympathy for their predicament?

And yet, both the man and his wife were still quite healthy. With the new treatment options, they might be alive indefinitely. In any event, why was such uncertainty acceptable for Ellie, who knew nothing of her parents' infections? What if *she* were suddenly left all alone?

The fact is, a boy with a disability didn't fit into Pat's idea of family. He was like a piece from another puzzle, somehow included in her box. I refused to accept this prejudice. And I refused to accept the idea that DJ simply wasn't her kid; *Ellie* wasn't her kid. I'd been fighting precisely this distinction for years: the American shibboleth of blood relations. Nevertheless, had the two of them shown any concern at all for DJ short of agreeing to parent him, I might have been able—might still be able—to understand their decision. At the very least, their money could have made a difference in his life: they could have arranged some sort of placement for him, helped out his foster mothers financially by providing clothes, toys, even a respite stipend.

But their operating assumption seemed to be: well, he's totally out of it; he wouldn't really know the difference between one home and another. Neither could appreciate the impact on him of losing his sister, the way it had made him withdraw even more deeply into himself. And neither could—or, rather, wanted to—appreciate the impact on Ellie of losing her brother. They underestimated what a relationship is, conceiving of disability only as deficits.

What had really gotten to me was their inability to recognize in this little boy someone just like themselves: someone to whom the fates had been similarly cruel and who thus also needed a second chance at life. Why should theirs come at the expense of his or, for that matter, Ellie's? What, after all, was the emotional cost of that life of "opportunity"? How could she not experience something like survivor guilt?

I remembered glancing, the morning we left for the Northeast, at one of the photographs DJ's birth father had sent of himself and Ellie at the beach. Because DJ had grown attached to the photo, we'd put it on the refrigerator along with the original one Ellie had sent. It had occurred to me the photo must have been taken by the man's wife; suddenly, Ellie's exuberance appeared entirely scripted, compulsory—the firm hand of the motherly photographer exerting a strict compositional influence. YOU SHALL BE HAPPY! YOU ARE SO LUCKY! Doubtless, I was reading into the photograph, but Ellie evinced the guilt her father did not, and she even seemed to acknowledge what was artificial about their neatly appointed life. It was as if she were standing at a blackboard and *writing*, over and over, "I SHALL BE HAPPY! I AM SO LUCKY!" Call it joy's detention—a girl kept long after school despite the vacation setting.

While Dan and I were doing battle, Ellie had become much more adventurous. She was now helping DJ down a flight of stairs in the hope of reaching some hilly terrain. "What are you doing, Ellie?" her stepmother asked.

"I want to pull DJ up that hill," Ellie answered. "I think I can do it. DJ, do you want to go? Hey, Emily, what's the sign for 'up hill'?" I prayed that DJ wouldn't fall and contribute to the already palpable tension by sobbing and hitting his head—his customary reaction to a negative surprise.

"You're going to hurt him," her stepmother continued. "Stop right now."

"It's all right," I yelled, wanting Ellie to have this experience and secretly reveling in aiding her disobedience. We walked over, and I remained just far enough away to allow Ellie to accomplish her goal, but close enough to come to the rescue if necessary.

Dan appeared increasingly desperate, like someone who'd started digging out from an avalanche but wondered just how much Pollyanna optimism had buried him. Gone was the obvious guilt of those preparatory phone calls. The more we downplayed DJ's disability, the more defensive he became. We simply refused to confirm the hopelessness of his birth son's condition. More important, DJ himself refused to confirm that hopelessness. But if DJ were not as irrevocably disabled as the man needed to think, then the charge of abandonment would stick—indeed, had already stuck. And the charge of separating the two siblings as well. The perfect clarity of these indictments hit him from behind, like a detective catching up to, and tackling, a criminal. The defensiveness gave way to silence and the silence to what can only be described as a tortured appreciation of the scene: his two kids together again.

21

For all of the man's dire predictions about DJ's future, he seemed positively confused about which prognosis, which understanding of disability, he was rooting for. I caught him intrigued by a report of DJ's progress at gymnastics camp. I caught him laughing at a story of DJ's first foray into the deep end of the public pool—he'd jumped in with all of his clothes on and sat peacefully at the bottom. And I caught him delighting in the image of his daughter straining to pull her brother uphill and then laughing as they began their precipitous descent: the image burned in his memory, I'm sure, as it is in mine. "Look at them go," he said. "They're really moving. DJ's got terrific balance."

The sky had grown darker, and a light rain had begun to fall. Pat said we should think about calling it a day, but Ellie pretended not to hear her stepmother. When DJ made the sign for "drink," she said, "Yes, I'm thirsty too," seizing upon an opportunity to extend the outing. I suggested we grab a drink at a pizza place we'd passed on the way down to the park. It was there the woman claimed to have wanted to parent DJ but feared she couldn't do it adequately. It was also there she announced, while the kids were playing pinball, that she was relieved to discover DJ was finally where he needed to be. It had been such a concern of hers, his finding a proper home. Pat was talking just loudly enough for Ellie to hear her, buttressing her case the way a lawyer might in closing arguments when something unexpectedly damaging has been revealed at trial. "DJ really seems to have bonded with you both," she said, "and you, Emily, with your expertise, you can offer him so much." Now, the woman was using DJ's progress as evidence of why he needed to be with us.

Dan took his wife's lead. He seemed to be searching for a way to fend off his low estimation of himself—a way to be positive about the decisions he had made. Positive about the long road leading to this spot. Positive about the visit, yes, very positive. Suddenly, he plunged into the well-lit space between us and, twirling repeatedly, landed on a tiny, elevated platform of sentimental gratitude. "You guys are my guardian angels," this edgy acrobat declared. As I had discovered passive aggression, so he had discovered gratitude. He could be grateful in spades. It wouldn't entirely take away his guilt but, at the very least, it would obviate the need to pick publicly at his sore. (The man's wife appeared to be annoyed by the amount of credit he was giving us; for her, each party had merely acted appropriately and, in doing so, helped to restore order to the world—the brown socks in one drawer, the blue disabled ones in another a thousand miles away.) And so, all of his contradictions the man wrapped up into the platitudinous bow of everything having worked out for the best. With the prospect of future visits—"We can get together again, can't we?" Dan said, as much to us as to his wife, who didn't respond—he was prepared to double his bet of gratitude.

Ellie didn't want to leave the pizza place. She started to cry and had to be reminded of the visit the following day. DJ had already withdrawn inside himself by the time her first tear fell: he'd long ago perfected this disappearing act, sniffing out any and all imminent farewells. He stood there serenely as his sister sobbed. "Stop right now, Ellie," Pat demanded "We have to go. You have homework to do. Now, say goodbye to DJ."

Once we had offered the assurances of tomorrow and finally parted, I began to ponder the notion of things having worked out for the best. In a way, Ellie's parents were right. DJ, to put it bluntly, was certainly better off with us than with them, but in order for him to have ended up with us he'd had to endure a vicious attack and all of the loneliness of foster care—far from salutary influences on any child, let alone an autistic one. DJ only became that much more fragile, defensive, and untrusting as a result of his experience. In addition, he'd been deprived of the kind of professional attention (speech pathology, occupational therapy) that might have made a difference in his development. To this day, Emily insists that had he received such attention from the age of three, his deficits wouldn't have been as significant as they were when he came to live with us. What is more, DJ's "good fortune" masked the fate of so many other children who never find parents. The chances of adoption for a child over the age of two are astonishingly low; the chances for a disabled six-year-old are virtually nonexistent. Finally, how happy could any ending be that separated two young siblings?

After a sleepless night, we greeted the morning much as we'd greeted the previous one: by killing time, by waiting for 3:30 to arrive. At 3:00 we left the apartment and wandered up to our meeting point; Emily insisted we were departing too early and, as usual, she was correct. We had to circle the block in order to vanquish the remaining few minutes. A light drizzle had begun—some massive low was stuck over the entire Northeast. When he spotted Ellie, DJ again ran up to her, this time simply taking hold of her hand. "DJ!" she exclaimed. "How are you?" We then all proceeded to the park near their place, consumed by a strangely expectant silence.

Before the kids went skating, they played for a while on the swings and then on a kind of merry-go-round: a number of tires chained together and suspended from a post. DJ loved this sort of thing, and the two of them rode it together, spinning arm in arm. Very quickly, however, Ellie started turning green. You could see she was dizzy, but she wouldn't get off. In fact, the more her stepmother exhorted her to get off, the more she refused, vigilantly upholding a smile and yelling, "I'm fine, I'm fine." Fearing Ellie might throw up and sensing trouble with the girl's mother, Emily intervened: she suggested the kids go skating before the rain worsened. She suggested this despite the fact that DJ wanted more—indeed, was signing "more."

And so, the kids resumed their tugboat imitation. Ellie found a hill to climb, and before long they were barreling down it, executing hairpin turns, weaving in and out. While we watched them, Pat asked about DJ's health, a question I finessed with breathtaking vagueness. I wasn't about to tell her of his seizures and thereby give her additional ammunition in the fight to prove she couldn't take care of DJ. She was someone whose judgment you never wanted to confirm.

The kids were now skating near a jungle gym, and DJ was pointing at it. "I think he wants to play on the jungle gym, Ellie," Emily said.

"OK," she replied, "but first we have to take off our rollerblades."

"Yes, you do," Emily agreed, smiling at Ellie's adorable earnestness. The kids came to a stop, and before Emily could get over to them, Ellie began to help DJ with his rollerblades. Emily stood back and watched, even as the girl appeared to be having difficulty getting them off DJ's feet. DJ, of course, wasn't helping any. In fact, he was still pointing at the jungle gym.

They hadn't been playing on the jungle gym for five minutes when a boy yelled at DJ, "Hey, out of my way." He was trying to make it across a long stretch, arm over arm, and DJ was hanging at one end, making it impossible for him to finish. "Out of my way," the boy repeated. But DJ just hung there, one foot resting on a lower bar to stabilize himself. He was clearly mesmerized by something in the leafless canopy above. The boy then muscled his way past—or, rather, through—DJ, causing him to fall. DJ shrieked and began banging his head against one of the bars. I ran up and said, without thinking, "Come to Daddy, DJ. Come to Daddy."

Ellie had been observing this interaction from about ten feet away, and when DJ fell, she climbed down and went over to him. But only after I'd referred to myself as "Daddy" did she start pummeling the boy who'd caused DJ to fall. "Ellie!" Pat cried. Dan quickly pulled Ellie off the boy and tried to explain to the boy's mother, who'd been roused from her magazine, that Ellie had misinterpreted her son's actions. At this point, Ellie started screaming at her father and hitting him: "You lied to me. He's not just living with them. He's fine. Look at him. He should be with us!" Over and over, she yelled, "He should be with us!" while sobbing and flailing at her father's midsection and legs.

Emily and I had agreed not to use the terms "Mommy" and "Daddy" in Ellie's presence; we didn't want to upset her. But not in our wildest dreams could we have imagined that she wouldn't be told of the adoption. The poor girl was discovering it accidentally on a playground, and now she couldn't stop crying. "All right, young lady," her stepmother said, "time to go home. If you can't behave yourself. . ."

"I hate you, I hate you, I don't want to live with you!" Ellie wailed. She seemed surprised by her words and a little scared but refused to turn back. An entire underworld had been exposed and subjected to the sun's perusal, like an ant colony some child had suddenly unearthed.

"You don't mean that," her father said nervously.

"Yes, I do," she screamed. "You're afraid of her. She doesn't want DJ because he's different. What if I was different?" Her words were barely discernible through her crying.

"Let's go home," the woman said.

"What if I was autistic? Would you get rid of me, too?" Passersby had stopped to take in the confrontation, as if watching theater in the park. The whole way back to our parting point, Ellie cried. When we reached it, she broke into uncontrollable sobbing. "When am I going to get to see DJ again? When?" Her father promised her she would see him soon, in the summer perhaps. I said she could come visit us in Florida or in South Carolina at Emily's folks' house. Now *I* was telling the girl half-truths. All of it sounded as desperate and hollow as a punctured drum.

DJ, in the meantime, had made himself into some sort of mental bat, narrowing his consciousness to the point that it had squeezed into the space between two particles of light. When Ellie went to hug him, he just hung there motionless. "I love you, DJ," she said, "I love you. I'll write to you." I couldn't look at anyone for fear of breaking down—Ellie was by this point gasping for air, so convulsive was her sobbing. Emily said we'd call when we got back to Florida, though she knew we probably wouldn't, at least not for a while. Then, she turned and told Ellie her brother loved her very much, that he pointed to her picture each morning at breakfast. "Remember how he kissed you, Ellie. Remember that." And then we started walking, the three of us, one foot in front of the other, hands clasped, concluding this impossible good-bye.

What's left of the story is sad and, in a sense, almost ridiculously foreseeable. To paraphrase the Russian playwright Anton Chekhov, if a gun should appear in the first act, it must go off by the third. Suddenly, guns seemed to be discharging everywhere.

DJ had a seizure at Emily's brother's house. We had put him down for a nap the following afternoon up in one of the kids' rooms on the third floor. He'd apparently awakened suddenly, which, as we found out, can set off an epileptic event, especially when anticonvulsant levels are low. By the time we made it to the third floor, he was screaming and banging his head against the wall. He seemed excessively disoriented and his eyelids were still fluttering. We rushed to the hospital where we waited for four hours while a very kind pediatric neurologist conducted tests and consulted with our doctor back in Florida by phone. The tests were inconclusive, but a seizure, he said, was certainly possible. I also think DJ must have panicked up in that room all alone. Emily's brother has five children, and the house might have reminded him of his first foster home. Maybe he even feared that we were leaving him there. Anyway, DJ was put on another anticonvulsant, and we were instructed to see our doctor first thing Monday morning.

On top of this, the flights back to Florida the following day were horrific. DJ experienced a full-blown rage attack—far worse than what had occurred on the flights up north. The trip to Jacksonville was especially excruciating. Picture a bobcat loose in coach. DJ mauled our arms and legs. He kicked the seat in front of us, spilling coffee on an elderly gentleman. Too far gone to stop himself, he bit the hand that held his mouth and clawed a careless forehead. Emily and I were like some desperate octopus, asked to fight a foreign foe: BATTLE OF THE SPECIES AT 30,000 FEET. We were squatting on DJ's legs, trying to immobilize his head, which he flung ferociously against the cabin window. A passenger shouted, "Control your fucking kid!" Another yelled, "He's going to break the glass!"

At one point, the copilot actually entered the cabin and asked if we needed him to "put down short of our final destination." It was almost laughable the way this stilted phrase resounded. No matter where we landed, we'd be short of our final destination, well short. (In language just as stilted we'd once described our goal on a DCF form as "a relatively open adoption with vigorous sibling birth ties.") We told the pilot we had to get to the hospital in our town—our doctor would be waiting—and begged him to bear with us.

Did DJ know the visit had ended disastrously? Did he know he probably wouldn't get to see his sister again? Was he spent? Had we pushed him too far and, in doing so, reactivated his trauma? Was something happening neurologically? Was he mad at us? What did he understand? We weren't sure of the answers to any of these questions. When you live with a nonspeaking child who is only beginning to learn sign language, you better be able to accommodate ambiguity. Because ambiguity is what you get—enormous crates of it, delivered every morning free of charge.

In time, I'd be able to say with confidence that DJ *had* been responding to the visit—indeed was still responding to it. Exactly what he understood remained unclear, but after we returned to Florida, he seemed to point more insistently at his sister's picture on the refrigerator. He seemed to want us to talk about her, to tell him what had happened.

Toward the beginning of June, we called DJ's birth father to inquire about the possibility of the kids getting together over the summer. We were hoping enough time had passed that everyone had recovered from Ellie's outburst; we weren't particularly sanguine about this prospect but we thought we'd call nevertheless. Dan told us that his wife had forbidden such visits, believing them too upsetting for Ellie. Ellie had been acting out in school, he said; there was no way his wife would allow another visit now. His hands were tied. He went through his usual routine of feeling bad and then a few days later sent some pictures from the visit and a present for DJ.

Six months after that, we received a call from the Department of Children and Families in the city where Ellie lived. It was investigating a charge of child abuse and was required by law to check on the status of any of the alleged victim's siblings. The records showed the alleged victim had a brother in foster care in Florida. After explaining that we'd adopted DJ, I asked the caseworker what had happened to Ellie. He told me that recently in the principal's office she had said that she was afraid to go home, that her mother would kill her for getting in trouble. She was hysterical; she wouldn't stop crying; she spoke of being beaten. The caseworker made it clear he didn't feel the accusations had merit, but he was required to investigate.

I was flabbergasted. I could only imagine the woman's response to the humiliation of an official DCF investigation. I'd seen what these were like. I knew that Emily and I were at least partially to blame for Ellie's downward spiral, and I felt awful. By championing DJ's progress, by refusing to accede to an exaggerated sense of his disability, we'd made her situation unbearable. Of all of the ironies in my son's story, that insisting on a full life for DJ would ensure his estrangement from his sister still seems the cruelest.

But the lesson of this debacle surely wasn't that progressive attitudes about adoption and disability had to be punished. Ours wasn't a case of classical hubris, of fatal overreaching. This wasn't art, however perversely "well-made" the chain of discharging events might have appeared to be. Whatever tragedy had ensnared us, it was that of particular human beings with highly particular foibles.

Each of us, at least to a point, could have put aside our respective resentments in the name of fostering the well-being of both children. Even Ellie's outburst could have been viewed as something positive: a chance to work through a heartrending predicament. God knows we've endured any number of outbursts from DJ. In fact, we've come to think of them as the necessary, if almost intolerable, prerequisite for healing.

In the three years since, we've had very little contact with Ellie or her father. We really don't know how she's doing. Shortly after our failure to arrange another visit, Emily began to assemble a scrapbook of DJ's milestones: a collection of photographs and report cards, school assignments and drawings—anything that might later give Ellie a sense of the time she missed with her brother. It contains copies of the Christmas and birthday cards DJ has written to her; after all, we can't be certain the originals ever reached Ellie. If they didn't, she'll be able to read these duplicates later. DJ enjoys assembling the scrapbook—cutting out the colorful matting paper, pasting the photographs.

At night sometimes, when I'm having trouble sleeping, I like to imagine the kids on another visit, except in my imaginings they're usually no longer kids when the visit takes place. Ellie's twenty-one, let's say, her brother's twenty. Her parents have died or perhaps they're still alive. It doesn't matter; she's old enough now to make her own decisions. The two siblings are in a roller-skating rink somewhere, maybe in Florida. DJ's just handed his sister the scrapbook and in sign has asked her to go skating. She can't believe how like a man he is. He takes her by the hand and directs her all over the floor, smiling. She can't believe how well he skates. He even skates backwards, something he learned to do, she discovers, when he was ten, just about the time his adoptive father decided to write a book about him. He struggled mightily to master this backward movement, figuring, he tells her, that once they did meet, he and his sister would have to go backwards if they ever hoped to catch up.

CHAPTER 2

More

The first time I met the three-year-old boy who would become my son we butted heads. Without any eye contact at all, without any animosity, without anything that could be construed as emotion, he took me by the second finger on my right hand to the couch in the family room, waited for me to sit down, sat down himself, and then brought our two skulls swiftly together. Emily, who was standing in the doorway, was as surprised as I—surprised that he'd even registered my presence, let alone that he'd approached me, doubly surprised the encounter was so intimate, so physical, so literally heady.

Working professionally with DJ, Emily had seen him use his head as a battering ram when angry, but she'd never seen him use it as a form of introduction: a forceful, but comparatively measured, hello. In fact, she'd never seen him seek out such close contact with anyone before. This version of an embrace—our two foreheads joined by the pressure of his tiny hands—left me dazed, a dull ache emanating from just above my nose. I was unprepared for the superfluousness of eyes, the heaviness of a child's breath. For twenty minutes we stayed that way: two bighorn sheep fallen asleep in play or combat.

Except we weren't asleep. We were both wide—or perhaps I should say, narrowly—awake, so restricted was our range of vision. Out of the corner of one eye, though, I saw Emily giving me a look that said, "Go with it, this might be promising." After all, the very point of having brought him home, and of having had me leave my graduate class early, was to see if there might be some way of coaxing this particular sheep away from the stark cliffs of perseveration that consumed him. All day long, DJ would flap his arms in front of a moving object—a fan, a spinning top, a passing car—and make an aggravated whirring sound much like an old prop plane in trouble. Emily had thought I just might have the same effect on him that I had on my ten nieces and nephews, whom I'd chase around their grandparents' home during holiday get-togethers: a mad, interactive excitement. Little did I know she'd also been thinking that in trying to draw out this boy, I (who in my thirties had become noticeably sullen, distant, at times even socially truculent) might be drawn out as well.

But more to the point, she was worried about DJ. Abandoned by his father, recently taken by the State from his mother, separated from his sister, placed in a foster home with five other foster children and a single foster mother who had no experience caring for a child with autism, DJ had become agitated. In fact, he'd taken to screaming uncontrollably while hitting himself on the head, jumping up into the air, and hurling himself onto the floor. The only thing that worked to calm him, his foster mother reported, was to put him in the car and drive, drive for hours: the specter of each Florida pine or fast-food restaurant magically rushing up to his window to introduce itself and then, just as magically, falling back into the distance. Opposed to placing DJ with this woman, Emily had agreed to provide some respite care for him. In short, the foster mother would get a break, and Emily would get to keep an eye on DJ. The woman had said she found his screaming and bizarre idiosyncrasies unbearable, but, according to the Department of Children and Families, there was no better placement for him.

When DJ was finished butting heads, he got up from the couch, took me again by the second finger on my right hand, and proceeded to explore the house—not once looking up at me. Tracing the structure's outside walls, we inspected each room, each closet even (so long as the closet itself was on an outside wall), eventually finding the kitchen where he stopped in front of a pantry filled with food. "Do you want something to eat?" I asked. No reply. "Something to eat?" I repeated. Again, no reply.

I pulled down an oatmeal-raisin cookie and some potato chips from a shelf and this time said, very slowly, "Which one do you want? An oatmeal-raisin cookie or potato chips?" I even used my arms to mimic the intonation of "this or this?" Still there was no reply. I hesitated for a moment, noticing DJ standing there staring at the food (without somehow staring at me), unable to make a decision but not, it seemed, because he was undecided. The very idea of a choice seemed to flutter like a bird just above his head. But what exactly was the autism at play here and what was simply a life of deprivation, a life without choices, was, Emily made clear, unclear.

And so, I chose some potato chips and placed them on the kitchen table in front of the nearest open seat. I then sat down across from that seat. A minute or so later, DJ went to the table and began to stuff his mouth with chips—at once like someone who hadn't been regularly fed and someone completely untutored in the act of eating. Bits of chips fell onto his shirt and lap; bits fell onto the floor. (Unaccustomed to children in the house, I had to resist the urge to pick them up.) Several times I tried to engage him, calling him by his name, asking if he might share his snack with me, but to no avail. Emily observed this new drama intently from the dining room.

The rest of that first two-hour visit was taken up with paging through a phone book I brought out, at Emily's suggestion, after DJ had finished with the chips. For nearly an hour he turned the pages, making that whirring noise and occasionally stopping to feel the thinness of the paper or to scrutinize its delightful crinkling. The visit ended with the sound of a horn on the street; DJ's foster mother had come to get him. Emily scrambled to collect his things while I helped him to put on his socks and shoes. Tying his shoes, I noticed just how quiet he'd become. It was a quiet beyond the general wordlessness or sensory blizzard of his autism; it was more like the flight response of some emotional gopher hurriedly burrowing into the ground to elude a predator. As Emily directed him to his foster mother's van, DJ let out a whimper, which gave him away, and he resisted getting in.

Subsequent visits with DJ would begin exactly like the first with the mashing of heads: that gesture of connection without eyes, that sensation of bone on bone, skin on skin. Quickly, however, we widened our circle of activities, venturing to the park where he enthusiastically discovered some rusted swings. On these outings, Emily would make sure to have with us two different snacks; she wanted to teach DJ how to make a decision, how to establish a preference. (His foster mother, by contrast, liked his passivity.) "Which one do you want?" Emily would ask. When he didn't respond, she'd hand him one of the two, careful to alternate, from visit to visit, the triumphant treat.

After a few weeks of compulsory sampling, she again held out in front of him a bag of Doritos and a chocolate-chip cookie while telling me to model the gesture of extending one's arm. "Which one do you want?" she asked. "Make a choice. Which one?" I remember watching in awe as he reached for the Doritos. Eventually, Emily was even able to use pictures of the snacks, instead of the snacks themselves, in this decision-making drill, thereby nudging DJ that much closer to necessary abstraction: the paradoxical remove of language.

The small victories sustained us even as we failed to get eye contact from DJ or to experience anything like a shared sense of joyful accomplishment. Sometimes we'd catch him glancing at us, but as soon as we did, he'd look away. He was certainly happy enough to be dictating his snack choice, and he certainly seemed unwilling to leave us at the end of a visit (a fact that was beginning to take its toll on Emily), but we hadn't managed a less anxious—which is not to say, more conventional—bonding.

All along, I'd been insisting that he was sad, that he was traumatized, that autism seemed merely to complicate the refracted manifestations of a child's grief. "Put it this way," I said, suddenly the boy's strident defender, "he is someone who has lost everything, *and* he has autism." His foster mother was in the habit of suggesting that his condition protected him from emotional trauma. "I've heard autistic people don't establish emotional connections," she'd remark. "He hasn't with me." I remember wanting each time to point to DJ's bighorn ritual or to his whimpering resistance at the end of our visits but always thought better of it. This woman, after all, sanctioned our visits. Emily would remind me that the task was to give DJ some way of more directly communicating his grief and, thus, of climbing constructively out of it—a challenge that paralleled the challenge of treating his autism. He was, in effect, at the bottom of two wells at once.

The truth is I didn't know much then about the relationship between trauma and autism. I was using the former term loosely, simply following Emily who, in her capacity as the Assistant Director of a Center for Autism and Related Disabilities, had long before rejected the dominant "theory-of-mind" hypothesis, which denied people with "classical" autism awareness of self and others. I was, in short, presuming the impact on DJ of loss, even as he responded to loss in an unusual and easily misinterpretable manner. I found myself strangely adamant about this point and, the more I got to know DJ, defensive of his humanity.

Just about this time, nearly all of my friends started having children—even the ones who had vowed they never would, who, like me, had seemed to enjoy reciting all of the customary reasons for not doing so: such as the falling off of one's relationship, the falling off of sex, the end of travel, the end of spontaneity, the end of youthful irresponsibility. These conversations, coming as they did on a night out, would inevitably drift toward ostensibly more significant, because less self-centered, reasons. Often phrased as rhetorical questions, they'd seem all the more satisfying for their apparently unassailable virtuousness. "Who," one of us would ask, "would want to bring a child into such a violent world?" Or, "With so many people already living on the planet, who could justify the egocentric need to reproduce oneself?"

While espousing such reasons, I had on occasion espoused some very different ones as well: reasons no less self-congratulatory than those already mentioned, and certainly no less grandiose, but at the same time neither illegitimate nor unimportant. These reasons were political, even ideological, and in late-night, liquored moments they'd find expression in a nearly hysterical attack on the concept of "family values." I'd take this contemporary shibboleth to be, among other things, a cynical encapsulation of the recent triumph of the Right: the headlong rush toward privatization, the foundational erosion of the public sphere, the relentless assault on "big government" with the resulting rise in corporate profits and an unbridgeable gap between rich and poor. "In place of social responsibility," I'd shout (to the horror of Emily and to the amusement of the nightspot's other patrons), "in place of a sober awareness of late capitalism's inequities and brutalities, in place of simple compassion, has come an ethic of personal and familial responsibility, like a trampling elephant with a smiley face!"

The educated son of happily moneyed, though not happily married, parents, I was certain I knew what families were for, and I was eager to impart my incontrovertible understanding. In search of an analogy to make my point, I'd look no further than the fashionable gated community in which my bickering parents lived. "The typical middle-class family already resembles the longed-for gated community," I'd harangue my friends, "by keeping out the riffraff, by inuring itself to the problems and pressures just beyond its filial walls (while paradoxically making its residents inside often thoroughly miserable)."

I'd quote from Friedrich Engels's *The Origin of the Family, Private Property, and the State*, a book I'd come across in a graduate class, leveraging this famous critique of family to expose our country's highly selective concern for children, so many of whom languished in extraordinary poverty: "With the passage of the means of production into common property, the individual family ceases to be the economic unit of society. The care and education of children becomes a public matter. Society takes care of all children equally." Like an overly dramatic high school actor, I'd emphasize that final word "equally," determined to ring a distinctly—and, to my mind, suggestively cracked—American bell and in this way jolt my friends from their egalitarian slumber. Engels—the very name seemed to evoke for them an image of some obsolete technology, which, like Betamax, had years ago lost out to a superior rival.

For all of my political bravado, I wanted to respond to the ailing world around me in however minuscule a way. The progressive writer Paul

Rogat Loeb speaks of "living with conviction in a cynical time," and I, the recipient of enormous privilege, set out to do this, believing that children constituted a major impediment. It's not for nothing that in some 30s-era literature, the activist figure is depicted as monk-like, spurning not only children but women as well. "I don't want to get nibbled to death," Jim says to the communist organizer in John Steinbeck's *In Dubious Battle*, a tale of a doomed orchard strike in California, when the organizer presses him on his reason for joining the Party and eschewing more conventional attachments.

Whatever the dubiousness of Jim's total commitment, having a family seemed conveniently to limit—certainly to sentimentalize—the burden of responsibility. Can one volunteer at a homeless shelter, I'd ask, organize collectively for the goal of a living wage, fight for universal health care, and raise children? Can one do these admittedly insufficient things while holding down a job and holding up a mortgage—especially at a moment when many middle class jobs have been under assault? If one can indeed do these things (and my observational experience suggested otherwise), *does* one actually end up doing them? Or does the unbearable harassment of an ordinary working day (not to mention the march of global capital) more likely than not find its protest in the form of a doting, after-dinner walk with one's son or daughter?

Back then, I was mostly aware of the contradictions that beset my left-liberal position, and yet I longed to have a position, to resist capitulating to some conventional middle-class identity. While earning a PhD in American literature and cultural studies, I'd devoted myself to a host of causes, becoming, in fact, the Friday manager at the soup kitchen. In addition to my concrete political commitments, I'd gone one melodramatic step further, without entirely recognizing what I was doing. I'd become hyperbolically, compensatorily gloomy. I absolutely relished the grim and grisly, imagining that I alone might cut the universal sugar. The radio bleating its monotonous witness—more famine, more war, more death, more disease. Who cared if most had decided they'd rather not listen? I would listen. Can one be too serious? Can one still live, as Thoreau once put it, "deliberately"? Or is such an aspiration now sadly passé or, worse, at least in this particular manifestation, its own form of cocoon?

When my friends' children were born, I noticed, particularly with the men, a further change in attitude. Some spoke of their own rebirth, of becoming suddenly less interested in business, of rethinking their priorities (within the boundaries of still having to work, still having to support a lifestyle). Some spoke quite touchingly of watching their children's progress, of taking pleasure in their physical and cognitive gains. I secretly resented these conversion stories, wondering at whose expense such joy, like a new sofa or refrigerator, had been delivered. Though a baby obviously differs from a consumer item, it seemed the crowning pleasure of upper-middle-class oblivion. I didn't at all see the extent to which a valid political argument might also serve an emotionally defensive purpose.

It was probably eight weeks into our regular visits when, having caught DJ studying me, I decided to take a gamble. I'd long registered the warning about tactile defensiveness in people with autism, but I thought that during our next cranial embrace I'd try to tickle him. I'd try to get him to laugh, insisting, on some level, that he was like any other kid. He, after all, had initiated contact; I'd simply respond with a gesture of my own. And so, before going to the park the following Monday and after being led—always by the second finger on my right hand—to the couch in the family room, I lifted up his Spiderman T-shirt and gently tickled him.

At first, he seemed shocked, even uncomfortable, but then he giggled: one tiny, sputtering, high-pitched sound. I tickled him again, and again he giggled, this time more full-throatedly. Emily, who was in the kitchen grabbing treats for the park, entered the room just as he looked up at me and smiled. "What's going on?" she asked. I tickled him once more and then left my hand hovering above his belly. DJ reached out and placed it back on his skin. "You want more!" Emily exclaimed, smiling ever broadly in return.

"You want more!" I repeated, smiling myself.

The following week, Emily had a plan to teach DJ his first sign: "more." She told me to tickle him and, as I'd done the previous week, to stop suddenly while holding my hand just above his stomach. Whenever he pulled it down, I was to make the sign for "more": the fingers of one hand, including the thumb, vertically meeting the fingers of the other, including the thumb, so that the knuckles of both were clearly showing. And then I was to continue to tickle him, making sure to stop every few seconds to repeat the cycle and, in a sense, glue the sign to the concept.

When DJ still couldn't produce the sign himself, Emily sat behind him like a deaf ventriloquist, helping to manipulate his tiny fingers. We now had him looking at us—in fact, we had him looking at nothing but us—but we couldn't get him to look at his fingers, to practice anything approximating hand-eye coordination. We'd eventually find out, after we adopted him, that he suffered from a serious vision problem, which, having been diagnosed but left untreated, had discouraged him from depending on his eyes. (A doctor had said that because he was so "developmentally delayed," there really wasn't much point in giving him glasses.) Indeed, when he'd begin to do puzzles, we'd notice he did them almost entirely by touch, ignoring what the individual pieces resembled, much as a blind person might. He'd have just gotten his glasses, and still he'd be doing a puzzle with his head turned in the opposite direction, his eyes investigating the sun-flecked leaves just beyond the window.

Finally, after much repetition and nearly half an hour into the lesson, DJ made the sign for "more" himself. Emily yelled, "You did it!" while I jumped to my feet, nearly forgetting to tickle him. "Tickle him," Emily said. And I tickled him. I tickled him furiously, alternately hesitating so as to emphasize the crystalline message of cause and effect. Again and again, he signed "more," now giggling in advance of the desired sensation, giggling for the control he'd suddenly discovered. Pardon the exaggeration if I compare the scene to a geological event: his hands coming together like oceanic plates in an earth-shattering gesture—molten rock where once there was only spangled water. My mind raced forward to the promise of fertile green. Having mastered this sign, DJ would never look back, signing, "more," "more," "more" each and every visit, though in the beginning we weren't ever entirely sure if for him "more" didn't simply mean "tickle." For upon arriving at our house, he'd already be giggling, already be bringing those two hands together.

It wasn't long before DJ began to use the sign for "more," well, more properly, though not less frequently, mobilizing it to indicate more food, more phone book, more water play, more swinging. In response to what seemed a veritable barrage of "more," Emily would say, "He wants more of everything"—a phrase that meant, we both well knew, in its darker inflections "he has so little." But in those first few months of playing with him, we simply took what progress presented itself, as fascinated by errors of cognition as by cognitive leaps.

I was particularly intrigued by his tendency to overgeneralize, as when he'd walk up to men in the park who were wearing jeans and stick his hands in their pockets. I, who always wore jeans on our visits, had taken to giving DJ a piece of candy, had taken to giving it to him in the park, so, to him, men in jeans in the park had candy. One man, I remember, seemed utterly flabbergasted. "What's he doing?" he shouted. While apologizing for DJ's rather forward behavior, I couldn't help but delight in his unwitting disregard for social protocol and in the adult panic it usually inspired. Of course, with each renunciation of the proverbial warning about not taking candy from strangers, I'd have to contemplate his terrifying vulnerability.

Gradually, DJ's visual thinking would become more sophisticated and discriminatory, though he'd continue to have trouble understanding spoken language, experiencing what Emily called an "auditory processing disorder," which was a big part of his autism. And gradually, *very* gradually, as he'd learn more signs, he'd say a few words or, rather, approximations of words, some of them humorously creative. His first would be tied, appropriately enough, to his favorite activity. "Tickadoo! Tickadoo! Tickadoo! Tickadee!"

Can ideological objections to family be trusted? By intimating that my political repudiation of family might have concealed a more personal repudiation, I don't mean to propose that I'd simply displaced the latter onto the former in some crude Freudian fashion. *Instead of confronting the problem of an unhappy childhood, the patient confronts the more manageable, because intellectual, problem of insidious privatization.* Or, *Instead of exploring the impact of his father's decision to stop speaking to him when he was seventeen because he'd once again sided with his mother during one of his parents' spiteful arguments, the patient drones on and on about the legacy of President Reagan's decision to fire the striking air traffic controllers and permanently dissolve their union.* However suggestive the pun in that final phrase might be, I object to the stark opposition of the psychological and the political, the reduction of one to the other.

Rather, I mean to say that the effects on me of my parents' punishing marriage and of my own rancorous and then nonexistent relationship with my father had found shelter in my political convictions, hiding like immigrant stowaways in my mind's darkened hull and under no circumstances allowed to appear on the official manifest. What could be more ridiculous, after all, than a wannabe socialist referencing his thoroughly bourgeois anguish? What did the personal matter? In retrospect, I can see how my father helped to fuel the development of my political sensibility, as if I were a character in Turgenev's *Fathers and Sons* and as if a primal struggle against authoritarianism were at the undiscriminating root of all such rebellions.

It had almost been too easy to make him the embodiment of capitalist antagonism, despite the fact that I'd clearly profited from the upbringing he'd provided and would later take advantage, among countless other things, of the beautiful waterfront home he'd build in Florida. (Summers, when my parents would be up north, Emily and I would spend weekends at this home, taking the boat out onto the intercoastal, indulging in breezy luxury.) An enormously successful corporate lawyer, a self-made man, my father was haughty, insensitive, self-involved, aloof, and, most important of all, never, ever wrong. Though he was quicker on his feet in an argument than I—he'd defeated the government in several high-profile anti-trust cases—I'd nevertheless insist on doing battle with him when I was in college. I'd mobilize every theory I'd learned from Marx in my political science classes: theories about commodity fetishism and false consciousness and alienation. Our battles, which would invariably degenerate into shouting matches, couldn't help but be vehicles for me to articulate a more personal version of that final, aforementioned concept. In other words, they couldn't help but express a wish, at least on some level, to be closer to this man. When I think of my father, I haven't a single memory of him being playfully physical with me, though I do remember his hearty form of discipline.

Years removed from such skirmishes, I'd imagine his smug retort to the facts and figures I presently summoned: 35.6 million Americans in poverty, with 500,000 additional children, since welfare reform, in "extreme poverty" (a woefully understated term denoting a household income of less than $6,403 per year); the loss of thousands and thousands of relatively high-paying industrial jobs, with only one-sixth of the jobs replacing them during the great technology-driven boom of the 1990s paying better than poverty-level wages; a staggering increase in the annual income, the annual *bounty*, of the top twenty percent—particularly the top five percent (of which my father could claim admission); two-fifths of the country without any kind of health insurance; crucial programs designed to aid the underprivileged under privileged attack; and all the while that very different, that much more vociferous, cry of "more" from Wall Street and consumerist America. Along with a host of other arguments, my father would inevitably respond to such a litany, or so I'd imagine, by dwelling on my own socioeconomic contradictions—in effect, by accusing me of insincerity. Then, he'd return to his favorite rant: "It's all about personal responsibility!"

The point, of course, was that whatever a person's contradictions or psychological stowage, those trends—and the people whose plight they encompassed—couldn't be dismissed. Clearly, with less and less for so many, not everyone could afford the dubious hot cross bun of family. Not everyone could purchase its delicately scrumptious social oblivion. At a moment when liberalism and its "Great Society" were in full retreat; when social obligation had been reconceived as an impediment to the nation's economic competitiveness, a pointless giveaway to the slothfully undeserving, and an historical failure; the effects of cultivating a private heaven (or hell) could indeed be devastating.

To me, the typical middle-class family still resembles the mythical gated community in which so many seem to want to live. I say this having long abandoned my unqualified opposition to family and the practice of ideologically pummeling my friends. I say this having abandoned any specific commitment to radical politics (Marxism included) in favor of a more modest approach to staggering inequality, an approach that only now seems radical in relation to the ascendancy of the Right. One in five children in America lives in poverty—more than thirteen million altogether. Nearly one in six people works full time and yet remains poor. Is this acceptable?

If, as the writer Marion Glastonbury puts it, autism, with its "aloneness" and lack of "knowledge derived from intersubjective reciprocity," afflicts an individual's ability "to link his situational center to a social circumference," then I'm tempted to propose that a vast majority of Americans are autistic. Though it's a definition of autism I now reject, the more I got to know DJ, the more autistic my father seemed. Suddenly, I had a way of thinking about my father's *volitional* "aloneness," his "lack of knowledge derived from intersubjective reciprocity," his arrogant refusal "to link his situational center to a social circumference," not only in the world at large but in his very home. Suddenly, I had a way of thinking about his more obdurate auditory and emotional processing disorder.

Once, in a poem, I joked, "When your father's a Republican, there are simply too many reasons/ to want to sleep with your mother." Although obviously unfair to many Republicans, I was trying to get at the way the psychological and the political might actually be connected. My father was the perfect manifestation of a dual self-absorption—a fact that allowed me to suppose that a wish for a closer relationship with this man might be part of a larger wish for social cohesion. I didn't know it at the time but in working with DJ I was working on this project, this dream. Watching him strive to connect with others, I'd come to perceive the need not only for a public transfiguration but for a private one as well.

Not too long after DJ learned his first sign, his mother emerged from rehab and officially requested to begin seeing him. Having quit rehab the previous July, Rhonda had returned at Emily's urging and this time completed the thirty-day program. At the court hearing in November, Emily volunteered to supervise her visitation and to continue providing support to DJ both in and out of school. She'd attended the hearing at Rhonda's request, and after asking Rhonda if she approved of Emily's proposal, the judge gave his assent.

In order that she might visit with DJ in a setting more relaxed than a conference room at the Department of Children and Families, Emily suggested that they gather at a park near Rhonda's rented trailer. Upon completing rehab, Rhonda had begged Emily for help in getting her children back, and Emily had agreed to give her money for a place to live: enough for a security deposit and the first few months' rent. She'd agonized over this decision, knowing that some sort of professional line was being crossed, but she felt compelled to give Rhonda a chance—and, of course, she'd hoped to save DJ from an entire childhood spent in foster care or, worse, an institution. I'd been in favor of the idea, and so with encouragement from me, she'd overridden her own serious reservations and given Rhonda the money.

The point had been somehow to keep the family together, to encourage Rhonda to meet her responsibilities. Emily felt for this single mother whose husband had abandoned her. She believed that the woman deserved support, that with it she could get sober and learn to be a more effective parent. Increasingly, Emily's job had consisted of exactly this sort of reunification or restabilization project. The combination of disability and poverty left families on the brink of collapse. She'd seen too many irrevocably destroyed and wanted to do more to try to save them.

We both knew about Rhonda's past (addiction, unemployment, homelessness) and chose, I think, to overlook it, or at least to undervalue it as some sort of prognosticator. I was still captive to the *idea* of helping people, understanding very little about the difficulty of actually doing so—beyond what I'd seen at the soup kitchen. Emily, in contrast, was seeking to fend off a nagging fear that she couldn't really make a difference in her job. In a strange way, her desperate need to make a difference paradoxically allowed her to believe in hope all the more, though her experience had taught her otherwise. This need and her fondness for DJ catapulted her over the walls of professional judgment. Revisiting the events leading up to, and following, DJ's removal from Rhonda's care, I have to pause at how fearless we were. A narrative of these events, ridiculously abridged, appears below.

In August of 1995, Rhonda, a thirty-eight-year-old white woman and single mother of two, had attended an outpatient consultation at the mental health unit where Emily worked. The unit was a five-day-a-week residential program for children with psychiatric disorders. At the time, Emily had been employed as an instructional trainer, later moving to one of Florida's newly formed Centers for Autism and Related Disabilities—in part because she found institutional care and the exclusion it symbolized so objectionable. Rhonda had requested that DJ be placed on the unit's waiting list, complaining that she simply couldn't parent her son full-time, at least not until they both received adequate instruction. While DJ remained on the waiting list, Emily provided direct services in numerous ways: observing DJ in his preschool classroom, offering ongoing support and recommendations to his teacher, attending DJ's IEP (Individualized Education Plan) (which resulted in a new placement at the center school for kids with disabilities—something Emily opposed), and giving parenting and educational advice by phone.

In January, the Department of Children and Families received an anonymous report alleging that Rhonda had threatened to harm herself and DJ. The ensuing investigation revealed that she had made these statements in order to secure a unit placement more quickly. Because Rhonda really was in bad shape (unemployed, drunk a good deal of the time, depressed if not utterly distraught), Emily worked behind the scenes to bump DJ to the front of the waiting list, and at the beginning of February he was admitted onto the unit. Having to parent DJ only two days a week improved Rhonda's mood, but it had the opposite effect of what Emily had intended, for Rhonda promptly asked for a meeting with Developmental Services in which she requested a permanent placement for DJ in a group home. She liked the current arrangement too much and sought to better it. She would legally remain his mother, she said, and would visit, but she wouldn't care for him. When she was informed that such placements are rarely—if ever—granted to children under the age of eighteen, she asked if DJ might stay indefinitely at the unit. Again, the answer was no.

Over the next two months, Rhonda's drinking worsened, and she seemed almost to strive to have DJ taken from her. In early April, a report came in alleging "substance abuse, neglect, confinement and bizarre punishment." The charge of substance abuse involved crack cocaine, and the other charges involved failing to look after DJ and locking him for very long periods in his room. In mid-April, the Department of Children and Families received five additional reports of abuse and neglect—this time the victim was DJ's four-year-old sister, Ellie. These reports spoke of Rhonda slapping Ellie on the face "with enough force to cause injuries/marks sustainable for more than three days."

By this point, Rhonda was in full-sabotage mode, drinking to the point of blacking out and having no recollection of her actions. She agreed to Voluntary Protective Services, a step short of losing her children to foster care, but before these services went into effect, Rhonda was arrested for disorderly conduct and public intoxication. Ellie had been with her at the time, and when Rhonda was released from custody, she left Ellie at the police station and didn't return to pick her up. The two kids were then placed in Emergency Shelter Care—Ellie with her maternal aunt in town and DJ with Edna Austin who would become his first long-term foster mother. Emily watched these events in horror, believing that if Rhonda confronted her alcoholism by entering a detox center, she might have a chance at doing right by her kids. It seemed the only conceivable solution, a dubious one to be sure, but what Emily had to hope for.

By the end of May, DJ and Ellie were adjudicated independent, meaning they were now officially wards of the State, and in June Ellie went to stay with their father up north. Though the Department of Children and Families generally tries to keep siblings together, it often can't find placements to do so, and in this case it had no choice but to separate DJ and Ellie. (Rhonda's sister had indicated that she could only take care of Ellie temporarily; like the kids' father, she, too, had declined to take care of DJ.) Ellie thought she was simply *visiting* her father and would be back in no time once their mother, in the Department's euphemism, had "gotten better"; Emily feared that she was leaving for good. What irked her most was the way that even DCF personnel used autism to downplay the implications of the siblings' estrangement—as if DJ had no feelings and Ellie couldn't possibly be attached to someone who didn't speak and often seemed not to register what was going on around him.

Shortly after Ellie's departure, Rhonda entered a month-long inpatient program for drug and alcohol addiction, which she left before completing on the eve, ironically enough, of Independence Day. In August DJ was discharged from the unit and began to live full-time with Edna Austin and her five other foster children. Emily remained in contact with Rhonda, encouraging her to return to rehab and to commence working on her case plan. DJ and Ellie, she said, were waiting for her. By early September, I'd begun to spend time with DJ at Emily's request; by early November, Rhonda had completed a second go at rehab—against all odds. And so, clinging to this slim cable of hope, as if it were a completed bridge and not its most rudimentary forerunner, we made our way above a gaping chasm.

In mentioning Rhonda's place, I used the word "trailer," but what I mean is half of a trailer: a run-down, single-wide, slapdashedly converted into two "apartments" by a greedy slumlord (or, in the language of the depoliticized market, by someone who'd simply identified an increased demand for substandard housing)—a wall put down the center, a door carved out at the other end. As part of her case plan, Rhonda had had to find a place that was "suitable for children." Because she'd been evicted from her previous apartment for failing to pay her rent, this place was at once the best she could do and a viable solution to the department's necessarily flexible mandate. Driving by the trailer on our way to pick up DJ for their first visit, I was relieved to find that Rhonda hadn't rented something more expensive. This decision would afford her an extra month or two to get back on her feet.

At the same time, I was appalled by her living conditions, and whatever liberal good will I accorded myself began to evaporate in the recognition of just how limited (and patronizing) was our concern for her well-being. People love to complain about welfare, but they forget what such minimal government assistance allows, preferring instead the image of the Cadillac-driving loafer who cheats the system and rakes in the dough. Sadly, the difference between our point of view and that of more mean-spirited conservatives who'd deny her any assistance at all wouldn't, in the end, be enough to hang our ethical haloes on. No matter how completely Rhonda would become the caricature people use to rationalize their indifference to human misery, there was always a more complicated story of forces both private and public that were determining her fate in dynamic, cumulative interplay. I knew this, even as I somehow expected her to turn her life around, Houdini-like, with minimal assistance from us.

The first visit couldn't have been more awkward. Whether it was his autism, anger, or psychological defensiveness, or whether it was some indecipherable combination of the three that rendered him more distant than usual, DJ seemed to spurn his mother. He didn't run up to her upon her arrival by bike; he didn't respond to her exaggerated entreaties; he didn't take to her smothering kisses. Instead, he remained on the first of a row of swings, kicking the dirt with his feet, his eyes conspicuously captivated by something on the ground. If there was anyone he paid attention to, it was me—a detail not lost on Rhonda and insufficiently finessed by the remark: "It's so nice to see him with a man; you know, he's never really had a father." She seemed stunned when, suddenly, DJ got up and initiated a version of our big horn ritual on the grass by the swings and then wanted to be tickled.

While on the grass, I could hear her tell Emily that she was working on her problems, going to meetings; that she missed Ellie, who hadn't responded to any of the letters she'd written in the previous six months; that she was looking for a job, which she found demoralizing. Eventually, she'd run out of money, she reported, in a tone that only half-hinted at the possibility of further assistance from us. Her welfare checks had been discontinued almost six months before her children had been taken from her, accelerating the plunge into uncontrolled addiction, parental neglect, and, finally, homelessness. DJ's disability checks had been discontinued the very month he was removed from her custody. Although she was willing, she said, to work, she didn't see how with a minimum-wage job she was going to be able to make a significantly different go of it, even after the resumption of the disability checks. At best, these checks would cover the cost of day care for DJ, leaving her to survive on roughly the same amount of money as she had (or hadn't) on welfare.

When that first two-hour visit came to an end, Rhonda proceeded, as she would during each ensuing visit, to conduct the most exquisitely painful of good-byes—drawn out, punctuated by breathless sobbing. It was as if she were preparing for some final farewell—as if she knew, I now suspect, that she'd never be reunited with her son. DJ either refused her the pleasure of his sadness or didn't register her distress, having found what seemed to be a preserve among the many birds that darted indifferently above our heads. As we walked with him to the car, he did turn, however, and look at his mother who was still waving on her bike. He then climbed into the back seat and, for twenty minutes, sat frozen, like a curly-haired Buddha who hadn't yet mastered his detachment from the world.

That night at home, Emily recounted a very different sort of good-bye between DJ and Ellie. I'd asked her how "the sister" (as I'd called her back then) had handled these occasions. During the brief period that the two kids had remained in town, Emily had taken Ellie to see her brother at the unit, where he was still residing five days a week. The unit had a playground in back, lodged between a series of enormous brick buildings that hovered over a sad little swing set. There wasn't a blade of grass anywhere; it was all macadam, fenced to be sure that the children didn't wander off and get lost in the massive complex of the sick and dying. Having regularly driven Emily to work, I knew the playground well, and it seemed the worst possible backdrop for such visits. Squeezed in between the sidewalk and macadam and staked to the ground, the young trees surrounding it looked like patients out for a stroll, their I.V.s in tow. Sometimes, dropping Emily off, I imagined that even the sunny Florida sky had been admitted into the hospital or was perhaps there to schedule an appointment for chemotherapy.

Ellie, Emily reported, had stayed assiduously upbeat during these visits, a four-year-old with a thirty-five-year-old's life experience, looking out for her brother until the very end. She'd tried to compensate for her separation from DJ by being as bubbly and affectionate as possible: hugging him, kissing him, holding his hand. DJ had seemed at once happy to see her and confused by their separation. Why was he staying with a stranger on the weekends and not his mother and sister? Where was his mother? Emily had no idea what he did or didn't apprehend. She'd been trying not to cry, overcome by the general sorrow of it all and fearing the demise of the sibling relationship if Ellie remained with their father. At the end of the final visit, Ellie had insisted, in a little girl's voice, that it wasn't good-bye. "I'll come back soon," she'd said. I wondered how long, after that visit, before DJ stopped believing she might return. Listening to Emily, I pictured him in a state of frozen expectation.

The visits with Rhonda got easier, though DJ seemed always to hold something in reserve, as if he were waiting for the next disappointment. But Rhonda, at least initially, didn't disappoint. She found a job in a supermarket bakery, stayed away from the booze and the drugs, and, for nearly four months, didn't miss a single visit. After a while, DJ no longer seemed quite as withdrawn in her company: he'd sit on her lap, he'd make eye contact with her, he'd even sign "more" to be tickled. Only her good-byes would provoke the emotional scurrying of a frightened animal or the hiding-in-plain-light routine we'd come to think of as a mind in brilliant camouflage. The visits would gradually lengthen, become unsupervised, change their venue from the park to the subdivided trailer, where Rhonda would make DJ a grilled cheese sandwich or a bowl of SpaghettiOs.

Emily and I would continue to pick DJ up from, and bring him back to, his foster mother's house. She lived some distance from Rhonda, and the Department of Children and Families, with its overloaded caseworkers and myriad crises, couldn't be counted on to provide reliable transportation. We didn't want the sudden specter of disappointment to interfere with either Rhonda's fragile recovery or the reestablishment of the familial bond. Besides, Rhonda enjoyed talking with Emily, receiving encouragement, venting frustrations and fears. Do I need to say that Emily and I longed to see DJ as much as possible?

Just when this fragile experiment in support needed no disturbance, the unthinkable—or, really, the all too thinkable—happened. The week before Christmas, on Emily's birthday in fact, we received a call from DJ's caseworker saying that DJ had been badly beaten. His foster mother was under suspicion, his birth mother couldn't legally see him, DJ was hysterical, an investigation had to commence, an exam had to be conducted, photographs had to be taken, couldn't we come down to the hospital? The call had interrupted a dinner party we were throwing for a friend from India. I'd heard the phone ring, and when I walked into the kitchen, I noticed Emily's eyes beginning to well up. Informed of the beating, I could only mutter, "On your birthday?"

We made our way to the hospital after instructing our guests to proceed with the party. The whole way there, I excoriated the Department of Children and Families, demanding to know how it could have placed DJ in a home with five other foster children and a foster mother who clearly didn't want him. Emily had begged the Department to place him elsewhere. "This is how children get killed!" I yelled in my usual dramatic fashion, desperate to undo what had happened with ample outrage. Of course, I knew how badly DCF suffered from a shortage of foster homes, and people like me weren't exactly vying to become foster parents. But my liberal rhetoric often got out ahead of my actions, bathing the world in legitimate but empty complaint.

Entering the room where DJ was being held, we spotted him pacing back and forth, frantically flapping his arms, as deeply in a fog as we had ever seen him. From a distance, he didn't look injured—physically, that is. His clothes were on; a nurse was trying to get him to sit down in a chair so she could take his blood pressure. The room—I don't know why I remember this—was pale blue, with animal pictures on the walls: realistic photographs with sweetly unrealistic captions. The fluorescent lighting made DJ's skin and curly, blond hair seem even lighter than they were.

51

Upon seeing us, he stopped in his tracks, paused (as if to allow some associative chain to complete itself), and then began, to our tremendous astonishment, to make the sign for "more." As he was doing so, a doctor came into the room, a middle-aged woman with a doctor's slightly harried look. "What's he doing?" she asked.

"He's signing 'more,'" I said, still in shock. "He wants to be tickled."

"He wants to be tickled now?" the doctor asked.

"It's the only sign he knows," Emily replied, fighting back tears. "We taught it to him. I think he's reaching for something familiar." Again, DJ signed "more," this time coming over to me and placing my hand on his belly. He even managed something of a giggle, while still flapping his free arm and continuing to make a sound I'd never heard from him before: what might be imagined as the sound of a gerbil being smothered by a pillow.

"I'm not sure you should tickle him," the nurse remarked. "Have you seen his chest and stomach?" At which point, the exam began. His clothes were removed—he winced when we took off his shirt. I winced when the doctor proceeded to inspect his anus for signs of sexual abuse.

"It happens," the doctor said casually, snapping photographs.

How can I describe DJ's battered body? Irregular streaks of blue, purple, and black along his chest, back, and abdomen; his left ear kicked in, also blue, purple, and black—hardly resembling an ear. (That side of his head had been turned to the wall, thus preventing us from initially detecting the injury.) His porcelain face untouched, as if the perpetrator had merely gotten careless with the ear, otherwise careful to beat him in places his clothing would conceal. His legs and arms similarly untouched. The perpetrator didn't have to worry, of course, about the victim's implicating mouth.

Who could brutalize a three-year-old? What kind of barbarism was this? I'd obviously heard about child abuse, but I'd never seen this sort of injury up close. The placement of the bruises suggested that the perpetrator was an adult, probably the foster mother, yet the police would finger someone else: another foster child—a thirteen-year-old purportedly jealous of our regular visits with his flapping housemate.

Anxious and alone, Kyle had been, up until the very moment of the beating, especially kind to DJ. He'd played with him, he'd talked to him, he'd looked out for him amidst the turmoil of a large foster home and a rather emotionless foster mother, and then he'd snapped. *He* wanted attention, or so the theory went. We didn't entirely believe this explanation, which the foster mother had too conspicuously cooked up, though Emily did remember the boy once asking her when she arrived at his house, "When are you going to come see *me*?" The line— delivered, according to Emily, so straightforwardly, so accusatorily— haunts us to this day. Whereas Edna Austin, who at best should never have left her foster children unattended and who at worst beat DJ herself, ended up incurring merely a reduction in her monthly stipend as a result of having one fewer foster child, this boy, we'd soon learn, was charged with battery and commenced bouncing, like the caption ball on some bad Disney sing-along video, from one foster home to the next.

A representative from the Department, who'd been making a phone call while the exam was taking place, came back into the hospital room and asked us if we might be willing to provide emergency shelter for DJ. He was familiar with us, she said, he was familiar with our house, it would only be for a few days, they were trying to convince someone who already provided foster care for a child with special needs to take another, it was the Christmas season, we'd really be doing him and them a favor, etc., etc. (People from DCF all seem to speak this way, running a series of sentences together so as to prevent you from even thinking of saying no to their requests.) We, of course, said yes. I say "of course," but the journey to "of course" had been a long one through hills with a heavy pack. As much as we'd grown fond of DJ, we were anxious about becoming parents. What did we know about caring for a child full time, even if full time only meant a couple of days? And the institutional nature of the request, the massive bureaucratic context, only aggravated our anxiety.

That night, after we returned from the hospital and after Emily unlocked the front door, DJ took me, as usual, by the second finger on my right hand to the couch in the family room and asked me in sign, as if it were any other visit, to tickle him. Our guests had long gone, leaving a barely touched birthday cake on the dining room table. "I can't tickle you," I said. "You're hurt." Not understanding me, though clearly understanding I hadn't yet tickled him, DJ signed "more" again, becoming particularly agitated and, in fact, smacking his head. "Here, let me tickle your feet," I suggested, bending down to untie his shoes. DJ stopped me from doing so and, as he'd done at the hospital, stubbornly placed my hand on his stomach. "I can't tickle you there," I repeated, agitated myself. "You're hurt."

DJ was now in a frenzy. He was hitting his head against the wall and shrieking and, every few seconds, continuing to sign "more." "Go ahead and tickle him," Emily said, standing next to me. "Just do it very gently." Lifting his shirt, I searched for patches of white among the purple, blue, and black. Finding a few—and there were only a few—I brought my fingers down and hardly moved them, hardly applied any pressure, at all. DJ, who seemed to know I wasn't really tickling him, calmed immediately. More than once, I made him wince, and in return he proffered a sad, half-hearted giggle. He was that disciplined in his quest for familiarity and dare I say love. It would take a lot longer, of course, to honor the full import of DJ's signed injunction. Only in looking back can I see something like the ceiling of my resistance to becoming a father, to moving outside of myself, beginning to collapse upon me.

The following morning, Emily spoke with Rhonda by phone, telling her all she knew and assuring her DJ was okay: injured but okay. The conversation grew strained when Rhonda learned that DJ was staying with us and that we couldn't allow her to see him because DCF regulations forbade it. She found the whole experience of being left out of the loop humiliating. Her son had been taken from her out of concern for his safety only to be savagely beaten while in the care of the State. Who was the better guardian, she wanted to know? She'd never hit DJ, only Ellie, and only when she'd been drunk and certainly never savagely, she insisted.

Emily recognized this tone—a mixture of indignation and self-pity—and worried that Rhonda might start drinking again. She knew enough about how the foster care system often failed its children and treated its parent "clients" (all of that condescension and control) to appreciate Rhonda's point. But she didn't want to get her any more riled up than she already was, instead suggesting she call her AA sponsor and try to go to a meeting as soon as possible.

The next three days went by in a flash. We took DJ to the park, the mall, a restaurant for dinner. We let him play in the bath, an oversized, antique claw-foot tub, which he absolutely loved. He'd get his hair wet and watch the water dripping from his nose; he'd stir up the bubbles, asking for more—insistently, obsessively. After the first bath, DJ's eyes became puffy and red, prompting us to buy hypoallergenic shampoo. The spectacle of neophyte parents learning on the fly wasn't lost on us nor was the spectacle of a battered little boy having fun in the bath. We charted the progress of DJ's bruises, watching them turn colors and begin to fade, and we charted the progress of the department's search for new foster parents. The caseworker wasn't having much luck, and she asked us several times if we'd be able to keep DJ through Christmas, maybe even the New Year. We agreed, secretly hoping we might be able to do just that, but we told her she needed to find someone soon; we couldn't do this permanently. We were just helping out.

At night we tucked DJ into our fluffy, queen-sized bed, piling comforters on him, giving him kisses, saying, "Night, little man. Sweet dreams." That first evening, he'd made whimpering noises, and so Emily had gone in and lain down next to him until he fell asleep. The following three nights, he directed Emily to the bed and even draped her arm around him. I slept on the couch, periodically getting up to check on our dozing charge.

On the fourth day, the caseworker called to tell us she'd convinced DJ's special ed preschool teacher, already a foster mother of a boy with a significant cognitive disability, to take DJ. A fiercely proud, African-American woman, she and Emily had something of a history, having been on opposite sides of the inclusion debate. This tension would end up troubling our relationship from start to finish. It manifested itself immediately when Emily asked Gladys on the phone if we might keep DJ for an extra day. "No," she said sternly; she needed to pick him up in a few hours and then, softening a bit, added that she was trying to buy a suit for him for Christmas services. She'd already bought one for her other foster child.

By the time Gladys's husband showed up in his van, Emily and I were beside ourselves with grief. I was carefully putting DJ's winter cap on his head and buttoning each of the buttons on his winter jacket, though it really wasn't very cold outside. We'd gotten a Christmas present for him, and I took it out with us to the van; Emily grabbed his things. DJ didn't seem to want to go, but he certainly went agreeably enough, quietly enough, without looking back. Emily kept it together until the very moment Gladys's husband started the ignition, and then she began to sob convulsively. (Later, on an errand at the pharmacy, she threw up in the bathroom and then fainted; she was having her period and felt awful, but I think it was the stress of DJ's departure that really clobbered her.) As I held Emily in the living room and watched the van pull away, I asked myself why we hadn't offered to become DJ's regular foster parents.

I asked the question repeatedly, dismissing a host of very reasonable excuses, including the fear that we couldn't shoulder the burden of fostering a child with autism and, as important, the worry that we'd be complicating our relationship with Rhonda. We neither wanted her to think we were trying to take DJ from her nor that she didn't have to stay clean— that we'd be available, in short, to parent him if she decided not to. We gnawed on this latter excuse as we drove to Vero Beach to spend Christmas with my family, but even it couldn't stand up to the picture of a boy who'd reached out to us being shipped off to yet another home. How could we both want DJ and not want him—or, rather, want Rhonda to have him? We still believed the best course of action posited Rhonda's and DJ's interests as identical; that this course of action also spoke to our own fears and selfishness made it that much easier to endorse. The entire time in Vero, lounging in the marbled lap of my millionaire father, we thought of DJ, wondering how he was doing, whether his bruises had healed, what he'd received for Christmas.

CHAPTER 3

Have You Tried In Vitro? or What's in a Name?

"I'm pregnant," Rhonda announced one Tuesday in March, roughly four months into our paying her rent. We were sitting in a McDonalds with DJ, I remember, who was eating fries: two at a time, one on each side of his mouth, like logs being drawn into an old Bugs Bunny saw-mill. She'd begun by congratulating herself on having met her various commitments—a long, drawn-out speech clearly paving the way for something awful—and then had sprung her surprise. She refused to have an abortion, she said dramatically (and at a volume that drew the attention of those nearby), but she was considering giving the baby up for adoption. Her obligation was to her son—she wanted us to know this—but she also had an obligation now to the little life inside her.

Though she seemed to understand the peril in which this pregnancy had placed her, she was strangely happy: aglow in the mistaken assumption of a universal and undiscerning reverence for expectant motherhood. She had no idea who the father was, even less idea how she might support two children: one, an infant; the other, a three-year-old with a cognitive disability. She confessed that she'd been drinking some and doing drugs, mostly on the weekends when she'd been lonely and, faced with too much time to kill, had needed to regard the wreckage of her life from a familiar barstool or a stranger's bed. She couldn't be forced to choose between the two children, she cried, and as she did I was sure I detected some registration of this possibility, some slowdown in the management of that otherwise efficient and oblivious sawmill.

Overnight, our interaction with her began to resemble a bad, made-for-TV movie, complete with facile foreshadowing and a not-to-be-resisted moral concerning the pointlessness of helping people. Rhonda quit her job—at forty, her back and feet couldn't take the strain of pregnancy and a full day's work—found the bottle again ferociously, and started canceling her court-appointed visits with DJ. Twice, forgetting to cancel a visit, she handed him a lollipop at the door of her trailer and stepped back inside, inexplicably refusing to see him. For periods at a time, she disappeared entirely, leaving DJ only that much more confused and isolated. After weeks without a visit, he'd stare so deeply into space upon seeing her that even tickling wouldn't rouse him.

How could she have gotten pregnant? How could she be drinking? We'd come so far, I told myself, having made it through the period of DJ's assault when she'd felt most vulnerable to a setback. Only recently she'd been, or seemed to have been, on something of a roll. But even my despair was self-congratulatory. Could I really have imagined that four months' rent and a bit of cheering from the peanut gallery would turn this woman around? Listen to my language: "this woman." As embarrassed as I was to admit it, I resented Rhonda. She'd sabotaged our day trip to beneficence, loosening the lug nuts on our naïve jalopy and then feigning surprise as the wheels fell off.

By mid-April, she was out of money. Threatened with eviction, she pleaded for further "assistance," coupling her requests with a cynical—or, at the very least, obtuse—complaint about DJ's "coolness" toward her. All along, we'd feared that the autism might allow her to think he didn't love her. "Don't you worry," she'd say, "I'm not gonna abandon him. I just need more." "More," she'd mouth while signing the word and awkwardly calling attention to her joke. As delicately as we could, we reminded her of the original agreement: a few months rent and a security deposit. Though we feared for DJ, we clung to our refusal, which was as much a part of this poorly scripted drama as her more obvious failures.

For the next two months, we implored Rhonda to stop drinking, to develop a plan for the future (which would have to include finding another, less demanding job), and, most important of all, to visit regularly with DJ. Only then—our resolve was crumbling—could we talk about more "assistance." How much assistance? Were we prepared to support her indefinitely? What precisely was our commitment to this family?

Rhonda saved us—I want to say thankfully—from having to answer these questions: first, by getting pregnant and, then, by adopting a tactic of merciless self-destruction. Knowing that she couldn't make a go of it with both children, she vowed, I think, to make a go of it with neither. She'd make the State, which moved like the slowest of locomotives, do everything, decide everything. She'd simply lie down on the tracks—booze in one hand, drugs in the other—and wait for it to cleave her in two. She wouldn't even try to get up, proclaiming from the rails her motherly devotion. She was, Emily said, a perverse example of the powerlessness that plagues poor women in the system and of the prevarication that plagues those who won't take any responsibility for their lives.

Although we could sympathize with Rhonda's unwillingness to choose between DJ and her unborn baby, we believed she had no choice but to surrender the baby and, in doing so, maximize the chances of a decent life for each child; the baby's prospects for adoption frankly far exceeded DJ's. But as quickly as she'd fallen off the wagon, it didn't seem that she'd arrive at such a conclusion or even try to slow her descent. And yet, she'd resurrected herself once before. Indeed, the four months of consistent visits, faithful employment, and relative sobriety had been tantalizing.

In early June, still a good month before Rhonda would give birth and only a week before she'd be evicted, Emily ventured to the trailer one last time to urge her to make a decision about her children. She simply had to think of their well-being; she couldn't wait for the State to make a decision for her. She was injuring her fetus and emotionally scarring DJ. Emily practiced making her points, before leaving, in a manner that would least inflame Rhonda. Though I'd wanted to accompany her, Emily insisted on going alone, believing they might talk more honestly just the two of them. She planned to offer Rhonda regular respite care if she once again committed herself to the goal of reunification. How she'd be able to take advantage of this help when she wouldn't have a place to stay or food to eat we hadn't exactly determined. We were like poorly prepared students taking a test, desperate for a point or two of credit and scribbling any old answer on the page.

When Emily arrived at the trailer, Rhonda was drunk, as drunk as she had ever seen her: flailing her arms, knocking things off the shelves, and screaming, as if she'd intuited the purpose of the visit. "How am I gonna bond with this baby when the fuckin' thing is gonna make me give up my son?" she yelled. Emily knew right then, of course, what Rhonda's preference was: some fantasy of a fresh start with a child who might naturally bond with her, but she also detected a guilt that would prevent Rhonda from ever actually choosing her daughter. The visit revealed the obscene intransigence of everyone involved: she refused to make a choice and drank, and we refused to give her more assistance.

Almost from the beginning the game had involved not directly linking our assistance to keeping DJ, though we all knew that was the arrangement. We'd hoped to avoid crassly defining the limits of our concern, and she'd hoped to prolong the experience of our affection. We wanted to help Rhonda, but only in the context of helping DJ. Now, with a week left on her rental, the cat was out of the proverbial bag (or, rather, the lion was out of its cage), and Rhonda sought control wherever she could find it. "*You'll* have to abandon me," she slurred. "I won't abandon my children," though the latter was precisely what she was doing.

Emily begged her to reenter rehab; she suggested that the program Rhonda had completed might take her back, but Rhonda knew otherwise. The only hope for her was some private detox center, and she had no money. Money—the very word unleashed a new tirade. "DJ misses you," Emily interjected cautiously.

"I can't help him," Rhonda sobbed.

"Try," Emily said. "We'll take care of him two days a week."

"Don't you fuckin' get it? I can't do it!" she shouted. "How am I gonna live?" Rhonda became so irate she seemed to want to hit Emily, staggering toward her and then half-falling, half-lunging in her direction. As Emily moved out of the way, Rhonda picked up something off the floor and hurled it against the side of the trailer, just missing Emily's head. The object fell into a borrowed baby stroller, as though it were some sort of omen. "Get the fuck out of here!" she screamed. When Emily tried to say something, Rhonda threw another object. The conversation was over, and Emily left as quickly as she could. Walking to her car, she saw two men lurking near the trailer, men she hadn't seen before. By the time she got home, she was still shaking.

"You should have seen her, Ralph, practically about to give birth on the sofa and taking huge swigs of beer. Utterly shitfaced. That kid's gonna have problems."

I've had years to ponder Rhonda's actions, and I still don't know what definitively to make of them. In their pleasurable demonization of "bad" mothers, many choose to ignore the link between income level and an intervention by the Department of Children and Families. Many refuse to acknowledge any relationship at all between a life of poverty and a habit of deplorable judgment or character (including the particular habit of substance abuse). "Choose to be rich," the self-help books and Sunday morning infomercials exclaim.

In Upton Sinclair's famous novel *The Jungle*, the Lithuanian protagonist meets every unendurable hardship with the line, "I must work harder," and still he can't get ahead. Writing during a period in which there wasn't any social safety net, Sinclair sought to dramatize the brutal repercussions of industrial capitalism, relocating the burden of responsibility from the individual to society. We've lost our taste in literature and life for strictly deterministic accounts and yet now favor a view just as extreme in its repudiation of the social and economic factors that shape people. It's all about personal responsibility, as my father would say.

Unable to reconcile my swaggering radicalism with a growing sense of the messiness of human experience, I lashed out at conservatives, though I'd already witnessed a hundred ways in which Rhonda, and not her material circumstances, had been to blame for her problems. (I know, you can't really disentangle these strands without being reductive, but sometimes a little reductiveness goes a long way toward helping you to see the strand you deny.) As a kind of compensatory hyperbole, I once suggested the State should take the children of the poor in advance of any particular grievance, to such stress does the ethic of smaller government and a "free" market now expose their parents. In this scenario, even the most diligent of mothers is crushed by naturalistic forces. With a critical shortage of foster homes, perhaps the older children, I proposed, could be sent to an abandoned military base where, like prison inmates, they could become another source of cheap labor, executing America's airline reservations or catalogue purchases.

A less inflammatory view requires less inflammatory rhetoric. So, let me ask: How was Rhonda supposed to have conquered her addictions, worked intensively with her disabled son, and held down a minimum-wage job that guaranteed she wouldn't be able to make ends meet? Even without a new baby she seemed doomed. And why, if we really could dismiss every last environmental influence in our assessment of character (and, as a consequence, imagine the woman becoming a different person once she'd just decided to do so), would we then test such a proposition with the worst sort of structural discouragement: unlivable wages, meaningless drudgery without the prospect of advancement, inadequate housing, lack of health care, lack of child care, etc.? The poor, certainly the recovering addicts among them, need no additional discouragement. Before too quickly declaiming the rhetoric of personal responsibility, before too easily hating a given mother for her weakness, her selfishness, even her violence, might we remember the *roughly* determinant conditions of her existence? Might our social analysis be a bit more complicated?

The truth is, for all of my liberal outrage at those who would demonize the poor, I found myself disliking Rhonda—her dishonesty, her selfishness, her weakness—even as I recognized I could afford to dislike her. I had a house, a job, all sorts of resources. She, on the other hand, was desperate. But knowledge just couldn't keep pace with feeling. I'd read, of course, about the merciless, post-welfare world in which we were asking Rhonda to make it on her own. I'd seen it from a distance at the soup kitchen. I understood the distinction between removing people from the rolls and finding them decent jobs. "Was our nation

62

focused on eliminating poverty, or just slashing caseloads?" the journalist LynNell Hancock asks rhetorically in her book, *Hands to Work: The Stories of Three Families Racing the Welfare Clock.* A study of PRWORA (Personal Responsibility and Work Opportunity Reconciliation Act) from the University of Wisconsin found that only one-fourth of those who had been on welfare had been able to lift their families above the poverty line in their new jobs. I knew that welfare spending on children with families had constituted only one percent of the national budget prior to the passage of PRWORA. How to conceive of it as the impediment to economic competitiveness that many conservatives claimed it to be? Such a claim was entirely cynical, as cynical as saying that Emily and I couldn't have afforded to continue paying Rhonda's meager rent.

And yet, the more I dealt with Rhonda, the more knowledge gasped and lumbered up the course of life, indeed the more my political convictions seemed like marathon dropouts: dehydrated, exhausted, in need of an I.V. In addition to the triumph of personal antipathy, the critique of PRWORA appeared increasingly inadequate, even slanted. It was as if there hadn't been any problems with welfare abuse, for instance, or with the not so subtle incentive to have more children. In his book *The Price of Citizenship*, the historian Michael Katz maintains that welfare reform represented a strictly ideological accomplishment, achieved through malicious attacks on poor women. Beginning in the late 70s, he argues, welfare began to "conjure a narrowly conceived image of morally suspect women." Within a decade it had become a "despised program of last resort primarily for the 'undeserving' poor—unmarried mothers, many of them black and Hispanic"—and it signified the "triple stigma of sexual licentiousness, willful poverty, and race."

But what if the stereotype in no small measure fit, at least for some? We knew that Rhonda had consistently spent a portion of her welfare and disability checks on booze and drugs. Moreover, after adopting DJ and receiving the mass of documents in his file, we'd discover that she'd lost custody of two other children prior to losing Ellie and DJ. Including the baby, whom she'd eventually lose as well, that would make five children altogether. *Five* children! It's cheating, of course, to drop this detail in here—we didn't know it at the time—but obviously some part of me thinks the case against Rhonda might be vulnerable without it. Another part concedes I've now tipped the scale in favor of outright condemnation and, in the process, made my own actions look better.

Values intrude at every moment, values that punish women far more than the men who get them pregnant and then promptly disappear; yet to talk about pregnancy and welfare or harmful parenting and welfare isn't (necessarily) to engage in misogyny. Gwendolyn Mink would have us believe the 1997 Adoption and Safe Families Act, which seeks to shorten the time that a child can remain in foster care before caseworkers pursue the termination of parental rights, was *simply* an attack on single mothers: "With a time limit on parental rights shorter even than the federal time limit on welfare, the adoption law hovers within the TANF [Temporary Aid for Needy Families] regime as the regime's final solution to independent motherhood." Final solution? Surely, feminist commitments must not come at the expense of children with equivalently urgent needs. DJ, to put a face on these abstractions, was crying out for help.

A few days after the blowup at the trailer, Rhonda began leaving messages on our machine demanding that we stop trying to steal her kid. Emily and I still hadn't spoken, let alone thought, of adopting DJ, and we were offended by the charge. He was Rhonda's kid—a logic we'd come to renounce, at least in its most restrictive meaning, but one that we were still trying to honor, especially in the case of a poor woman at odds with such powerful forces. Moreover, we ardently believed that Ellie and DJ ought to be able to live together, and Rhonda offered the only chance of making this happen.

Though we understood how excruciating her agony must have been and how she must have needed to hate us for our comfortable good will, which we'd dangled before her and then so piously retracted, we couldn't believe the irony of her accusation. Rhonda had doubted whether *she* could parent DJ. "We've been trying to help this stupid woman get DJ back!" I yelled, foregoing all sensitivity. "No one sets out to steal a kid with autism." If anything, we'd been pushing even harder than before to compel Rhonda to assume her responsibility. We'd begun to focus on the prospect of DJ having no one and, despite our great fondness for him, feared being fingered as potential parents. It was one thing to agree to a four-day emergency placement, quite another to agree to a permanent one. The riptide of our involvement had already pulled us so far out that we thought we'd never make it back to shore.

But why was Rhonda leveling such a charge? Because she sought to avoid responsibility for losing DJ? Because she felt guilty? Yes, of course, though I want to believe she was also asserting the value of her son over and against any calculus that would find him lacking. A battle for DJ would mean that he was loved, desired. She could love him through this act of half-hearted paranoia. Though she no doubt sensed our feelings for DJ, she must have known we'd never have actively vied to take him from her, at least not at that point. Sometimes, I think she might have been *asking* us to take him—in the form of an accusation that planted the seed and allowed her to preserve her resentment of us, of us and of a world of choices in which she had none (or at least none she found satisfactory). Perhaps I give Rhonda too much credit when I suggest she was finding DJ parents. And perhaps I once again let myself off the hook for abandoning her, for making such a "happy" ending inevitable.

In any event, Emily and I grew into the accusation. I still can't isolate the moment we first mentioned the word "adoption," but shortly after the fateful encounter in the trailer and Rhonda's phone messages, we started throwing it around—half like a football that two eight-year-olds might use to act out some future heroics, half like a hot potato that threatened to burn anyone foolish enough to linger over it. For hours on end, we'd discuss the possibility, delivering arguments like law students at moot court. How much longer can DJ wait to have parents, one of us would ask? How much longer can he wait for the joys—yes, the profitably insulated joys—of a middle-class childhood? Or, more crucial, how much longer can he wait for the kind of one-on-one therapy that might still bring him language and a chance at an independent life? How can we not do this? one of us would say. How can we do this? the other would reply. Emily was concerned that we not frame our decision around the idea of cognitive progress. She didn't need that kind of pressure, and, more important, she wanted to love DJ for who he was and what he could do now. We both knew that he could do more, but that couldn't be the precondition for deciding to adopt him.

I couldn't believe we were even talking about this. Like me, Emily had previously sworn she didn't want children. When she'd chosen to work with kids with neurological disabilities, she'd claimed she couldn't have both a family and a vocation. Surely, what she was doing for DJ, the reasoning had gone, wouldn't be possible if she were busy raising children. And if she were busy raising DJ, well, a vocational commitment would cease altogether, what with the sheer intensity of his demands. Such a scenario would constitute the most perverse kind of anti-utilitarianism: the good of the one coming at the expense of the many. All of those weekend visits, after-dinner visits, and endless telephone calls about alternative forms of communication (such as picture schedules and adapted sign language), play-embedded learning, redesigned classroom environments, interventions for self-injurious behavior, toileting strategies, strategies for managing extreme food selectivity, strategies for pressuring unsympathetic school administrators, strategies for negotiating due process hearings, ways of accessing service providers, ways of coping with parental disappointment and fatigue—all of those extras would have to be curtailed were she to become a mother, let alone DJ's mother.

As important as the threat to a sense of vocation had been the threat to our relationship. Eight years into her marriage, Emily still found her husband's green eyes and deteriorating runner's build attractive and wanted to spend time with them, with me! She'd relished our many shared activities, even as she'd apparently perceived me to be tunneling each week further inside myself. (That romance might constitute a retreat from the world hadn't concerned us. Like social geneticists, we were certain we'd identified the elusive marker for the dreaded bourgeois trait: a minivan! Moreover, like the overblown Warren Beatty character in the movie *Reds*, I'd declared romance to be an integral part of political commitment.) Should I have known that as Emily had expressed these fears she was harboring a passionate desire to do what she'd foresworn: have, or at least raise, a child? Should I have detected in her voice the empty auditorium of argument's rehearsal, the underlying wish to have a shot at it all? Had she simply been a better actor than I, or just more sensitive to her partner's contradictions?

Once again, at a key moment in this drama, Emily and I went on vacation, this time to Emily's folks' cottage in Northern Michigan. Even more than at Christmas, we thought about DJ and missed him terribly. We hadn't seen him in weeks, as Rhonda had stopped visiting with him. Speaking to our friend Nancy on the phone, I heard for the first time a description of my feelings that fit, a description I'd resisted, suppressed, like some popular uprising of the heart. "You've fallen in love with that boy, Ralph."

She was right. I couldn't bear the thought of DJ in foster care while we had fun at the lake, taking the boat out, playing tennis. What was he thinking? Did he wonder why we hadn't come to pick him up and take him to his mother's, why we hadn't tickled him and played at the park? I couldn't bear the thought of moving forward with our lives as he stood, his meager possessions beside him, in some fatalistic station of neglect, trains arriving and departing and no one, no one, sweeping him up and ushering him lavishly into their lives, making him feel special, loved. If this sounds melodramatic, so be it. It's what I felt. I woke up one morning at the lake and said to Emily, "We have to do this. We have to try. If Rhonda won't get him back, we need to step forward."

"Yes," Emily responded, surprising me. I'd meant what I'd said but almost hoped to be talked out of it. Emily, after all, was the more sober and sensible of the two of us, rarely allowing her enthusiasm to commandeer her common sense, and here she was responding "yes"—an entire, vexing quandary reduced to one word. "Let's wait till the baby is born and see what Rhonda does. Maybe she'll change her mind and fight for DJ. Otherwise, we should adopt him."

Having arrived at this momentous decision, fear promptly set in. Could we really do this: adopt a child with a significant disability? I mean, could we *really* do this, not only do this but do it well? We agreed not to say anything to anybody (our friends and family would think us insane—how insane we'd soon find out) and instead just wait for further clarification of Rhonda's ultimate intention.

I wish I could explain *precisely* how we came to our decision. At least for me, it felt like the overdue recognition of a need. Back before meeting DJ, I hadn't yet discovered a way of attending to the dream of a more inclusive happiness that wasn't also a form of parodic self-punishment or abnegation. In that signing three-year-old, however, I'd come to see the dream's continuing possibility and the fulfillment of my own nagging, if fearful, desire to be a parent. Under DJ's tutelage, I'd already found myself hunting amidst the news for a place to laugh, a place in which to move resolutely forward. I knew that caring for DJ would preclude doing other political work, but caring for DJ was essential.

There's so much to say about the duty to respond to the world beyond our noses, but instead let me quote from Molly Peacock's poem "Altruism." Though it doesn't mention autism—a word that literally means "self-referring"—the poem echoes what I've been presenting as our common predicament, even as the setting is conspicuously and comfortably suburban.

> What if we got outside ourselves and there
> really was an outside there, not just
> our insides turned inside out? What if there
> really were a you beyond me, not just
> the waves off my own fire, like those waves off
> the backyard grill you can see the next yard through,
> though not well—just enough to know that off
> to the right belongs to someone else, not you.
> What if, when we said *I love you*, there were
> a you to love as there is a yard beyond
> to walk past the grill and get to? To endure
> the endless walk through the self, knowing through a bond

that has no basis (for ourselves are all we know)
is altruism: not giving, but coming to know
someone is there through the wavy vision
of the self's heat, love become a decision.

I've spent a lot of time thinking about the phrases "to endure the end-less walk through the self," "a bond that has no basis," and, of course, "love become a decision."

After Rhonda gave birth to the baby, she moved in with her sister, who told her in no uncertain terms that the arrangement was tempo-rary. Rhonda asked to see DJ in early August, and we suggested that she get someone from DCF to transport him from, and to, Gladys's. We thought she wouldn't want us to be there in light of her caustic accusa-tions, but, in fact, she did. I had to stop myself from divining the pur-pose of the visit—to tell DJ good-bye? To move forward with her case plan? To try to make a go of it with both children? I could actually feel my heart racing as we drove up to Rhonda's sister's apartment.

Why I imagined she might actually have some definitive pronounce-ment for us I don't know, because she didn't. She acted as if it were any old day, hugging DJ (who immediately performed his emotional disap-pearing act), saying hello to us, exchanging pleasantries. "This is your new sister," Rhonda remarked, holding Hannah out in front of DJ, who refused to look at her. "Isn't she cute?" The awkwardness, at least from our perspective, was unbearable.

"We'll be back in a couple of hours," Emily said, cutting Rhonda off. When we moved to leave, DJ tried to follow us.

"No, you stay here," I said. "We'll see you soon." He seemed not to understand, again trying to follow us.

"Come to Mama, DJ," Rhonda half-shouted, and when she did we could hear the garbled final syllable of her son's name.

In the car, Emily asked if I'd noticed the beer in the baby stroller, a six-pack of Pabst Blue Ribbon poorly concealed beneath an infant's color-ful onesy. Later, collecting DJ, we offered Rhonda a chance to tell us whatever was on her mind, staying a bit longer than perhaps we should have, but she said nothing, nothing but "Bye, DJ, bye."

Two weeks later, after dropping the baby at her sister's, Rhonda began wandering the eastern coast of Florida. When it seemed she wasn't coming back, we had a meeting with the head of the Guardian *ad-Litem* program in our town, a wonderful woman, one of the toughest (and sweetest) child advocates I've ever come across. We told her that we might be interested in adopting DJ, and we wondered how in the meantime we could see him regularly. The woman, Bobbie Johnson, had gotten to know Emily through the various proceedings involving Rhonda, and she'd been impressed with how much support we'd provided her and DJ. She knew that Emily was an expert on autism, and she could imagine, she said, no one better suited to being DJ's parents. "You're the kind of gift from God we almost never receive, no matter how hard we pray," she stated plainly. I didn't feel like a gift from God; I felt like an all too imperfect convert of another sort: a secular proselyte who finds himself, dream-like, at the door of a crumbling institution. "At the hearing in late September, let me propose the possibility of liberal visitation, with the idea that you and your husband have been the one constant in this little boy's life. I'll suggest you've indicated a willingness to adopt DJ should his mother continue to defy her case plan. The judge just might go for it." And he did, though Gladys was none too pleased. She didn't like being ordered to accommodate our wishes, even as she and her husband had said they didn't want to adopt DJ. (In Florida, foster parents are given preference when it comes to their foster child's adoption.)

And so, we began our weekly, three and a half hour visits with DJ. Accustomed to such a short time with him, we reveled in the luxury of so many minutes—two hundred ten of them, lined up like dominoes and falling the moment we got him into our car, falling the moment he signed "more." I had gotten it into my head that we should teach DJ how to rollerskate. Emily had her doubts. With his vision, body awareness, sensation overload, and coordination problems, rollerskating seemed the last thing he might take to. But I was insistent. I wanted him to have fun. I wanted us to be active. I wanted to expose him to new experiences.

Monday night, we discovered, was Christian music night at Skate Station, our town's rollerskating rink. Beyond the pulsating, heavy metal refrains of JESUS that shook the building, Christian music night offered a distinct advantage over other nights at Skate Station: it was miraculously uncrowded, and beginners could feel comfortable skating slowly and, if they had to, collapsing onto the floor without fear of being run over. At first, DJ was like some sort of drunk Gumby; he seemed to have no muscle groups or vertebrae. Emily and I each took hold of an arm and tried to propel him forward, but he immediately did the splits. It took a while, but eventually (several weeks into these outings) we taught him to keep his knees locked and his legs rigid so that we could pull him around the rink. He loved the colored disco lights, which caromed off the ceiling. As we strode in tandem, he followed the lights with his eyes, moving his head as he would have his hands had they been free. He'd gone from putty to steel with his constitution. Though he didn't appear to respond to the greetings of the kids who passed on either side of us—African-American kids from Gladys's neighborhood and church, we surmised—he wore a smile that broadened slightly whenever "Hi, DJ" came our way.

Over the course of the next year, we'd get better at this synchronized event, falling much less frequently and improving our speed. In addition to rollerskating, we took DJ to the mall, to restaurants, to a neighbor's heated pool, to the park, to the fair when it came through town. We let him play in the bath. We wrestled with him and, of course, tickled him. We also began to experiment with toilet training, letting DJ forego the diaper during the period he was with us. Emily actually knew quite a bit about toilet training kids with cognitive disabilities—she'd presented at conferences on this topic—and Rhonda, before dropping out of the picture, had expressed an interest in having DJ master this basic skill. We utilized the Miller Method, which emphasizes a highly predictable routine, broken up into a series of accomplishable motoric events: walking into the bathroom, unbuttoning your trousers, pulling down your underpants, sitting on the toilet seat, etc. The idea was to make the child an active participant in toileting rather than the passive object of diaper changing. We took a picture of poop and urine in the toilet so as to underscore the proper place for such waste and made certain to have DJ perform this ritual at the same time each visit. Emily believed that if you could get a child to invest in the ritual, the final productive achievement would come naturally—like the urge, she said, to place the last piece in a jigsaw puzzle.

Our five-year-old diaper-wearer caught on almost immediately. We didn't tell Gladys about this training, aware of both her prickly control issues and oft-stated concern that DJ wouldn't be able to sit through long church services on Sundays and Wednesdays without a diaper. How was he going to indicate the need to go to the bathroom? She wasn't opposed to toilet training, she said. She just didn't think he was ready for it. After one visit, we forgot to put DJ back in a diaper, and later at Gladys's he peed in his pants. She was furious; she even complained to DCF about our interference. We were furious with her for retarding DJ's development. This fight over what was best for DJ became the vehicle for expressing otherwise unarticulated racial and economic tensions. No matter how superior our more progressive understanding of disability, we presented ourselves as, well, superior: upper middle-class white people telling lower middle-class black people what to do. Gladys and her husband had seen our nicely renovated Victorian bungalow (situated, provocatively, at the edge of a black neighborhood), and we had seen their semi-rundown doublewide on the outskirts of town.

Once, as we were picking up DJ, Gladys's husband quipped, "Ya'll sure do have a lot of cars." Because Emily's job required her to travel quite a bit, she was frequently rushing back from some distant county and often had a rental car on the day of our visits. The man mistakenly assumed we owned these cars. When he made the remark, I had a better sense of how we must have come across to him and Gladys, and I began to understand how a commitment to inclusion, at least at that particular point in history, seemed a sign of privilege. Again, however, rational understanding couldn't keep up with actual experience: the messiness and complication, the untameable feelings. Gladys and her husband resented us, and we resented their resentment.

In early November, Rhonda's sister phoned to say that Rhonda was back in town and wanted to speak with us. She was staying with a man and hadn't retrieved the baby; the sister didn't know much more. When we called, Rhonda asked if we could come to the man's apartment the following Saturday to talk about DJ. Still committed to helping her, yet ever more deeply attached to DJ, we decided to reiterate our offer of regular respite care and to mention the possibility of adoption. We wanted to push Rhonda, as gingerly as we could, to make a decision about DJ: either recommit to the case plan or terminate her parental rights. We worried that the offer of adoption would provoke another round of child-stealing charges, but we had to do something. We knew that an involuntary termination of parental rights could take forever, despite the new law that required DCF to move toward TPR after a child has been in foster care for fifteen months. In the meantime, DJ was waiting for permanency, therapeutic intervention, and love.

We showed up at the apartment where Rhonda was staying, and the man opened the door. I immediately wondered if he was the baby's father—the baby looked vaguely like him. "My friend here's letting me live with him," she said in a tone intimating something untoward, a kind of bartered business arrangement. The man hovered over Rhonda, giving her directions, and she seemed to compensate by being too cheerful, too solicitous of him. When the conversation finally turned to DJ, she paused and said, "I think I'm gonna sign away my rights. I know I can't parent him." We couldn't believe our ears. It wasn't a definitive pronouncement, but it was close to one. Emily reminded Rhonda of our willingness to provide respite care, and then like someone who's been digging a tunnel for years and hoping her counterpart across the channel has been similarly diligent, she pushed forward and proposed to adopt DJ. As Emily said the word "adoption," I looked for the telltale sign of light from the other side, light and crumbling earth. "Let me think about it," Rhonda said. "I know you care about him. I know you'll both help him." Risking pushiness, we talked about the difference between a voluntary and involuntary termination of parental rights and how the former would allow us to help DJ sooner.

"Only if you can't parent him," Emily clarified, her voice ever so slightly disingenuous. We were now rooting for Rhonda to sign away her kid.

"Let me think about it," Rhonda repeated.

Over Thanksgiving she left a message on our machine thanking us for all we had done and asking us to adopt her son. Her voice was strong and firm, cracking only at the end. When we got back from Hilton Head, where we'd spent the holiday with Emily's parents, we tried calling Rhonda at the man's apartment but learned that she had left, taken off without telling him or anyone else where she was going. What to do? We phoned Bobbie Johnson, the Guardian *ad-Litem* supervisor, and explained the situation. She suggested we pursue our adoption plans by enrolling in the next available MAPP (Model Approach to Partnerships in Parenting) class at the Department of Children and Families in January with the idea that we'd be ready to move when Rhonda signed surrenders. If she didn't reappear, we'd have to wait for the process of involuntary termination to unfold in all its dilatory splendor. (Bobbie had once remarked that it was easier to execute a person in the state of Florida than to terminate that person's parental rights.) Either way, we had to enroll in the MAPP class, be interviewed extensively, have a background check with fingerprinting, and complete a home study. All of this would take time, giving us the opportunity to search for Rhonda, which we did—everywhere: at her sister's, at her previous place of employment, at her favorite bars, at the homeless shelter, at a couple of old boyfriends'. She had a habit of popping back into town, and we wanted to be sure to catch her when she did.

The writer Annie Dillard has an essay called "Living like Weasels," in which she derives from the weasel's habit of biting his prey at the neck and not letting go a figure for purposeful living. One particular weasel, she reports, having been pounced on by an eagle, "swiveled and bit as instinct taught him, tooth to neck, and nearly won." The eagle, once it died, was found with the "dry skull of a weasel fixed by the jaws to his throat." Dillard extrapolates, "I think it would be well, and proper, and obedient, and pure, to grasp your one necessity and not let it go, to dangle from it limp wherever it takes you. Then even death, where you're going no matter how you live, cannot you part. Seize it and let it seize you up aloft even, till your eyes burn out and drop; let your musky flesh fall off in shreds, and let your very bones unhinge and scatter, loosening over fields. . . ."

Now, I love this passage even as I recognize its unbounded hyperbole. Something like this had taken hold of me—exactly as I had taken hold of it. For the next seven months, I devoted myself to freeing DJ from foster care and becoming his father, calling DCF practically every day to urge them to accelerate the process. I'd picture DJ in that station of neglect and have the feeling you get when you're late picking someone up, very late. Did the little guy understand that we were coming? That we were stuck in the traffic of a congested bureaucracy? The romance of my "one necessity" was romantic enough to drive me onward yet realistic enough to allow me to know, at least to some extent, what we were getting into with DJ. And it was conflicted enough to remember the plight of his mother. Our noble ambulance run had, after all, left an injured party at the scene.

How can remorse seem anything but an empty gesture, a mere narrative requirement? Why bother to go back in these pages, sirens blaring, knowing full well that Rhonda no longer lies there on the ground? Because her story is complex, more complex than either side of the welfare debate would generally concede. Though Rhonda appeared to be the very embodiment of conservative complaints—having babies, refusing to work, unable to stay clean, parentally negligent—she was more than this. In addition to learning about the other children she had lost, we'd also learn that she'd been sexually abused as a girl and abandoned by her own mother. Without directly correlating childhood injury to adult action, I want to honor these formative traumas. At the same time, I know that other addicts, abuse victims, and welfare recipients have managed, against insuperable odds, to rise above, plow through, maneuver around their circumstances—circumstances both of, and not of, their own devising. (These two points of view line up in my head, as in an old-fashioned duel, and repeatedly, though not mortally, wound each other. Guilt and a natural propensity to analyze things keep the duel going.)

While the historian Michael Katz rightly insists that the "idea of the welfare state codifies our collective obligations toward one another and defines the terms of membership in the national community," a central component of that agenda—government programs to help the poor—was woefully inadequate and often destructive. Plenty of people benefited from the government's helping hand, using the safety net as a way to regroup and then climb back out onto the economic wire, but plenty became trapped in a cycle of poverty and powerlessness. The Left loves to promote the claim of social constructionism, but why on this issue doesn't it ever speak about the culture of *welfare* as a determining force? God knows how dependent it had made Rhonda.

The fact that many politicians have exploited the problems with these programs by pushing through an agenda that abandons the poor altogether isn't grounds for invoking some idyll from the past, whether that idyll be liberal or even Marxist in character. We ought to acknowledge the failures of previous ameliorating schemes, pushing back against self-serving ideological spin, to be sure, yet responding to new developments pragmatically and imaginatively. At the same time we mustn't resign ourselves to the ruthlessness of late capitalism.

There will always be a gap between dream and world, but why turn on the former? Renouncing a speculative mathematics that no one's ever properly worked out, many now profess the easy algebra of greed: "X squared equals ME!" We need new equations, new solutions, however imperfect and inadequate. As the historian of social policy Linda Gordon succinctly puts it: "For whom are we responsible?" The children of questionable mothers, but not the mothers? Not even the children? How to deal with profound human fallibility? Should anybody be thrown away or left to die no matter how self-destructive?

Christmas came and with it no sign of Rhonda. In the middle of January, we commenced taking the MAPP class at the Department of Children and Families. Walking into the room, I was stunned to see about seventy African Americans and two other Caucasians. Like many white people, Emily and I rarely find ourselves in the racial minority, and we were uncomfortable. Or perhaps I should say that this discomfort aggravated a larger discomfort about the strangeness of what we were embarking upon. Before we'd even sat down, one older African-American man said to another, "What are *you* doing here? You already got plenty of money." At the time, it was easy, too easy, to racialize the crass intentions of the "average prospective foster parent," that mythical being. (The MAPP class consisted primarily of prospective foster parents with a few prospective adoptive parents mixed in. In our case, we were hoping for a "foster-to-adopt" scenario where DJ would come to live with us before he was technically eligible for adoption, but the Department was only willing to move him from Gladys's once termination proceedings had begun.) Six weeks into the course, when the DCF leader announced that anyone with a felony conviction for aggravated assault, rape, and/ or sexual abuse was ineligible to become a foster parent and no fewer than seven people got up and left, people with whom Emily and I had role played, well, you'd have thought we were voters in the 1988 election for president falling for those Willie Horton ads.

Foster care *is* a supplemental income program for a lot of poor people, and in our town—the south generally—many of those poor people are black. Many have minimum-wage jobs that don't allow them to survive and thus do foster care on the side. Many already parent the children of family members and seek to be remunerated for it, as long as such remuneration is available. Helping people and getting paid (minimally, I might add) to do it are not mutually incompatible. Emily and I would end up receiving a $500 per month stipend as DJ's adoptive parents, though we wouldn't really need the money in the way that many of our classmates did. (We would, however, need the free medical care, as DJ's health issues would prove very expensive.) I want to be careful not to presume a problem with remuneration, and yet I do worry about the motives of some foster parents. There are plenty of stories of abuse (DJ's, for example). At the same time I wonder why so few middle- and upper-middle-class people become foster parents. There's something perverse about creating a system of compulsory volunteerism for the poor, a volunteerism that's then demonized as suspiciously motivated, while the affluent just play golf. With such a shortage of foster homes and with so many kids in foster care (well over half a million nationally), we need a common commitment to the well-being of children, not some fatuous cultural sentimentalization of them. Maybe then the system of foster care as we know it would be utterly transformed.

As with the image of welfare queens that President Reagan so popularized, the simple stereotype of the racialized, predatory foster parent should be resisted. We met some of the most extraordinary people, most of them women, in our MAPP class, and in meeting them and hearing their stories, we came to look at Gladys differently. Here was a woman who, before bringing DJ into her home, had agreed to parent a severely emotionally disturbed boy whom no one else would parent. The boy had witnessed the murder of his seventy-year-old father by his twenty-five-year-old mother and been left in the trailer with his father's decomposing body for a week. The boy had regularly been wrapped in electrical wire and shocked as a form of discipline. Gladys wasn't in it for the money, and her ferocious pride increasingly seemed a reasonable response to the racial and economic inequalities she'd encountered in her life.

Aside from meeting some extraordinary people, the MAPP class itself wasn't terribly useful, in the way that any abstract preparation isn't terribly useful when compared to the overwhelming experience just ahead of you. It was a bit like, I imagine, listening to your skydiving instructor tell you what position to assume while you plummet to the earth. You listen intently, of course, but then discover the difference between measured instruction and terror-filled actuality. As I mentioned, we role played quite a bit, watched DCF films about thorny fostering situations (where foster kids accuse their foster parents of abuse), learned about abandonment issues, attachment issues, food-hoarding issues, rebellion issues. We heard stories about the difficulty of dealing with birth parents and of saying good-bye to foster children. The whole program seemed designed to inform but not to discourage—to the extent that you could feel the delicate calibration. If we inform too much. . . . If we inform too little. . . . The looks in the eyes of the DCF personnel seemed to say, "If you only knew how hard this was going to be, you wouldn't do it, but we need you. We desperately need you." One woman, who had herself adopted a child from foster care, actually ventured the following comment, to the surprise of her colleagues: "My little girl cried for an entire year when she came to live with me. All day. All night. Literally. An entire year. And that was just the beginning."

As the MAPP class progressed, we started filling out the voluminous paperwork required to become foster and/or adoptive parents. There was a personal profile, a questionnaire, worksheets with sample parenting predicaments. We had to secure numerous references in addition to the official background check and fingerprinting. We had to sit through long, astonishingly intrusive interviews, which, among other things, inquired about our first sexual experiences and whether or not they were "enjoyable." (The reason for asking such a question was to determine, the interviewer said, if we had any sexual hangups.) There was also a question about whether we walked around in the nude and had sex in places other than our bedroom. Whereas I can understand the need to protect children from potentially deleterious habits, the questions made for a kind of awkward and voyeuristic theater. "Yes, I enjoyed my first sexual experience, so much so that I wanted to repeat it almost immediately!"

The home study wasn't any less ridiculous. The woman doing it couldn't believe how nice our home was. She went on and on about our furniture and the bungalow's intricate Victorian features. "I've never seen a foster home quite this nice," she declared. (Our home *was* nice, but we rented it, and it wasn't a mansion: three bedrooms, one and one-half baths, a living room, dining room, kitchen, and front parlor. "People in houses like this don't do foster care," she seemed to be saying. "They don't have to.") I'd been led to believe that I'd be asked to wash dishes for the woman in order to demonstrate proper hygiene skills, but taking in the house, she waived this requirement. Her assumption? Upper-middle-class people must be clean. When I pushed the woman on the purpose of the home study, she said, "You wouldn't believe the homes I'm asked to approve. I mean homes without bathrooms, homes with kitchens so disgusting you wouldn't let your dog in them." After waiving the dishwashing exhibition, she didn't bother to check if we'd purchased the required temperature gauges for the hot water heater and bath. Again, on the basis of our enviable bungalow, she simply presumed sufficient diligence.

With Emily and me having jumped out of the plane, or at least having climbed into it and begun to take off, I started telling friends and family about our intention to adopt DJ. Their reaction surprised me, particularly the anxiety it seemed to provoke. Again and again, we heard the following question, aggressively posed: "Why don't you have your *own* children?" Even my mother, who would actively support the adoption and cherish her grandson, was unable to stop herself from saying to Emily, at least twice in passing, "You know, the two of you are wasting such good genes." When we weren't encountering objections to adoption per se, we were encountering objections to this particular adoption. "Why would you adopt a child with a disability?" or, as a colleague of mine put it, assuming there was something wrong with either Emily's or my reproductive equipment (there isn't), "Have you tried in vitro?"

Because it had taken me time to work up to the idea of adoption myself, I could understand people's reservations, but there was something excessive about them. Once the word got out, mere acquaintances felt free to comment on our plan. Several people inquired about the difficulty of adopting white children, noting that DJ was "not an infant and, well, in a sense, damaged." No paragon of racial sensitivity, I was nevertheless appalled by the idea I'd go out of my way to avoid adopting a black child, say, or a Chicano one. As offensive would be the assumption, ostensibly from a different point of view, that Emily and I must be devout Christians: hyperbolic, designated do-gooders with a joint eye firmly on some final prize (a house on St. Peter's golf course, say, in the truly gated community of Heaven). "You two are soooooooooo nice," we heard repeatedly, as if our future son deserved pity and we were allowed neither our flaws nor a different understanding of social commitment. The journalist Adam Pertman, in his otherwise excellent book *Adoption Nation*, reproduces exactly this logic when he speaks of "children so challenging that only the most *saintly* among us would think of tackling their behavioral and physical problems (though, thankfully, there are many such inspirational foster and adoptive parents) [my italics]." Exactly how inspirational? one might want to ask. Though Pertman includes a chapter in his book on state-supervised adoptions, he and his wife "certainly didn't turn to the public system after we accepted the finality of our infertility." For Pertman, adoption is the last act of a desperate couple, and it involves steering clear of both damaged kids and exasperating bureaucracies.

Selected not as a last resort, adoption—particularly of a disabled child—seemed to constitute a challenge, even a threat, to the comfortable assumptions of our friends and relatives. Nearly everybody wanted to identify the adoption as, on the one hand, an act of altruism and, on the other, foolhardy, even self-destructive. Who in their right mind would abandon the relative safety of neighborhood (and gene pool) and, driving to the wrong side of town, offer some injured stranger an extraordinary lift? The answer to the question "For whom are we responsible?" or, rather, "For whom *will* we be responsible?" seemed implicitly "one's blood relations" and if not one's blood relations because one's reproductive equipment doesn't work and technology can't be made to correct the problem, then a kid from overseas (an infant), or one obtained through private adoption, not a foster child above the age of two, perhaps with medical and/or psychological issues. "White, middle-class, married couples are not flocking to get" this latter sort of child, Pertman bluntly states.

Having witnessed up close the problem of poverty and the crisis in foster care, I found myself pondering the coincidence of traditional family structure (genetic citadel) and the late twentieth-century aversion to the public sphere—that space of common good and what I called earlier "ameliorative schemes." Though by this time an ardent, if aspiring, family man, I nevertheless wondered if the concept of privatization, a word denoting the triumph of smaller government (at least with respect to social programs) and the extension of the profit motive, hadn't intruded into the very way we conceive of love or, put differently, if it hadn't taken advantage of a trusted arrangement for raising children and for retreating nightly into a more personal space. Born out of despair over the failure of grand government programs and, as important, an ideologically driven consensus about the inevitability of economic winners and losers, the responses of friends and family oscillated between a desire for something like social justice and a sense of its impossibility. While I've criticized the knee-jerk rejection of welfare reform—or at least the idea of welfare reform—by some, I do worry that the decline of the welfare state has only intensified the fetish of blood relations, thus narrowing the scope of ethical concern and working against the idea of a larger human family to which we might feel obligated.

Of course, adoption itself is ultimately a privatizing gesture (the public ward made private, given a new name), and as an ameliorative scheme it merely helps this child or that. Call it patchwork rescue. It doesn't address the forces that generate the need for amelioration in the first place. Still, it's worth remembering that American families haven't always been so biologically determined, or so closed to the outside world. As E. Wayne Carp, an historian of adoption, writes, "What is noteworthy about the history of adoption in America is that, at its beginning, colonial Americans showed little preference for the primacy of biological kinship, practiced adoption on a limited scale, and frequently placed children in what we would call foster care." Referring to the recent rise of open adoptions, a practice that works against the ideals of secrecy, complete assimilation, and parental ownership, the adoption scholar Barbara Melosh similarly contends, "Open adoption has been touted as an innovation, but in many ways it represents a return to the kind of child exchange that has prevailed for most of American history." In this way, fluid and transparent family making reminds us of possibilities for reorganizing both affection and responsibility. It points to broader obligations. I hope that I can make such an argument without ignoring the pain of giving up a child or of being given up—without ignoring our own failure in reaching such an ideal arrangement with Rhonda.

In late March, DJ's case came up for review in family court, and in preparation for it, Emily composed a long letter to the judge officially withdrawing her support for reunification and explaining how we had come to offer to adopt DJ. Bobbie Johnson wrote a letter as well. Her letter contained sentences such as "The hope we have had for Rhonda's success at sobriety is gone," and it recommended immediate termination of parental rights, citing the fact that DJ had spent the previous twenty-two and a half months in foster care. "I believe Ms. Savarese in her letter to the Court, on page 3, paragraph 3, explained DJ's autism more aptly than any of us are able," the letter's conclusion began. "It is clear the importance of making a decision for DJ's future: so he can settle into a permanent family who knows and understands thoroughly his disability and who is astoundingly sensitive to all of his possibilities." Having identified us as the perfect parents for DJ, she then treats the issue of our ambiguous relationship to Rhonda:

> It is her sensitive and loving heart that has cast [Emily] in this dual role with this little boy. She has been with DJ consistently these past three years—from the time he was a precious two-and-a-half year old baby to a complex and intense five-and-a-half year old child. Every step of the way, Ms. Savarese and this wonderful man who is her husband have constantly cared for and supported Rhonda Swanson. They have been totally appropriate in this shifting role of responsibility, and I can personally represent their astounding commitment to DJ's continued progress, safety, and permanency with a loving family whoever that may be. It is quite moving to see a young couple, both of whom are committed to fine, personal achievements in their own careers, care so deeply and lovingly for a young child's welfare.

I quote from this letter less to toot my own horn or to contradict myself—God knows that Bobbie's words cast their own "saintly" shadow—than to demonstrate how hard she was working, rhetorically and otherwise, to help DJ. Consider this climactic passage: "There is no more time to give—Rhonda's son's life is in the balance. His early years are almost over—the time is so vital for his own survival. DJ must be freed by the termination of parental rights of his mother. This child will have a future only with this decision." Bobbie saw a chance for DJ, and she took it. This was her primary duty as a child advocate, and I am grateful for her commitment. And yet our duty, as I've been maintaining, wasn't as clear. We wanted DJ, knew he would be better off with us, felt justified in arguing for TPR, and still, underneath it all, felt remorse. In suggesting that Rhonda's hope of sobriety was gone, Bobbie wrote that the "loss is mainly due to Rhonda's own choice." "*Mainly* due"—that qualification condenses an entire tortured argument.

In preparation for the March hearing, Bobbie also called DJ's birth father. She'd spoken with him before, and he'd indicated a willingness to terminate his parental rights if a suitable adoptive family could be found and if his ex-wife surrendered her rights first. The latter demand seemed clearly a function of marital hostility, not fatherly devotion, as he hadn't bothered to do much for DJ since he'd entered foster care. Why seek to preserve control? The former demand seemed self-congratulatory, as he hadn't worried about the suitability of DJ's first foster mother, for example. Why feign concern now?

My bitterness is showing through, but that's how I felt when Bobbie reported that Dan wanted to speak with Emily and me personally before signing anything. He'd abandoned DJ, and now he got to interview us? Would he play games? I wondered. Would he say yes, then change his mind? Would the Department have to take him to trial as well, extending what was already an agonizing limbo for DJ? Was he equivalently attached to irresolution?

I shouldn't have worried. We weren't two sentences into our conversation when the real purpose of the interview became apparent: I was to evaluate *him*. I was to hear about his paternal failures—how he'd wanted to take his son but his wife wouldn't let him, etc., etc. (exactly what I'd confront when, a year or so later, I'd call to set up a visit between DJ and Ellie). I'll come off looking even worse than I do if I tell you that I'd like to fill the page with et ceteras—a train so long the reader would have to wait for hours at this crossing for the narrative to continue. I knew that he'd left Rhonda, paid no child support, and now was living a very comfortable life.

At the end of his self-pitying rant, Dan said he was only too happy to terminate his parental rights; he'd been waiting for people just like Emily and me to come along and fall in love with DJ. Again, he'd wanted to parent his son, but his wife had been unwilling to. Though I said nothing in response to his edgy protestations, Dan could sense how difficult it was to make his case. We'd solved a problem for him, but in doing so we'd created another: guilt somehow worse than that of abandoning DJ in the first place.

Armed with the man's agreement to sign surrenders and a proposal to adopt, we went into the hearing. At the previous hearing, the judge had wanted to give Rhonda another shot. He'd discoursed extensively on the problem of alcoholism. This time, we honestly didn't know what he'd do or how he'd react to our changing sides and proposing to adopt DJ. Would he, like Bobbie, see the proposal as a one in a million chance, a seat on the last flight out of some circumscribed existence, an opportunity to be grasped—ethics and legalities be damned? Would the awful logic of DJ's undesirability and our rare saintliness save him and us in a way that it wouldn't had DJ not been disabled? Rhonda, of course, had made it easy to justify termination, and after the fifteen-month limit in foster care had passed, it was entirely within the judge's right to move in that direction. But such decisions depended on the particular judge, and we had one who was famously liberal, sensitive to the plight of poor women with addiction issues, someone whom I, ironically enough, admired.

The judge *did* decide to move toward termination—reluctantly. I remember sitting in the gallery and breathing an enormous sigh of relief. He recommended that DCF try to get Rhonda to sign voluntarily, knowing that a trial would prolong everyone's misery. He asked the lawyer who was representing Rhonda to help DCF to locate her. By this point the lawyer, too, had given up on the goal of reunification; her client hadn't even shown up for the hearing. She told the judge that Rhonda was somewhere in Daytona, and he requested that she and a member of the Department of Children and Families travel there at the court's expense to find her. She agreed.

We left the hearing feeling both elated and anxious. Bobbie Johnson reminded us that Rhonda could very well refuse to sign surrenders and that we might still have a long road ahead. She could tell we wanted DJ yesterday; in our minds we were already tucking him into bed, unraveling our earlier doubts about parenting him, like some poorly crocheted sweater. I fear that I haven't adequately conveyed the frustration of working through the State system, the painstakingly slow pace of the proceedings. We wanted this drama to be over. After nearly two years in foster care, a vicious beating, three judges, six case workers, Rhonda's protracted vacillations, our own protracted coming to terms with what we wanted to do, countless hectoring phone calls to DCF, multiple court hearings, the MAPP class, paperwork, fingerprinting, interviews, it was time for DJ to go home. It was time for DJ to *have* a home, a permanent one. And it was time for us to live life in something other than a constant state of expectation and alarm.

About a week after the hearing, we returned one night to a message from Rhonda: "I knew you fuckers were after my kid!" She'd obviously been informed of the judge's decision. So much for the dream of voluntary TPR, I thought. Rhonda's words once again infuriated, but at least this time they were accurate. We *were* after her kid. Even now, it seems like something of a conspiracy, our ending up with DJ—an odd conspiracy to be sure. A conspiracy aided and abetted by Rhonda herself: by her poor life decisions and by her strange, face-saving dance of accusation and request. However finally unjustified, the charge served as a reminder not of practical exigencies (DJ needed responsible parents) but of loftier possibilities unfulfilled (Rhonda needed more help, our social arrangements could be fairer). At least in part, some larger "we" *had* stolen her son.

Two weeks after we'd received the message on our machine, Bobbie Johnson called to say that Rhonda had finally terminated her parental rights at a Burger King at six in the morning so as not to be drunk or stoned when signing the papers. She'd sobbed uncontrollably throughout. When we heard the details, we sobbed ourselves. I don't think Bobbie understood we also felt terrible: tears of joy complicated by a hundred darker emotions. It had taken the lawyer and the DCF representative one trip to find Rhonda and a second to secure her signature. In the end, she'd come around to the logic of looking out for her son's welfare, or so Bobbie reported. "I think she honestly loved him," I stammered, wanting to think well of her, wanting to imagine the whole, long ordeal as akin to a planned adoption—difficult, excruciating even, but ultimately successful. How successful? I knew that Rhonda was on the streets; indeed I pictured her, as I sometimes pictured DJ, calling out for help in every way she knew how and having no one, absolutely no one, come to her.

As the surrenders were presented in court three weeks hence, DJ's birth father, who was speaking by phone from a notary's office in Manhattan, noticed that the name the judge was reading off the form was incorrect. "My son's middle name is Joseph not James," he said. The caseworker had made a mistake, and in her anguish at signing the document, Rhonda had missed the error. The judge had no choice but to throw out the document and to start over.

"Start over?" I shouted, actually rising to my feet. "How can you do this? How can you do this to DJ? How can you do this to us, to Rhonda? How could the caseworker have been so careless?"

"I'm sorry, Mr. Savarese, but these documents need to be correct," the judge replied.

"Rhonda might not sign surrenders again. We might not be able to find her. It's not like she has a permanent residence. She's been moving up and down the coast."

"I understand your frustration, but you don't want someone later making a claim on your son. Your right to this child is a function of properly executed surrenders." The judge ordered the attorney and DCF representative to go back to Daytona, and then, with unimaginable discipline and not the slightest glance in our direction, moved on to his next experience of exasperation. Outside the courthouse, Emily and I were reeling. "What's in a name," I screamed, "a fucking middle name?" Of course, I already knew the answer: assumptions about children as property—*private* property. In recognizing only one set of parents, the law tells us they are not to be shared or cared for in common. It seemed absurd that we would have to learn this lesson again.

CHAPTER 4

He's So Fine

It turns out the caseworker hadn't made a mistake in copying DJ's name onto the TPR documents. She'd simply used what was in his file. When DJ had been taken into custody initially, someone else had failed to secure his birth certificate—a legal requirement. The error was only one of many committed by DCF. When I think of how this institution failed my son—from placing him in an inappropriate home and endangering his life to ignoring his need for all sorts of therapies to delaying his adoption—I want to descend on Tallahassee like those gigantic villains in the Christopher Reeve *Superman* movies. The temptation to engage in an attack on big government remains as tempting now as it was back then. I'll never excuse the Department's failure to test DJ for HIV, though it knew that his father had been positive when he impregnated his mother. (The materials we'd later receive about DJ's case state, almost nonchalantly, "David has the possibility of the HIV virus. No testing has been documented thus far.") With early treatment the key to long-term survival, not testing DJ ought to constitute a felony. When Emily and I demanded that he be tested, the Department seemed to stall, and we wondered if it feared we might rescind our offer to adopt should he come back positive. "We'll take him either way," we kept telling his

caseworker. "Jus...
back negative, tho...
time that could ha...

And yet, as muc...
DCF, I knew how u...
and inhuman caseloa...
and they certainly we...
As angry as I was, I sou...
tors who saw an oppor...
to privatize services, for e...
this corrective, I was rep...
children whom foster care...
rifically (you add your own...
fair, standing up at synchro...
the newspaper only to be dr...
various commentators' pingii...

much for the white night of privatiza...
easy answers to the challenges of c...
familial conflict is messy, ine...
best of circumstances. Ou...
out, the jury hasn't ev...
is better.

Emil...

DJ's...

...u in
...genuousness of the

Not too long after adopting DJ, I'd be asked to serve on a committee to explore the privatization of our county's child welfare services. A number of pilot programs were up and running in other counties, and Jeb Bush, Florida's governor, had instructed the entire state to prepare for privatization. My initial response to the governor's plan? Complete opposition. I'd envision companies making money off the misery of fractured families, and I'd go on the liberal warpath: "Three cheers for the opening of new markets of grief!" Though there was talk of allowing for-profit outfits to bid on service components, in the end the model would involve the "third sector": nonprofit, community-based organizations. When I'd actually listen to the various proposals, I'd hear fresh solutions to intractable problems. At the same time, I'd discover that a majority of the pilot programs in Florida had failed, some miserably, and that the governor was nevertheless moving forward with his plan. The pilot in the county directly south of ours, for instance, had had a child die in its custody; it had also failed to predict the number of children who would require services and, as a result, had requested additional money from the state. What's more, it hadn't proved any better at making decisions about removing children from, and returning them to, their families. So

on, I'd think. There aren't any
ild welfare. Dealing effectively with
act, inefficient, and expensive under the
goal has to be to do a better job, but the jury's
n been seated, on the question of which approach

and I spent the next several weeks pressuring DCF to ready
transfer. Though we were far from certain Rhonda would sign sur-
enders again, we didn't want to delay it any more than it already had
been. However fraught with potential disappointment, such a strategy
seemed better than staring at the minute hand and wondering if Rhonda
had been located. We also prepared the house for the little guy's arrival,
turning the upstairs into a playroom with a pillow pit for roughhousing
and a newly painted boy's bedroom. We delighted in these preparations;
we even enjoyed trading in our sporty sedan for—you guessed it—a
minivan.

Almost a month to the day that Rhonda had signed the first batch of
surrenders, she signed the second. She'd remained in Daytona but at a
different place, and so the lawyer and DCF representative had to drive
around looking for her. The meeting was once again tearful, though not,
apparently, as frantic. We'd asked the lawyer to convey our intention of
sending regular photos of DJ and news about him as he got older—a far
cry from a truly open adoption but all we thought possible and prudent
under the circumstances. Little did we know how quickly we'd lose touch
with Rhonda. Not three months after signing the surrenders, she'd disappear for good; even her sister wouldn't have any way of contacting her.
Either she'd be dead or all too disciplined about giving her son the space
he needed to forge new attachments.

Once the surrenders had been filed, we'd expected to become DJ's
foster parents immediately, until the adoption could be processed. That
had been the plan. But, suddenly, we started experiencing resistance: from
the caseworker, the adoption supervisor, and, most of all, from Gladys.
No one would tell us what was going on. Only after bringing Bobbie

Johnson in and going over the head of the adoption supervisor did it come out that people were questioning our decision to remove DJ from the center school for kids with disabilities and enroll him in our neighborhood school. In speaking with the adoption supervisor, we'd previously indicated our intention. The supervisor had balked at the idea, but Emily had reminded him of her training as an inclusion specialist, and he had backed off. But now some nameless person was suggesting we might be putting too much pressure on DJ and, even more outrageous, that Emily considered him her "little experiment." In sum, our fitness as adoptive parents was being challenged.

I blew a proverbial gasket—hot liquids were flying everywhere. I told the supervisor it was well within our right to make educational decisions concerning our future son. Would there have been objections if we'd decided to homeschool him or to have him go to some Christian academy? I reminded him that no one else had offered to adopt DJ, to provide a warm, safe, loving environment in which he could reside permanently; in light of such an offer, objections to our educational philosophy seemed at best trivial and at worst mean-spirited. (We'd later hear that the principal of the center school had been stirring up trouble. She knew we objected to the very idea of a center school, and she and Emily had clashed over the issue of inclusion before.)

A higher-up at DCF called a meeting that nearly all of the central participants attended. Sensing a frontal assault from us, and the threat of a very public dispute, the administrator laid down the law: we were indeed entitled to make decisions concerning our future son's education. We didn't have to wait until the adoption was final, as some had insisted. But before we could celebrate, the administrator turned to Gladys and her husband and asked them if they wanted to adopt DJ. I couldn't believe it; they'd already been asked officially and had said no. Why were they being given a second chance? I worried that Gladys's resistance could be attributed precisely to second thoughts about having said no. Perhaps she couldn't bear to give him up. Perhaps we'd lose DJ at the very moment we were about to get him, after having come so far. When I think now of how many things needed to happen in order for us to become DJ's parents, I shrink in fear at the utter contingency of our lives.

Pausing, Gladys once again said no, though she seemed to fight back tears and engaged in a long, tortured explanation about being older and needing to retire soon and about already being responsible for another foster child. A date was set—June 1st—for the transfer. We told Gladys and her husband they could see DJ as much they wanted, but it was clearly the wrong thing to say, as if we, in all of our Caucasian generosity, were bestowing something on her—a free gift, like a "Rolex" watch everyone knew was a bad replica, not something to be fallen for. It felt as if we'd won a battle and not allowed her to save face. Gladys told us we could pick DJ up at school on the 1st; she would drop his stuff off sometime before. Her tone was tense and proud. The details of the transfer seemed half retaliation and half desperation: the gesture of a woman who wouldn't let us see her pain, who'd treat the transfer as the most banal of occurrences.

That night, Emily and I sat down to write Gladys and her husband a letter. The adoption supervisor had previously recommended we do so—in part to say thank you to our child's foster parents and in part, if we were willing, to invite continued participation in his life. We genuinely wanted them to remain in DJ's life; he clearly loved them, and he certainly didn't need another lesson in loss: love someone and they disappear—inexplicably, irrevocably. We thought a heartfelt letter might clear the air, forge a new beginning. We still have a copy of the letter:

Dear Gladys and Nate,

As we sit down to write to the two of you, it is hard not to think back to December 21st, 1996, the day Nate came to pick up DJ at our house and bring him to live with you. On the one hand, we hated to see DJ leave—we cared so much for him and had secretly hoped he would be with us through the Christmas holidays; on the other hand, we were relieved to know that he was going to stay with the two of you, people who were not only familiar with kids with autism but were familiar and friendly faces to DJ. We remember being concerned at the time that he would think we were "giving him up" or "deserting him," and how difficult it was not to be able to assure him of our care and concern.

As DJ leaves your home to begin a new life with our family, you must be experiencing a degree of sadness and loss. DJ has so clearly become a full-fledged member of your home these past months, and we know that you and he love each other very much. He wouldn't have made all of the gains he has made without the establishment of that special bond. The depth of our gratitude is difficult to express; however, you need only to think of DJ's infectious laugh or serene smile to appreciate the depth of his!

Allow us to thank you, too, for respecting and supporting our ongoing visitation with DJ. We know that in the past there were times when we seemed to misunderstand one another. We hope, in retrospect, it is clear we all cared a great deal for DJ and wanted what was best for him. We are grateful for the opportunity to have witnessed your love and support for DJ firsthand, and we hope you will remain an active part of DJ's life for many years to come.

Sincerely,
Emily & Ralph Savarese

When we spoke with Gladys a few days later, she didn't mention the letter, though she appeared to have read it, for she said she thought it best for DJ if they made a clean break. "He doesn't need any confusion about who his mother is," she explained, a bit too insistently. Emily repeated our desire to have her and Nate stay close, but Gladys demurred. "It's better this way," she said. We could tell she'd made up her mind and that the more we pushed, the more resolute she'd become. We hoped in time she might soften her position.

How could an adult put her own needs ahead of those of a wounded child? Grief does strange things to people, especially someone as proud and collected as Gladys. At the time, I didn't fully appreciate her pain, but later I'd come across a book by a former foster mother called *They're All My Children* that would stun me with its anguish. In it the author interviews women who've experienced the heartbreak of losing foster children. One woman made me think of Gladys immediately—how at the very last minute she'd objected to DJ's transfer:

I have been getting the boys ready for their new home for a long time now. But now that the time is here, it is really hard. I'm scared of letting them go. I know them so well. I just wish I could put the whole thing on hold and wait for a while and let them stay longer.

Another woman brought home the sheer impossibility of temporary attachment:

You have the agency on one hand saying, you've got this child coming to your home and you're supposed to love it for however long you have it in your home. Then all of a sudden, a year later, you've got this agency saying, now you've got to stop loving this child because it has to go some place else, but we've got this other child and now we want you to love it.

Still another woman spoke about the impact of losing a foster child on her family:

It messes up your whole life. . . . It's hard for your spouse, it's hard for your family because they've grown attached to each other, especially when you've got adopted children, because it reminds them that they're vulnerable. . . . You end up lashing out at everybody, if you're like me. I'm a very emotional person. . . . You'll be busy washing dishes and you'll just stand there and cry. For no reason. Because . . . that's the grieving process.

Finally, a fourth woman compared losing a foster child to "handing over a part of your body, like your arm or your leg." "Sometimes I couldn't do it," she said. "Sometimes my husband had to do it." Gladys must have been feeling these emotions, for compounded by the difficulties in our relationship, handing over DJ seemed to prompt a paradoxical response:

she could master the pain by refusing limited contact. She could control it by losing DJ absolutely.

Just how much she must have loved DJ, and DJ her, would manifest itself in the weeks after he came to live with us when, in the grocery store near our house, he'd walk up to pretty, African-American women and try to hold their hands. He was like that bird in the children's book *Are You My Mother?*, searching high and low for his mother. And yet, this wasn't a lesson in species discrimination: a bird discovering that a bird, and not an elephant, or a construction crane for that matter, must be his mother. This wasn't a lesson in racial or even genetic/biological discrimination. DJ's first, unambiguous experience of being loved had been with Gladys, and he was looking to recover it. One woman, I remember, responded to DJ's overture by saying, "Come here, sugar" and enveloping him in her arms. She didn't even know DJ, but she saw the plaintive look in his eyes and reacted warmly and magnanimously.

Now, I don't want to make too much of this, but there was something inspired about DJ's lack of understanding of race. For all we knew, he might have thought of himself as black. He'd certainly taken in much from having lived with Gladys and Nate—from pork rinds to jazz to heartfelt caring. My friend Steve Andrews, himself an African-American and Korean adoptee, would later quip, "You can take the white child out of the black family, but you can't take the black family out of the white child." And he was right.

All of DJ's worldly possessions appeared on the Saturday before the 1st of June—in trash bags and cardboard boxes. Nate dropped them off silently, nervously, as if he'd been instructed not to converse with us. It was a sweltering Florida day and he perspired profusely, but he declined our repeated offers to help. "No, I can do it," he said. And then he was off, the sound of his van lingering long after it had disappeared down our street.

There were many more bags than when Edna had dropped off DJ's stuff after the beating. Gladys and Nate had bought him all sorts of things, and they were neatly folded and organized according to clothing type.

We made a point of leaving the bags and boxes in the front parlor so we could unpack them with DJ. We wanted him to be able to visualize permanence. I hated the idea that he must have seen Gladys and Nate gathering his things and then had to wait the entire weekend to find out where he was going. Though we'd tried to tell DJ he was coming to live with us, we feared he hadn't understood, or at least hadn't registered the news. Either way, the wait for confirmation must have been excruciating.

On Monday, we retrieved DJ at school and drove him back to our house. He saw his things in the parlor and smiled, not extravagantly but noticeably. I want to say that even the trash bags breathed a sigh of relief, for once living up to their product name: GLAD. DJ then took me by my finger and led me upstairs to the pillow pit, where we sat down together. We'd shown him the new space—playroom and bedroom—during our last visit, and it seemed as if he were trying to christen it, make it officially his own. After we sat for a while, Emily had DJ help her put his possessions away. Then we prepared to go swimming at the public pool. We'd gone swimming with DJ before, and he loved it, so we thought that right from the beginning we'd literally bathe him in fun.

That night, when we put him to bed in his new room, DJ acted as if he'd been living with us for years. He didn't hesitate at all before entering the room or climbing beneath the covers. Emily and I each gave him a kiss good night, and together we said, "We love you, little guy." We then closed the door and waited outside to see if he'd fall asleep. After about twenty minutes of making pleasant, unintelligible sounds, he quieted down. When we looked in on him, we saw DJ using his two prayerful hands as a pillow, at play among the angels. He was with us! Asleep in our house! It seemed surreal, the more so for how naturally he'd responded to the move. Emily and I stayed up for hours talking, planning, rejoicing. By breakfast the next morning, we were like any other couple with a child: scrambling to meet the demands of the day. Except our child didn't speak, and his hapless parents had missed the first six years of his life.

The month of June whizzed by—on skates, if you will—with only a few minor mishaps. Emily had taken some time off from work, and I'd taken some time off from writing my dissertation, so we were able to devote ourselves to parenting tasks of all kinds. Between toilet training, photographing nearly every object in our house for DJ's picture schedules, setting up doctors' and occupational therapy appointments, exploring future day care options, continuing with the sign language, taking him to the park, giving him baths, and going swimming and skating, we kept busy. DJ remained cheerful throughout, though quite autistic with his flapping and repetitive behavior, which included staring at people's shoes and beseeching them to move so that he could create his own flip book cartoon when squinting his eyes.

The only evidence we had of visible distress was a fierce refusal to enter anyone else's home. Friends would invite us to dinner, and DJ wouldn't go in, pulling on our arms to indicate his refusal. We chalked this up to anxiety about foster care, as if he thought our friends' homes were new placements. For almost two years we'd encounter such a reaction—to the extent that we'd almost never socialize outside of our house. Our friends would be marvelously understanding of this idiosyncratic friendship requirement, sometimes having us to dinner by carting the food over to our dining room table. Meeting this need of DJ's was the first of many experiences of a diminished adult life, and though we were too absorbed in parenting to complain (at least initially), we did notice the change.

That summer DJ attended an inclusion camp sponsored by the University of Florida. It was there that he met Tracy and Linda, the first of many excellent young people who would come into our lives and help him and us immeasurably. Because we planned to enroll DJ in a regular school, we were anxious to give him some experience learning and playing with typical kids. The camp proved quite difficult for him in almost every respect; you name the developmental area, and he was delayed. If most of the kids resembled frequent fliers traveling to Chicago or New York, then he was stuck in Omaha, his plane grounded due to mechanical difficulties. And yet, the repairmen were at work; the airline spokesman had promised everyone the plane would take off. Though DJ had a very limited attention span and couldn't do such basic things as sit for story time, he *was* watching the other kids and sharing intermittently in their fun. Emily had insisted DJ would profit from imitating the behavior of typical children and that, whatever his cognitive limits, he had a right to be part of life.

The camp experience clarified a number of areas in which DJ needed a lot of help. He had all sorts of motor planning difficulties. He couldn't figure out how to move around a jungle gym, for example, or negotiate a crowded classroom. His hand-eye coordination was virtually nonexistent, in part the result of a vision problem that had gone unaddressed and in part the result of his autism. DJ's gait was noticeably different, and he didn't process sensorial input in the way a neurotypical person did. He was both hyper- and hyposensitive. Indeed, at times he seemed to jump and flap in order to know that he was there, that he had a body.

In addition to the unofficial therapy of swimming and skating and wrestling and tickling, we signed DJ up for occupational therapy with a dynamic and innovative therapist named Angie. If I had to point to one person who had a significant impact on his life—who literally made DJ's future possible by helping him to organize his relationship to the world of objects and people—it would be Angie. She understood the connection between movement, cognition, and emotion, and her infectious enthusiasm was like a crane at a construction site: it made significant building possible. She'd put DJ on a swing in her therapy suite and get him to throw a ball through a hoop while moving behind him and calling out his name. When he'd turn, she'd yell, with a smile as long as any suspension bridge in the world, "You did it! You did it!" At the same time, we started speech therapy with another terrific woman named Linda, who didn't think it crazy that a nonspeaking six-year-old with autism might one day speak.

In July we traveled to Vero Beach for my mother's sixtieth birthday party. My mother and brother had already met DJ, but no one else in my immediate or extended family had. Emily and I were apprehensive about the occasion: how DJ would do, how everyone would respond to him. I feared the casual remark of a sibling or in-law, which might provoke from me an explosive retort. People tend to stare at odd behavior, and in the short time we'd had DJ, I'd already become frustrated by my own conflicted response to this reaction. The behavior itself didn't bother me, but I hated it when people stared, so I found myself telling DJ not to flap or stim in public. No disciple of conformity (or peddler of oppressive notions of normalcy), I'd disappoint myself time and again.

I also had no idea what to expect from my father, the emperor of self-absorption. How would he receive DJ, his nonbiological grandson? Would he overlook our historical disagreements and see in this wordless little boy a chance to make amends, to love me through my son? It seemed the easiest solution to the debacle of the past and the uneasy, superficial truce of the present. Who could fail to be moved by a wounded Little Prince? DJ's story regularly evoked the sentimental good will of others (when they weren't making judgments about his difference). Would my father respond in kind? Would he meet me a quarter of the way? More practically, would he accept the presence of an extraordinarily messy child in his waterfront palace? The place was immaculate and filled with expensive antiques.

Finally, Emily and I worried about DJ's aggressive outbursts, which had begun recently, after something of a parenting honeymoon. Directed only at Emily, the outbursts seemed a reflection of his need to test her to determine if she might abandon him, as Rhonda had. Before investing emotionally, he'd try to sabotage the relationship to see if it was worth clinging to. These outbursts could be fairly intense, involving hitting, scratching, and head banging. We didn't want my relatives to see such outbursts, if only not to have to be the recipients of worried looks and the "I told you so" conclusions about adopting foster kids. More important, we wanted DJ to shine, like the jewel we knew him to be.

The birthday party was a great success. My mother cried when her brother, sister, and children spilled out of the rooms of her house, shouting, "Surprise!" Everyone treated DJ generously. Everyone, that is, but my father. He treated DJ the way he treated me, Emily said: with haughty disregard. An initial hello, and then nothing. I wondered if perhaps he'd been unnerved by encountering a being as ostensibly distant as himself. (Once in a poem I described the man as a spacecraft moving through the heliosheath, some fourteen billion miles from the sun, wracked by interstellar winds and headed for deep space.) But that was just wishful thinking; my father didn't care enough to be unnerved by DJ. And anyway, DJ wasn't distant or aloof. He reached out in all sorts of subtle ways.

After getting over the shock of my parents' house—how big it was (you could play full-court basketball in the great room)—he settled into the luxury of a private pool and boat. (I honestly believe the house had stunned him: round and round he walked, looking up at the sixteen-foot ceilings.) My brother, James, played with DJ in the pool, and DJ did his best from that point on to get his uncle to accompany him whenever he went swimming. He did this by standing in front of James with his bathing suit on, sometimes even turning off the TV James was watching. Though he didn't have words, DJ could tell you unequivocally that he was having fun. Giant smiles, shrieks of laughter, and the sign for "more." More, more, more, more!

He was fearless in the water. We'd throw him up into the air and watch him descend to the bottom of the pool, as far down as his little life vest would allow. He was equally fearless in the ocean, actually loving it when a wave crashed into him and knocked him over. He'd get up, clear the salt water from his eyes, do a little movement jig, stim at the ever-fascinating surf, then head back out again, grabbing me or Emily or James or my Aunt Maureen (a consummate body surfer) by the arm. Though you could quickly lose DJ to his water reveries, we definitely experienced the joint attention that experts speak so much about. He was present, even if he couldn't communicate his inner life with any degree of specificity or sophistication.

The last two weeks of July and the first week of August were consumed with getting ready for school and the dreaded IEP meeting. (The acronym stands for Individualized Education Plan, and every student in special ed must have one, with carefully elaborated goals and a strategy for achieving them.) Emily had requested an IEP and "change of placement" in June but had been told that with various vacation schedules, August 10th would be the earliest we could meet. The first of many attempts to sway the outcome of the proceeding, it had alerted us to just how much opposition we'd encounter, and Emily had wisely decided to confront such chicanery head on. I remember listening to her conversation with the county's ESE supervisor. "August 10th is far from ideal, but if that's all you can offer me, we'll have to meet then," she said. "But let's be clear: this is the county's decision, not ours. It'll have no effect on what together we decide. We won't listen to any arguments about delaying DJ's transfer due to a lack of time to set things up." After a pregnant pause—sextuplets could have been pulled from that womb—Emily added, "You may think I'm strong-willed and difficult, but you haven't met my husband. He just fought to get this boy out of foster care, and he's adamant about giving him a chance at a regular school."

When necessary, I'd played the role of dogged belligerent with DCF (about DJ's HIV test, for example). It's a role that comes naturally, as my friends point out, and I was prepared to play it again with the school district. In fact, I was too prepared—at once justified in my outrage at the tactics of the anti-inclusion crowd and less than psychologically astute about how to accomplish our objective. I was a bit like the sort of heavily armored vehicle that urban SWAT teams now employ, capable of knocking down an entire house, let alone its front door. Political struggles sometimes require such a posture, but at least as frequently they do not. Emily, who had a better sense of when to coax and cajole and certainly a better understanding of the state educational apparatus, developed a system whereby she'd kick me under the table to indicate a particular need: once to call in the attack dogs; twice to call them off. We made a good team, both of us passionate in our own way.

I'd invoke DJ's life story, what had happened to him, in order to appeal to people's better instincts, to remind them of why they'd chosen a career in education in the first place, to insist they go the extra mile to help this kid when we, after all, were going the extra marathon. You might say I bullied them into virtue, bullied and stroked, finding, in the end, that nearly everyone wanted to help out, wanted to feel good about themselves. Any close reader of this text will notice that I repeatedly contradict myself: I say I loathe the logic of virtue for fear of its demeaning effect on DJ, and then I mobilize it myself. I'd learn from Emily, however, that it's better to get what you want for your child than to be indignantly right (or commendably consistent). Use what's available. Besides, it's possible to aid someone without pitying him. That adoption would turn out to be an advantage in the inclusion struggle is an absurd irony. Perhaps it suggests that people's altruistic impulses really do extend beyond the parameters of family that customarily constrain them.

Emily did two things before the IEP on the 10th. First, she met with the principal of our neighborhood school. Without this woman's backing, we'd be lost: the battle not so much uphill as completely vertical. The woman, Sarah Bollinger, listened to Emily's request, DJ's story, our promise of intense involvement, and agreed to have DJ at her school as long as the county funded a para-educator, someone to help him in the classroom. At crucial moments in our educational journey, people of enormous sympathy have appeared almost magically. Twice—twice!—we have run into principals who'd adopted children, and she was one of them. The other had even adopted a child from foster care. Having secured Principal Bollinger's support, we now had to get the team to agree that F.F. Linney, our neighborhood school, was the best placement for DJ. The way the IDEA law is written, you articulate goals for your child and then decide which school will best allow you to meet these goals. You can't just say that you want your child to attend Linney, though that's in fact your explicit desire. So, you end up crafting your goals in such a way that only your neighborhood school will fit the bill.

The second thing Emily did to prepare for the IEP was to collect information on DJ's experience at the summer inclusion camp. I defer to Emily's account of this preparation and of the IEP that followed. Written initially as an extended journal entry and then later adapted for a paper on the importance of inclusion, it captures the tense perversity of the IEP tribunal. The section from which I quote begins with an epigraph from the black revolutionary writer Frantz Fanon: "Where am I to be classified? Or, if you prefer, tucked away?" Like Arthur Frank, author of *The Wounded Storyteller*, and others in the burgeoning field of disability studies, Emily borrows from postcolonial theory a notion of the violence of colonization to understand the plight of the disabled, who must wrest from medical practitioners the right to describe, in a very different language, the nature and meaning of their conditions.

Emily doesn't seek to dismiss medical understanding outright, but rather to complicate it, even humble it, with evidence of its erroneousness and the view from the inside of its declared pathologies. In the case of a boy tucked away under "autism" and "profound mental retardation," who couldn't (yet) tell his own wounded story, she strives to hold in abeyance definitive proclamations, opting instead to advocate for possibility. For her, the center school was the spatial fulfillment of the oppressive classificatory gesture. I quote from the paper because, as I said, it evokes the perilousness of the meeting but also because I want to include Emily herself—her words—in this book. She made inclusion happen. Moreover, so much of my thinking has been influenced by this intelligent and deeply humane woman.

> Prior to our first IEP/Placement Meeting for DJ, the burden of proof sat squarely on DJ's and my shoulders. I knew that I must come to the meeting with some school-acknowledged proof of DJ's competence. That's how it works. And so I'd enrolled DJ in a grant-funded inclusion camp at the university. I'd met with the director after the first week, and she'd seen to it that ample videotape was taken of DJ, showing him looking over from a distant corner to observe what the other children were doing during Circle Time; on a few occasions, he was even seen participating directly in the organized group activities. (No small feat for a tiny boy of six who had lost his entire family, been neglected and abused in foster care, recently changed homes for the fifth time and—oh yeah—who didn't speak.)
>
> The director had also written a letter, drawing a picture of DJ as a child who was becoming more and more interested in his peers' actions, increasingly independent in toileting, and more and more willing to coexist in a group. She had asked if I wanted her to attend the meeting, and I had politely said, "no." This meeting would require a delicate balancing act of letting the district know we knew the law and trying to convince people to put aside all of their

preconceived notions of who DJ was and, more important, of who he could become. The letter from the university professor/director would let them know the former; her actual presence at the meeting might cause them to raise their defenses.

I knew that toileting is a popular gate-keeping skill, so I planned to repeat what the letter said, "He is totally toilet-trained." Playing dumb, Ralph would follow with the remark: "It was amazing really. In ten days he was bladder-trained; in three weeks, bowel trained." I gathered my line graph to show that when given a mini picture schedule of four separate activities, DJ was able to stay on task for twenty to twenty-five minutes, eighty percent of the time. Lastly, I listed some examples of activities we'd been doing: ABC form puzzles, initial sound/object puzzles; one to ten number puzzles, listening to me read a book, learning to sign, building with Legos, and creating tanagram pictures.

Emily's account goes on to list the various people in attendance at the IEP—the ESE county supervisor and moderator of the meeting, the vice principal of the center school (we had explicitly asked for her instead of the principal), a prospective first-grade teacher at the center school, the principal of F.F. Linney, a prospective first-grade teacher at Linney, the resource room teacher at Linney, and, finally, the guidance counselor at Linney—and it relates what had been the first major obstacle: where the meeting would take place, at the center school or Linney. "The county supervisor," Emily writes, "had tried to insist we'd need to meet at the center school, DJ's *current* placement, until the IEP *team* decided otherwise."

"Listen, Cathy," Emily had replied. "We can either do this in a friendly manner or an unfriendly manner. My husband and I vote for the friendly manner at DJ's neighborhood school, but, of course, the choice is yours." The woman wisely agreed to hold the meeting at Linney, ascertaining, I think, that we were the wrong people to mess with. She could make things as difficult as possible, but she'd heard in Emily's carefully modulated tone a will and resources that could come back to bite her if she went too far.

I pick up Emily's account with a kind of pre-game pep talk:

> The strategy was this: remain calm, kind, and firm. Prepare for a barrage of hogwash and condescending "expertise" with a varnish of charitable "good intentions" for "what's ultimately best for the child." Do not, repeat, do NOT be incited to anger by nonsensical remarks—most likely to come from the special education teachers and/ or possibly the county ESE supervisor. Remember the cognitive behavioral strategy you use to teach anger management: take a deep breath, remind yourself that none of these people know how to teach kids with autism. (There had never been a non-speaking child in a regular classroom in the county's history.) Remind them that this is a partnership and you'll be there to help. Use things they've said to prove your point.
>
> The law mandates that IEP decisions be made in this order: first, establish goals; then, decide what "level of support" is needed to reach those goals. In other words, what is innocuously labeled "Description of Current Level of Functioning" serves, in fact, as a prescription of who that student can become in the future. We emphasized three key areas: literacy, social-emotional development, and communication. We crafted the goals to dictate teacher instruction—the kind we wanted for DJ. My husband's insistence that we include the phrase "to begin to ask him important questions about his life" took an hour to get on the IEP and was scoffed at by the center school crowd. The first half of that goal—"Will learn to answer 'wh' questions"—had taken forty-five minutes, so averse were these people to imagining DJ's future competence.
>
> Once the goals were in place, the county argued for a class at the center school with "more emphasis on academics." "It'd be hard to have any less, that's for sure," I thought,

but then smiled and said, "That would be great if our only concerns were for academics. To be quite honest, I feel I can teach DJ lots of his academic skills one-on-one at home. (And I had. In the previous month, he'd learned a lot; in the previous three years at the center school—they'd documented it themselves—he'd learned nothing.) What we can't give him at home and what the center school can't give him at school is constant exposure to peers who model verbal communication and social skills. You mentioned earlier that DJ has shown no competence in receptive language skills. If, in fact, he is able to think only visually, then for all we know, DJ has concluded that when he gets to be as tall or as old as an adult, he'll magically be able to speak. And if socializing is very difficult for DJ because of his autism, then he needs to be around kids for whom it's easy, so that some of them might begin to reach out to him."

"At this point, DJ has not been able to achieve a single IEP goal. How could he possibly make it in a regular kindergarten class?" the resource room teacher at Linney asked.

"I agree with you," I responded. "It's disturbing that DJ has not met a single IEP goal in his three years in school. But I would be more concerned about trying something else if he'd made some progress. [These goals had included buttoning and unbuttoning his shirt, putting pegs in a pegboard and staying on task for ten seconds.] Now, correct me if I'm wrong, but I think the law states that children must start out in the least restrictive environment and only be placed in more restrictive environments if it's absolutely necessary. So, aren't we coming at this from the wrong direction? Shouldn't we be seeing if his learning rate improves in a regular class? Aren't we actually obligated by law to do so? Perhaps now that he has glasses [the school district and the Department of Children and Family had done nothing to address a lazy eye that had gotten so bad that DJ's face, neck, and chest muscles had atrophied] and a safe and stable home, he might thrive. [Here, Ralph chimed in with his ready-made exhortation about saving underprivileged kids, giving them a legitimate chance to prove themselves.] I don't really see that the law affords us any other choice."

"OK," the county supervisor reluctantly conceded, "then he'll start first grade at F.F. Linney."

"First grade?" I queried, looking to the Linney principal. We'd never discussed first grade, only kindergarten. The county was trying to increase the likelihood of his failure.

"Well, he graduated kindergarten last year," the vice principal of the center school stated.

"Look, he may have completed his third year of attendance at the center school, but you certainly aren't saying DJ has mastered the kindergarten curriculum."

"Well, no, but—"

"Plus," I added, "his birthday's in July, so he'd be one of the youngest first graders in his class. [DJ had just turned six.] Certainly DJ wouldn't be the first young first grader to repeat kindergarten?"

"Well, no, but—"

"This strikes me as a no-brainer. Somebody tell me what's at stake here. You're all experienced and dedicated educators. You can't tell me you support his promotion to first grade because it's 'in his best interest.'"

It was the Linney principal who spoke up, winning my trust with her honesty: "The district is strongly discouraging retaining ESE students. It's concerned the students might remain the responsibility of the school district until they're twenty-three or twenty-four, and it doesn't think that's a good idea." [Aha, the logic behind the irrational. At that time in Florida, ESE students were being "excused" from standardized testing, and no alternative means of assessing student learning had been put in place. Concerned about the prospect of indefinite retention, schools were promoting students who hadn't met their goals. On the one hand, DJ wasn't competent enough to attend Linney; on the other, he had to start in the first grade, though—that's right—he hadn't achieved first-grade competence. The point was to take DJ's learning seriously, not to envision a better, less depressing holding facility for the cognitively disabled.]

"We don't intend to have DJ in secondary school past the age of nineteen," I insisted. "Is it possible to sign a document attesting to this fact?"

"I've never heard of such a thing," the Linney principal said. "But I think I have a way around the issue. How would you feel if I turned DJ's class into a kindergarten-first grade classroom? That would enable DJ to be in a kindergarten class. No one would even have to know he was a first grader on paper."

I believed, right then, that we could make it, though the skirmishes weren't over. The resource room teacher who'd have DJ thirty minutes a day for extra cognitive learning would remain our biggest concern (until the latter part of the year when, noticing he possessed an astonishing visual memory, she'd decide that she might actually be able to teach him how to read). But we now had in our corner a very decent, problem-solving principal who'd adopted a child herself and understood how people work. She had heard us, I felt certain. DJ had gained an advocate.

As the group dispersed, Ralph and I were approached by the vice principal of DJ's former school, who knew we'd explicitly asked that she—not the principal—attend the meeting. With tears in her eyes, she said, "DJ is certainly very lucky to have such well educated, articulate, and devoted parents as the two of you."

"Thank you," I said, half-stunned by her comment. At the time, I'd have forgiven my worst enemy, so profound was my relief at having sneaked DJ through the gates of Ellis Island, but I wondered what it was like for her to leave that meeting. Did she feel any discomfort acknowledging to her fellow teachers that DJ hadn't learned a single thing at her school? Was she ashamed that when asked what his greatest school-related strength was, she had replied, "His good looks. He's a physically beautiful child."?

Emily had done it. Like Jennifer Garner in *Alias*, she'd vanquished the enemy and completed the mission without disturbing a single hair on her head—this despite the rhetorical somersaults and tonal duck and dodge. Driving home, my inclusion superwoman confessed that she'd stood in front of the mirror that morning and cried, wondering if she really could pull off a miracle. I thought back to how, once, picking up DJ at the center school, I'd heard a teacher refer to her class as "God's little idiots." I understood why Florida ranked second from the bottom with respect to services for the disabled and why families without our resources, in such a subtly acrimonious and obstacle-ridden struggle with God's special educators, often didn't have a prayer of mainstreaming their kids.

There were only ten days before the kindergarten open house, and the principal still needed to assign a teacher and hire a para-educator. At one point, amidst the panic and commotion of preparing for the start of the school year, she suggested we might be better off delaying DJ's arrival for a couple of weeks. It would allow them time to fill his aide position and to firmly establish the school routine, something she'd gathered a child with autism required. Emily and I objected vociferously. Though we understood the awkwardness of using temporary paras for the first two or three weeks, we knew that part of belonging to a group is being there from the start. If DJ's anxiety and confusion were ever going to fit in, they would do so alongside the discombobulated responses of the nineteen other first-time school children.

On the Thursday before school began (Friday was the open house), Emily met for about forty minutes with the woman picked to be DJ's teacher. Alice Thompson had taught kindergarten for years and seemed relatively receptive to, though completely ignorant about, having a child with autism in her classroom. She said she'd done some reading about autism on the Internet, which made Emily cringe, as she knew the picture provided was invariably grim, if not downright hopeless. In fact, she was certain Alice had come across the phrase "devastating developmental disorder" because that descriptor ("devastating") always seemed to come attached to the phenomenon, like some standard finish on a piece of furniture. Emily explained she'd be in the classroom for the first two weeks to train the aides and to get DJ acclimated. She had tons of sick leave available, and she planned to use it to keep close tabs on how things were going. Her colleagues at CARD were very flexible, understanding Emily's absence *as work*: a kind of outreach that might end up helping kids other than DJ, for if he could be included successfully, then maybe they could as well.

The three of us went to the open house like defendants awaiting a verdict, defendants who hadn't yet been tried! We were that nervous. Whether DJ understood what was awaiting him wasn't clear, though he'd certainly picked up on the vibe of his parents and was flapping vehemently. Emily looked like she was about to vomit, and I was telling everyone to relax in the most unrelaxed manner. We'd reached the moment when a beautiful idea—inclusion—alights on the ground of reality, like a snowflake on warm macadam. We found DJ's classroom and entered tentatively. Once inside, it seemed as if no one would speak to us. The other parents were standoffish, and as soon as DJ commenced flapping, people began to stare. We were too immersed in our own anxiety to recognize that many of the parents were probably sending their first child off to school and so were themselves preoccupied. Mrs. Thompson came up, knelt down to be at eye level with DJ and told him something encouraging. DJ was unresponsive, and this surprised her, as if she'd never before tried her kid-centered greeting and had it fail. Near the end of the open house, a woman approached, saying, "Are you Emily and Ralph Savarese?"

"Yes," we replied. She turned out to be a former colleague of our friend Caroline. Caroline had been in a car accident that had left her a quadraplegic and ended her career as a gynecologist. The woman, who had a daughter in DJ's class, had heard a lot about the fundraiser Emily and I had organized to buy a van that would accommodate a motorized wheelchair.

"You're legends at the hospital," she said. The woman was incredibly kind and kept the day from being a total disaster.

We were glad from the moment Monday began that we'd decided to have DJ start the year with everyone else. It was clear that Mrs. Thompson's teaching style was going to help DJ and that she was going to have time to work with him. "She can teach kindergarten in her sleep," Emily said. She was that good. She truly understood young kids: the importance of predictable routines and the advantage of kinesthetic learning. Valuable to typical kids, these things are essential for kids with autism. It would end up being a tremendous boon that Mrs. Thompson knew sign language, as we'd already discovered sign's usefulness in escorting DJ into the province of abstraction. Combining photographs, words, and signs would prove decisive in helping DJ to acquire proficiency with representational systems. Moreover, because DJ didn't seem to understand spoken language, sign language allowed us to exploit his obvious visual strengths.

But it was the kids' reaction to DJ that really confirmed our decision. At our first PBS (Positive Behavioral Support) meeting, Mrs. Thompson remarked, "The kids have convinced me this is the right thing to do. I was shocked to discover our adult concerns about their acceptance of DJ were just that: *adult* concerns. They absolutely love him and don't question for a second whether or not he belongs." Such a remark, so early in the school year, helped to set a tone of enthusiastic endorsement, especially at meetings intended to confront problematic behavior. Mrs. Thompson was right: the kids did love DJ. A boy named Austin regularly offered Emily words of encouragement: "DJ was a little nervous today, but I bet he'll feel better tomorrow." His would be the first of multiple birthday invitations DJ received—each of them treasured but Austin's particularly sweet for two reasons: first, except for one other kindergartener at Linney who lived across the street from him, Austin invited only nonschool friends, and second, he told his parents he wanted to have his party at Skate Station because he thought DJ would love it. Kids used his photo schedule to see what classes came next, whether they had PE or library that day. Other kids volunteered to be the recorded voice on his communication devices, to be his partner in line, to sit beside him in circle. Three little African-American girls flirted with DJ, admiring his curly locks and slate-blue eyes. "He's so fine," one of them said, giggling. "He's sooooooo fine," another replied.

Still, at times the task of settling DJ into the classroom was daunting. For starters, he had a very hard time physically supporting his body in the cross-legged position required of every Circle Time participant. After two or three minutes, he'd grow weary and lie down unless propped up against one of us or seated in a chair at the end of a table that abutted the Circle rug. Later in the year, we'd decide that letting him "draw" with markers at the table enabled him to sit most independently during Circle Time, so that's what we did.

DJ's way of coping with stress was to go to the bathroom (which was located *inside* the classroom) and repeatedly flush the toilet. He loved to watch the swirling water, and he'd flap, whir, and moan in a frenzied manner. This particular coping strategy made Emily very uncomfortable because Mrs. Thompson was married to a firefighter, and, more than anyone at Linney, she understood the importance of conserving water. All summer the state had been plagued by terrible fires and drought conditions; one fire had made it within a few miles of our town. Along with his periodic meltdowns and occasional hitting and scratching, DJ's perseverative tendencies taxed everyone—though, interestingly enough, the adults more than the children. Late in the year, after most of our fears about DJ making it had subsided, the principal would tell Emily a funny anecdote about the first time Mrs. Thompson showed up at her office, beaming about DJ's success. "He's doing much better," Mrs. Thompson reported. "Today he only flushed the toilet three times." Mrs. Bollinger remembered being unprepared for such a report. She'd say it was a turning point for her, a moment when she realized that "DJ's gains would be numerous and quite different from those of his peers."

As the first month wore on, Emily and Mrs. Thompson developed a sturdy, even affectionate, bond. Because she hadn't attended the IEP, Mrs. Thompson hadn't heard about DJ's heartrending past. Emily was so modest and discreet that she'd neglected to use this Archimedian lever, assuming, I think, that the principal must have informed her. When she finally learned of the abandonment, abuse, and separation from his sister, Mrs. Thompson committed herself even more to DJ's inclusion. "I want you to know I'm a hundred and fifty percent behind making DJ's year in kindergarten a success," she told Emily one morning. "I don't know all of the answers, and I'm sure there will be hiccups along the way, but I feel strongly that DJ's in my class for a reason. It's clear the children know he belongs with them, and we understand each other well. Having you in the class periodically is easy, and I feel like I can ask you for help whenever I need it." Emily wanted to collapse in tears, she later told me, so grateful was she for Mrs. Thompson's boundless generosity.

By the end of the year, she'd barely be able to say good-bye to Alice. As Emily would explain, the woman had possessed the same power so many other teachers possess *and use* to remove children from their classes, but she had never, ever used it. Nor, finally, had any of DJ's other teachers at Linney, even when legitimately provoked. Mrs. Thompson, however, had welcomed hope when hope seemed most alarming. If you consider how poorly paid American teachers are and the many hardships they put up with, it's amazing they aren't all incorrigibly jaded and resentful. It's amazing, too, what kind of cooperative community can be forged when parents involve themselves intensely in their kids' educations, volunteering time, offering support and gratitude.

With the conclusion of the second month of kindergarten, even some of the parents had joined in their kids' delight at DJ's presence in the class. The mom of a girl named Julia shared a conversation that she and her daughter had had at the dinner table. The mom had asked how DJ was doing. "Mom," Julia had replied, "it's Deege. His family and his good friends all call him Deege, not DJ." The mom of another girl, who was volunteering with Emily on school picture day, admitted that at the open house she'd been very concerned about seeing a child with a cognitive disability in her daughter's class. She'd worried that DJ might take teacher time away from the other students. "Now," she said, "Karl and I are thrilled. I can't put my finger on all that it's done for Nikki, but it's something no book, no talented teacher, no terrific curriculum could ever teach. She's inspired by him. She tries harder, worries less, and smiles more. She really adores him." The father of a boy named William regularly came into the class in the morning and made a point of saying hi to DJ. "I love that kid," he'd tell us. "This is a great kid." The sister of a boy in his class, herself a fourth grader at Linney, would similarly go out of her way to say hello to DJ, always waiting for him to reply by looking up at her. The entire family raved about our son.

Come June, the parents of seven classmates would actually *request* that their children be in DJ's first grade class. In addition to the many intangible benefits to his being there, they'd know that Mrs. Thompson had referred the fewest kids for extra reading help in all of her fifteen years of teaching. The theory, supported by some research, was that the use of sign language facilitated literacy generally but especially helped so-called slow or problem readers. Mrs. Thompson's class had had its share of "at risk" kids, so the decreased number of referrals was even more striking. Having another adult in the room—DJ's aide—obviously helped as well. Though focused on DJ, the aide was intermittently available to assist the other kids. That Emily provided nearly all of the curricular modifications (a daunting after-work challenge if ever there was one) ensured that Mrs. Thompson wouldn't be consumed by the needs of just one child.

As DJ progressed at Linney, we discovered additional benefits. DJ's first grade teacher reported much less test anxiety when the kids took the ITBS (Iowa Test of Basic Skills) and, in general, a greater sense of cooperative learning. A psychologist for the school district conducted a study of time on task in DJ's classroom, and it turned out to be quite high. There had been some concern about whether DJ and his penchant for making noises were "disruptive to the attention flow of the class." Over the summer, Mrs. Bollinger had accepted an administrative job in the district, and so a new principal was at the helm at Linney. In Mrs. Bollinger's absence, a long-time vice principal aired her previously unspoken opposition to inclusion. The only person from Linney we'd ever clash with, the woman demanded, in the most disparaging tone possible, that the aide "get him the hell out of the classroom when he made noise." Right there, in the middle of the PBS meeting and in front of the new principal, I shouted, "How dare you talk about my son in that way? I won't stand for it. You're ignorant and mean-spirited, and you've had absolutely nothing to do with the success of this venture." (Emily didn't have time to kick me under the table; I was too quick with my retort, but after the meeting she thanked me for saying something.)

I understood what the ADA's principle of "reasonable accommodations" meant. DJ's needs and/or tics weren't absolutely protected, especially if they interfered with the learning of others. And yet this woman, who knew almost nothing about DJ, had popped her head into his classroom, heard him making noise, and presumed he was a disruption. No, *hoped* he was a disruption. Emily and I had been incredibly sensitive about DJ's noise, ushering him out of the classroom whenever it seemed like it might be a problem, but we also knew the other kids had very quickly stopped noticing his flapping or hearing his odd sounds. They were a model of accommodation; DJ's difference no longer stood out. Yes, there were days when he *was* too loud and the kids did look up, and we did "get him out of there," but most of the time the hive of learning kept on humming (quietly), kept on meeting its honey quota.

Thankfully, the psychologist's observational data ended up confirming our own undocumented assessment. DJ's classmates remained on task well over eighty percent of the time. As the report concludes, "On task for children is considered good at fifty percent. Average is fifty to seventy percent. It should be carefully noted that, even during special times such as fall festival, time on task was exceptionally strong in this classroom. . . . This is a high attending level class for young children." Even DJ's time on task, the report found, was higher than average. What a joy it was to receive this data, though we were denied the consummate pleasure of the vice principal's attendance at the PBS meeting where it was presented. I think the woman might have been told not to appear by the new principal, a warm African-American woman who was still finding her bearings at her new school but who offered us as much support as we could have hoped for. Looking back on the initial reactions of some of the parents and of the vice principal, I detect a logic that seems to rule our historical moment: the idea that one group's well being must come at the expense of another. Call it competitive happiness (with dubious, even crooked, referees). In this northern Florida elementary school, we had proven that a different logic might prevail.

CHAPTER 5

Guidance

That first year in kindergarten was also DJ's first year with us, and there were plenty of ups and downs at home. DJ kept hitting and scratching Emily in moments of panic while being ridiculously sweet and affectionate with me. I don't know how Emily withstood his constant testing; I wouldn't have had the roles been reversed. But she was as patient and steady as the morning sun, illuminating every corner of his room and rousing him from bed. Light and warmth no matter how he behaved.

The Wednesday before Thanksgiving, DJ experienced a monumental meltdown. Because we planned to spend the holiday in Hilton Head, South Carolina, where Em's folks lived and where the entire Thornton family would be gathering, we'd packed the car on Tuesday night in the hope of leaving straight from school the following afternoon. We took DJ to Linney in the car, and about halfway through second period, he exploded: kicking, screaming, scratching, biting, and sobbing—convulsively sobbing. Though there's always the danger of projection, we couldn't help but conclude that he'd seen his packed belongings and thought he was moving to another home. We'd never witnessed an eruption that ended with him in tears, clinging to Emily. "You're here for good," she told him, over and over, in the lobby of the school—as if that simple idiom could assuage his panic or resolve the awful ambiguities of his life. To win a set of caring parents, he'd had to endure so much. Those first couple of years, we devoted ourselves to the challenge of developing a communication system—sign, pictures, and, one day, we hoped, words—so that whatever the difficulties of spoken language, we might be more responsive to his needs and he might be able to work through some of those awful ambiguities.

December commenced with DJ awakening in the middle of the night and refusing to go back to sleep—a pattern that would continue on and off for months. On the 21st the adoption became final. We'd served as DJ's foster parents for as long as it took the court (about three weeks) to accept Rhonda's second set of surrenders, and then we'd waited for the mandatory six-month adoption trial-period to conclude. At last, we'd reached the familial finish line. The night of the 21st, my mom threw the three of us a celebration dinner in Vero; we couldn't determine if DJ understood the reason for the party, though he clearly liked my mother's food (especially her homemade rolls). In January we received the official document attesting to his new identity. The document reads:

Therefore, it is ordered and adjudged that

A. The minor child born on July 18, 1992, in the State of ——————, is declared to be the legal child of petitioners, Emily T. Savarese and Ralph James Savarese, and is given the name of David James Savarese, by which he shall be hereafter known.

B. This adoption decree creates a legal relationship between the adoptee and petitioners and all relatives of petitioners that would have existed if the adoptee were a blood descendant of the petitioners born within wedlock, entitled to all rights and privileges thereof, and subject to all obligations of a child born to Emily T. Savarese and Ralph James Savarese.

Done and Ordered in Chambers at ————, ———— County, Florida, this 21st day of December, 1998.

Notice the document's constant privileging of blood relations. Notice, too, the name we gave to DJ. Rather than keeping his middle name Joseph, we decided to change it back to what we'd thought it was until the hearing the previous spring. Vulnerable to exactly the sentiments I frequently condemned, we'd relished the fact that DJ and I shared a middle name and decided to re-correct the error. Hence, in addition to receiving the last name Savarese, he received the middle name James.

I'll happily plead guilty to the charge of political insincerity, but I think a lesser count is more appropriate. We wanted to symbolize our intimate bond; declare the presence of a family; have DJ feel that he belonged, was one of us. We also, frankly, desired full legal control so that we could make decisions regarding DJ's future without having to worry about anyone's interference. With its declaration of a new identity, the legal document gave us certain rights, but it also contributed potentially to the circumscription of social concern I lamented. How I still wish to believe that a name can do its positive symbolic work without effecting the latter.

From January, we limped into spring—literally. A few months before the infamous trip to see Ellie, we received the diagnosis of partial-complex and/or absence seizures. There was the possibility of hemiplegic migraines as well, which could also explain the intermittent paralysis in DJ's right leg. With inconclusive CAT scans and EEGs and only observational data from us, the neurologists had a very difficult time arriving at a determination. In fact, the neurologists disagreed—one saying seizures, the other hemiplegic migraines. Without the skillful mediation of our developmental pediatrician, a woman named Carol Delahunty, we'd have been having seizures (or hemiplegic migraines) ourselves.

We put DJ on an anticonvulsant whose added benefit was some mild mood stabilization. (Later we'd find a drug that could take care of both problems.) This period of DJ's "neurological episodes," as one doctor put it, was immeasurably stressful. The sleep-deprived EEG put us in the position of CIA interrogators, torturing our suspect by refusing to let him sleep. DJ looked at us like we were crazy every time we shook him awake or rang a bell or played some music. He hated having the electrodes attached to his head and chest. For two straight hours he screamed, as Emily and I struggled to immobilize him. Sadly, the MRI wasn't any less traumatic. Because he couldn't lie motionless, a nurse had to administer a sedative, and DJ, always in the statistical minority, vomited as a result—right inside of the tube—and then nearly aspirated on what came up. "Get him out of there!" the technician yelled to her assistant. "That's a million-dollar machine!" Later, when the vice principal would use the exact same phrase in the PBS meeting, I'd think of that barking woman who cared little about our groggy, choking six-year-old.

Throughout this period, Em's parents and my mother offered lots of support by calling regularly on the phone and coming to visit us. From my father—nothing, not a single call, not even when for a brief spell one of the neurologists had us worried about a brain tumor. His utter disregard for DJ infuriated me a thousand times more than his disregard for me, and I think he knew it. Certain I could escape my father's orbit and, as in a sci-fi novel, settle on some distant planet of neglected sons, I discovered that his response to DJ just drew me back in. My engines weren't strong enough to defeat his indifferent, gravitational pull.

Summer came and with it the introduction of three new members to the Savarese team: Jennifer, a graduate student in psychology, who was working, interestingly, on a study of the role of irregular gaits in autism; Evan, an older undergraduate whom I met through my friends Peter and John (Evan worked at the independent bookstore in town, which my friends helped to manage); and Kathy, a fellow foster mother and paraprofessional. Jennifer and Evan each took care of DJ two days a week until Emily and I came home, and Kathy became DJ's new aide at Linney in the fall, spending time with him over the summer as well. All of these people played an invaluable role in DJ's development. Jennifer could handle anything—from temper tantrums to medical crises. Once, as she was driving DJ home from OT, her car was hit by the tire of a dump truck, which had come loose because the tire shop that had just serviced the vehicle had forgotten to resecure the lug-nuts. Out of nowhere this giant, bouncing tire struck the passenger side windshield, shattering it. Had DJ been sitting in that seat, he might have been killed. When Emily and I showed up at the scene of the accident, the police officer commented about DJ, who was sitting like a statue on the curb, "Ma'am, your son is incredibly well behaved."

"He's in shock!" Emily exclaimed, and indeed he seemed to be, staring out into space, refusing to move.

Evan was the older brother that DJ never had: at once Captain Fun and Mr. Responsibility, exposing him to new experiences and holding him accountable for his behavior. There was a sweet earnestness about his commitment to DJ: he knew that he was a role model, and he wouldn't smoke, for example, or swear around him. Kathy was the aide we could count on—astonishingly reliable and competent. She, too, knew sign, and she was eager to be part of an effort to include a child with a cognitive disability in a regular school. Moreover, she understood what we were going through as parents. She and her husband, Chris, had fostered kids whom they later adopted. One glance at her on a morning when things hadn't gone well for us at home, and she could deduce the entire exasperating scenario. All three of these people quickly became our dear friends.

Compared to that first year, the second was much easier—if not a breeze then a gale force wind, an improvement upon the daily hurricane. I worked on my dissertation, taught classes at UF, and looked after DJ; Emily continued to work at CARD and spent lots and lots of time at Linney. During this year, DJ made significant communicative leaps. His signing improved to the point that he could say, "I want to eat" or "I want to take a bath," though it remained strictly utilitarian and very repetitive. Issues with finger dexterity suggested that sophisticated signing might not be in DJ's future. Although he recognized more and more signs, he couldn't produce them himself, even after much practice. We continued to cover our house—all of the objects in it—with sign diagrams, picture symbols, and words, especially words, immersing DJ in what experts call a "print-rich environment." We also pressed on with speech therapy and, of course, OT.

If the primary goal of kindergarten had been to acquaint DJ with the expectations, routines, and activities of a regular school, then the goal of first grade was to begin the long march to literacy. Though Emily didn't know whether or not he was a gestalt learner, she'd suspected he had great trouble deciphering spoken language and thus believed it pointless to teach phonics. Instead, she focused on sight recognition, utilizing his cultivated familiarity with puzzles and his desire to close the system (as with toileting) to build alphabet, number, and word awareness. The reading program DJ worked on began by asking him simply to find a word printed on the left hand side of the page in a grouping of first two, then three, then four, then five words on the right side of the page. The words would be accompanied by picture symbols or diagrams. "Point to same," we'd tell DJ in sign, and he'd take the word on the left, which had Velcro on its back, and attach it to the proper word on the right. Before he'd actually attach the word, we'd make sure it was correct by asking him to point to his answer. A proponent of "error-free learning," Emily believed that it was important to keep him from memorizing the wrong answer and to relieve the pressure of being right (especially for a kid with fragile self esteem who hadn't yet secured his place in a regular classroom). The physical act of velcroing the word to its partner closed the system in a definitive manner.

At the beginning, DJ was correct only about thirty percent of the time, and so we'd have to ask him to reconsider. "Find same," we'd say over and over, and he'd point to something else. Endless (and I mean endless) repetition accustomed him to English letters and letter groupings. Seeing the corresponding picture and sign helped to connect these graphic symbols to the things they represented. When we began, we had no idea if this literacy strategy would work or how far it would take us; we just knew that what had been tried previously hadn't worked. Early in the first grade, the resource room teacher at Linney saw that DJ was having success in matching words, and fairly soon she became one of DJ's most ardent advocates. In fact, when Mrs. Bollinger left to take an administrative post in the district, she assumed the PBS and IEP leadership role, problem solving creatively and intelligently.

Getting DJ to focus continued to be a problem, but we were making progress there as well. Having read a number of autobiographical accounts of autism, Emily advanced the theory of sensory input difficulties as a major impediment, perhaps *the* major impediment, to learning.

Lack of input, too much input, a system of sensory processing wildly out of whack—these were the issues confronting kids with autism, kids who couldn't seem to focus. At times, the everyday world was like a siren blaring in their ears or a fireworks display before their eyes. At other times, a void: a blank, operating room white, with the Autist like a patient on a table who doesn't feel a thing—a patient in search of his body. The challenge was to tame the distractions the rest of us knew how to tune out and/or to provide the missing sensation. Somehow we convinced the folks at Linney that DJ needed regular sensory-input breaks: moonshoes, a mini-trampoline, brushing, swinging, walking. You can't imagine the look on the new principal's face when the resource room teacher suggested that the courtyard outside the first grade classroom might be a good place for DJ's trampoline. Envisioning a fourteen-foot trampoline that only DJ could use, the principal seemed shocked. "No, a much smaller one—like they use for aerobics," the resource room teacher said, appreciating the principal's concern. That almost no one scoffed at these unconventional pedagogical methods spoke to how invested the school had become in DJ's success.

Once DJ had mastered the task of matching words, we moved on to fill-in-the-blank sentences. Again, we employed pictures to help convey the meaning of a sentence, focusing on one part of speech, one part of the sentence, at a time. Here, "error-free learning" was even more important, as DJ, at least initially, couldn't pick the proper word from the assembled word bank. For a good long while, we simply modeled the right choice, conceiving of the exercise as intensive spelling and vocabulary training. After we pointed out the correct answer, we'd have him attach it with Velcro to the blank in the sentence. Over and over, we repeated this process, hoping that meaning might stick and that eventually syntactical relationships might become evident. Although we saw signs of improvement, the going was very slow indeed—slow and erratic, with tiny bursts of insight and knowledge consolidation, followed by inexplicable setbacks.

In the resource room, where he spent one period per day, DJ moved through a series of stations. One involved the hand-over-hand tracing of his name or the completion of alphabet pages where he had to cut out a letter and glue it on the page and then color all of the pictures of the objects that began with that letter. One was a puzzle of some sort. Another was a picture with the shape of the corresponding word carved out. DJ had to spell the word by putting the correct plastic letter in the correct cut-out letter space. This he could do errorlessly on his own, and then a device called "Leapfrog" would say the word out loud. A fourth involved one-on-one reading with the resource room teacher. Though DJ didn't experience any genuinely explosive eureka moments, we felt as if we were laying a foundation: tediously, meticulously. Yes, his concrete was taking longer to set, but we looked forward to helping him frame the sturdiest of structures. It seemed as if a house was coming, or at least we thought it was. By the end of the year, Kathy noticed that DJ was focusing on learning tasks more easily, beginning to recognize new vocabulary/spelling words by the third or fourth time they had practiced them, and moving around the school and the resource room more independently.

The summer after first grade Emily and I bought a house. After eight years of renting, we decided that it was time to accumulate some equity. I'd come to the conclusion we'd probably remain in Florida after I received my doctorate. I'd apply for jobs in other places, and if I got a good one, well, then we'd think about moving. Otherwise, I'd teach at the community college. Emily loved her job, DJ was thriving, and we had a dynamic circle of friends and support we couldn't imagine giving up.

Less than a half a mile from Linney, the house had a small swimming pool and room for the principal's worst nightmare: a fourteen-foot trampoline! Ever since we'd thrown DJ a birthday party at the local gymnastics center and he'd jump on the many large trampolines, I'd had it in the back of my mind that we should purchase one. I'd buy an enclosure to make it safe, and I'd put it under the shade tree in the back so that the black nylon surface wouldn't get too hot. I'd once read an essay by Oliver Sacks about a family of autistic people who all jumped on a trampoline: a trampoline, if I remember correctly, that they kept in their living room. Though I pitched the idea to Emily as a kind of at-home OT, I was really envisioning all of the fun DJ and I would have bouncing and laughing and wrestling and moving in circles.

124

It took DJ a while to get acclimated to the unsteady surface, and at the beginning he wanted to hold my hand, but very quickly he got the hang—or, rather, the fall—of it. I couldn't believe how talented he was! On land, as it were, he was almost entirely uncoordinated, but at sea, at air, he had an uncanny sense of body position. He wanted to jump all day long. "Jump, jump, jump," he'd sign, refusing to let me stop, no matter how much I was sweating or panting. "Break, break, break" I'd beg, falling to the surface and performing exhaustion. Emily and I would use the trampoline as a behavior reinforcer. If DJ had a good day at school, I'd jump with him for as long as he liked. If he didn't—if, for example, he hit or tantrummed—then the trampoline sat empty and I ignored his signed entreaties. I'd point to the daily report and tell him that he had to work hard and learn to control himself.

Just before we moved into the new house, I had a fight with my father on the phone. My sister had started an Internet company, and as she was raising money for it, she approached me about giving her the names of some of my wealthy friends, guys who had gone into business and done quite well for themselves. I did give her some names, and two of my friends decided to invest, with the proviso that at least one of them be appointed to the board of directors. My father, who was acting as my sister's primary advisor (read: he was the de facto head of the company), left my friends off the board and then played dumb when I confronted him about it. It quickly became apparent he'd thought he could snow them (and me), though my friends had contributed a substantial portion of the total sum raised. In his slick, lawyerly voice, he prevaricated: truth's masseuse, inviting me to lie down on the table of his crass manipulations. Twenty years' worth of anger came pouring out, and I actually screamed, "I'm not one of your clients. Don't speak to me that way. You're a fucking asshole." And then I hung up.

Two months later, my mother called to say that she and my father were getting divorced. He'd left her for another woman and was already playing games with the money they'd soon fight over. In fact, he'd given himself a legal head start, hiring a lawyer before announcing his intention to split up. What lay ahead was a titanic battle over significant assets. Thank God for the no-fault/50-50 divorce rule in the District of Columbia, where they legally resided; without it, my mother might have gotten much less than she did. I felt sorry for her. Though I knew she was better off without my father, I also knew she was now alone.

As we settled into our new house, buying furniture and various household items, we received the last of a bunch of calls from DCF asking us if we wanted to adopt another child. The Department was desperately trying to find homes for its many eligible kids. "We can't possibly take another kid," I'd say in a cranky voice. "Get someone else to do their part." On the one hand, I resented being put in the position of having to say no. It was like giving money to a cause only to be called back and asked for more precisely because you'd just given some. On the other hand, I felt guilty. I knew how badly these kids needed homes. They were just like DJ. I'd recently watched a *Sixty Minutes* episode that depicted foster kids at a mall being paraded before the shopping throngs, and I was horrified. The kids walked glumly down a runway, the kind used at a fashion show. Very few shoppers even stopped to acknowledge this grotesque spectacle of need. But there *we* were, as comfortable as could be, luxuriating in our new swimming pool while the world and its misery carried on unabated.

For the first time since adopting DJ, I took stock of our present situation. In some respects, all of the things I feared would happen to Emily and me had indeed happened. We'd withdrawn into a much narrower sphere. I no longer volunteered at the soup kitchen or anywhere else for that matter—I didn't have time. Emily didn't devote herself as fully to her job—she didn't have time either. Our relationship had suffered: it was neither as romantic nor as intensely companionable as it used to be. And yet, we were doing important work on the disability front and providing a home for a deserving little boy. Moreover, we loved parenting, however tired we were. Almost from the beginning, I'd seen the possibility of a very different kind of relationship with DJ than the one I'd had with my father. I'd delighted in our much less burdensome silence and mutual eagerness to bridge the communicative chasm—with, for example, that more creative head-butting. I refused to apologize for domestic happiness even as I thought maybe I should.

There's a poem by Bertolt Brecht, one of my favorite poets, that declines to shrink from the world while honoring a child's sense of wonder and uninhibited duty. I like to think of it as a father–son piece for the socially committed, where metaphor does the work of reconciling public and private. Written in 1939 on the eve of World War II, the first section goes like this:

> To-day, Easter Sunday morning,
> A sudden snowstorm swept over the island.
> Between the greening hedges lay snow. My young son
> Drew me to a little apricot tree by the house wall
> Away from a verse in which I pointed the finger at those
> Who were preparing a war which
> Could well wipe out the continent, this island, my people,
>   my family
> And myself. In silence
> We put a sack
> Over the freezing tree.

The fate of the tree, Brecht tells us, is the fate of the larger world. Analogously, the poet's time with his son is time in the world. (I admit it: I've read all sorts of things into the line about their shared "silence.") Though it's no doubt preposterous to compare our own era to that of Nazi imperialism, I defy anyone to tell me this country couldn't be fairer, more compassionate, less consumed with the inane.

And so, remembering those left behind by joy—Rhonda, that sad, bouncing ball of a boy who was accused of the beating, all of the children who don't find parents—and, yes, remembering the larger "more" still left to do, I'd nevertheless look forward to DJ's nightly tickling ritual. Shirt up, grin from ear to recovered ear, he'd race into the family room, become airborne, and then land bottom down, giggling, on the couch. Although in command of many more signs and a few more words, he loved to revert to the hilarious basics of "more" and "stop," this latter sign learned, at Emily's insistence, just after the beating. He'd deliver the sign, a sort of karate chop, one-handed against my chest or leg—

against any available and extended plane—his other arm pinned as part of our game. "Tickadoo! Tickadoo! Tickadoo! Tickadee!" And then, having gotten me to stop, he'd once again sign "more."

In many respects, second grade was a continuation of first. We added more words to DJ's word banks (thereby giving him more choices) and, eventually, more blanks to his sentences. We encouraged him to point as much as possible, making sure to correct him before he closed the system. Where second grade differed from first was in the introduction of hand-over-hand typing. He'd use a labeler to do his work, a portable machine that printed out full sentences that could then be stuck to a piece of paper. Emily figured that DJ would likely continue to have finger dexterity problems and thus she believed that typing—not writing—would constitute his primary means of communication. She also thought typing would serve as yet another way to expose him to print. The keyboard would stabilize the location of letters and standardize them as well. From a practical standpoint, the machine was very convenient—much, much better than the Velcro system, as the worksheets that comprised so much of elementary school life no longer required the same tedious preparation.

It's important to underscore that at no time did we think we were practicing facilitated communication, that controversial communication technique from the 1990s in which someone supports the hand, wrist, or arm of a nonspeaking person with autism as he or she types. We knew that *we* were doing the typing, just as we knew back when we commenced the fill-in-the-blank exercises that *we* were answering the questions. We sought simply to model every aspect of the exercise through repetition and full immersion. We'd seen progress with the fill-in-the-blanks and so hypothesized that we might one day see progress with the typing. When we eventually did see significant progress, we still didn't call it FC—not because we were afraid to stir up controversy but because our path to success had been so atypical, involving years of practice and explicit literacy instruction before we even expected the kind of results normally associated with FC. If, as the religiously inclined might propose, the average FC triumph was like the resurrection of Jesus on the third day, then ours was like the resurrection of Lazarus on the fourth or, rather, four hundredth day. It wasn't really a resurrection at all but a slow coming forth to communicative life, as if the cave in which Lazarus resided were several miles long and it had taken him years to limp out. And yet, in emphasizing the gradual achievement of literacy, I need to make room for some sort of notion of a sudden, inconceivable burst—both with respect to the pace of DJ's subsequent communicative achievement and, even more important, to the concomitant psychological awakening. Only after DJ had been walking among us for months and months did we begin to speak of facilitated communication.

With the typing, we continued to follow the principle of error-free learning. We'd read the fill-in-the-blank sentences aloud to DJ along with the possible answers and ask him to choose. We wanted to work on his oral comprehension while we worked on literacy. If DJ was wrong, we'd point to the correct answer, type it with him and then have him place it on the page. We'd star those questions he got correct on his own. If DJ pointed at four incorrect answers in a row, we assumed the information was too difficult for him and reverted to the cueing protocol used in the first grade. When DJ's classmates began writing simple sentences and very simple stories, we'd do a version of the same with fill-in-the-blank sentences and word banks composed of equally acceptable answers. This gave DJ a chance not only to complete writing assignments on his own but also to make choices, even if the choices he made he didn't always understand.

In the resource room, the *Edmark* reading program focused on nouns: find the yellow car, the green car, the small car, the large car. After stabilizing the noun, it then stabilized the adjective: find the red car, the red apple, the red house, etc. Instead of worrying about the names of different parts of speech, we emphasized practical application. We took advantage of DJ's ability to "find same," breaking the category of "same" into smaller units of similarity and difference. After lots of practice, he could identify the verb in a grouping of, say, *apple*, *go*, and *purple*. In the resource room we began to leave three and four blanks in sentences or, for shorter sentences, to require DJ to assemble the entire sentence himself. He had some success with these tasks. By the end of second grade, DJ was able to stay in class with few, if no, breaks, provided that he was actively engaged. He was able to do the various exercises described, with the exception of the sentence assembly, with a seventy-five percent accuracy rate. He was also able, with minimal cueing, to use his *Cheaptalk* device, which Emily would load with lots of answer banks, to participate in class.

What did DJ's progress amount to? Where were we? We hadn't the foggiest idea. Could DJ move from rigid drilling, as in a foreign language course, to something like fluency? Would the rigid drilling help us achieve literacy but paradoxically reinforce his autism? Anyone even remotely familiar with autism knows about the infamous tics and obsessions. Maybe DJ would perseverate on *Edmark* exercises, insisting on finding "the red car, the red apple, the red house," over and over. How to get him to the point of meaningfully expressive communication? How to get him to talk about his life and the feelings we knew he had?

In January of that year, I interviewed at a small liberal arts college in the Midwest. I'd attended a liberal arts college myself and loved it, and I'd always wanted to teach at this sort of institution. When the opening appeared at Grinnell, a very progressive, highly selective college in Iowa, I was ecstatic. Not about Iowa (I preferred the warmth of Florida), but about the teaching and writing possibilities. The job would allow me to be both a scholar and a creative writer. I knew the school devoted a substantial portion of its large endowment to financial aid and scholarships—ninety percent of the student body received some kind of help—and I knew as well that it explicitly understood its mission as instilling in its students an ethic of service. These things attracted me enormously, especially as I pondered a self-imposed obligation to work in public education. A product of private education through college, I'd just received my doctorate from a state university, where I'd spent the previous seven years teaching. I knew what sort of work needed to be done in public education—home of the underprivileged and underprepared. It was a public school, after all, that had met DJ's needs, not some highly selective private school.

I didn't think I'd get the job—the competition was fierce—and when I did, Emily and I had a big decision to make. She generously encouraged me to accept the position; it was my turn to prompt a career move, she said. I worried about uprooting DJ, about having to include him again in another school in a strange place where we didn't know anyone and didn't have any clout. I felt guilty about wanting to teach at a private institution where the pay was better, the students were motivated, and the school felt free to define its mission in the way that a public university couldn't. Shouldn't I be teaching at a community college? I asked. (Ironically enough, I'd applied to the one in town, and the hiring committee had rejected me on the grounds that I seemed too intellectual.) When, Hamlet-like, I lost myself in the irreconcilable pros and cons, Emily stepped in: "It's an opportunity you can't pass up. DJ will be fine. We promised ourselves before we adopted him that we wouldn't entirely restrict our lives. Don't worry about me. I'm fine with it. I need a break. I'll focus for a year on including him in Iowa. Take the job."

Our friends were distraught when they learned we were moving to Iowa. As with so many things in life, you only appreciate their full value when you're just about to lose them. The day before we were set to leave, a crowd showed up to help us load the trucks—two giant U-hauls, one with a trailer for our Isuzu. Peter, John, Elaine, Evan, Jennifer, Nancy, Kathy, John, Stephanie, Rick, and Raina—each of them helped to close the system of community.

I don't know what DJ made of our preparations. He had to understand that we were moving; he'd been through it the year before when we bought the house we were now vacating. We'd tried to explain it to him in words, signs, and a picture book, but he just stared off into space: his customary response to stressful things. That episode at Thanksgiving had convinced us of DJ's abandonment worries, as had his refusal to enter other people's houses. We hoped that the moving trucks might signify something different from a packed minivan (though our minivan was packed to the hilt as well). As I watched him stim by the pool, I heard, in the back of my mind, the little girl's voice in Randall Jarrell's poem "Moving":

Butter the cat's paws
And bread the wind. We are moving.
I shall never again sing
Good morning, Dear Teacher, to my own dear teacher.
Never again
Will Augusta be the capital of Maine.

Changing the point of view toward the end of the poem, Jarrell writes,

The little girl
Looks over the shoulders of the moving men
At her own street;
And, yard by lot, it changes.
Never again.
But she feels her tea-set with her elbow
And inches closer to her mother;
Then she shuts her eyes, and sits there, and squashed red
Circles and leaves like colored chalk
Come on in her dark head
And are darkened, and float farther
And farther and farther from the stretched-out hands
That float out from her in her broody trance:
She hears her own heart and her cat's heart beating.

She holds the cat so close to her he pants.

Never again. Was DJ privately saying this to himself, insofar as he could *say* anything? Had his past experience of loss come bubbling up? Had it induced an analogous trance—part autism, part anxiety? At the end of the poem, Jarrell captures the child's visceral response to change, and it's about as close as I can come to describing DJ's reaction to the move. Just when he'd thought it safe to care and bond, safe to relax, his dad was yanking him by the tangled leash of his heart into another state, let alone another yard. Sensing how bad I felt, Emily assured me that the move would be good for DJ. "He'll see that he'll always be with us," she said. "Being dragged across the country is much better than being left behind."

My mom had flown out for the move, and our friend Nancy had driven up from DeLand. A devoted friend, she'd offered to drive one of the trucks to Iowa as part of our three-vehicle caravan. This was a woman who'd biked across the country by herself and attempted to kayak the entire eastern seaboard—she was game for anything. As if we needed confirmation of DJ's anxiety about the move, the morning we left, he awakened at six, went to the car, and, sitting in his customary seat in the back, waited for five hours in the blazing sun. By the time we loaded the final odds and ends, he was as red as a beet. I kept trying to get him to drink some water so that he wouldn't become dehydrated, but he refused. Perhaps he thought my concern a diversion from the calamity at hand. Perhaps he thought it a last act of kindness before another abandonment.

Driving away was hard: our friends waved from the front step of our now old house. I waved from my truck; I couldn't see Emily in the car, but I'm sure she was crying. She hates good-byes. DJ? I'm sure he was looking away. The whole endeavor seemed unreal. Never again will Tallahassee be the capital of Florida. Never again. Only after we'd crossed the Mississippi and entered Davenport, Iowa, two and a half days later did I believe we were moving to the Midwest.

We spent the month of July settling into Grinnell and preparing DJ for school. We met the principal of Davis Elementary, a man named Doug Cameron, who was very warm and accommodating, especially when he learned that we'd adopted DJ from foster care. He'd adopted a girl from foster care himself. When he learned that Emily was an expert on autism and would be offering her inclusion expertise free and spending lots of time at the school, he practically did jumping jacks for joy! Unlike many other school administrators whom Emily had come across, Doug considered the enrollment of a child with autism, and the help Emily offered, an opportunity to learn how to do something they really ought to be doing.

Much of that first year in Grinnell we tried to get DJ used to his new surroundings. Emily trained the two aides and discovered that the quality of DJ's work and focus had decreased dramatically, especially when he wasn't working with her directly. He was also acting out quite a bit: making noises and being silly. The afternoon aide, Jane Lohman, reassured a panicked Emily. A woman of enormous experience who was fluent in sign, she suggested that perhaps she and DJ needed to start at the beginning and move through each stage. Much to our relief, she turned out to be right. The biggest problem in third grade was convincing the regular ed teachers to get their lesson plans to Emily a day in advance so that she could do the modifications necessary for DJ to participate. She was often standing in the doorway at the beginning of class, still waiting to commence this process. Because Emily was doing all of the modifications herself, she grew more and more frustrated when these teachers couldn't accommodate this request. That year DJ received his most valuable learning experiences one-on-one in the resource room and in speech. If we included Mrs. Lohman in the world of special ed, it seemed as if he was learning *because of* special ed, not in spite of it: an irony that wasn't lost on Emily and me. Still, we were glad DJ was exposed to the comportment and friendship making of his peers.

In January, with DJ still unsettled and sullen, I proposed that we build a garage on the back of our property that could house DJ's fourteen-foot trampoline. In fact, I proposed that we put the trampoline in the ground (i.e., make it level with the floor) so that it would be easier to climb onto. I also proposed that we install a woodstove to heat the building. Thank God Emily had had some experience with my zany ideas, or she might have called the nearest loony bin. DJ hadn't been able to jump since the weather had turned cold and we hadn't found an OT, so I thought that this might be a solution to both problems. I wanted to teach DJ that we could respond to change positively, creatively. If winter in Iowa made outdoor jumping impossible, well, then, we'd move the trampoline indoors. We'd find a way to do what we wanted.

"Truth is, you miss jumping yourself," Emily said with a smile, and I did. My new job was stressful and taxing; there were lots of demands on my time, and I was trying to prove myself. I loved coming home in the fall and jumping with DJ. All of that stress would spiral upward like smoke from a portable fire pit: we were the flames dancing within the circular, metal grate. The response of our neighbors to this odd construction project was hilarious. After the excavator prepared the four-foot deep "basement," we could hear people walking by who said, "Are they building an indoor wading pool?" "No, that's so the guy can work on his car. He'll be able to get down below it." When word got out that the pit would house a trampoline, we became known as "that family with an indoor trampoline." We were legends in the hinterland of Iowa— people who had vanquished winter in the name of that loftiest of principles: fun. DJ and I took our first well-roofed bounce in March, and his familiar grin returned.

By April, Ms. Leathers, the resource room teacher, and Mrs. Lohman reported that DJ seemed to be moving their hands when typing. He'd point independently to a word in his word bank and then initiate the typing procedure. They felt him guiding their hands to the appropriate keys. Suddenly, he was able to read a story and complete six to eight worksheets on it. The questions asked DJ to pick out relevant information: the color of the car, for example, or location of the hot air balloon. For the first time, DJ was answering "wh" questions with complete accuracy. Because we saw DJ first pointing to the correct answer in his word bank, we didn't doubt for a second that he was guiding Ms. Leathers' or Mrs. Lohman's hands when typing, but we didn't make a big deal of it. We focused on the cognitive accomplishment, and, familiar with his finger dexterity and hand-eye coordination problems, simply assumed that DJ needed this kind of physical help.

Again, we didn't call this help facilitated communication, either privately with each other or publicly at school or in the community, though that's what it was. It didn't occur to us to ask DJ questions unrelated to the worksheets—about what he wanted to eat, for instance, or what he was thinking. I can't entirely explain why, especially since I'd made such a fuss at his first IEP about including the goal of asking questions about his life. We were locked into our routine of using sign and pictures to determine DJ's needs and using the labeler to work on his literacy skills.

Perhaps we'd grown too accustomed to the absence of more sophisticated expressive communication from DJ, underestimating what might have been possible right—or should I say, *write*—then. We were still relying on fill-in-the-blanks, however, and we honestly didn't think he could compose an entire sentence on his own. Still, we could have set up a worksheet that said: I feel a) sad, b) happy, or c) mad, and the fact that we didn't bothers me to this day. His most passionate advocates were probably holding him back.

About this time, we noticed that DJ was showing more interest in his regular ed math teacher's instruction than in the basic addition/subtraction money worksheets we were having him do with his aide. He literally seemed to crane his neck to see what was being written on the blackboard instead of concentrating on what was immediately in front of him. Early on, we'd decided to focus exclusively on literacy and had only just begun to give him math materials. Here, too, he shot forward, like some sort of spaceship assuming warp speed. He'd clearly apprehended the concept of place value on his own, for he started solving more complicated problems, embarking, it seemed, on a daring space walk in the thin universe of numbers. At the IEP in May, Ms. Leathers and Mrs. Lohman reported DJ's progress and asked sheepishly if we'd ever consider just trying him out in the regular math curriculum. For the first time, school personnel were setting the bar higher for DJ than we had. It was quite a moment. We found it ironic that the subject we'd entirely neglected might turn out to be DJ's strongest. His teachers for the following year, Mr. Abarr and Miss Louden, were present at the meeting. Though apprehensive about the experience that lay ahead, they were open to it, and they asked what they could do to help. "Have your lesson plans ready in advance and expect DJ to actively participate in your classes," Emily told them.

We spent the summer in Hilton Head at Em's parents, where Emily continued to work with DJ on his alternative reading program, which she'd borrowed from the school. DJ looked forward to his daily reading lessons, completing five to six worksheets a day and taking only two days to complete each story. On a short trip back to Florida, we had lunch with our friends, the Rifkins, who have a son with autism. Just home from a weeklong intensive seminar on using technology to access literacy for kids with autism, Margo inspired us to do more with computers. We planned to apply for a state-funded Gemini: a high-powered Mac with touch-screen and voice capabilities that cost about seven thousand dollars. DJ needed to be able to "speak" more than the prerecorded messages on his *Cheaptalk* would allow.

The week before school began, he experienced his first expressive breakthrough. Up until this point, all of his worksheets involved either fill-in-the-blank comprehension tasks or sequencing tasks, not open-ended questions. Emily and DJ had been reading the program's version of "Jack and the Beanstalk," and they had arrived at the conclusion of the story where Jack and his mother sit enjoying their triumph. The last question on the last page surprised—and worried—Emily. Instead of asking for factual information from the story, it asked the student to imagine what the mom might be thinking. At this point, DJ was still conveying his answers by pointing to words in word banks and adhering them to the page in the appropriate place. How could he possibly answer this question? Emily thought. She considered either skipping it or offering three valid ideas of her own from which he might choose. Before she could decide, DJ picked up his labeler and turned it on (something she'd never seen him do before). He took Emily's hand and purposefully guided it from letter to letter until he had typed out: "where a dad." The incorrect grammar, the obvious way in which this statement reflected his own life experience, and the fact that Emily had no idea what he was going to type (in the past, they'd simply typed his already identified answer) stopped her dead in her tracks. With tears in her eyes, she called me into the room and narrated for me what had just happened. I was dumbfounded. "Where a dad?"—an exceedingly relevant question from a boy whose family life had been so unstable. "Wow, DJ!" I exclaimed. "Wow!"

A week later, after he'd correctly solved a math problem, the worksheet asked him to explain his answer. To which DJ replied, once again picking up his labeler and taking hold of Emily's hand, "becuse just." So, DJ understood colloquial English as well, except he'd transposed the two words, producing that brother-from-another-planet translation effect that seemed like poetry. The fall was one long whir of accomplishment. "What is a subway?" "subway is underbus," DJ answered, either coining his own clever definition or simply failing to hit the space bar on the labeler. "What is a pyramid?" "opyramid us [is] sand triwangle." This answer floored Emily and me—once, of course, we'd accustomed ourselves to the characteristic errors in his typing: in particular, hitting the key next to the one he wanted. We'd encountered these errors before, but now we had no idea what he was going to say. "A sand triangle" seemed as good a short definition of a pyramid as I'd ever come across; you could tell it was the product of a visual thinker—almost painterly in its minimalist, compositional emphasis. "What is a mummy?" "kijng tut," DJ answered. "What is a capital?" "big ciuty." "What is a festival? "uit iws sa pwarty." "What are monuments?" "detad people live there."

How did DJ know the answers to these questions? Had he been reading before we knew he was reading—not only reading but thinking, processing, refining? His answers suggested something far different from rote memorization or rigid regurgitation: the expected mastery of someone autistic. Hyperbole can't do justice to our excitement, our awe, at DJ's achievements. Our friend Judy Barber, the district's speech/language person, said in disbelief, "This isn't supposed to be happening. The kid isn't falling farther and farther behind; he's catching up!" As excited as we were, we consciously decided not to bombard DJ with questions about his life. Before, we'd failed to move quickly enough; now we wanted to focus on integrating the labeler into everyday routines, careful about overwhelming him emotionally. But what was he thinking? I had to resist handing over the stacks and stacks of pennies I'd saved for precisely this moment—a whole piggy bank's worth to make up for lost time. We'd let him choose when he wanted to weigh in on his past or present. He seemed to need to get used to this new ability or, if not the ability itself, the experience of reciprocal exchange in a nonschool- or school-related setting. He needed to get used to having unscripted conversations. Though he appeared genuinely pleased by his accomplishments, he also appeared to be more nervous than usual, edgier, at times even frantic.

By mid-fall, DJ was doing regular fourth-grade math, amazing every-one. On his first test he received a B-, but after that, nothing but A's. Mr. Abarr had started DJ out on a calculator but very quickly realized that he was doing the problems in his head. With a 100s chart he could simply point to the answer and then with assistance write it and place it on the page. One day in language arts, at the beginning of a unit on the *Titanic* disaster, when Miss Louden was trying to determine the kids' familiarity with the event, DJ typed out, "There were rich people on the boat. There were poor people down below. I was poor person once." (It's one of the few things DJ's typed that I don't have, so I can't reproduce his characteristic typos, but I saw the page and memorized the remark.) Everyone was stunned by what DJ knew of the less ro-manticized version of the incident and how he'd identified with the ship's least fortunate travelers. When Miss Louden asked the class what it would have been like to be a passenger on the *Titanic*, DJ typed, "Scared to die."

How to account for a neurologically disabled fourth-grader with both class and existential consciousness? How did DJ know these things? How, with almost no training in math, could he do complicated addition, sub-traction, multiplication, and division problems in his head? How? How? How? How? Later, when I'd start investigating this phenomenon, I'd discover that nobody really had an adequate theory beyond a notion of the child with autism somehow storing information (without exactly understanding it) and accessing it once he or she had come to commu-nicative life. There was, however, precedent for such progress and a theory—indeed, an entire perspective on autism—that had been dis-carded in the 1970s as neurobiology began to triumph over psychology. At a hearing before the Congressional Committee on Labor and Public Welfare in 1957, the Director of the League School for Seriously Dis-turbed Children gave the following testimony:

> In 1943 Dr. Leo Kanner, of Johns Hopkins, diagnosed many of the pseudo-defective children as suffering from "early infantile autism." Lack of response, Dr. Kanner be-lieved, had led to the suspicion of innate feeblemindedness.

The league school, a psychiatrically supervised nonresidential school, has been working with 30 of these schizophrenic and autistic children for four years. We have found from clinical observations and psychological testing that the majority of these children are of normal and superior intelligence. Most of them have phenomenal memories and exceptional gifts in particular areas—mathematics, music, mechanical aptitudes, etc.

Our children's resistance and emotional blocks to learning are part of an all-pervading fear of exploring anything new. They feel safer with rigid routines and stereotyped activities and yet when these emotional blocks are removed many of our children have made amazing progress, often achieving 3 or 4 years of reading or arithmetic skills within a period of one year.

However unfashionable (and politically incorrect) it was to do so, I'd come to think that autism could have, in part, a psychological etiology or, at the very least, that serious "emotional blocks" could contribute to the neurological phenomenon. The very word "block" calls to mind some sort of dam or obstruction, behind which there exists enormous pressure. What if DJ's own all-pervasive fear of anything new was a manifestation of both sensory input disturbances (with their subtle social and emotional effects) and traumatic injury? Once those problems had been partially ameliorated by all of the things we were doing, including teaching him how to read, perhaps he was then ready for release. How else to account for the speed and force of his progress? Whatever the case, DJ's development presented a significant complication: his intellectual gains seemed to be creating additional "emotional blocks." As language allowed him to begin to explore the past, anxiety began to clobber him.

"Where a dad?" DJ had asked. "I was poor person once," he had reported. As the year unfolded other momentous statements followed, particularly at Christmas and then again in the spring. He was agitated enough in the fall that we decided to try him on a course of Prozac and, later, Zoloft—both with disastrous results. We'd heard of other people with autism benefiting enormously from taking these drugs, which curbed their jitteriness and anxiety. But DJ, once again in the statistical minority, experienced a number of adverse side effects, including profound disinhibition (especially uncontrollable silliness and laughter). These side effects were so bad that Emily and I had to keep him out of school. One day, I kid you not, he laughed for six straight hours, disturbing us more than any tantrum ever had, what with the laughter's incongruous relation to his actual feelings.

Around this time, I received some awful news about my own health. I'd been bothered by intense pain in my groin on the left side, pain that had been getting worse and worse over the course of the previous summer and right into the fall. It had gotten so bad I'd stopped playing tennis. Certain I'd torn a muscle, I was entirely unprepared for what the orthopedist said upon reading my x-rays: "You're going to need a total hip. Actually, you're going to need two." I looked at him blankly. Total hip? The orthopedist was talking about joint replacements—two of them, in fact. "Mr. Savarese," he told me, "you have some sort of arthritic disorder and you need to see a rheumatologist immediately." Then, he was out the door, rushing to the next patient, leaving me in my underwear to absorb the news.

I honestly don't know how I made it home from the doctor's office. I kept thinking of all the things I'd never do again: run, play competitive tennis, jump on the trampoline. Jump on the trampoline—what would DJ say? How would he understand? I vowed I'd jump with him as long as I could bear it, delay the surgery, because afterward mine would be a life of little impact. The strained pun suggests how self-pitying and melodramatic I became, understanding this news as the very end of the world. And in a way it was. How could a thirty-eight-year-old need not one but two hip replacements? How could this be happening to me? I spent the rest of the fall seeing specialists in Iowa City and New York in an attempt to determine what was wrong. Believing I had an autoimmune disorder and wanting to arrest the rapid pace of degeneration in my joints, the rheumatologist in Manhattan prescribed a powerful immunosuppressant, which I'd begin taking in January. The drug—Remicade—was administered through a series of infusions in the chemo ward at our local hospital.

The day after Christmas, as I was preparing to leave for the annual meeting of the Modern Language Association, Emily had a conversation with DJ on his laptop. DJ had awakened at three in the morning and hadn't been able to fall back to sleep. Em's folks, who had purchased the laptop for DJ when it became clear that the Gemini would take months to get and that he really needed something more portable anyway, were sitting in the living room watching the conversation unfold. Throughout the fall, they'd heard about DJ's amazing progress but now they were getting to see it for themselves.

"What woke you up this morning?" Emily asked.

"adr A dreammmmmm," DJ typed.

"About what? Do you remember?"

"i dont know," he replied.

"My dream was about _____." Emily hoped that the fill-in-the-blank procedure might help him to answer.

"a saaaad nityes"

"Your dream was about a sad night?" she asked. "What made the night sad?"

"hdeerd heard hide deadddddddddddddddddd," DJ typed. He had a habit of depressing keys and watching the computer reproduce the letters endlessly. But DJ was also becoming upset, and when he was upset his typing faltered more than usual.

"What was dead?"

"giiiiirl," he said.

"Did you know her?"

"yes"

"What was the girl's name?"

"eklki," he typed.

"Sister Ellie?"

"yes"

"In real life sister Ellie is OK. She lives in _____," Emily explained. "Would you like to write talk see her?" she asked.

"se33e," he answered, letting out a loud shriek and starting to cry.

"Do you remember skating and swinging with her?" Emily possessed unfailing judgment, and she'd clearly decided this was the moment to pursue the past.

"ues," DJ replied.

"Ellie is very nice."

"when you were giiomg giuither [going get her]," DJ typed, now sobbing. So, he knew I was traveling to _____ and thought somehow I might return with his sister.

"You miss Ellie. She loves you very much."

"yesw."

"when you ftherrrrrrrrrrrrrff,"

"When you find her?" Emily clarified.

"findhergoinggither," DJ typed insistently. If the house had been a mine shaft, we would all have been falling through it—Emily, Rachel, Phil, and I. As impressive as the demonstration of cognitive competence had been, it was DJ's heart that moved us most, his commitment to his sister, confirming what we'd always known: he missed her terribly.

Just before Christmas, DJ had produced his first story—his first sustained piece—about Frosty the Snowman and his pal Jimmy. The story concluded with the following lines, and we thought of them again when DJ inquired about his sister. If the story seems more composed than his customary communication, it's because he worked on it endlessly. Every element of it is his; Emily and I simply asked him if a given word or sentence was correct, and slowly but surely, he came up with this:

> They were standing on the dock, standing and looking at the stars. They turned and ran away. They flew home. They hugged, then waved goodbye. They were sad.
>
> Jimmy is dreaming about Frosty. He is sad because Frosty is melting. Jimmy is going to miss his friend Frosty.

The deep longing in these utterances and their obvious resonance with DJ's life had stunned us. I was particularly impressed by the syntax of the first line (a construction I'd been trying to teach my creative writing students). It fixed the two characters on the dock in a posture of earnest contemplation, the way an image in a poem might. "What's the meaning of it all?" "Why is there loss?" the story inquired, half-expecting the stars to provide an answer.

Miss Louden conducted a creative writing workshop with her class, and one of the students responded to DJ's story with a suggestion: in effect, that the problem of Frosty's melting ought to be introduced earlier in the narrative. DJ went bananas, screaming, hitting his head. When Mrs. Lohman walked him out of the classroom and calmed him down, he typed on the computer, "dont want yelp [help] its my story." Even Mrs. Lohman, who had been struck by DJ, delighted in the pride he was showing in his work. Emily joked that DJ took after his father. While getting an MFA in poetry writing, I'd found receiving criticism similarly unbearable.

It had taken DJ forever to write the story. The one-finger typing, the autistic fading in and out, the process of asking for clarifications and corrections, the multiple drafts—all of it made for very slow going. Miss Louden and Mr. Abarr were terrific about granting extensions. They were terrific in general, waiting for us at the door when we picked DJ up to tell us about his latest accomplishment. They always had their lesson plans ready well in advance so that Emily could do the modifications. Mr. Abarr worked with DJ sometimes one-on one, as did Miss Louden. Miss Louden learned lots of useful sign language, incorporating it into the daily routine. She had the class, for example, sign the "Pledge of Allegiance" each morning. She also used the finger alphabet in spelling exercises. Both frequently called on DJ in class. For the first time in Iowa, he seemed like a fully active participant in his regular ed classes.

DJ had an excellent stretch from January to late March. He continued to make progress in his academic work, though there were signs of agitation and, occasionally, panic. At home, he spoke of people being killed in his dreams, and several times he went to pieces with his college buddies—sobbing and sobbing. To the question "Why did you get so agitated at the Forum [a college hangout]?" DJ typed, "becausddddd

144

nobodymightknow whertriammghtfg [where I am]." We began to notice that DJ's communicative command would especially falter whenever he was distressed, and so we had to work harder then to get him to make sense.

In early April, a guidance counselor at Davis spoke to the fourth grade about the problem of child abuse without alerting us beforehand. We'd have never allowed DJ to be present for such a talk, fearing precisely what happened: a huge upset. Such an encounter with the past, we believed, would have to be carefully planned for, managed. The guidance counselor framed her talk around the imperative to disclose—"You need to tell an adult if you know of anyone who is being abused," she said—and DJ took her literally. Shortly after the talk, he erupted and began to hit Mrs. Lohman. The outburst was so aggressive and disruptive that Ms. Leathers had to be called in. Having played a crucial role in teaching DJ how to read, Ms. Leathers would now play an even more important role in talking DJ through his crises.

"What are you trying to tell me? What do you need?" Ms. Leathers asked.

"i need to tsalk," DJ said.

"What do you want to talk about?"

"guidaNCVE"

"What are you thinking about?"

"i mb thinlking about erin she visv vstioll [is?] in gtrouble"

"Who is Erin and how do you know her?"

"shde ies from vbflorida v." At this point DJ apparently started screaming and hitting again.

"Remember that fingers are for typing and that everything here is OK," Ms. Leathers said. "Everyone here at Davis loves you and cares about you."

"yes iknow"

"We are so proud of all the hard work you do. You have done great work this year."

"i want to taslk abougt edrin," DJ said, again becoming agitated.

"OK, we can talk about Erin. I will listen but you need to use your fingers for typing and not hitting."

"ok"

"Can you tell me how you know Erin?"

"mfostervcar," he replied.

"Do you remember how old you were?"

"3"

"Was Erin a boy or a girl?"

"gifrl"

"Was she younger than you or older?"

"older." At this point DJ signed "all done, all done," and Ms. Leathers didn't want to push it. During her lunch break, she called to tell us what DJ had typed. We surmised that Erin must have been the victim of child abuse and that DJ had been reminded of it by the guidance counselor's talk—indeed, that he was now following her instruction and reporting it to an adult. There was something unbelievably touching about DJ's sense of responsibility. And something eerie as well: the imperative to disclose coinciding with his fall into language.

At home, he didn't mention the problem of "guidance," but the next day in the resource room, DJ became distraught and once again struck Mrs. Lohman. "i want to talk about guidance," he typed.

"Tell me what you are thinking," Ms. Leathers replied.

"scared," DJ said.

"Why are you scared?"

"friend iunn erin"

"Where is Erin?" Ms. Leathers asked.

"florida sbhe is hurt," DJ answered. His use of the present tense suggested some kind of flashback. "she does not like her dad," he explained.

"Did she tell you that?"

"hhyes"

"What happened with Erin and her dad?"

"he hnit hwer"

"Does Erin still live with her Dad?" Ms. Leathers asked, trying to escort DJ into the present and to bring the conversation to a positive conclusion.

"noo"

"I bet that she is like you and is in a very safe place now."

"yes im ook now," DJ said.

"So, by hitting Mrs. Lohman you were trying to say you were worried about Erin and wanted to talk about it?"

"yes"

"Next time go to the computer. Don't hit. OK?"

"ok," DJ said.

That evening with us, DJ started to cry for no apparent reason. "What's the matter? Are you nervous?" I asked.

"yes becaued guidancd," DJ said.

"What happened in guidance?" I was hoping to get him to elaborate on the phenomenon I called a flashback. I also thought he might want to address his own experience of abuse. Since the past had shown up unannounced, it seemed better to offer this traveler a room than to leave him seething in the rain.

"i thonk about florida hry ii i"

"What about Florida?"

"i was sczredfh scared"

"What scared you in Florida?"

"going to fostetcsre"

"It must have been very scary. You were very brave. Can you tell me what scared you the most? Did some bad things happen?"

"hurt," DJ said simply.

"Do you remember being hurt by someone? Who was it? Do you know?"

"sertyyygtfrom restgupopufdfggg"

"I don't understand. Tell me again."

"it was girouphome"

"Someone at the group home?" I asked, but DJ wouldn't respond.

The very next night more came out, including the answer to the question of who had beaten him. DJ had become especially agitated and violent. "It's not OK for you to hit, bite, or bang your head," Emily yelled. "Why are you doing this?"

"i am hitringfor badboyn," he replied.

"Are you remembering this from when you were little or from now?" No answer. "Do you see this bad boy in your mind? Do you know his name?"

"kykle," DJ said.

"Did he live with you at Ms. Austin's house in the country?"

"yefs"

"Did he hit you?"

"yes he hurtgirltoo." So, Kyle *had* been the one who beat DJ mercilessly. It was all so much sadder and more complicated than I'd wanted to imagine: a boy working out his problems on small children who were completely vulnerable, a woman taking on too many foster kids and leaving them unsupervised, a community failing to produce enough socially engaged citizens.

At the end of this conversation, DJ responded to our familiar request to control himself by typing, "dad. i ferce [fierce] not ok." And yet, despite his self-understanding, he persisted hitting and screaming. With DJ having told us about Kyle, the young man now moved into our house—permanently, it seemed. He was everywhere. "i saw kyle just now," DJ told us.

"Where?" we asked.

"in my bedroom." DJ was terrified. "i sede kyk." "i am nervous that i will sfde kyle." "kyle is going hurt me?" he asked, half as a statement, half as a question. Even when we could distract him from his foe, anxiety remained a constant companion. The day after attending an assembly with a shuttle astronaut, DJ let out a scream that could be heard in the exosphere. When asked to explain himself, he typed, "i remembered the spaaceshuttle explioding." The guidance we collectively offered seemed to be leading him further and further into a cavern of fear. The more we headed for the light, the darker it became.

148

CHAPTER 6

Read the Book

I'd gone off the Remicade in late April and went to see a specialist in Indianapolis right before my brother James's wedding. This doctor had been using Doxycyclene to treat obese women with arthritis of the knees. The official trial wasn't yet complete, but the Doxyclyclene appeared to slow the rate of degeneration by inhibiting an enzyme involved in cartilage loss. The drug hadn't been tested on anybody with arthritis of the hip, but because it was fairly innocuous, compared with the potentially life-threatening immunosuppressant Remicade, the doctor agreed to put me on it. With my left hip having deteriorated so quickly and my right one following suit, I was desperate for a remedy. The doctor in Indianapolis believed my problem was "mechanical" not systemic, though the doctor in New York thought just the opposite, and the doctor in Iowa City told me he didn't know. Once the condition had run its course, he'd be able to rule things in or out, he said, but of course by that point I might not have much cartilage left. DJ wasn't the only one whose condition the medical profession understood poorly, and I experienced for myself the strange victimization of fumbling expertise.

What we did know, what we all agreed upon, was that the Remicade hadn't worked. I'd done badly on it, acquiring various infections.

Moreover, it was very, very expensive, and the tests hadn't ever indicated an inflammatory problem, the kind associated with autoimmune arthritic disorders where the body visibly attacks itself. On the other hand, the sudden rapid loss of cartilage suggested a problem different from your run-of-the-mill osteoarthritis, even in a person like me who had so taxed his joints with years and years of highly competitive tennis. Something unusual was happening, and I couldn't bear to sit idly by, stiffening into despair.

I'd planned the Indianapolis trip so that on my way back to Iowa I could meet Emily and DJ in Michigan for the wedding. I'd been so absorbed by DJ's turbulent emergence into language, my own medical problems, and the grueling pace of the spring semester that I hadn't really had a chance to focus on the fact that my family would be congregating for the first time since my parents' divorce. I hadn't seen or spoken to my father in three years—not since we'd had that awful argument on the phone. The estrangement had been a long time in the making, but once my father announced his intention to divorce, it became too easy to imagine that the two events were connected—indeed that the latter had precipitated the former. My father no doubt welcomed the opportunity to write off our estrangement as an immature response to divorce: a grand irony, for I'd been pleading with the poorly matched pair to split up from the very moment I became a teenager. Had they divorced twenty years earlier, my mother might have had a second chance at love. In this culture older women generally don't get such a chance.

As weird as it would be for me to see my father with another, younger woman (he hadn't invited me to his nuptials, so I hadn't met my new stepmother), it would be even weirder for my mother—weirder and sadder and more infuriating. She'd be without an escort for the weekend, and the mere sight of my father with his new wife might provoke a fit of rage, especially if my mother were to drink excessively. The smug romantic and financial triumph of men of my father's generation was enough to make any fair-minded person a Leninist of love. Come the older woman's revolution, my mother's anger proclaimed, and they'll line the bastards up against a wall and let their hearts flow. Maybe then these men would understand what it's like to give of themselves so completely.

However over the top, my mother's anger was legitimate, even as she ought to have assumed more responsibility for her own happiness—at least after we kids had left the house. My brother was worried enough about our causing a scene that he'd taken precautions, such as seating us as far away from the old man as possible and ensuring we wouldn't have to pose for pictures with him. I regret the stress we added to James's wedding preparations, and I can only imagine what Eileen, his fiancée, must have thought of all of this, coming as she did from an exemplary family. In the end, however, these precautions saved everyone, allowing the lovers what they deserved: a joyful day free of Sicilian-Irish drama.

James had emerged from a painful divorce, met a remarkable woman, and discovered a future better than he'd ever imagined. My mother, who'd worried terribly about James, hosted a rehearsal dinner under a tent in the back yard of the soon-to-be newlyweds' summer home on Lake Michigan. She was determined to make the event memorable for all of the right reasons, and she did, offering up the first toast: a moving tribute to her new daughter-in-law. She said nothing about my father; there were no digs, no veiled allusions to faithless men. I commended her upon the dinner's conclusion. I could tell how difficult the occasion had been for her, but she's a goodhearted person through and through.

The wedding the following day was spectacular. Almost too beautiful with her white dress and jet-black hair, Eileen provoked a kind of intense nostalgia. It was as if we were already recalling her. Standing next to my brother as he said his vows, I remember thinking how grateful he seemed for another go at love, another, deeper plunge into commitment. In contrast to my father, he'd struggled to save his former marriage, and when his ex-wife ended it, he couldn't have been more giving in the settlement proceedings. I admired him immensely for the way he'd handled himself, as hurt and exhausted as he was. He really wished his ex-wife well. How many men have their former fathers-in-law call to congratulate them on their impending marriages? When James kissed Eileen, it seemed as if life might work out: the two of them like rivers that had traveled thousands of miles to empty into one another.

Everyone had a good time at the reception. Emily and I knew DJ liked music—later that summer he'd tell us he "like[s] jazzc because it uis sascd

[sad] it taps into my heaer [heart]"—but we had no idea how much he liked dancing. From the moment the first song began until nearly 10:30 at night, he danced, some three hours straight. My mother had bought DJ a dark blue suit, and he looked quite dapper in it with his Harry Potter curls and glasses. But for all of his wholesome good looks, DJ danced like a punk rocker, moving strictly from the knees up and throwing in plenty of vigorous head bobbing. Periodically, he'd sign to us, "fun, fun."

And boy was it fun! We danced with my aunts, uncles, cousins, nephews, siblings, and mother. Perhaps the best part of the reception—and really of the wedding in general—was how much Eileen's family and ours intermingled. On the nights leading up to the wedding, we'd spent time at the hotel bar with her brothers and sister and their respective spouses, and at the reception we all danced together. We were like one giant octopus or family of octopi, unconcerned with formal boundaries, refusing to match up specific arms or legs. We just moved—joyously. I had taken as many pain pills as my stomach would allow; I didn't want to miss out on the dancing, though I knew the next day I'd be in trouble, and I was.

In retrospect, I see that the weekend, with its emphasis on family, triggered in DJ a sustained reflection on the meaning of relation—how people are connected to one another. The anxiety about Kyle and foster care, which had briefly subsided in the late spring, resurfaced as we traveled to the Poconos for a Thornton family reunion and, later, to South Carolina and Florida where we saw a host of old friends. DJ was moving into language with breathtaking speed, and language brought with it awareness at once integrative and disintegrative. Moments of penetrating insight would be followed by periods of extreme panic and upset. It was as if language were the hand that had brought the lens of the past into focus and that focus caused the photographer to hurl the camera onto the ground—over and over and over again. Language meant anxiety. Language meant fear. The experience of being with family and old friends whom he missed provoked fits of comparison and association.

These episodes throughout the summer were but the prelude, however, to the real crisis of the fall when DJ entered middle school. The big kids there reminded him even more intensely of Kyle which made him think of Ellie which made him think of Rhonda which made him think of foster care—round and round in a mad whirligig of pain. The past was like some carnival just on the outskirts of town to which DJ was constantly catching a ride, sneaking out of his present window under the cover of silence. I'm not sure I can convey the extraordinary difficulty of this period—the ferocity of DJ's attacks, our sense of helplessness and despair. It was the only time I ever thought that our best efforts might not be enough. But I get ahead of myself. The Australian poet Les Murray has a magnificent poem in which he speaks of a "woman walking ahead of her hair." It's a windy day and she races, he says, "comet-like right into the sun." I am a narrator walking ahead of my despondency.

The Thornton family reunion took place at a lodge called Skytop in Pennsylvania, and it encompassed Emily's mother's side of the family. In total, there were fourteen adults and fifteen young people present—the young people ranging in age from seven to twenty-two. The place had a large swimming pool, golf course, fishing pond, hiking trails, ping-pong tables, tennis courts, and God knows what else. DJ loved swimming with his cousins and Uncle Tim, to whom he seemed especially drawn. Tim had taken us to the hospital those many years ago when DJ was having a seizure in his house. Everybody was terrific about including DJ in activities, and he really seemed to be having fun. We attributed his periodic meltdowns to autistic overload and obstinacy, but then one night while waiting for dinner to be served, he suggested another reason for his behavior, allowing us to see what was bubbling just beneath the surface.

Emily and I had been trying to keep DJ occupied until the main course arrived. The protocol for meals—all of them sit-down, all of them formal and requiring for men and boys alike a sports jacket—had proven especially challenging for DJ, who that night had taken to signing, "all done, all done. go" before the salad had even appeared. In an effort to delay our departure, we attempted to get him talking on the computer. "Who helped you go back to our room and find Dad?" Emily asked. Earlier that afternoon, DJ had become distraught when Emily briefly left him with her brother Tim and his wife Kathy.

"sdunt kathy," DJ replied.

"Are you happy to be at dinner with your family?" Emily inquired, unaware of the wave about to swamp us—unaware, that is, of how the most positive experience of family could prompt in an adopted child feelings of profound loss and disconnection. When DJ made a move to leave, I asked him a question that I'd been curious about for some time.

"DJ, did you know that your Daddy is writing a book about you?"

"yerd" he said.

"How did you know?"

"i hearc ykj rewqding [you reading] it to mom," he answered, shocking me.

"What do you think about it?"

"kig [it] is breaking my heart," he said. I think Emily gasped when she saw DJ's reply.

"What do you mean? Does it make you sad?"

"yes"

"Why do you think I'm writing a book about you?" I asked.

"becazusde you lov mde," DJ typed.

"Yes. I love you and think you are very brave. I want the whole world to know how smart you are. Why does Dad's book make you sad?"

"becazuse I misds edllie," he explained. So, he was referring to the chapter about our trip to the Northeast. There were only two chapters I'd read to Emily, two chapters I'd written—both of them recounting the period before DJ acquired language.

"You know she misses you too," I said. "DJ, I wrote about Ellie so that one day she can know how much you have missed her." By this point, the waiter had begun to serve our entrees, and DJ once again signed, "all done, all done"—this time with an anxious flourish that hinted at an ensuing outburst.

When I'd asked the question about my book, I'd expected DJ to indicate perhaps a general awareness of its existence, not that he'd been listening to me read from it. At the time, I thought his ability to decode spoken language minimal at best. Indeed, later that summer he'd still describe autism as a problem of apprehending what other people say. The conversation would begin with a question about facilitated communication: "Why do you need Mom's finger to type?"

"becaUse it helps looo [look] both at key and screeb [screen]"

"Do you know what autism is?"

"yes it isnvt funm"

"Why not?"

"be cause it os hard tyo understand other people"

"How is it hard?"

"it is not eas ti [easy to] hdear"

"What helps you understand what other people are saying?"

"ty;ping is gooc"

"Is it easier to read than to hear words?"

"read," he said. DJ wouldn't always feel this way; in fact, becoming literate would improve his auditory comprehension, eventually making it nearly one hundred percent reliable. At the beginning of the summer, and certainly during the previous spring when I'd been reading versions of the first two chapters aloud to Emily and we were, in general, still typing all of our communication, DJ had to have been well on his way to full comprehension, perhaps farther along than he knew.

Just how much he'd understood of the book became clear in Hilton Head not two weeks after he first mentioned listening to it. DJ had been complaining of nightmares and insisting we might return him to foster care. That particular afternoon, he'd experienced a major meltdown: screaming, hitting, banging his head. "DJ, do you understand that Mommy and Daddy adopted you five years ago?" I asked.

"yes"

"What are we?"

"mom and dad"

"Do you ever have to worry about leaving us?"

"you read the the girl that read her that you t," DJ typed cryptically. He was still very agitated.

"Are you talking about the book that Daddy is writing? Does Daddy's book make you worry?"

"yes"

"Why does it make you worry?"

"read read that girl is my sister that girl girl." However fractured the syntax, DJ's answer was very telling. At its most basic level, it was asserting his relationship to "the girl" in the book: that girl was his sister, and he ought to be with her. If the Thornton family could have a reunion, then why couldn't he and Ellie? But the repetition of the word "read" suggests something more. At least part of DJ's worry concerned the act of reading itself. He seemed to be trying to express the shock of literacy, of communication: the moment he'd entered the social world of meaning. By "reading" my book, he discovered his sister. That moment, as I've already hypothesized, brought both clarity and anxiety: the camera in pieces on the ground. "read read that girl"—the transitive verb and the unusual direct object capture the force of his discovery.

Americans have little patience for psychoanalysis. It's almost too easy to parody Freud's focus on sex—the centrality of terms like "castration complex" and "oedipal fantasy." But what other field of knowledge seeks to explain the birth of desire and its evolving operation in and through language? Americans want less a theory of desire than a watered-down psychology of self-help, and they certainly don't want a theory that overtly sexualizes the family unit. The family unit, though, is precisely where desire first apprehends, first names, its available objects. The family unit is where difference first becomes a problem: the problem of "the other." It's where the social first manifests itself as a pressure of identification. I wanted a framework for understanding DJ's emergence, and I wanted to take seriously the discovery of his sister in language. Hence, I turned to psychoanalysis.

If, as some psychoanalytic theorists propose, language is a kind of surrogate parent (or in this case, sibling) that instills a longing for oneness exactly as it reminds us of this impossibility, then DJ's life story literalized a fundamental paradox: the acquisition of language betokens loss. Put provocatively, language is the group home of life. By the time an infant recognizes his separation from his mother and can speak of her as a discrete object, he is already racing toward the lonely singularity of adulthood. Of course, for DJ this crisis in the short term afforded no compromise: most of us get to preserve the illusion of oneness in the persons of our family, as at a reunion; he did not. Ellie thus became the name he'd track like a bounty hunter through the swamps of longing, a bounty hunter who wouldn't give up.

"Where do you think your sister is?" I asked.

"_____," DJ responded.

"Yes, you are right. Why is Ellie in _____?"

"because i read it," he said. He'd misunderstood my question, but his misunderstanding revealed in the most disconcerting fashion the contribution of my book to his emergence.

"Do you remember visiting her in _____?"

"yes"

"What do you want to tell me about the visit?"

"that it was fun"

"Why do you think Ellie lives in _____?"

"likes to be with her family," DJ said, skirting the issue of his own displacement and adoption. Did he, too, like to be with his birth family? He'd begun the conversation by expressing a fear of losing us.

"Yes, that is true. Do you remember living with Ellie?"

"yes"

"Whom else did you live with?"

"rhnda"

"That's right. Do you know what happened to Rhonda?" As I posed this question, I almost had to pinch myself. Five years after suggesting at his first IEP that a legitimate goal would be giving DJ a way to talk about his life, he was actually doing it. I had been laughed at by the special educators, but there he was inquiring about the things any child in his circumstances would inquire about.

"read ity the book," DJ replied, once again reminding me of the significance of my book.

"So, what did you read about Rhonda?"

"her readhy to live by herself." I hadn't actually said that in the chapter he'd heard, but it wasn't an entirely erroneous account. In a way, I think he was trying to tell us that *he* hadn't been ready to live by himself, that *he* hadn't wanted to give up his family. The issue of living by himself would end up haunting us, as DJ imagined that achieving independence, however slowly and gradually, would mean returning to foster care.

"Rhonda was sick," I said. "She wasn't well. She couldn't take care of you and Ellie. Do you understand?"

"yes"

"That's why Mommy and Daddy worked so hard to make it possible for you to live with us. Is there anything you would like to know or ask about Rhonda or Ellie?"

"yes"

"What would you like to ask?"

"that shd visit." I was afraid he might say this—the one thing we couldn't make happen.

"You mean Ellie?"

"yes"

"Do you understand why you and Ellie do not live together?" I asked.

"no," DJ replied.

"Do you want Daddy to try to explain?"

"yes"

"When Rhonda got sick, Ellie went to live in _____, just as you went to live in foster care. Do you understand?" My explanation seemed so matter-of-fact, neatly equating the two destinations: _____ and foster care, a dozen roses and a pile of crap. I said nothing about him not being wanted. Though DJ claimed to have "read the book," I wasn't sure what he knew specifically, and I didn't want to punish him with the truth.

"yes," DJ said.

"When we visited Ellie several years ago, who were the people with her?" I asked.

"father," he replied in tantalizingly ambiguous shorthand. The lack of a possessive pronoun seemed significant: he both did and didn't want to clarify his relation to this man.

"Whose father?" I asked, wondering if maybe he didn't know that he and Ellie shared a father.

"her fagther," he typed.

"Do you understand that I am your father now and that Mom is your mother?" I asked a bit too defensively. DJ had indicated a desire to end the conversation, something I was all too happy to do. Whatever my commitment to open adoption, I was starting to feel insecure about my status—my claim, as it were, on DJ.

"yes," he responded.

"This will be true forever. So, you don't have to worry about leaving us." Of course, my final statement neglected the possibility of DJ's ambivalence: whatever longing he had to join his sister in the Northeast.

The following morning, while reading with Emily, DJ brought up Ellie again. Emily had wanted to get a head start on fifth-grade reading, so she'd asked for a list of stories and books and had commenced reading them with DJ. Many of these stories were sad and violent. Along with the decision to assign them, they reflected, I believe, a comfortable middle-class take on the world, a liberal interest in suffering—one might even say a kind of spectatorship. The desire to expose children to the plight of others less fortunate is noble enough, but there needs to be more awareness of those kids for whom the story isn't just a story. Like my own unwitting assignment (the reading aloud of the first two chapters of this book), the fifth-grade reading syllabus contributed to DJ's shotgun emergence into language and what we would come to call "post-traumatic stress."

The story that morning involved the death of a seeing-eye dog. "Why is Leslie worried about being able to love Ursula, the dog?" Emily asked.

"bexcaUSE she is in love ewirth marit, the old dog. i understanr."

"Tell me more about what or how you understand her feelings."

"i k ow thge old dog is ikk i knowe whastg it feeos l9ike toi lose sokeone."

"Tell me whom you have lost."

"ellie"

"Think about the text structure. What important thing happened before the story even began?"

"the olod cog [old dog] diewd"

"Can we talk for a minute more about Ellie?" Emily asked. "You think about her a lot, don't you?"

"yes i lo ve heer," he said.

"You know she loves you, too. Do you think she thinks about and misses you often?"

"yes i di undedsabndr"

"Do you have any questions you want to ask me?"

"yes i waqbnt to iknosw why ii do jiot [not] lige [live] w" Before he'd even finished typing the crucial preposition "with," he'd signed "all done, all done." We'd already answered this question; the fact that he was asking it again indicated a desire to go beyond any of the easier, logical explanations.

Later that day, while taking a bath, he erupted—banging his head, screaming, sobbing, smacking his thigh. DJ loved taking baths; sometimes he took three a day. It was relaxing for him, and we were especially surprised by his eruption there. Once we'd gotten him out of the tub and dried off, we had a conversation on the computer. "DJ," I said, "you need to work harder to control yourself. If you want to go to school next year with your friends from Davis, you cannot scream like that. You need to go to your computer and tell people what's bothering you. Do you understand?" With the transition to middle school ahead of us, I was paranoid about DJ's behavioral issues, trying to work on them at every possible moment. I feared that the folks there would be much less forgiving than the folks at Davis had been. "Why did you scream in the bathtub?" I asked.

"treated to read tears," DJ replied. Again, the notion of reading and sadness and this time the strange use of the word "treat." I remember being stumped by his response, having a sense of what he meant, but needing confirmation.

"Why were you hitting your leg in the bathroom?" Emily asked.

"read tto dad," he said, mystifying us. Whenever he was totally distraught, his command of usage and grammar seemed to become unhinged. Was he talking about the book, which *I* had read to Emily? The concept of reading seemed especially unstable—what it was, who did it, and to whom.

"I don't understand. Can you say it another way? Why were you screaming in the bathtub?" Emily reiterated.

"to tear teazr,"

"I want you to answer my question," Emily said, with some annoyance. DJ was starting to become silly. He sometimes did this when discussing difficult matters. His emotions were a bit like an accordion, sliding easily from one to another.

"dad readt," he said. Now DJ was really laughing, but in a jittery sort of way.

"Do not be silly. I want you to answer my question: why did you get mad in the bathtub?"

"because tteared tears," DJ said.

"Are you saying you were sad?" Emily asked.

"yes"

"About what?"

"read rread read girl read."

"Who was the girl? What happened to her?" Emily knew the answer to this question, but she didn't want to assume anything.

"read girkl girl was wellie."

"What made you think of her?"

"the story in the book"

"What should you do when you get sad?" I interjected. "Should you scream or should you go to your computer to tell everyone you are sad?"

"go to computer"

"Yes. You need to work harder to control yourself. Next year, if you scream at school they will ask you to go home. Do you understand?" As excited as I was about the conversations we were having about DJ's life, I was a sober pragmatist when it came to inclusion's opponents.

"yes," DJ said.

"I want people to think you belong at school like all of the other kids. Do you have anything you want to say to Ellie?"

"you are my sister you love me," he replied. The stark declaration of siblinghood and the attribution of love to Ellie as a function of that relation were rejoinders to any adult reason for their estrangement.

The very next day, another outburst—this time at the kitchen table. "DJ, why did you scream and hit the table?" I asked, with the tone of someone taken entirely by surprise.

"because you were speaking about me," he replied.

"Why does speaking about you make you mad?"

"because you werwe making fun of me"

"DJ, how was I making fun of you? I love you. I have never made fun of you."

"near everyb thing has gone," he typed.

"What do you mean? Can you say it another way?" Emily asked.

"you you read go you be tears read dad's," DJ responded. Had he been trying to say before that he'd lost everyone—his father, his mother, his sister?

"You were thinking again of Dad's book?" I said.

"yesd"

"But why do you think I made fun of you?"

"because thne bhook is wbout me abnd i havenot6rread it." What to say? Having been introduced to the story of himself, DJ wanted more. Just how badly he wanted more would become apparent as he pestered me throughout the summer and fall, querying, "do you have ready the biook foer me?" It was as if the book might not only awaken him but also guide him into the future, as in a tale by Borges. His eagerness reminded me of the imperative to talk things through, confront the past directly, and thereby make "the book" less important, even less magical. I'd proposed the book as an act of sympathetic representation and political advocacy. I'd wanted poor kids and disabled kids and especially poor, disabled kids to get a fairer shake of the political dice. With DJ starting to represent himself, my conception of the book was beginning to change. I knew I wanted to incorporate his words into the story of his life.

"Do you understand that Daddy's book is not yet finished?" I asked. "I am still writing it—in fact most of it is still yet to be written. Though the book is sad in places, finally it is happy because it is all about the family that you, Mommy, and I have made. It is all about how smart you are. When the book is finished, I will show it to you. OK? But what should you do when you get mad or nervous or sad?"

"go tyo n tthe computer," DJ said.

No matter how many times I told DJ to express himself in words, he remained committed to self-injurious outbursts. The following morning, Emily led him down the cliff-laden trail of loss, his mule stubbornly intent on peering over the edge. "DJ, Daddy asked you not to scream. Why are you so mad?"

"because the girl read," DJ typed.

"Which girl?"

"elli"

"What were you thinking about her?"

"dread her not being here," he said.

"I'm sorry she is not here. Do you understand that Mommy and Daddy have tried to ask her parents if she can come for a visit?" In negotiating the tricky terrain of adoption, Emily didn't want to demonize Dan and Pat, but she needed to make clear our willingness to let DJ see his sister.

"yes," DJ replied.

"We have not heard back from them yet. Remember when Daddy and Mommy took you to _____ to visit Ellie?" Emily asked, providing proof of that willingness. "We want you to be able to see her. But we cannot make her parents agree to a visit."

"the girl is my sister," DJ declared—again, the assertion of relation and the rational expectation of contact.

"I know. Her parents fear that if you saw each other that you would want to live together. If you were able to see each other, would you be mad when you had to leave?"

"no," DJ answered, somewhat unbelievably.

"Do you understand that Mommy and Daddy cannot make Ellie's parents set up a visit? We keep trying to set one up, but so far they haven't gotten back to us."

"yees"

"Are you mad at Mommy and Daddy?"

"no"

"We are trying to make it possible for you to see your sister. But when you think of her, you need to try not to scream. OK? Do you have anything you would like to ask?"

"her parehtys are gone to her youth," he said, stumping us.

"I don't understand," Emily replied. "Can you say this another way?"

"thew girlo is fooli ng them her dad is my dad," he replied. Perhaps DJ was saying simply that Ellie had lived with him and Rhonda, not Dan and Pat. Her parents were thus gone to her youth—they weren't present. The notion of Ellie "fooling them" may have come from the chapter about the visit, in which I suggested that Pat's approach to the past was to pretend that it didn't exist. Sharing a dad made DJ and Ellie siblings, but that relationship was being denied. Though DJ's syntax was unreliable—he often attributed actions to incorrect subjects—he may also have been wondering about Ellie's part in this charade. Was she agreeably fooling them herself?

"The word I would use for him is 'birth dad,'" I said, entering into the conversation. "Do you understand?" Reading this remark in the notebooks, I cringe at my defensiveness.

"no"

"Who am I?"

"dad"

"Yes, I am your dad now."

"DJ, Ellie wants to see you, but her dad and his wife think it will make you two sad because you now live in different families," Emily explained.

"please tell them that i want to see heer," he replied. Such longing—his heart was an unfenced field, a plain the size of North Dakota.

"We *have* told them, and we will tell them again," I said.

"DJ, what did you mean when you typed that Ellie was fooling her parents?" Emily asked.

"she is my sister," he repeated.

"Yes, she is," Emily said. "Do you understand why you do not live with her?"

"becanuse they duid not want me," he answered. His response caught us off-guard. Emily had planned to present the most generous explanation possible for their separation so as to help him come to terms with it, but now she had to reckon with a deeper, more accurate understanding. If I'd had any doubts about what DJ had ascertained from the chapters he had heard, they were gone, and I felt terrible. I'd inadvertently delivered this crushing truth. Though I resented the hell out of Dan and Pat, I'd never have chosen to tell DJ such a thing, risking his fragile self-

164

esteem. I'd believed the auditory processing theory wholeheartedly, and I didn't know that by learning how to read a nonspeaking person with autism might then be able to decode what he heard, attaching graphic signs to previously unintelligible sounds.

"DJ, Ellie wanted you to live with her very much. But her parents felt that they didn't know enough about autism to be able to help you to learn to read and to write and to communicate," Emily said. She'd wisely adopted a middle-ground approach, insisting on Ellie's ardent desire to be with him and softening Dan and Pat's callousness. Even though the cat was out of the proverbial bag, there was no point in dwelling on their motivation. "Do you understand?"

"yes"

"So, Mommy and I will try again to call them to see if we can set up another visit," I said.

"gredat," DJ replied.

"We want you to be happy," I added.

Our heads were spinning after these conversations like tops on the floor banging into the legs of all sorts of emotional furniture. Enormous excitement mixed with enormous concern about DJ's well being. There comes a time when any adoptive family has to talk about adoption, but DJ's adoption was compounded by the issue of disability. Moreover, our discussion of it coincided with his emergence into language. Very few adopted children come to terms with the loss of their birth family as they learn to communicate, and if they do, it doesn't happen as quickly and in as compressed a fashion as it did with DJ. Adoption was the script of his emergence. His primer, as it were, had been my book—not some story of Dick and Jane. This coincidence (in the word's less common usage) caused tremendous upheaval in DJ: fits like we'd never seen before. "dread going to bed," he'd tell us at night, afraid of the nightmares that plagued him. By mid-summer he was a dynamic wreck: a car that kept crashing over and over into the same wall.

As DJ fixated on Ellie, he also explored the meaning of family in other ways. He seemed bent on deciphering the logic of human connection and what one might call, if one were a sociologist, the social organization of feeling. As somebody only recently and incompletely acculturated, he offered a unique perspective on the common preference for "natural" families. As Barbara Melosh puts it, "Adoption is Other in a culture and kinship system organized by biological reproduction." In such a culture you encounter, among other things, the "search" phenomenon, where adoptees look for their biological parents out of a "feeling of loss . . . some essential void in my connection with the natural order of origin—or birth," in the words of Elizabeth Cooper Allen. DJ's views on adoption and family allowed me to test the fundamental assumption of a genetic link that, in the absence of any contact or care, demanded obeisance. Of course, whatever my personal convictions on the matter, there was the simple fact of adoptees in pain. Feelings don't give a hoot about their ideological underpinnings. They're like marionettes that have quickly achieved a life of their own, dismissing the cultural puppeteer.

Shortly after the Fourth of July, our friends John and Leslie visited us in Hilton Head, and DJ told them, "i love you you ar one nice inlaw." He'd clearly picked up the concept of "in-law" as a type of family relation, perhaps at the wedding or reunion, and applied it to our friends. John had been a professor of mine, and over the years we'd remained very close—to the extent that I had become, in effect, a member of his family. DJ seemed to have detected this, and no doubt he remembered visiting John and Leslie at their home in Connecticut.

When Emily asked DJ, "Who are John and Leslie? How do we know them?" he replied, "they are dad brother."

"So, you think John and Dad are brothers?"

"yee b," DJ said.

"Why do you think that?"

"they look like eacgh other." The funny thing was that we didn't look like each other—John was twenty years older than I, had olive skin, and appeared very Italian. DJ had moved from the concept of "in-laws," which implied no physical resemblance, to brothers, which did.

"You are right that John and Leslie are like family to us," Emily said, "but actually John was Dad's teacher."

"i know thbery [they] are famippy [family]," he replied.

"How do you know that?"

"yoiu look like each othr i look likjee ellir." Truth be told, Ellie and DJ didn't look much like siblings either. So, what was DJ up to? Why the emphasis on physical resemblance? Clearly, he'd learned enough to know the cultural power of the biological argument, which is a fancy way of saying that DJ had apprehended the most basic definition of family, and that he had used that definition to insist on contact with Ellie. Indeed, his associative mind had extrapolated from my visit with John the right to a visit with his sibling. What we were witnessing as DJ rushed into language was a very different sort of "search" phenomenon: that of affect, as my friend Johanna put it, in search of a story. The words "sister," "brother," "father," "mother" were all compressed cultural narratives that offered their services in the way that, say, the Mafia offers protection: for a price. My analogy is inflammatory, but I'm not really attacking the institution of family. All language has its way with us—at least in part. Before acquiring language, DJ knew only the experience of care (or its lack). He didn't need to look like his sister, just as he didn't need to look like me.

But even as he paid his protection money, DJ retained a fluid sense of family, applying the term (or some variant of it) to a range of people technically unrelated to us. Three weeks after John and Leslie visited, their younger daughter, Sarah, flew down for the weekend. "DJ, who is Sarah?" I asked.

"she is youfriend," he said.

"Yes, she is. Do you remember John and Leslie?"

"yes"

"Sarah is their daughter. When Sarah was little I used to babysit her. What would you like to say or ask?"

"her father is nice he is her father." Once again, the assertion of relation. I thought about how much we identify people by means of their family.

"Yes, he is her father. What would you like to ask Sarah?"

"yopu are pretty," he said.

"What else?"

"you are splendid." I'd been teaching DJ new vocabulary words, and he chose this moment to practice using one of them.

"You remember the new word that Daddy taught you. Do you think it's funny to say that Sarah is splendid?"

"yues"

"I think it's funny, too. You have a splendid sense of humor. What else would you like to say?"

"you are her brother," he replied. There was certainly something stereotypically autistic about this perseverative declaration, but the repetition served another function. DJ had begun by saying that Sarah was my friend, and then, after calling her splendid, he said that I was her brother. The boy who had been without a family, the boy who pined for his sister, wasn't simply projecting his predicament onto everyone he encountered. He was a socialist of connection, albeit an unwitting one. He was like an armored vehicle with its back doors open and filial declarations falling all over the highway. "Brother" was his word for love, for relation. He used it both literally and figuratively, as in our colloquial usage: "He ain't heavy, he's my brother."

"I am like her brother, but she is not actually my sister," I said. "I treat her as if she were my sister. Do you understand? What else would you like to say?"

"you feel her like a sister"

"Yes, that's it. Anything else?"

"you are her brother," he repeated. The insistence on family—that figure—as if without it he couldn't convey the bond: the depth of feeling, the closeness. When DJ said you were like family, he meant it; it wasn't a trivial analogy. Here autistic perseveration reminded us of the way we might feel about those with whom we have no blood ties.

"you love her," DJ said.

"Yes, Mommy and Daddy love Sarah, her father John, and her mother Leslie. We also love her sister Becca. You haven't yet met Becca."

Sometimes Emily and I felt as if we were conducting a seminar in human feeling, but one that we hoped wouldn't entirely reproduce our culture's customary habits and attitudes. Part of what we were doing was compensating for the autism, but mostly for DJ's belated emergence. In fact, DJ would end up becoming a great professor of feeling, understanding it in its innumerable cultural inflections—all of this a rejoinder to the autism experts and their "devastating" theories. In the beginning, though, his knowledge evocatively faltered. Even his most literal understanding of family seemed a marvel of alternative thinking. "DJ, who is Nancy?" I asked, alluding to our dear friend who had driven up from South Florida to see us.

"nancy is mom's sister"

"Why do you think Nancy is Mom's sister?"

"she visits us in lots of places."

After DJ had explored the notion of siblinghood, he turned to that of fatherhood. It was one thing for him to say of Ellie, "she is my sister"; it was another for him to say of Dan Swanson, "he is my father." The latter set off alarms. Because there wasn't any competition in the sibling slot, our narrower dream of open adoption seemed both feasible and unthreatening (if, that is, we could get the two kids together). Anything more ambitious—shared parental love—we weren't ready to entertain. The circumstances of DJ's abandonment had saved us, we believed, from needing to worry about this on DJ's end, especially now that DJ was aware of those circumstances. But we were wrong.

One morning, out of the blue, DJ asked me, "how is your father?"

"Have you heard me speaking about my father?"

"yes." Again, the problem of being overheard.

"What have you heard?"

"that he is mean," DJ said.

"What do you think about that?"

"he is bad"

"Did you see my father at Uncle James's wedding?"

"yes"

"DJ, Sarah's father John is like a real father to me," I said, wanting him to know that I had someone who cared about me. "Would you like to ask me something about my father?"

169

"you love him," DJ said. His question took the form of a statement and seemed almost like a sophisticated interpretation of my behavior: the contortions of resentment and longing that often pass for love.

"Why do you ask this? Are you thinking of your birth father?"

"yes"

"How do you feel about him?"

"love," DJ replied.

"Do you remember him? He left you when you were only one year old."

"yes"

"Why do you love him?"

"because he is my father," DJ said. I was stunned. Had he simply applied the logic of loving his sister to his birth father, discerning some general cultural mandate to love one's relations? Ellie had cared for him, so I understood the ascription of love to her. But I found it hard to believe that DJ remembered Dan Swanson. How, then, could he love him?

Beyond the obvious way in which DJ was working out the problem of abandonment, psychoanalysis once again offered some instruction. DJ's emergence seemed to clarify the nature of desire: how the objects we want, whether present or not, are always just out of reach—the words we use to describe them at once instantiating their allure and rendering them strangely immaterial, even ghostlike. A notion of lack in a general psychological sense was moving in tandem with an adoptee claim of primal loss, creating a powerful mechanism of longing—what DJ termed love. Physical distance was the key element here. It allowed DJ to substitute one object (Ellie) for another (Dan), starkly dramatizing the ordinary operation of desire. But there was also in DJ's declaration of love for his birth father a need to know where he came from, to collect the missing pieces of himself: a task that seemed synonymous with language use in general. This need should neither be dismissed as exclusively cultural, as I'm sometimes tempted to do, nor held up as exclusively natural. The point would be to distinguish between the general concept of language use and the specific values of any given language at any given moment in history. (And the point would be to concede the interested nature of this adoptive father's rampant intellectualizing. Any argument coming from a member of the adoption triad ought to be viewed with some skepticism.)

"Who am I?" I asked, anxious to retain a place for myself in DJ's family tree.

"dad," he responded simply. So, DJ had already mapped out a crucial distinction: "father" for point of origin, "dad" for day-to-day sustenance.

"Yes, I am your dad. What would you like to say to your birth father?"

"that i miss yioun"

"You miss him or Ellie?"

"both," DJ said.

"Do you understand that you, me, and Mommy are a family?" I asked. I was trying as hard as I could to conduct the conversation in an impartial manner so that DJ might say what was on his mind, but I was obviously anything but impartial. Reviewing the notebook entries for this period, I cringe once more at my insecurity. I feared a request from DJ to visit his father—not only to visit his father but also to live with him. I feared the mechanism of longing. I couldn't compete with an unobtainable object of desire that our culture presented as superior to me, indeed as essential for happiness. I could critique adoption ideology until the cows came home and went back out into the Iowa fields again, but my insecurities remained—including those that lurked beneath the righteous contempt I had for my own father. And DJ had to have picked up on them.

I asked my question again. "Do you understand that you, me, and Mommy are a family?"

"yes," DJ said.

"Does that make you happy?"

"yes"—the answer I was looking for, but what else really could he have said? The question, while necessary for drawing out his thoughts, was unfair.

"Good—because we love you very much. Is there anything else that you would like to ask me about my father?" If DJ was using my relationship with my father to talk about his relationship with his father, then I thought I'd give him another chance to work through difficult material.

"yes," he responded.

"What is it?"

"he is mean." How to answer? After all, he'd already heard me express this sentiment in the book and in conversations with Emily. I decided to be honest.

"Yes, he has been mean to Grammy and to Mommy and me. He doesn't want to see us." As I typed these words, I didn't appreciate how loaded they were. DJ was clearly asking me if I thought his father was mean—something I'd also expressed, albeit in a more complicated way, in the book. I was reeling from DJ's declaration of love and, in general, from the fact that we were even talking about his life. The conversation wasn't a chess match, mind you, in which a player can take some ten minutes to plot his next move.

"it is sad," DJ said.

"Yes, it makes Daddy sad. That's how I understand what makes you sad sometimes." I figured that DJ and I might mourn the loss of our fathers together. I didn't realize, strange as it might seem, that in fully acceding to this parallel, I was instructing DJ in the very enterprise of desire that I feared.

"i sad about you."

"Thank you, DJ. It means a lot to me that you care about my feelings. Even though there is a lot of sadness in the world, there is also lots of happiness and lots of fun and good times," I said, trying to maneuver us through the rapids of reflection and out onto calmer waters.

The extent to which I had tutored DJ in the art of missing his birth father would reveal itself in late October—right in the midst of DJ's major bout of post-traumatic stress. Trauma was what we were experiencing and what, alas, we still had very much ahead of us: full-blown attacks whose violence would make a mockery of anything so far encountered. "What makes you suddenly think about sad things?" I'd ask him.

"you," he'd say.

"Why do I make you think about sad things?"

"because yuo are sad"

"Why do you think I am sad?"

"because you miss yourv dad"

"How do you know that?" I'd ask, astonished by DJ's simple wisdom.

"because you are angry"

"So, when a person is angry, he or she is missing someone?" I'd say.

"ytyes," he'd reply.

"You are very insightful. Do you know what that word means?"

"no"

"Someone who is insightful is very smart about people and the world," I'd explain.

"read the book," he'd say.

Missing people was the theme of that summer. If Emily and I were teaching a seminar in human feeling, then how to have a relationship at a distance was its central question. When DJ's college buddy Marie came down to Hilton Head for DJ's birthday, he got mad at us for talking to her. "she is *my* friend," DJ told us.

"If you have your own special times with Marie, is it OK for Mom and Dad to be friends with Marie, too?" Emily asked.

"nl [no]," DJ said.

"Why not?"

"becaudr she is here just to see me." I had told him this in order to make him feel better about not being able to see Ellie, thinking a friendship exclusive might serve a similar function.

A whole host of people traveled to South Carolina that summer, and we traveled to Florida, where DJ saw Jennifer and Evan and Kathy and Eric Studley, an old friend from school. Each of these visits prompted an expression of longing in the face of absence, and collectively they provoked anxiety about his placement with us. Leaving Florida seemed to have merged with all of DJ's other losses, and at times I think DJ imagined some sort of idyllic return. The night before their departure from Hilton Head, DJ had told John and Leslie, for example, "i weill miss ygtoy [you]." He also spoke of "ignoring theioe [their] housr" when we had visited them in Connecticut.

"Why?" I asked.

"i was fraic [afraid] because i thokught youj leavinj me there." After his visit with Jennifer in Florida, he announced, "i wanty to jhave grirlfriends one in one"

"Did saying Dad and I were going on a date make you think of girl-friends?" Emily inquired.

"yes"

"Do you realize that at eleven years old you are still very young to have a particular girlfriend to date?"

"oi know one girl i really like was jennifer and i miss her by nn"

"She loves you very much," Emily said.

"i love her took [too]. i fesrt have tresst ini hher [first have trust in her]."

He listened to Evan on the phone and in response to Emily's question "How did you feel about hearing his voice?" said, "i sas [was] vdery i interested to k noe hoiwe hne id [how he is]." Later, after playing with Evan, he remarked, "i want to live where he lives." When Emily said that we'd make an effort to see Evan more than once a year, DJ responded, "it is ok but i wiuld rather livenear him." That night at Skate Station with Eric Studley, he typed, "i like being in _____. i misd beinh here," following it up with "I have missed you" and "i want to go to linney."

The trip to Florida would have been unsettling enough, but about two days before we traveled there, a very good friend of ours died suddenly of an undetected heart problem. A woman in her mid-forties, Joyce had been a former professional tennis player, having played Martina Navratilova on center court at Wimbledon, and she was still in excellent shape. Emily and I juggled the funeral with seeing friends, all the while trying to remain as upbeat as possible. We didn't want DJ to become anxious, so we didn't tell him about the funeral, instead presenting our brief time away from him as an opportunity to hang out with Jennifer by himself. I'm certain, however, that he heard us on the phone, even as we whispered, and he must have sensed our shock and sadness. The day of the funeral we were supposed to have had lunch with Joyce and her husband, Mike. We hadn't seen them the summer before, and I was angry with myself for not having made the effort. At the funeral I wept openly, feeling Joyce's absence. Sitting there in a pew in the funeral

174

home chapel, I recalled DJ's phrase for Ellie the previous Christmas—the "dead girl"—and thought of how he understood long-distance relationships: one side pining for contact; the other, beyond all reply.

When we returned to Hilton Head, DJ's regular fits intensified. Kyle started popping up like a jack-in-the-box, surprising us long after it should have been possible. "i wsas think9ng abouit kyle k k k," DJ would tell us, once we'd gotten him calm enough to communicate on the computer. After a fit in which he'd try to scratch and hit us, he'd say something like, "i tried to be good i wilo [will] keep trying" and "i wajnt to bd with you foreverc i want you to be oproud of me." Once, he remarked, "i eant [want] ytou bto poriudf of me iu [I] dfeam offv [of] that becasuse in the fdtercare i had no one who ffed [?] ylou bare [are] the only ones who carwed [cared] agout me really." Such statements would slay us, and we'd feel him both pushing away from, and clinging to, his adopted life. He resented losing Ellie but feared losing his new family.

One afternoon, DJ let out a shriek in the TV room. "What are you upset about?" Emily yelled.

"i am worfdc wrd worriedwas that grandy was ready bdead," DJ said.

"You were worried that Grandy was ready to die?" Emily asked. "What made you think that?"

"i saw her lying in a coffin you were ready to kiss her"

"Do you know what brought that picture into your head?"

"i was thinking about the girl in tat movie."

"A movie that you were just watching a few minutes ago?"

"uyes tat girl was sad in that movie i dread that her death"

"Is Grandy alive and well and up at the Lake with Bop?" Emily asked, commencing her home therapy routine.

"yesa"

"Do you need to worry about her?"

"nko"

"Does she love you very much and want you to have lots of fun and laughter while you're here?"

"yeds i love her very much she is so nice to me and she thinks i am seciao speciap [special]"

"You are right. How does she let you know that?"

"she writes me cards and tells me that i am very smart ane important to her that she is glad i am her grandson that she wants me to be happy and feel great so ive grateful to hedrvfd grandy hds [has] realkly bg [big] heaert," DJ said.

"Do you know yesterday Dad was telling Grandy all of the terrific things you are sharing with us on the computer. She was so happy. She told Dad that dancing with you in Pennsylvania was one of the true high-lights of her life!" At Skytop, Rachel and DJ had danced to a couple of songs by a jazz band—they were the only two out on the dance floor.

"grear [great] tune ty dance ty i was resreally happy her dandfing [dancing] is greast."

These moments of intense bonding were inseparable from moments of resentment and panic. You couldn't have the former without the latter. At my mother's in Washington—we stopped there on our way back to Iowa—DJ pitched a fit, then told his Grammy that he liked her apartment.

"What do you like about Grammy's home?" I asked.

"becausr sxje [she] is hre [here]," he said sweetly. He reported that he loved her "vbderyt vsuft becds [very soft beds]." When we wondered, "Is your bed at home hard or soft," he replied, "jt bis hbard but i like it bgecause uigt ius my hgede [because it is my bed]." With our friends Caroline and Philippe, who came to dinner at my mother's apartment, he wanted to know, "how d idc ypou find us?" "mmyh hom isd long frfm hered [my home is long from here]." He'd used the word "find" before. About Ellie, he'd typed famously, "findhergoinggither," and of Evan he'd asked once, "has he trie4d to find me." Back home in Iowa, a few days before school, he'd use the word again. He'd wake up in the middle of the night and discover that Emily and I weren't in our bed. It would have been too hot upstairs, so we'd have decided to sleep on a mattress in the front room. He'd practically do a jig when, after searching for us, he'd see the mattress on the floor. "i found you," he'd type, breathing heavily. Life was like that. Everything seemed a loose working through of loss, a constant fantasy of reunion.

Long before DJ came to live with us, I used to tease Emily about Daniel Day Lewis, an actor she found irresistibly sexy, especially in the

176

movie *Last of the Mohicans.* Day Lewis plays Natty Bumppo, and there's a scene where Natty Bumppo's beloved has been captured by a warring tribe, and he shouts, "Stay alive. I will find you." I tried to imagine DJ in foster care—his own captivity narrative—waiting for someone to find him, but no one does. I tried to imagine him *with us*, waiting for someone to find him, but no one does. What must that have been like? How much worse, strangely, once the fog of limited communication had lifted?

A few days before we left Hilton Head, DJ saw a program on Antarctica on the Nature Channel. "What did you think?" I asked him.

"not fur livi [living]," he typed inventively. He could have been talking about foster care—the past in general. Like those ludicrously equipped, nineteenth-century Arctic explorers, DJ seemed poised to embark on an expedition, a dangerous one, and we were going with him. I'd feel a bit like the Englishman who brought all of that fancy silverware, full place settings, and sat freezing in his tent.

CHAPTER 7

Poking

We returned to Grinnell in time for DJ to begin a week of "Extended School Year." It was a chance for him to meet his new teachers and aide and for Emily to provide additional training to the staff. We were petrified about the transition to middle school. DJ was still talking about Kyle and foster care and, in general, acting very anxious. His tics had acquired a fierce concentration. "i bite my arm because i am nnervous about school," he told us. "i feel insecudre." We were grateful that DJ's resource room teacher from Davis, Tina Leathers, had followed him to GMC, upset that the school had failed to put the kids we requested (kids who knew sign language and had learned to overlook DJ's stereotypies) in his various classes, and apprehensive about the new schedule, which required a good deal of scrambling from one room to the next.

DJ faced the challenge, at least initially, with fortitude. After the first day of "Extended School Year," he reported, "i liked ity [school] i thought it took me a while to gget usedv to thr buildintg but then ih it waas grest [great] i tried real,y hsard." He told Ms. Leathers, "ithink that uyou are going tyo open new doorws for me." He said that he was "nervous abouy meeting mrs. pearlson," his new aide, but then he gave her a big smile and waited patiently for Emily to explain a host of things, including

178

the phenomenon of facilitated communication. He loved his locker—especially opening it with the key, which he decided to keep in his notebook. He had a good time working with the district's speech therapist, Judy Barber, whose husband was a colleague of mine at the college. He managed to remain relatively calm the entire day, and he didn't sign, "go, go": something we were certain he'd do within a minute of entering the building. All in all, a success.

The second day, however, he hit Ms. Leathers—just after she'd finished saying that everybody at the school knew he was smart. "Can you tell me why you just hit my face?" Ms. Leathers asked.

"i domnt want to fcome to school," DJ answered. Tina once again assured him that everybody knew he was smart, and DJ once again slapped her.

"It hurts my feelings when you hit my face," Tina said. "I care about you a lot and I know that you are smart and I know that every day you continue to amaze me by what you know."

"i am sorfry tha5t i hit yolur face ij m nervkous," DJ said. It was as if hearing the thing he most wanted to hear generated anxiety—perhaps because it meant having to prove himself all over again. But DJ's anxiety appeared to exceed any specific cause; in the jargon of psychology it was free floating. That night, he bit his arm ferociously, and when I asked him why, he said, "i don;rb know." As the sun went down, he announced, "dread going to bed." Did anxiety bring back foster care, or did thoughts of foster care bring back anxiety, or did the issue of intelligence (as the thing that had once left him parentless and now allowed for communicative self-discovery) bring back both in a never-ending circuit? If the latter, not wanting to go to school meant so much more than a general aversion to change or a particular aversion to the building, say, which he'd soon come to dislike.

The next morning, we found DJ in bed, having pooped in his pants. "Did that happen when you woke up in the morning or in the middle of the night?" Emily asked.

"in the middle of the night"

"I'm sorry you were uncomfortable from the poop. You are a tough, brave guy," Emily said.

"that's ok i forgive cyou but i dread going to bed," DJ replied. Forgiving us for not knowing about his toileting accident and for not coming to him sooner seemed significant, even symbolic.

"You do? Why?"

"i have justb nightmares," DJ said, inverting the verb and adverb. How many times with him did an error resemble a Freudian slip?

"About what?" Emily asked.

"i just huv nightmares in which i ed [end] up in fostercare"

"I am so sorry. Mom and Dad wish that those nightmares would go away. You have done such an incredible job of growing and learning and becoming confident and independent."

"i know but i still worry you tryn to put me back"

"You worry we would do that to you?"

"yes," he said.

"Honey, Mom and Dad would never ever do that to you."

"i knkiw [know] but i still worry," DJ explained, aware of the irrationality of his thoughts.

"What could we do to assure you so you will trust us one hundred percent?"

"i don't know"

"Have Mom and Dad ever sent you to foster care before?" Emily shouldn't have asked that question. I could tell where we were headed.

"yes"

"When?"

"asfter getting me atg the hosptal," DJ said.

"Are you talking about when you came to stay with us for four days?"

"yes"

"So, you're wondering why you left our house to go live with Gladys and Nate?"

"yes."

"DJ, when you went back to foster care, we were not yet your Mommy and Daddy. The law said that we had to take you back to foster care. But I promise you this: from the moment you were in the hospital, we vowed to ourselves to get you out. But it took a long time. Daddy and Mommy

180

worked every day for two years to make it possible for you to live with us. We took classes, met with judges, and did everything the law required until finally the court said, 'YES!! DJ can come live with you forever. You will be his Mom and Dad, and he will be your son.' On that day, your last name became our last name, which meant we were a family: Emily Savarese, Ralph Savarese, and DJ Savarese. Do you understand?" No response. "DJ, we wanted you to be able to stay with us. We didn't want you to have to go someplace else. But because we were not your mom and dad then, the law said we had no choice."

Over the next year, we'd return to this question again and again, constructing slightly different responses. Here, Emily didn't tell DJ about our evolving commitment to him or our initial loyalty to his birth mother, and I wondered how much he knew of these things. After all, in the first of the two chapters he'd heard me read aloud to Emily, I explicitly regretted sending him off to Gladys and Nate.

"Do you understand?" Emily repeated.

"yes"

"You are the best thing that ever happened to Mommy and Daddy," I declared. "I loved you the first time I saw you."

"Now that we all have the same name, no law or judge can ever put you in foster care again," Emily told him, the logic of name an obvious strategy of reassurance, but an ironic one in light of my aversion to regressive symbols. Was foster care, I wondered, intrinsically damaging or damaging to the degree that the care provided was insufficient and unstable (not to mention violent)? Had the word "family" come to mean something against which no alternative arrangement could compete? If so, was there any way to give children what they need without giving in to the practice of exclusive concern?

"i know," DJ said, "but trybv to underetand that i still worry i amn terrtfred terrified that i wreturn theref i dreadv itgv youj justg haveb to believe me." DJ was shaking as he typed this, and both Emily and I could feel palpably his terror. If it was becoming real to him in the telling, it was becoming real to us as well—not something described or alluded to but experienced.

"I do believe you, DJ," Emily responded, her eyes filling with tears.

"i knioe you returned yoiu greatv," he said, wanting, I think, to comfort her. We'd abandoned him like everyone else, but we'd come back.

"DJ, I am so sorry that the first five years of your life were often sad and scary."

"i know youn really lovwec me," he typed.

"Yes, we sure do love you!" I said. "And you deserve every ounce of our love."

"i know."

"Part of why Mom and Dad wanted you to learn how to read and communicate is so that you would feel empowered," Emily said. "Do you know what that means?"

"yes it means great"

"Sort of. Empowered means you feel like you have the power to stand up for yourself."

"ok"

"Why do you think Mommy and Daddy didn't have any other kids?"

"in yhe fvasmily there were lots ofr kidsv," DJ guessed, alluding to his many cousins. The boy was a budding population control advocate.

"yes, but not in our immediate family. Why do you think Mommy and Daddy didn't have any other kids?"

"because you wanted to bev my psarennnts," he typed tentatively.

"THAT'S RIGHT!!!! We wanted YOU. We thought you were so special."

"good i lo bve you"

"We love you with all of our hearts! Please talk to us about all of the things you think about and feel. It's so exciting to be able to communicate with you like this now!"

"ok you rfeaskly reallu makr mer feel greast."

Unfortunately, feeling great was not something that DJ did for any sustained period of time. Anxiety kept sticking out its frothy, white tongue. No matter how quickly we reinforced the sandcastle walls, the next wave was upon us, breaching the enclosure. The tide seemed to be coming in, though we didn't really have a sense of time or of the forces regulating the waves' movement—we were like fledgling physicists in an alien world.

DJ got through the week of "Extended School Year" and actually had a solid couple of days right at the beginning of the term, though the hitting resumed, as did the screaming and bouts of primal insecurity. He also started poking: reaching for people's faces and eyes with his finger. We didn't know what to make of this behavior; DJ had lots of behaviors, so we chalked it up to the odd partnership of autism and anxiety. Most disconcerting to us was the aide situation. Without a good aide, we were lost. Though the woman had previously worked with a non-speaking boy with autism, she'd done so in a self-contained classroom at the high school. She hadn't a clue about inclusion and seemed fearful of what it involved: a kind of dynamic yet largely invisible orchestration. She needed to know when to remain close and when to foster independence. She needed to be inventing ways for DJ to participate in classroom activities. All of this was unfamiliar to her. Moreover, she couldn't get the hang of facilitating DJ's communication—admittedly a tricky thing—but she didn't seem to want to get the hang of it either. She refused to step in and take charge, preferring to watch Emily.

DJ sensed her unwillingness and insecurity—a lethal scenario. With DJ you needed to appear supremely confident, whether you felt confident or not, or his nervousness would take over. Very quickly, he started closing the laptop whenever Mrs. Pearlson did try to work with him. He also began to fixate on her breath. "i fearv her . . . ," he told us, "her breath smells like rhonda's." The woman reeked of cigarettes, and DJ had connected her with his birth mother, who also smoked. It wasn't long before he was hitting Mrs. Pearlson and begging Emily to work with him. "dreadc beiung with her," he said. It was just our luck that one of the first assignments in language arts involved a personal history. The students had to write something for each year of their lives. "i dointf like gthkis bassignmdentg," DJ complained, "it b4ri9n gs bavbcjmk vbmedmlor ies [brings back memories]." The past had launched a full-scale invasion, and both his aide and his teacher had unwittingly abetted it, like sentries too accustomed to cards and banter to see the figures moving in the woods. Three weeks into fall, after being absent a good deal of the time, the aide quit, leaving us at square one.

The principal, Frank Shults, wanted to pay Emily to be the interim aide. I was adamantly against it. I feared that there would be little incentive to find a replacement with her on the payroll and, even more important, I believed that Emily needed to concentrate on being DJ's mother. She needed to get out of the school as quickly as possible, and she needed, if I may say so, to recommit herself to her own ambitions, professional and otherwise. She had to find a better balance—within reason, of course. She was still the one with inclusion expertise; she'd never be able to withdraw completely. Hence, while we waited for the principal to post the job and interview applicants, Emily served as DJ's unremunerated aide. This period would stretch into November, almost six weeks, and even then she'd have to stay at school to train the new hire. She'd end up surrendering her whole semester as DJ's outbursts worsened and the principal wanted someone on call to intervene when necessary. In retrospect, I'm not sure that anybody but Emily or I could have borne the brunt of these attacks, the most violent of which occurred during the period between aides.

At first, DJ seemed relieved to be working with Emily, telling her "i kneed yohu to bebnb strfrvbng great redx happyh." He was like a manager at McDonalds giving his employees a customer satisfaction pep talk.

"You need me to be strong, great, relaxed, and happy?" Emily asked.

"yed," he said. The pressure was tremendous. How to keep DJ in school when all of the previous strategies for managing his behavior no longer seemed to work? How to remain relaxed when at any moment DJ could erupt? Contributing to the pressure was my absence during the day, the feeling, Emily said, of being in this alone. My third-year review had commenced, and I was working harder than ever, preparing for a full round of class visitations by my senior colleagues. At Grinnell, passing the third-year review is in many ways more difficult than getting tenure because the college uses the third-year review to indicate the likelihood of that outcome. Since Emily and I had switched positions as primary and secondary breadwinners, I was indisputably doing less than she was with DJ, and we had vowed that after the third-year review was over and DJ had transitioned to middle school, we'd even things out. As it was, I'd rush home between classes to offer moral support, strategize, and talk with DJ when Emily had had to take him out of school. But no matter how many times I'd rush home, I'd feel like some sort of military advisor who drops into a combat zone by helicopter and then departs just as quickly, leaving the grunts on the ground to fend for themselves. At night and on the weekend, *I* was a grunt, but during the weekday I enjoyed conspicuous privilege. That I was working like a dog and in considerable pain did not lessen my guilt.

The third day with Emily at his side, DJ experienced a total loss of control; having lost control, he found it difficult to recompose himself. By the end of the week, he seemed to be aggressing, in one way or another, about every twenty minutes. "DJ, you are really struggling right now, aren't you?" Emily asked.

"yezs," he said.

"Whom have you hit in the last two days?"

"mom daaazxdxd miss leathers"

"When you look at us, what do you see?" Emily had noticed that DJ's eyes glazed over whenever he really lost it. She wondered if his memories were somehow more than memories. Together, we'd bandied about the idea of post-traumatic stress, and she wanted to pursue it with him.

"i see my mom," DJ answered.

"Whom do you mean?"

"rhonds," he clarified.

"So, when you hit at us, whom are you hitting?"

"atrhonda," he said.

"Do you know at the time that you're really hitting me or Dad or Ms. Leathers?"

"yed." So, it wasn't psychosis, but it was some sort of reenactment or reliving. In the throes of an episode, DJ appeared to be sufficiently gone that he couldn't know the difference between past and present, Rhonda and us, but he claimed that he did.

"Why do you want to hit Rhonda?" Emily asked.

"she gave me away," he replied.

"I can really appreciate your anger toward her. But if you are angry at Rhonda, how does hitting Mom and Dad and Ms. Leathers help you? What are you trying to accomplish by hitting us?" Emily understood full well the psychology of self-destructive acting out, but she wanted to see if DJ could articulate the logic of it for himself and, still more important, she wanted to lay the groundwork for rational self-correction. Besides, she wasn't entirely convinced that DJ did keep things as distinct as he claimed. At the Wall Street firm of Worry, Fret, & Stew, his highly associative mind specialized in corporeal mergers.

"i kind of hatr you," DJ said with astonishing self-awareness. Were we headed back to a discussion of our having initially failed him?

"What makes you think you kind of hate us?" Emily inquired.

"you hate me like she," he typed, stopping mid-sentence. If we were like Rhonda, then we must be planning to give him away as well. His insecurity moved through the streets of our lives like the Bad Humor Man.

"DJ, Mom, Dad, and Ms. Leathers are so very different from Rhonda. We want to have you in our lives. We feel so fortunate to know you and to be able to watch while you become everything you want to be. We think you are tremendous!"

"i kind of know tynbhatg [that]," DJ said, once again employing the newly learned colloquialism.

"I'm not sure you do know it," Emily countered. "If you truly felt the love and admiration and respect that we have in our hearts for you, you'd understand there couldn't be any hate at all. Do you want us to love you?" Emily asked, trying a different tack.

"yesx b"

"Is it possible that you wish we didn't love you?"

"yes"

"Why? What would be accomplished if we didn't love you?"

"you woulkd give me away," DJ said. We'd seen this sort of reversal before, where the thing worried about was also the thing desired.

"Are you saying that sometimes you wish we would do that?"

"yesx"

"Why? What would happen then?"

186

"i would go to live with elkie."

"Aha, so you are trying to do whatever you can to go see Ellie?"

"yes," DJ said.

"I can understand that you must desperately want to see her. We are very sorry that you don't get to live with her. I am sure you both miss each other tremendously. Do you ever just let yourself cry and get some of the sadness out?"

"no," DJ replied.

"DJ, what would you think if Ellie were to visit from time to time? Then, when you two were older, you could decide to live in the same town and see each other whenever you wanted. Remember how I said the same thing about Evan this summer?" Emily vowed at that moment to fly to the Northeast and knock on Dan Swanson's door, if she had to, to make this happen. "We simply can't continue to take no for an answer," she'd later tell me.

"yes," DJ said.

"Mom and Dad think it's very unfair that you and Ellie don't get to live together as children, but there is nothing that any of us can do to change that. What we can try to do is to convince Dan and Pat to let Ellie visit you regularly so that when you are adults you will know each other and can live near each other if that's what you want. OK?"

"good idea," DJ responded.

"If we called them and asked if Ellie could come visit, do you think you could settle down and enjoy being here with us?"

"i dont know," he said truthfully.

"So, there must be more reasons why you kind of wish we didn't love you so much. What are they?"

"i want to live with mym sister."

We'd end up having multiple versions of this conversation and others, too, in which DJ's complicated resentment expressed itself. In the same breath he'd ask to be abandoned and then state, "i was ready tl think you dresaded havinjg me as a son." We'd also discover additional evidence of his associative thinking—the way his mind could move effortlessly from one person or thing to another. "What are you trying to tell Mom when you poke her throat like that?" Emily asked one morning.

"i poke your throat to poke your throat," DJ replied.

"Do people ever poke your throat?"

"no"

"Why?"

"poking isn't nicer"

"So, what made you feel like being not nice to me?"

"you poked poked med in the throat," DJ typed, apparently contradicting himself.

"When?"

"poking iin the throat means you have badcv bfreath," he explained, like a translator at some International Congress of the Unconscious. Poking was now a metaphor that condensed a whole host of things: abandonment, Rhonda, Emily, bad breath of any kind. He literalized the offense of bad breath in an action (poking) that he knew his proclaimed antagonists had not committed, but he nonetheless insisted on an equivalence. The intensity of this equivalence, the way DJ gave in to its dictates, suggested something other than complete awareness. How to describe a state of mind that seemed semi-delusional?

Around this time, DJ composed his prairie dog acrostic (which appears in the introduction). This poem engaged in a similar process of analogical equivalence, using the details of animal trapping and maternal viciousness to evoke his life. You wouldn't know what the poem was really about unless you were familiar with DJ's past. Only when I pressed him did he concede that the poem was "about fostrcared." But DJ also confronted the past more directly. When asked to write a short personal narrative, he decided to tackle the visit to the Northeast to see Ellie.

> The day Ellie and I met on a busy street in _____
> I walked up to her and planted a kiss on her cheek. I was seriously plotting her return, plotting us living together again. Ellie told me, "I missed you so much." I felt as happy as I could be! I took her hand and walked toward the park. We went rollerblading together. Pleased, I looked everywhere.
> Ellie met my Mom and Dad. I think she liked them because she played with them, too. Possibly possibly I met

my Dad. He looked just like me with his hair red. I was trying to please people as much as possible. Ellie liked me. Ellie
played with me the whole time. I loved that I pleased people.
I felt delighted!

DJ was narrating his life! *We* felt delighted, delighted and, yes, scared.
How could the plot to live with his sister succeed, no matter how much
he "pleased" people? How could the "bond" of red hair ever live up to
expectations? Then again, how could that bond trump the bond of actual devotion?

The more DJ confronted the past, the more frantic he became, hitting and poking in a blitzkrieg of violence. We were starting to have to
hold him down and immobilize his head so that he wouldn't injure himself during his outbursts. It was like being on that plane all over again, except he was bigger now, much bigger. Conversations with DJ had usually
been able to bring him around to a sensible understanding of his actions.
"i was miudbeha vi9ng tofay at s chopolk [misbehaving today at school],"
he'd say. But his outbursts had become so common that retrospective acknowledgment of them no longer helped in the present. It just seemed
part of a cycle that had us spiraling downward. Bouts of panic would follow moments of striking clarity—bouts in which DJ's command of English faltered, became fragmentary and figurative. The relative equanimity
of, say, his reunion paragraph, itself achieved after much revision, was a
far cry from the strange shards of distress he also produced.

The problem felt larger than losing Ellie, even as Ellie functioned as
DJ's primary object of desire. What I knew of trauma suggested a failure of language in the face of devastating injury, but here language failed
as DJ acquired it. Language allowed him to organize experience but that
organization ("I lost my sister," "I was beaten") prompted a crisis. It
didn't, in other words, contain the trauma as Freud thought narrative
would. DJ's mind was like a *Mission Impossible* communiqué, combusting
immediately after it's been read. Perhaps the only way out was through,
as in a movie where the hero escapes amidst a hail of bullets. We'd have
to escape amidst a hail of words, and I had my doubts.

189

We were tired of talk, and yet talk we did, sitting on the couch in the den for hours, trying to get DJ to stop being violent. We had put off calling his psychiatrist, hoping to solve the problem without new medicines. The experience on Zoloft the year before had really spooked us. It didn't matter that DJ had reason to be angry. Ours was a practical predicament: he had to stop aggressing. We were already pushing the limits of teacherly patience. Only because Emily had been camping out at the school and ushering DJ from the classroom whenever he appeared on edge, and only because we'd exploited shamelessly his life story (the very thing we denied DJ as an excuse for his behavior) did the school, I think, cut us so much slack. The folks there were decent and caring; this, of course, helped enormously, but how much could we continue to demand of them?

Soon we'd have to do something. Time-outs, no matter how long, had ceased working, as had the suspension of privileges, such as taking an extra bath, going for a drive, or jumping on the trampoline. In fact, DJ had begun to laugh at us in time-out (when he wasn't banging his head or shrieking), and it seemed as if we were granting him the very thing his demons wanted: a rupture in our bond. At the same time, we couldn't just ignore his behavior, showering him with affection and fun the way we always did. The notebooks from this period indicate an obvious and escalating frustration.

"I am furious with you," Emily declared in one entry. "I am not hitting or banging my head or acting silly even though I am FURIOUS with you. That is because I know how to control myself and to act grown up. If you think it's funny to see Mom mad, go ahead and keep behaving the way you did today. You will have no drives, no baths, no choices about food. It's your decision. . . . Mom tries very hard to make life interesting, to help you learn to read and write so you can have fun, make choices, meet friends, and do with your life whatever you want. Today your behavior said, 'I don't care one bit about anything you do for me. I don't care about you. I just want to misbehave because that's just what I want to do.'"

The very next entry in the notebooks shows Emily responding to an explosion at school and then a gargantuan fit in a convenience store.

Emily had told DJ that we only needed one bottle of juice, not two. "You were repeatedly hitting me in a store. That disgusts me," Emily said. "I do not want to be with you when you choose to be mean. I am more serious about this than I have ever been. YOU MUST CHOOSE NEVER TO HIT. IT MUST STOP COMPLETELY. You must decide whether you want to be smart, grown up, nice, and friendly or if you want to be mean and aggressive. . . . If you choose to be MEAN and HIT AT ALL, life will be boring and empty and sad. . . . You know that we have three or four bottles at home already. You may not grab a ton of bottles off the shelf and just bully your way to what you want. You may NOT do that. It was stupid from my vantage point for you to decide to hit and scream over that or anything else. My feelings are VERY, VERY hurt. I am sad to think that you think it is more fun to hit people than to love them."

The tension in our household had become unbearable. Emily and I were bickering constantly. We didn't know what to do. One minute, DJ acted like a spoiled brat; the next, like a ghost-ravaged war veteran. I wanted to pursue a harder line with DJ, thinking we had no choice, but Emily worried about him detaching from us altogether. She'd been reading about attachment disorders and talking to people on the phone; they counseled against extended time-outs or anything too Draconian. I thought we should follow the approach that had gotten us where we were—only much more stringently. We should provide for his basic needs, I said, but withhold affection. The approach had worked before when DJ acted out, so long as good decision making was then greeted with exuberant praise, warmth, and fun. Of course, we'd never encountered anything as extreme as what DJ was presently doing.

One afternoon, he said that he hated Emily and wanted to live with me, and Emily for the first time intentionally scared him with the prospect of her absence. She was still the obvious target of DJ's maternal anxiety, but she also suffered from the plight of stay-at-home moms who spend long hours with their children: the children come to spurn their mothers and adore their absent fathers. This, as you can imagine, did not thrill Emily, and it aggravated the rift between us—to the extent that

DJ started thinking we were planning to divorce. He couldn't have been more adept at manufacturing a problem that he then cited as the cause of his anxiety. Emily was quietly angry with me for not being home enough; I was loudly angry with her for not appreciating how much I was in fact doing: the stress I was under at work, with DJ, with my body. The conversation in question went like this. "Why do you choose to poke and hit?"

"i hated you"

"Do you still hate me?"

"yesd"

"Do you want me to go away from you? I don't want to. I love you and believe in you, but if you hate me, maybe you wish I would go away. Who will take care of you?"

"dasds"

"So you want me to leave and you will live with Dad? Who will help you at school?"

"possibly mom," DJ said, recognizing a major problem with his wish.

"Not if you hate me," Emily replied. "Who else?"

"love you," he typed, quickly changing his mind.

"You hate or you love me?"

"i love." Upon saying this, he began to bang his head and signed, "all done, all done."

"Why are you so upset?" Emily asked.

"i love you," he explained, and it *was* an explanation, if an entirely condensed one.

"Why does that upset you?"

"i think you hate me," he said. His insecurity was masterful—like a wrestler who chooses to be on the bottom and then performs an escape. Whatever Emily's feelings, *he'd* elicited them.

"How can you think that? Do I hit and grab and poke you?"

"nbo9"

"What can I do to assure you that I love you?"

"just look happy," DJ said. He was back to testing his employees with the worst treatment conceivable. Could they remain imperturbably upbeat?

"I will look happy if you will stop poking me in the face."

"ok," he replied, but no sooner had DJ typed that word then he started poking again.

"You have NOT stopped. You cannot expect someone who is being poked and hit and grabbed to be happy," Emily said, reproving him.

"i hate you," he repeated.

"Why?"

"yoiu hate me." Again, the charge that Emily had started this. As I said, DJ's anxiety had no use for conventional causality. It was enough that she was now mad at him. Once his discomfort reached a certain level, he almost needed to engineer a disturbance. The problem, at least in part: he couldn't find a way of expressing his ambivalence that didn't incite panic. He both hated Emily and loved her.

"I do not," Emily said. "Why do you think I do?"

"i hear what you anfcd [and] dads say"

"What do you mean?"

"I hear you say that you might get diviorced." So, hating him meant threatening the family unit, and yet his behavior had—you guessed it— caused the tension that, from his perspective, signaled divorce. Emily and I *were* fighting, but we weren't planning to dissolve our marriage. Exhausted and frazzled, we simply didn't know how to help DJ, and we feared that we might be in over our heads. How to get someone to stop striving for the thing he dreaded? For so long, we had been the resourceful pair who had proven the experts wrong, but now we were floundering.

The very next day, DJ couldn't stop washing his hands; he was as obsessive as I had ever seen him. "Why do you keep wanting to wash your hands?" I asked.

"i feel like I can't stop," he said.

"That's what I was wondering. You feel compelled to keep doing it over and over again?"

"yes"

"So, you feel you have to rather than you want to?"

"yes." Not too long after this conversation, he started becoming agitated whenever a train moved through town—the tracks were probably less than two football fields away from our house. After some prodding from us, DJ said that the trains "remind me of kyle," adding, "i think seed libdedf nezsf trsin trazckxsv [we lived near train tracks]." DJ's first foster home in Florida had indeed been near train tracks, but we reminded him that this train was very different from the one there. This train carried corn syrup, and though it made a similar sound, it should cause him to think of happy things like candy. If I were to write DJ's emergence as a play, I'd borrow from Eugene O'Neill's *Long Day's Journey Into Night*, giving the train the role he gave that haunting Connecticut foghorn. Our days were punctuated by the train's whistle, and it did seem to evoke, once DJ had called my attention to it, the struggle we were engaged in. Could the sweetness of positive thinking win out over the sheer force of negative association? Still later, as if we needed any more proof of his anxiety problem, DJ saw a report about the insurgency in Iraq and immediately screamed and banged his head. "i really get scaded [scared] because i worry thsafg bwe might get killed by a bomb," he told us. Threats were now everywhere—ballooning and proliferating.

Smack dab in the middle of our crisis, Ellie's stepmom called to say that she would allow Ellie to visit DJ in December. There aren't words to describe the shock of this news, so long hoped for, so long denied. Emily had been calling and leaving messages on Pat and Dan's machine, and we think that Ellie might have intercepted one. Pat said nothing to Emily about the failure to respond to our previous efforts at communication, nor did she provide an explanation for why she had suddenly relented to the visit request. She did say, however, that she wasn't opposed to future visits, which gave Emily and me hope about tempering DJ's longing. If he could see his sister regularly, then maybe he might be able to relax—especially now that the offer wasn't simply hypothetical. We decided to wait until Pat had booked Ellie's flight to tell DJ the news; we didn't want to risk disappointing him. But the following morning, Pat called with the details of the reservation.

"Did you hear me say that Ellie's plans are made for her visit?" Emily asked after hanging up the phone.

"yevsd. when is she coming?"

"December 27th, two days after Christmas. She is staying for six days. Wow! That's a long time!"

"i possibnly possibly drdead her havinmg to leaver," DJ said soberly.

"Of course, it will be sad to have her go, but what fun you'll have for six whole days with no school and nothing to do but get to know each other and laugh and talk and jump and skate and sled and be happy together! And also, we'll have the next visit to set up before she goes home, so this time you'll know you can see her again before long. For sure you will get to see her in the summer and maybe you will get to see her for a long weekend sometime in the spring." When DJ did not reply, Emily started up again, eager to get out ahead of his negativity. "Pat says Ellie wants to see you many, many times and she and Dan are OK with that. That's a big change from the past three or four years. It's something to be very excited and happy about, isn't it?"

"yesd"

"Grandy and Bop will be here until December 29th, so they will get to meet Ellie, too. Will it be nice for you to introduce Ellie to Grandy and Bop, and them to her?"

"yes"

"What do you think Ellie will think of Grandy?"

"that she really," DJ typed, then stopped. He wanted to close the computer.

"Have I upset you by talking about Ellie and her visit? I hear you breathing heavily."

"yesx"

"I am so sorry. I thought it would make you happy and give you something exciting to look forward to."

"i possiblh saw kyul in e [Kyle]," DJ reported.

Had he "seen Kyle" because Emily raised the issue of family relations or because his sister was inexorably tied to the string of events that had left him alone and beaten in foster care? Was she now, like so many other things, a trigger for stress, despite his ardent desire to see her? The speed with which he moved from Ellie to Kyle scared me. I imagined Ellie arriving in Iowa with Kyle in her luggage. Whatever the case, the prospect of an actual visit didn't assuage DJ's anxiety; it made it worse.

Hand washing, train worries, war worries, Kyle fears—all of these things became more and more unmanageable. DJ continued to express his desire to live with his sister, but this desire couldn't go anywhere without the past. The past was like some government minder who made it impossible to speak freely. "i possibly play poker," DJ said one day, at first confusing us.

"What does that mean?" I asked.

"it means i might be being bad because i want to live with ellie." "Poking," DJ had already suggested, was what Rhonda had done to him, and the word had started to feel like a catchall metaphor. We knew that bad breath meant bad mothering, and the injury of each DJ called "poking." But perhaps "poking" also referred to the loss of his sister and the beating from Kyle. No matter how many times we told him that he could be our son *and* see his sister, that he didn't have to choose between us, he insisted on living with Ellie. Ellie's visit underscored the need for a visit and brought with it the whole mystifying mess of what had happened to him.

I knew we were in trouble. I remember telling Emily that we needed to call Dr. Babson and try some sort of medication. DJ was just too stressed out. Emily had been speaking to various professionals on the phone, but we weren't making any headway. After listening intently to our descriptions of DJ's behavior, Dr. Babson said that it sounded like post-traumatic stress disorder (what we had thought for some time). He laid out the medications that might help DJ's range of symptoms— nightmares, flashbacks, anxiety, rage, obsessive compulsion—and landed on two: Zoloft and Risperdal. Just hearing the word Zoloft made me flinch, but hearing the characterization of Risperdal as an "antipsychotic" had me doubting my desperate lunge toward pharmaceuticals altogether. The possible side effects of the latter drug were terrifying, and the fact that it was new and relatively understudied only scared me more. DJ was already on Topamax for his hemiplegic migraines, and we were worried about adding another powerful drug to the mix. Hence, we declined the Risperdal, even after Dr. Babson cited a study that showed very promising results in reducing aggression in children with autism. But if we weren't going to try the Risperdal, were we really going to give the Zoloft a second chance? Dr. Babson believed Zoloft to be fairly innocuous, and he didn't think it would result in disinhibition again. In fact, he wasn't entirely sure that the Zoloft had caused DJ's disinhibition previously. After agonizing for two days over this decision, we decided to put DJ back on the Zoloft. We felt as if we had to do something; the present situation was untenable. Unfortunately, it would take a good month to notice the drug's therapeutic benefits, so in the meantime we explored counseling options within an eighty-mile radius.

Finding someone to do therapy with DJ was no easy feat: we called and called and called. "PTSD in a nonspeaking eleven-year-old with autism, somebody who uses facilitated communication to communicate?" A vast majority of the people we spoke with might as well have said, "You're joking." We found no one even remotely helpful in psychiatry at the University of Iowa or Iowa State; a woman at the Autism Society listened to our problem but couldn't direct us to anyone. We contacted innumerable counseling centers—in Newton, Marshalltown, Des Moines, Pella—and each time the person on the other end of the line pleaded ignorance about one aspect of our problem or another. We ended up calling the crisis center in Grinnell and found a woman who had experience with adoption and abuse issues. She'd never worked with someone who didn't speak, but she was willing to give it a try. Later, we'd find a woman in Cedar Falls, some seventy miles from Grinnell, who'd also never worked with someone who didn't speak, let alone someone with autism. But she was quite familiar with PTSD and, detecting the desperation in our voices, agreed to help us.

With Ellie coming in December, Emily and I decided to finish the trampoline house. At the time we built it, we could only afford an uninsulated shell, which made heating the structure a challenge. On a really cold day, the woodstove could get the temperature to about fifty—just warm enough to jump on the trampoline. We wanted the kids to have a cozy place to play, so we looked around for someone to do the project. Emily and I joked that we needed to post an ad in the paper: "Looking for a builder and a therapist." That way, we whose nerves were shot might get some counseling as well. In truth, managing a minor construction project gave me something concrete to do, something whose progress I could chart. I also hoped that DJ might see how hard we were working for him and his sister.

The other thing I did during this period to reduce my own anxiety was to read up on trauma and autism. I knew a good deal about the latter (Emily was a specialist, after all) and a bit about the former, but I knew nothing about the relationship between the two. The fact that for a while autism had been thought to be a psychological disorder whose symptoms often resembled those of trauma significantly complicated the matter. I can't pretend here to map out in elaborate detail the distinctions between the two phenomena. What I'm interested in is the shift from psychology to biology in the study of each. I found this shift worrisome because it seemed to lose the person in the condition and, in a cold, clinical way, to render it hopeless.

Even in work on trauma that was dedicated to an interdisciplinary perspective—what's called psychobiology—I encountered a quasi-fatalism:

> The traumatic event, which started out as a social and interpersonal process, comes to have secondary biological consequences that are hard to reverse once they become entrenched.

> Roughly speaking, it seems that the chronic hyperarousal of PTSD depletes both the biological and psychological resources needed to experience a wide variety of emotions.

> Kolb (1987) was the first to propose that excessive stimulation of the central nervous system (CNS) at the time of the trauma may result in permanent neuronal changes that have a negative effect on learning, habituation, and stimulus discrimination.

In this view the human body changes, and these changes appear to be immune to treatment, particularly psychological treatment. The irony, of course, is that with trauma the initial injury is not physiological: something happens to the mind that initiates a series of physiological responses. This has been the fundamental conundrum of trauma ever since the mid-nineteenth century when John Eric Erichsen tried to figure out what was wrong with apparently uninjured railroad accident victims. Such a paradoxical fatalism manifests itself in a range of social practices and attitudes, including an aversion to adopting kids from foster care because the kids are thought to be hopelessly damaged. But might the physiological be vulnerable in turn to the psychological? It's hard not to read into the proclaimed triumph of the former, a kind of insecurity, one that reflects a larger repudiation of psychoanalysis and a consensus about what does and doesn't constitute "science." At least with the study of trauma, some form of psychology *has* to play a role in understanding the condition. As the above authors make clear in distinguishing between the traumatic event and its aftermath, the "intrusive reliving, rather than the traumatic event itself, is responsible for the complex biobehavioral change that we call PTSD."

Unfortunately, with the study of autism, there really isn't an analogous notion of "complex, biobehavioral change." For the last several decades, it's been all brain and no mind. Ever since Bernard Rimland's seminal 1964 work, *Infantile Autism: The Syndrome and Its Implication for a Neural Theory of Behavior*, rescued mothers from the accusation of responsibility by insisting on a biological etiology for autism, the field has largely eschewed psychological, and especially psychoanalytic, understandings. Yes, all sorts of cognitive and experimental psychologists have weighed in, but starting from a notion of biological/genetic causation they have attempted simply to delineate the fundamental pathology: that triad of deficits the *DSM-IV* lists (communication, social interaction, stereotyped behavior). The picture that emerged was of a devastating disorder that robbed a person of his or her humanity. The dominant "theory of mind" hypothesis and the more recent, updated "mindblindness" defined that humanity in terms of a crucial awareness of self and others.

I remember thinking back then how the denial of mindfulness to persons with autism oddly mirrored the field's preference for "science" over psychoanalysis in understanding the phenomenon. Repudiated once as cause, psychoanalysis couldn't help but be repudiated again as remedy. Temple Grandin, the most famous American with autism and someone from whom we've perhaps extrapolated too much, has said that she doesn't have an unconscious. Of course, the rest of us don't have one either, as "science" would insist, but *she* really doesn't have one. She's wired differently, she says, and that wiring makes social-emotional life an enormous mystery to her. I remember thinking as well about the rejection of facilitated communication and wondered if it couldn't be attributed to the impassioned restoration of the *person* with autism, on the one hand, and the failure to account adequately for why the technique works, on the other.

For all of the harm that Bruno Bettelheim did with his theory of the refrigerator mom, he still held out for the possibility of the child's improvement and, despite his admittedly perverse methods, honored the child's complex psychological makeup. Now, in order to avoid blaming the mother, we must in effect blame the child. The current thinking is excessively binarial—psychological *or* biological—and very fatalistic. A recent study of Romanian orphans by Michael Rutter and colleagues came to the shocking conclusion that trauma, in this case extreme deprivation, could produce the symptom set we call autism. So aware of the politics of resurrecting such a claim, Rutter couched his findings very carefully: "In terms of what is known about the organic basis of autism and the very strong genetic component that is involved . . . autism would not be expected to arise as a result of severe privation." He studied 111 children and found that one in sixteen exhibited significant autistic behaviors and a further one in sixteen exhibited mild autistic behaviors, as opposed to the overall figure of one in one hundred sixty-six in the population at large. That's twenty times the normal incidence rate. Significantly, many of the children improved after being adopted and living for some time with their new families.

Remembering that nowhere near a majority of the orphans became autistic, we must nevertheless acknowledge the impact of environment in generating the condition in some of these children. At the same time, we must be careful not to conclude that all of the cases had an environmental origin, and we certainly shouldn't map back on to ordinary families a theory of traumatic deprivation—at least not necessarily. That said, we should expand our sense of what autism is, why it occurs, and how it can be helped so that our account might accommodate the full range of factors in their dynamic interrelation. Rimland's advice to parents "to refuse psychotherapy" is not helpful, for such therapy could allow someone like DJ to reflect on the events of his life (whether or not those events were a precipitating influence in the development of autism) and to deal with the issue of being different in a stigmatizing world. It could also model for those befuddled by a complex social-emotional life a kind of feeling exchange. The point is to restore complexity to the debate and to the individuals under discussion.

In her book *A Positive Approach to Autism*, Stella Waterhouse does just that by refusing to naturalize apparent deficits as autism. Attending to pressing physiological issues, she nonetheless wonders if the prevailing view is wrong. Might the "very strong genetic component" about which Rutter and others speak express itself not as the familiar deficits themselves but as a perceptual problem whose primary byproduct is social withdrawal? Waterhouse focuses on the effect of anxiety as a function of "abnormal sensory perceptions," and she cites the work of Lauretta Bender who as early as 1959 was attempting to "bridge the gap" between psychological and biological understandings. Bender, Waterhouse writes, "felt that autism was not an inborn impairment of the central nervous system but rather a defensive reaction to such an impairment, suggesting that the child withdrew in order to protect himself from the disorganization and anxiety which arose from an impairment . . . 'in their genes, brains, perceptual organ or social relationships.'" In short, "It's the problems they have that drive [people with autism] toward isolation." Drawing on the writings of Donna Williams and on her own extensive experience providing therapy to children with autism, Karen Zelan says something very similar: "I believe the social withdrawal of autists—sometimes accompanied by an utter dismissal of social stimuli, sometimes by their single-minded absorption in nonhuman stimuli—leads them to act *as if* they have no sense of mind. In other words, their hypersensitivity to human and other stimuli invites them to withdraw and pressures them to ignore the mind's social workings."

Imagine the cumulative impact of such a withdrawal. Rather quickly, the apparent deficits would seem to be essential to autism: fixed, immutable. Indeed, they might even become actual deficits! We need to resist any theory that assigns a narrow biological or psychological cause, and we need to understand the role of culture in producing precisely those phenomena that purport to nullify cultural influences. By cultural influences I mean, among other things, both the interpretive lenses through which we see autism and our consequent responses to it, all of which can operate as reinforcers. People with autism don't like to be touched, we say—and, surprise, surprise—our failure to patiently familiarize them with touch creates an even more pronounced aversion to physical intimacy. As a result, they miss out on all of the benefits of such intimacy.

In his well-known profile of Temple Grandin, "An Anthropologist on Mars," Oliver Sacks alludes to Hans Asperger's idea of an "intelligence scarcely touched by tradition or culture . . . strangely 'pure'" as a way of explaining Grandin's sensibility. Isn't it time to eschew this idea in favor of Grandin's own discarded speculation that "impoverishment of experience [is] . . . a contributing factor in . . . autism"? In other words, what both Sacks and Grandin naturalize as a fundamental social and affective deficit is, at least in part, culturally fabricated. Why should we read Grandin's great affection for cattle *entirely* differently from any single, neurotypical person's preference for an uncomplicated relationship with her pets? Why shouldn't we suspect the climate of scientific rationality in which she dwells professionally of having an influence on her manner of being? In this way, our very theories of autism, along with our predilection for a certain kind of science, can themselves be formidable influences on a person's life.

Waterhouse's approach offers a dynamic account of a biopyschocultural condition and, for my purposes, a plausible explanation for DJ's emergence. This emergence by a boy with "classical" (or "low-functioning") autism, I should point out, was unthinkable according to the dominant theory-of-mind hypothesis. For Waterhouse, if you can tame the sensory barrage and attending anxiety, then you can reintroduce the person with autism to the social sphere. Indeed, I think this is what happened with DJ. Through a mixture of sensory integration, occupational therapy, jumping on the trampoline, mood-stabilizing drugs, and facilitated communication (touch-based talking), he was able to focus enough to participate. (To this day, DJ refers to neurotypicals as "easy breathers," an appellation that nicely underscores the fundamental problem of anxiety in autism. "You free great people breathe easily," he wrote recently in a letter to his classmates. "I'm hoping to do the same. Desiring to be relaxed and to start having friends.") Of course, DJ had problems in addition to his sensory processing; he couldn't—and still can't—speak. Only after he had learned how to read and then to decode spoken language (achievements that were perhaps a function of the earlier sensory adjustment) could he truly explode into sociality.

But DJ also had psychological problems stemming from his abandonment and beating. Before finding him therapists, we in a sense provided that service by cuddling with him, holding him, tickling him, wrestling with him—activities designed to facilitate emotional bonding but also aiding, I believe, the sensory processing adjustment I just spoke about. Could DJ's life events really have brought about his autism? I don't think so, but they might have worsened it. In any event, getting to the bottom of DJ's autism is impossible. On the one hand, he was diagnosed with autism at the age of one and a half—*before* the abandonment; on the other, life with his mother had been violent and unpredictable. Moreover, he'd lost his father. Bettelheim would have had a field day with these events, interpreting physiological symptoms in strictly psychological terms. But why do the opposite: interpret physiological symptoms in strictly biological terms?

Rather than despairing over the indeterminacy of exact causation, we should take a lesson from autism about the radical polygenic character of life itself: that ever-evolving, complex interrelation of nature and nurture that engenders every last one of us. We need approaches to, and treatments for, autism that emphasize this interrelation. If performed imaginatively, occupational therapy, for example, is never just occupational therapy. It's speech therapy; it's affect cultivation and motor coordination; it's—the list goes on and on. Again, the point is to restore complexity to our investigative proceedings. All forms of reductionism should be contested.

Although I worry about the easy war cry of complete social construction in academic circles, I worry more about the hegemony of scientific determinism in medicine and the culture at large. In their essay "Traumatic Stress in Childhood and Adolescence," Robert Pynoos, Alan Steinberg, and Armen Goenjian lament a "biological reductionism" in the study of trauma, arguing that it "under-represents the extraordinary activity of children's minds in the experiences and remembering of the moment to moment aspect of traumatic situations." Seeking to honor the richness of traumatic expression and the experience of injury, they cling to a concept more capacious than "brain," one greater than the sum of brain's mechanistic parts: namely, "mind." Judith Herman similarly worries about biological reductionism, especially as it neglects the politics of injury and healing. For her, the study of trauma requires the most extensive holism possible. I quote her in full because she offers a model for how we might think about autism:

> The next generation of researchers may lack the passionate intellectual and social commitment that inspired many of the most creative earlier investigations. In this new, more conventional phase of scientific inquiry, there is some cause for concern that integrative concepts and contextual understanding of psychological trauma may be lost, even as more precise and specific knowledge is gained. The very strength of the recent biological findings in PTSD may foster a narrowed, predominantly biological focus of research. As the field of traumatic stress studies matures, a new generation of researchers will need to rediscover the essential interconnection of biological, psychological, social, and political dimensions of trauma.

Finally, a few words about autism and trauma together—in the same person. Reading Waterhouse and others at the time of DJ's descent into post-traumatic stress allowed me to speculate about the relationship between two kinds of anxiety: the anxiety of abnormal sensory perception and that of trauma. Waterhouse usefully conceives of autism as existing on a continuum of other conditions such as obsessive compulsive disorder, Tourette's syndrome, attention deficit hyperactivity disorder, and schizophrenia, and she focuses on the role of anxiety in each. Determining whether trauma can cause autism quickly became less important than noticing the way different kinds of anxiety could overlap, aggravate, supplant, and even perversely complement one another. DJ would later write of our "losing [him] to [his] fort," but even before that I began to think about dissociation and its connection to what Donna Williams describes as "being swept away . . . in an all-consuming tide of total mental and sensory blankness where 'the world' stood irrelevant and uncountable leagues away." Whatever their differences, trauma and autism seemed to produce a similar state of withdrawal. Consider this description from Herman of the dangers of dissociation, and notice how reminiscent it is of Williams or of the quotation from Tito Mukhopadhyay that follows it:

> The extensive recourse to dissociative defenses may end up aggravating the abused child's dysphoric emotional state, for the dissociative process sometimes goes too far. Instead of producing a protective feeling of detachment, it may lead to a sense of complete disconnection from others and disintegration of the self. The psychoanalyst Gerald Adler names this intolerable feeling "annihilation panic." [Eleanore] Hill describes the state in these terms: "I am icy cold inside and my surfaces are without integument, as if I am flowing and spilling and not held together any more. Fear grips me and I lose the sensation of being present."

In *The Mind Tree*, Mukhopadhyay concludes the first long section of his autobiography by saying, "Today, the fragmented self of hand and body parts, which I once saw myself as, have unified to a living 'me,' striving for a complete 'me.'"

Understanding DJ's sensory adjustment as an uneven and discontinuous accomplishment, I came to believe that he had in part traded one form of anxiety and disorganization for another. Once a "living me" had appeared on the scene as a result of the various multidimensional interventions we performed, that "me" had to confront the full horror of what had happened to him. The acquisition of language allowed, paradoxically, for its complete failure in moments of extraordinary distress. If, "during flashbacks, specific areas of the brain involved with language and communication may . . . be inactivated," as trauma experts suggest, if "the central nervous system reverts to the sensory and iconic forms of memory that predominate in early life," then what we were witnessing with DJ was an emergence that frantically undermined itself. The story he had to tell perpetually undid the self he had made, had organized, in the telling. Again, think of the image of the camera hurled to the ground or of the *Mission Impossible* communiqué.

Perhaps I've deferred concluding these speculations because I can't bear, even now, to say what happened next. I can't bear to reveal the depth of Emily's and my despair as DJ grew ever more violent and agitated. We watched the oscillation between mental states and wondered if the pendulum of his mind could withstand the furious rocking motion. Might it tip over? Where were we headed? For all of my objections to the fatalism of a narrow physiological approach to trauma, I began to think—privately—that we might be stuck.

Almost immediately after going on the Zoloft, DJ started behaving oddly. We didn't have the hysterical laughter from before; we had a wild impulsiveness—like reaching into the oven and, with his bare hands, picking up hot food. He was telling us, "im nerbouh about evdrhgthjg [nervous about everything]," and he was having more dreams, dreams that prompted what soon would become a compulsive, catatonic-like response: "poking is bad." He'd clearly taken to heart our condemnation of poking, but he couldn't stop pointing in the direction of people's faces and, in slightly calmer moments, actually touching their eyes. Kyle continued to roam the house and began showing up at school. "i see kyle," DJ would say during our customary debriefings in the resource room or principal's office. When asked about his behavior, DJ reported, "the pill um takijng is making mew act stfranhge. i try to fiocuys [focus] but i get diustracted by my thoughts." Dr. Babson had asked us to be patient with the Zoloft, but we were becoming gravely concerned.

By the third week in October, after some two weeks on the medicine, we had a long conversation with Dr. Babson by phone. DJ wanted to stop taking the "green pill," and he had responded to the question "What should we tell Dr. Babson?" by typing, "i ca ntm pokder i cZAnt stop pokking just that." Dr. Babson suggested that we increase the dose. He knew that we were opposed to some of the more aggressive drugs for DJ's symptoms, and thus he believed that we really had to give the Zoloft a try. Bailing now would tell us nothing and send us in the direction we most feared. DJ was saying things like "im really ttyi ng rto beehavfe," but he couldn't do it. In addition to the kicking and screaming and scratching and poking, he began to bite. The glazed look in his eyes terrified us. It was as if he were in another world entirely, fighting invisible antagonists. During these states you couldn't talk to DJ, and he couldn't talk to you. Sometimes for hours we'd have to sit on top of him so that he wouldn't hurt himself or us. Other times, he'd just lie on the beanbag in his room, a lifeless lump, withdrawn into some equally unreachable space.

The day after Halloween, he made a loud noise in the grocery store—half-scream, half-growl—and later in the car explained, "il fefgt [feel] really weifrd."

"Can you say more about the weird feeling?" Emily asked.

"ik felt like everyoner was watching me and lpokinmh." It turned out this was a common occurrence for DJ. I hadn't ever used the word "paranoid" to describe his demeanor, but that's what I'd been thinking.

Three days later, on November 5th, DJ experienced the meltdown of all meltdowns. I'd come home from work to grab a book, and when I went to return, I saw Emily pull into the driveway with DJ in the back seat. Emily was crying. There was a trickle of blood on her hand. DJ had bitten her wrist, actually puncturing the skin; she had scratches everywhere. DJ, in contrast, was calm, too calm, though he seemed to know he was in trouble. If he didn't know it when they pulled up, he knew it when I opened the passenger door. I immediately started screaming at him, yanking him by the arm. "What the fuck are you doing?" I yelled. "How dare you hurt your mother?" I pulled him into the house and up to the beanbag in his room. "Sit the fuck down!" I said. "You're going to sit here for the next three months!"

Could anger solve a problem that patient caring had not? It didn't matter. First of all, I was spent, literally at my wit's end. Second, his aggression had to cease. Whether volitional or not, it was terribly destructive.

How much more insanity could the school take? How much more could we? Though it occurred to me at the time that my own helplessness, which engendered rage, mirrored DJ's, understanding this was hardly balm for my frustration. As I just demonstrated, I could spout trauma theory all day: "Helplessness constitutes the essential insult of trauma." That insult requires "the restoration of a sense of efficacy and power." "Trauma impels people both to withdraw from close relationships and to seek them desperately. The profound disruption in basic trust, the common feelings of shame, guilt, and inferiority, and the need to avoid reminders of the trauma that might be found in social life, all foster withdrawal from close relationships" (the measured tone a testament to empathetic understanding of the plight of the traumatized but not, alas, of the plight of their forlorn caregivers). If it didn't make life any more manageable for us, what good was such knowledge?

After planting DJ on the beanbag, I went downstairs to speak with Emily, who seemed in shock. The drive to school, she reported, had been fine. They were standing in the front hall at DJ's locker when suddenly he screamed, hurling his lock at the big, glass trophy cabinets a few feet away. Somehow he missed hitting them, but having missed them he commenced attacking Emily. Emily did all she could to get DJ out of the building and into the car where she could restrain him privately, or at least semiprivately.

In the light of the living room, I took in her full injuries. She looked as if she'd hit her head then crawled through a jagged window. Her face was scratched and bruised; her arms were a railway yard of intersecting tracks. I knew what DJ's fury was like; I'd wrestled him to the ground when he was having a flashback. I hugged Emily and told her that we would get through this. To which she replied, sobbing, "I don't know. I really don't know." I didn't know either, but we'd agreed that we'd try never to collapse at the same time. Hence, I adopted the tone of the confident tough guy. By reassuring her, I might reassure myself. Emily knew I was faking, of course, but faking was preferable to a common acknowledgment of complete despair.

Later, she did what she always did: talk DJ through the day's calamity. She was like a therapist who'd just been traumatized herself, eerily capable of going through the proper therapeutic motions. She'd emerged from her shattered train compartment window and commenced counseling her fellow passenger. "Tell Mom what happened this morning."

"i saw ,kyklr"

"When?"

"sew him whdn k looked im the glazss [when I looked in the glass]."

"Tell me what he looked like and what he was saying or doing."

"i saw him poking me in thre frace"

"Was he saying anything to you?"

"yes pokibngh iol I kill you"

"Tell Mom what you did after you saw Kyle's face in the glass."

"i threw my lock at him"

"Then what did you do next?"

"ik staryed screaminbg and hittimng you"

"Why did you start hitting me?"

"he tole me to"

"Why do you listen to what he says?"

"i am safraid of him"

"What exactly do you hear him say to you?"

"i hear him dasy poke poke poke"

"But did you poke me?"

"yes"

"I don't remember you doing that. I remember you hitting me and banging your head on me."

"i was afraid."

"What else did you do to Mom?"

"i bkt her [bit her]"

"Why did you do that?"

"im trying to br good"

"Why did you bite me?"

"im wrong to do that"

"Yes, you are, but I'm asking you why you hit and bit me and tried to do whatever you possibly could to really, really, really hurt me."

"dreeazd pokingh [dread poking]," DJ said.

"You dread poking someone or you dread being poked?" Once again, DJ's abbreviated response encouraged us to think that he didn't understand the difference between subjects and objects, between Kyle and him. The very idea of a flashback seemed already to confuse distinct entities (past and present). Was DJ reenacting the original assault and belatedly fighting back or was he trying, in a sense, to be Kyle?

"drtesd being po,merfd [dread being poked]"

"How will attacking Mom and really, really trying to hurt me help?"

"pokking is bad"

"Tell me more about this poking you dread. What exactly happens and what does it feel like?"

"poking is s cstry [scary?]"

"What exactly is done?"

"poking is when he takerd hisd fi nger zand puts it in my ests eye"

"Why does poking scare you so much?"

"it hujjrts"

"Does he actually touch you?"

"yes"

"Where?"

"etecc eyes"

"DJ, when you were poking at me a lot the last few weeks, it annoyed me BUT it never hurt physically. What you did to me today was much, much worse. I do not understand why you would act SO dangerously and hurtfully just because you thought someone might poke you. Can you explain why you got SO violent and aggressive and out of control?"

"ijuxst lost control"

"Why?"

"Was breally mad at you because you looked really mad"

"DJ, we were in the front hall at school after a nice morning at home. I was looking forward to your having another good morning like you did yesterday. I was NOT DOING ANYTHING to provoke you."

"yes"

"WHY?"

"you lookd like ktle3 [Kyle]," DJ said.

"What do you mean by that?"

210

"i saw kyle when i lolkd at hou [looked at you]"

"But earlier, when I asked you what happened and what you did, you said that you poked Mom. That makes it seem like you knew as you were hitting me that you were actually hitting me and not Kyle. Did you?" Emily was trying to get to the bottom of DJ's flashbacks. How could DJ know that he was hitting Emily and act as if he were hitting Kyle? What was this state of mind?

"yexsd," DJ replied.

"First, you looked and thought Mom was Kyle but before you started hitting and biting me, you knew I was Mom and not Kyle. Is that right?"

"yres"

"So, were you able to erase Kyle before you started hitting and biting me?"

"poking poking," DJ typed, clearly upset.

"What does 'poking poking' mean?"

"it measns he was threragening"

"Threatening?"

"yes"

"What was he saying or threatening?"

"he really was sc ary because poking is hiikkimj hikkimg just trhying to kill ngvb sdomeoned"

"There is usually a big difference between poking and killing. Explain to me how they are similar and what it has to do with Kyle."

"pokkinbg hurts"

"What is poking exactly?" We'd already seen DJ use the word "poking" as a metaphor for bad breath, metonymically moving from breath to Rhonda to his former aide to Emily. It seemed a metaphor for the past generally, but here it had specific, literal content, or at least that's what Emily thought. She was trying to discover the precise nature of the violence to which he'd been subjected.

"putting yer fingrr ijnn someonede rexctv rrrrrrreeyec," DJ answered. "rexctv." Had we paid even more attention to the keyboard—which letters are next to which and might have been struck accidentally—we'd have had evidence of the thing we half-suspected but didn't want to presume.

211

"That can hurt but it is not able to kill you. Why when he threatens poking do you think you are in danger of being killed?"

"pool,iknmg is very scsary"

"Does poking always stop at poking or does it become something else?" Emily asked, gingerly inviting him to say more about what Kyle had done to him.

"it ju7ust is ijjn ookim poking," DJ replied. He seemed to be fending off Emily's inquiry, or had he simply misunderstood it?

"Has Kyle ever actually poked you?"

"yes"

"When?"

"ikn fodtercare"

"What else did he do in foster care?"

"it is tg trying to kjill me," DJ said.

"Do you mean 'it' or 'he'?"

"it"

"What is 'it'?"

"pokiiknh"

"What do you mean 'poking is trying to kill me'?"

"opoki npppppp=p[" DJ was now typing nonsense. Why had he moved from Kyle to "it"?

"Can you answer the question? What else did Kyle do to you in foster care?" When DJ didn't respond, Emily typed out one of those sentences designed to get him started: "So, when you were in fostercare, Kyle poked at your eyes and. . . ."

"thrfdrs [threw?] three bv balls at me"

"And. . . ."

"and hhhhhhit med in the poking b"

"Try to tell me more about this poking. He poked you in the eye and. . . ."

"pokking in the pokinmg," DJ said then signed, "all done, all done."

"You are scared to talk about the poking?" Emily asked.

"yesd," DJ said.

"OK, we can stop for now if you want. I just need to explain to you that you REALLY LOST CONTROL this morning at school. You

MUST NOT ATTACK ANYONE like that EVER. It is very, very dangerous. Not even Kyle deserves to be attacked like that. Even when he did terrible things to you and frightened and hurt you very much. If Kyle appears in your thoughts and pokes or threatens to poke, you need to tell him to go. If you need help, you should sign 'help' to an adult you know. If looking at their faces means you might see Kyle, then look away or down at the floor. That will help you remember that Mom is Mom, or Dad is Dad, or Molly is Molly. [Molly was one of DJ's college buddies.] That will help you remember that no one here is Kyle."

I marveled at Emily's ability to talk DJ through his behavior—patiently, calmly, lovingly. That night, we consulted with Dr. Babson and decided to discontinue the Zoloft. We went back and forth about the Risperdal, but agreed to give it a try. We really had no choice. While going off the Zoloft and on the Risperdal, DJ stayed home from school. We couldn't risk another assault. During this ten-day period, he wrote two letters—one to his classmates, the other to his Positive Behavioral Support Team—that underscored the sad intractability of the situation: DJ wanting to behave but his demons refusing to let him.

> Dear Class,
> We are trying to help me. lYou possibly look at me as crazy. I am not crazy. I am scared to be at school because mt t [my] temper is like a raging an. Im really glad im in your class. Pretty soon I will be back.
> Love,
> DJ

> What I Want My PBS Team To Know
> Before you write me bad, please give me chance to show my true self. I need an assistqance with my never being bad. I feel scared because pople be bigv.

DJ's classmates wrote incredibly touching replies to his letter, replies that reduced me to tears when Emily showed them to me. One began this way: "Everybody misses you. We are having fun at school, but not as much fun as when you were here." Another began, "we all really miss you and we all want you to come back to school." A third was covered with smiley faces and DJ's initials in brightly colored magic marker. It opened with the line: "I miss walking down to Gym with you. Come back soon." A fourth presented a series of math problems to solve. This student knew that DJ excelled in math and sweetly offered him a chance to show his skill. A fifth letter referred to DJ as the student's "best friend." A sixth complained that things had been "kinda quiet" without him, a remark that made me laugh out loud because DJ was often quite noisy, even when calm, clapping his hands and making his signature vocalizations. Each of these replies demonstrated just how well inclusion can work, how generously accommodating kids can be, and together they made it all the harder to entertain the possibility of DJ not being able to return.

When he did return in mid-to-late-November, we saw signs of improvement. The disinhibition had decreased significantly, but DJ was still anxious and hitting people, though not with the same ferocity as before. He seemed committed to changing his behavior, saying such things as "i want to gettg betgtdd agt not hitgtimg [better at not hitting]" and "i feefl terroible" when he did hit someone. Once after slapping Emily, he typed, "is yourf pretty face ok?" I can't thank those who worked with DJ enough—his teachers, aides, speech instructor, college buddies— for sticking with him during this period. The principal, Frank Shults, was beyond generous and flexible. Almost everyone got hit at one point or another. Each time, DJ claimed that he "saw kyle," and each time we reminded him that Kyle was in the past.

If I make it seem as if all DJ was doing was hitting people, it's because that's what I was focusing on. In truth, he was doing very well academically and could go long stretches—three quarters of a day, sometimes a whole day—without aggressing against anyone. We had debated keeping him out of school longer but feared losing too much ground. DJ also started saying that he didn't want to go to school. "I am nervous because im hurtinbg people," he'd say, and we knew that we couldn't let him think the answer to his problems lay in hiding at home. We were trying to make it to Christmas break, hoping that the Risperdal would kick in even more and that Ellie's visit might somehow calm him. In the midst of this turmoil, the school hired a new aide, whom Emily trained. I give this woman credit as well because she moved bravely forward in spite of DJ's sometimes wild fluctuations.

Ten days before Christmas, he asked one of his therapists, "when do the mytrying to forget what really ha [happened]?" The following morning, after a very restless night, he typed, "three ,liyttle ..kids.. th, mhurt .fee my f. [they hurt my feelings?]" He was very agitated. When Emily asked him, "What woke you up last night?" he replied, "the. treewas the tree was hote. really. i. tried to.forge. fok." We couldn't understand what he was saying, and when we pushed for clarification he signed, "all done, all done." That afternoon, he let out a shriek while staring at our Christmas tree. "tree really might cause rememberub..," he said. "we got a tree that day. when we got home kyle was mak. topay cfir [for] the dread . really. i saw reallyscar y things. really really scary that tree seemit fired . . . . was a. long drivehome wein really close . . . . . . we really pretty scare. . arevery plwtploik."

So, DJ was trying to tell us that our Christmas tree reminded him of getting a tree when he lived with Edna Austin, but why was the tree "hot"? Was DJ speaking metaphorically of the lights, which generated heat? Over the next couple of days, more came out. "i.ve seen scary. 1they. tease really really scary etrtz he saifd i was really fucking freaky.c." Eventually, DJ explained that the older foster kids had made a bonfire after they returned from getting the tree and that Kyle had tried to burn him. In his mind, he probably conflated the Christmas tree and the wood on the bonfire. "i am nervous because i .saw .what happened . . . we were playing .out in the yard. three little kids.daw.daw. me kylertn. [DJ was speaking of another foster child Dawn, who was a year younger than he.] thewind was really firey.. thefire was hotfires. he was really mad reallytrying to bring my handveryclose to the fired . . . trying to make me touch the fire." By the time he finished typing this last sentence, DJ was clapping his hands and clenching his jaw. His face was beet red. "you read this because the true version bf," he continued, alluding to my book, wanting, I think, to set the record straight. "poked me repeatedly with acaneveryhard reallyreally hard never stoppiefer [stopped]."

215

CHAPTER 8

Have You Missed Living with Me?

Christmas was nearly upon us and with it Ellie's visit. We were all anxious and exhausted. I was trying to give exams and grade my seminar papers while pressing to finish the inside of the trampoline house. Though we were only insulating the structure and putting up wood paneling, the building was large—21 feet by 34 feet, with eleven-foot walls and a cathedral ceiling—and it was taking forever. The fellow I'd hired to help me with the project could only work at night, after he'd finished his day job as a carpenter. The building, I kept telling him, had to be ready for the kids' reunion, and Jack assured me it would. The stepfather of a young man with autism, he'd been so moved by the story of these two siblings separated by disability that he'd been willing to work weekends as well.

And thank God, because if he hadn't, we'd never have finished it in time. As it was, the final week was total madness. In order to stain the ceiling, Emily and I needed to take advantage of Jack's scaffolding while it was in the trampoline pit. This meant staying up all night, for several nights, breathing in horrendous fumes. Once Jack removed the scaffolding and we reassembled the trampoline, we'd never be able to get at the ceiling. Perfectionist that I am, I wanted the building to be *the* fantasy play space, complete with brightly colored walls, decorative mobiles, and a stereo system to drive the neighbors crazy! Nothing less would do. I wanted it to be a space where Ellie and DJ might literally stun the past with joy or, in one of DJ's obsessive idioms, "be free," bouncing beyond or over grief—the music from *Shrek I*, say, in the background. Hadn't I learned my lesson about lost time? Didn't I understand that compensation was impossible? No lump sum settlement of fun could ever make up for the previous five years. And yet, there I was acting as if it might.

Finishing the trampoline house was bittersweet. By that point my arthritis had gotten so bad that I didn't know how much longer I could put off a hip replacement. My left hip throbbed all the time, so much so that my doctor had prescribed the painkiller OxyContin. I had, of course, dramatically cut down on my jumping: the activity, perhaps more than any other, that had enabled DJ and me to bond so deeply, what with us moving and shrieking in tandem so many wordless hours a day. DJ had experienced this change as yet another crushing blow, telling me on the computer that I "find great reasons not to play with him." Occasionally, I'd jump when we had a party, but whenever I did I paid for it afterward, sometimes unable to walk or to sit for days. From his perspective, I'm sure he couldn't believe he was being asked to accommodate this particular disappointment. "Let's jump," he'd sign, over and over again, until we'd both become exasperated.

DJ was especially mad at me during that period in December when we were rushing to finish the trampoline house. No matter how many times I explained that I was trying to make the trampoline house nice for him and Ellie, he accused me of ignoring him. Maybe he thought the building was pointless once we could no longer jump together; he wouldn't say. I kept thinking that he and his sister needed a place to hang out; winter in Iowa—winter in the middle of nowhere in Iowa—can be a real drag. I also hoped to use the room as a way for DJ to work on his social skills, to make the friends he so wanted to have. Only later would we learn he'd once again convinced himself that we were getting "diborced." "Why did you think that?" we'd ask. "You were trying to gdt lots of furniture," he'd reply. Emily's folks, who'd flown in from South Carolina for the holidays, generously purchased couches

for the new space. Her Dad rented a U-haul and, even more generously, drove to Des Moines to pick them up. When DJ saw the couches,
he thought that I was moving out—moving out to the trampoline house!
Apparently, he'd witnessed his birth parents divorce when he was not
yet two and remembered his birth father leaving with furniture. If DJ
was nervous, you simply couldn't keep pace with his associative proclivities, his mind a search engine frantically tying the world together
in a vast network of dread.

By the evening of the 24th, two days before Ellie's visit, we'd finished putting the final touches on the trampoline house. We'd moved in
an old rug, rearranged the couches, purchased a small refrigerator, and
set up the stereo. By all accounts but the one that mattered most, the
room was spectacular—a kid's paradise. DJ, however, didn't want to be
in it. In fact, we could hardly get him to jump. He did so perfunctorily,
for a few minutes, once he'd noticed our very long faces. But he was
distracted, agitated. In the middle of Christmas Eve dinner, he heard the
train that rumbles regularly through town and told Emily, for the umpteenth time, "train makes me poke." Emily, as she always does, reminded
him of the train's very pleasant mission: to move corn syrup from one
end of the state to the other. "Yes," DJ typed, "train for candy."

Later, discussing Ellie's visit in his bedroom, he confessed, "I worry
that I will poke. i think Christmas is scary and sad i hate christmas becaye
it is when i injured by Kyle."

"You are right," Emily typed, all too aware of the memories that even
a happy event could bring back. "Those scary things did happen near
Christmas a long time ago. But this Christmas promises to be so very
different from that one," she said. "You are big and strong and smart
and safe. Your sister is coming to stay with you for six days and six nights!
You will have a chance to skate and sled and jump and smile and laugh
together. You will plan your next visit for the spring or summer. This
Christmas is a time of joy and family and fun and love and moving into
the future!"

Unmoved, DJ responded sullenly, "i know but nothing wreally
changese what22happenefd." He had a point, this eleven-year-old with

the insight of a depressed historian. He couldn't disentangle the bad from the good: losing Ellie initially from seeing her once again, being beaten in foster care from having a safe home now with a fourteen-foot trampoline, the only indoor residential one in all of Iowa! Being abandoned was the big bang that had authored his universe, everything rotten and redemptive issuing forth from that explosion.

We tried to keep the conversation going. DJ had a habit when tough stuff came up of shutting down, signing, "all done, all done." Emily reiterated the importance of choosing to move forward when, suddenly, he interrupted her. "You need to understand thst you do lots of things you m ight notb realize hurt bmy feelijgd [feelings]."

"Can you give me some examples so I can understand?" Emily asked.

"ypu try to be muy mon [my mom]," DJ said. Accustomed to this sort of turn in our conversations with him—the all-roads-lead-to-adoption theme that so typified DJ's thinking—Emily simply tried to sustain the exchange.

"Why does that hurt your feelings?"

"becausde im nolt yiur son."

"Whose son are you?"

"i'm rhonds."

"You're right," Emily replied. "You have two moms. Lots of kids do. Some kids' parents get divorced and remarry. Then the kids have two moms. Dad has a friend who has four moms. Having a lot of family is usually a very good thing."

"I,l acceptb thar c," DJ offered. Emily then went on to mention the various father figures who had stood in for my estranged father.

"Our lives are enriched and made stronger by all of the good, kind people we know; whether they are family or friend doesn't really matter so much. What matters is that we love them and they care about us. We would help them and we know they would help us whenever we needed it."

"possibhly that vmaakes sense," DJ typed. The conversation then seemed to stall when DJ stared off into the distance.

"What are you thinking about?" Emily asked.

"i think free people are happy," he said.

Later, after he'd gone to bed and Emily began wrapping presents, I started writing the lecture I was to give in San Diego on the very day Ellie was to arrive. I'd committed to giving the lecture long before I knew that she'd be coming to Iowa. Once I learned that she was coming, I told Emily that I wanted to cancel the engagement, but she encouraged me to go, reminding me that I'd only miss the first half of the visit and that because the lecture was all about a more progressive understanding of cognitive disability, I would in a sense be with DJ and his sister while I was lecturing. Emily is a very generous person, but she also knew, as she later revealed, that I'd be exceedingly apprehensive about how the visit would go. I'd be wanting it, needing it, to go swimmingly—or perhaps I should say jumpingly. I do get revved up, and DJ is a vibe person, so the arrangement was probably best for everyone involved. Well, maybe not for me. The whole time out in San Diego, I'd be on pins and needles wondering what was happening, trying not to call every half hour. "What are they doing now?" "What are they doing now?"

Christmas went more smoothly than had the previous few days, though DJ still didn't want to be in the trampoline house. In the late afternoon, before dinner, Emily and I involved him in a conversation with his grandparents. "DJ," I said, "tell Grandy and Bop one of your jokes."

"why does santa have a garden?" DJ typed.

"I don't know," Emily's mother replied. "Why does Santa have a garden?"

"so he can ho ho ho." We all laughed uproariously, at which point DJ remarked, "really funny joking becaude im mommy's joking boy you thinkm i'm funny." I then got Grandy to ask DJ what he wanted to be when he grew up. His therapist in Grinnell had been so impressed by what DJ was saying in their sessions—the sophistication of his insights— that she'd suggested he might want to be a professor like his father. Questions about the future invariably agitated DJ, so before he responded to his grandmother, we had another minor bout of poking.

"How about it, DJ, do you want to be a professor?" I asked, trying to bring DJ back from whatever reverie had taken hold of him.

"i will, not be a pto because they read tioo, much," he typed, the font on his computer suddenly shrinking. Either some mysterious key had been struck or the *Intellitalk* program was malfunctioning; it required so much memory that sometimes the laptop couldn't shoulder the burden. "i mightb be a teacher of politic s," DJ continued, "he can speak up for the poor poor poorbb poor. . . ." Now the computer was behaving very strangely, repeating the word "poor" ad infinitum, as if it thought we upper-middle-class people needed to have it drilled into our heads. I let out a loud guffaw, shocked by DJ's political commitment and feeling a bit guilty about my habit of reading whenever conscious. "you laugh," DJ said, "please lpoliutics are important," the font now even smaller, almost too small to read. "they try to mhurt the poor," DJ typed, adding, apropos of nothing, his nervous mantra: "ploking is bad." Emily rubbed DJ's hand, trying to calm him, trying to get him to finish his thought. "politics help police look for bad people tghf ggive pople tge right ti vote they give popl the right to go to school." A very important declaration from someone who had lived in poverty and who had been condemned to a special ed school where he did nothing all day but stim at moving objects and practice buttoning and unbuttoning his coat, not to mention someone whose attacker had been carted away by the police. The astonishing thing about DJ was his earnest desire to make a difference, even as his anxieties sometimes got the best of him. I remember my in-laws, who had bought DJ his talking computer, sitting in disbelief. We were all sitting in disbelief, marveling at what he could now communicate.

I'm obviously not the best person to narrate the beginning of the reunion, but I have Emily's journal notes, the two siblings' conversations on the computer, and a video taken by my father-in-law. After the hour drive to Des Moines, Emily, DJ, and Phil seemed to wait forever at the airport before spotting Ellie, accompanied by an airline employee. Emily had worried about recognizing her; the last photo we'd received was almost five years before. In the video you can see Ellie walking tentatively toward her brother, thinking something like, "It must be him. I tried to prepare myself for how old he'd be, but I hadn't anticipated he'd be that old." DJ was pacing and distant, not letting on that he'd seen Ellie. No running up to her and kissing her this time. Rather, it was as if he were enclosed in a plexiglass bubble: a boyish pope who wouldn't acknowledge the crowds before him. With DJ there was a constant struggle between emotional participation and withdrawal. As Emily moved to greet Ellie, the airline employee demanded identification, something that only seemed to exacerbate an already awkward encounter. The intrusion was reminiscent of other legal intrusions into the kids' lives—yet another official handover. Emily can be heard on the video trying to speak for DJ, compensating for his apparent indifference. "Isn't it great to see Ellie after all of this time?"

In the car, Ellie called her father and stepmother, who had insisted she contact them the second her plane landed. DJ didn't want her to be on the phone; in fact, he tried to take the phone from her: their first real interaction. He generally doesn't like anybody to be on the phone. Whenever we're on the phone, he says that we're ignoring him. Ellie was trying to respond to her father's many questions. Having been discouraged from coming to Des Moines, he was eager to hear about his birth son. Surprised by DJ's actions, she moved the phone from one hand to the other in order to keep it out of his reach, which only made DJ that much more insistent. Ten minutes into the ride home, and tension filled the car. Once Ellie said good-bye to her father, Emily turned on DJ's favorite song and began telling Ellie all of the amazing things that DJ had learned to do since she saw him last, including communicate with a computer. She told her about the method we'd been using called facilitated communication. In retrospect, Emily wished she'd brought the computer with her, but she'd feared it might be too difficult to facilitate DJ in the car. The car only has two bucket seats in the back: if the kids sat together, Emily wouldn't be able to provide the physical support that DJ needed.

After they returned home and Ellie introduced herself to Emily's mother, the siblings had their first conversation ever, a conversation that brought a lump to everyone's throats. Ellie began with a kind of letter, thanking DJ for the picture album he had gotten her for Christmas.

> Hey D.J.,
>
> I am very excited that I am here with you and your mother, grandfather and grandmother. I have been looking forward to these days for a long time. How is school going for you? I hope it is going great and you are enjoying it. Have you made a lot of friends at your new school? Thank you very much for the presents. I love them. I will keep all of my pictures of you in there and I will write in it too! I hope you like the clothes I gave you for Christmas. They will be great on cold days. Thanks so much for inviting me over to your house and letting me stay with you for a week. I hope to get to see you more often than every five years!
>
> Love, your sister, Ellie
> P.S. I am having lots of fun here. THANKS!

Ellie's assiduously upbeat tone, a requirement for life with her step-mother, didn't sit well with DJ. He began to reach for his sister's eyes, a gesture we explained as a kind of nervous tic. We had decided not to tell Ellie of the abuse DJ had suffered in foster care, about which we'd learned a great deal more in the preceding few months, preferring instead to let him choose what he wanted her to know. Ellie had been told by her parents that foster care was a good, safe option for DJ, which of course it wasn't. We feared that if DJ told her about the abuse, it might unsettle her and encourage her parents to ban any future visits; at the same time, there wasn't any way of adequately accounting for DJ's behavior without referencing his horrific past. The bind was exquisite. Five years later, we were all playing a version of the game we'd played in the Northeast, and it wasn't clear that this game would end any better.

When DJ didn't respond to Ellie's letter, Emily asked him to tell Ellie a joke. "what is worse thjan rudolph with a coldf/" DJ typed. "frosty with a fever." Ellie couldn't believe it: her brother was using words to communicate. Her brother was communicating! She started to cry. At which point, DJ again reached for her eyes. Emily stopped him and he typed, "judst be patient i am trying to tr.ll you how i feel i love you i poke because i get nrvous nnnn please don't cry i love you very ve4y much."

Ellie seemed dazed, the inhabitant of a dream world. "Thanks D.J." she typed. "I am crying because I am very happy to see you and it has been so long since I have seen you."

"i try=please you," DJ said.

"I try too," Ellie replied. "So how has fifth grade been going for you? Do you have lots of friends? Are you learning a lot and like your teachers?" Even a fairly innocuous question could bring on a fresh round of poking, which left Ellie confused, slightly sullen. If we were worried about the visit disturbing Ellie, we should have been worried about it disturbing DJ. The glazed look in his eyes suggested the return of flashbacks. Emily stroked his arm, retrieving him from the past.

"i pok please be patiejmt please," he urged. Ellie took the computer from Emily and commenced typing with two hands, as she had all along, but now this bothered DJ. He wanted her to type like him—with one finger.

"I am sorry," Ellie said. "I am just so used to typing like this and soon you will be typing just like me or even better." Ellie was terrifically supportive, but she didn't understand that even the slightest difference between them DJ read as a kind of betrayal, somehow linked to the decision to send him to foster care. DJ signed "all done," and after it was clear that pressing him to continue would not work, Emily suggested that they go order pizza for dinner.

That night, after everyone else had gone to bed, Ellie and Emily spoke for several hours. Ellie had all sorts of questions about autism, about why DJ couldn't talk, about how and what he was learning at school, about sign language, about facilitated communication, about poking. She wondered why DJ seemed so mad at her when he typed such loving thoughts on the computer. She wondered why he was so anxious, sometimes even telling her "bye" (one of the few words he could say). Emily did her best to answer Ellie's questions, talking at great length about some things, skirting others.

The next day, Ellie wanted to see the trampoline house. DJ went out there, but only reluctantly, and he wouldn't jump. The weather had turned much colder, so Emily had gotten a fire going in the wood stove. Ellie kept saying that she wished she had a trampoline house. "Come play, DJ, come play." When DJ refused, Emily again tried to engage the two siblings in conversation.

"pl ease be pagient," DJ typed.

"Sure," Ellie responded. "You are a super brother. I love you very, very much."

"ellie," DJ asked, "hasb you missd livinh with md?" The question should have broken Ellie's heart, but she calmly answered, as though having memorized in advance the perfect reply: "Yes, very much, but I am glad we are not living with Rhonda in Florida. You are in a great place with a great family that loves you and cares for you a lot." This was her parents talking, committed proponents of a happy ending, no matter at what cost it had come for DJ. Utterly reasonable, her remark seemed to slay him. How could it be even a moderately good idea that they lived apart?

"Do you remember Rhonda?" Ellie inquired.

"Yes," DJ said.

"She was not very nice at all, but now you are in a wonderful place."

"i knos but i miss you you understand me vlik no other kid," DJ persisted.

"Mostly because when you were very little, I took care of you. I am also your sister, that helps a lot."

DJ paused, then stated plainly, "i'm tryingh to forgetv the mmm past tgheee past was very scary for me." He seemed to want to puncture his sister's pleasant argument.

"Yes, it was very scary. Luckily, we both have great families that care for us very dearly," Ellie said.

DJ was now distraught, flapping his arms and making a loud moaning sound. He seemed about to cry. "What is the matter, DJ?" Ellie asked. "Are you OK? Is there something wrong? Please tell me."

"hav'v patience i really wantb to jump with you but i was badly poking poked by realky mean fire when1 i 4f was ljitlle amd i scared." In the blandest way possible, Emily explained to Ellie that DJ had been mistreated in foster care.

"I know the fire bothers you from when we were little," Ellie said, "but if we jump the other way we could have lots of fun! Please! Would it help if your mother jumped with us?" Her tone was so sisterly. She'd fallen back into her role as DJ's caretaker, but she didn't know the half of it. DJ was trying to tell her about the windy afternoon in Florida when Kyle had hit him with a big stick, then dragged him toward the bonfire and stuck his hand in the flames. Emily realized that DJ had connected this fire with the fire in the wood stove, which he could see through the stove's tempered glass. We'd encountered such a pattern before: once a piece of DJ's past had surfaced in his writing, shortly thereafter a fear of some familiar object or place developed. He'd been in the uninsulated trampoline house the previous two winters and hadn't ever objected to the wood stove. In fact, he actually seemed to like fire, always eager to help me when I was cooking out on the Weber grill. Now he was panicked.

"Mom and Grandy will watch the fire so you and Ellie can have fun jumping with no worries," Emily told him.

"look are youn 56666really sure the fire is locked in there b," DJ asked.

"Absolutely! I promise with my whole heart it is locked in there and cannot get out."

"So you will jump with me and give it a try?" Ellie pleaded.

"ok," DJ typed, but as he headed for the trampoline, he signed "all done" and "go"—"I want to go." Ellie looked depressed. Rachel began to talk to her as Emily packed up the computer and headed back to the house with DJ. Emily feared that his stress level was just too high. He might really blow, and she wanted to avoid an ugly encounter. As they walked back to the house, DJ turned around and saw his sister jumping on the trampoline without him and, what is worse, his beloved Grandy looking on admiringly.

Much of the rest of the day proceeded like that, with Emily's parents consoling Ellie and Emily prodding DJ to have fun with his sister. But DJ had taken down his circus tents, packed up his animals, and he had done so at the very moment his audience had arrived. He needed to punish that audience with disappointment. Because the show had once gone on without him, it would now not go on with him. He wanted Ellie to feel his pain; he wanted her to have his past. They'd been in the same lifeboat together and then a luxury liner had come by and picked her up, leaving him all alone.

Later that second night, when Ellie and Emily again stayed up to talk, Ellie confessed she was mad at her stepmother for worrying—indeed predicting—the visit would trigger difficult memories from Florida. The girl was caught between a kind of compulsory cheerfulness that assuaged the woman's anxiety and a terrifying despair that honored her brother's injuries, which she had only just begun to sense. She wanted Emily to tell her the story of how we'd come to adopt DJ, a story whose ambiguity she flirted with acknowledging, peeking every now and then beneath its happy ending to see what lay inside. She refused to implicate her father, who had rescued her—she loved him too much. And so she blamed her mother's sister who had a daughter who was deaf and who, Ellie believed, should have taken DJ. (Emily allowed the faulty logic of this assertion to pass without mention.) Toward the end of their conversation, Ellie let slip that she hadn't been able to refrain from telling her parents about DJ's experience in foster care, which had made her stepmother very defensive and had caused her once again to question the value of the visit. Hearing this later from Emily on the phone, I grew furious, knowing too well where they—we—were headed.

In the morning, before the kids went ice skating in Iowa City at a mall with a rink attached to a giant food court, DJ told his sister that he wanted to "please her," but he was fixated on poking. "ploking is bad," he typed.

"Why have you been thinking about poking so much? When you do it, it is not a big problem," Ellie said.

"i really, wangt to stop pokinb but 8i can;'t."

"You have not poked me today, so I would think that you are getting a big start to ending the poking. I still do not know why you worry so much if it has not been going on today."

"poking has been omewhat of a problem at schooo," DJ replied.

"I think everyone understands that moving to a new school with lots of big kids and very busy, noisy hallways is scary at first," Emily interjected. "But you are doing a really great job there now. Should we have a fun day in Iowa City?"

"yes I rrtry," DJ said.

And try he did, but he was just too wound up. When, after an hour's drive, they reached the rink, DJ immediately signed "all done, all done." Emily knew then that they were in trouble, but she pushed forward, hoping to get some skating in, hoping somehow that DJ would not erupt. While Phil and Rachel waited on a bench by the skate rental counter, Emily helped DJ lace up his skates. She then escorted him out onto the rink. Ellie kept wanting him to skate with her, but he signed, "go, go" and clung to Emily. The rink was incredibly noisy. The sound system blared some sort of pop song, and the food court echoed with chattering lunch-goers. The combination of stress and too much sensory input almost always proved disastrous. In fairness to DJ, he was behaving like an utterly diligent volcano, giving off all of the appropriate warning signs and allowing the local denizens to flee to safer ground. But Emily was stuck. Ellie was just too happy to be out on the ice, eager to have fun, expecting her brother to hold her hand as he had while roller skating those many years ago. She kept pestering DJ, encouraging him to skate on his own if he wouldn't skate with her. A very competent skater, DJ seemed rapidly to regress, becoming unstable and petrified, as if he needed to act out the past, demonstrate the helplessness of an abandoned three-year-old. But Ellie missed this warning sign.

The explosion came when she began to converse with Emily. DJ had directed Emily toward the side, anxiously signing, "all done, all done." Once they had stepped off the rink, Emily removed DJ's skates. Ellie then launched into something about her life in the Northeast. As Emily bent down to pick up her own skates, trying all the while to respond to what Ellie was saying, DJ smacked her in the nose and started screaming as loudly as he could. Before Emily could recover from the shock, he bit her breast, actually clamped down on it. In a flash, the two of them were locked in a desperate struggle, the kind of encounter we'd experienced numerous times the previous fall. Priority one: stop him from injuring you. Priority two: stop him from injuring himself. When he exploded, ferocious head-banging invariably followed. Priority three: make for the exit as quickly as possible.

Emily knew the drill. Like some sort of secret service woman, she neutralized the situation, then expertly ushered her charge to safety, leaving a shocked crowd behind, a crowd that included her parents and Ellie. The attack was as bad—and as embarrassing—as any that Emily had suffered; DJ had never bitten her breast before. Once in the car, she began to cry, in part relieved that her parents had seen just how under assault we'd been for the past four months, in part fearful of Ellie's response—what she might tell her parents. DJ sat motionless in the back seat, having delivered himself to a space of impenetrable placidity: his customary, if paradoxical, resolution to an outburst. After a while, Emily did what she always does: discover new veins of energy, new veins of motherly generosity, in that strip-mined heart of hers. "We need to talk, DJ."

"I want ellie to go home," DJ typed.

"Why?"

"because i don't poke when she's not here"

"Really? What happened at the ice rink?"

"ibit you really hard because you were talking to ellie"

"You got that mad and tried to hurt me that much just because I was talking to Ellie?"

"yes"

"DJ, why did that make you so mad?"

"really hurt bmy feelings because ypu were ignor58jgy meb"

"DJ, I was not ignoring you. I was skating with you. I am just trying to make Ellie feel welcome because I know she is important to you and I want her to come back to visit you." The mere mention of another visit set DJ off again, as he reached for Emily's eyes and then banged his head once against the back seat window. "You cannot get THAT irate about something like this. It is OK to feel mad or hurt and to tell me, 'Mom, please let me know how much you love me.' BUT I do not deserve to be bitten and hit and grabbed like that, and you don't want to lose control of yourself," Emily told him on the computer. Pausing, she then asked, "Why do you keep asking Ellie to go and not want to play with her? I am sure you are feeling lots of different things at once. Can you talk about any of them?"

"i feel mad at hder for pleasijg yoiu because I didn';y you lije [like] her"

"Do you like her?" Emily asked.

"yes but ylu like her btter than 2"""""""""""""""me"

"DJ, that is not true at all. I like Ellie because she is your sister and important to you, but I love you. You are my son and extremely important to me. I was trying to keep Ellie company because you are being so distant with her. Why are you telling her to go all of the time? Wouldn't it be more fun to use these days to talk and support each other and have fun together?"

"i feel sad that she has to have me for a brother. no one shoukd have to doi that"

"DJ, you are saying lots of very negative things about yourself. Are you trying to make Mom feel sorry for you?"

"yes"

"I don't feel sorry for you. I think you are a strong, smart, competent, lovable guy who has a good home and can choose to pick up and move forward in life or can wallow in self PITY."

"i known please be the best mom I have evferevgdf," DJ replied. He had a tendency, whenever his own behavior was in question, of making emotional demands on his parents, exhorting *us* to do better. Emily moved right past this remark and said, "Please do not ever attack someone like you attacked me unless you are in a life-threatening situation. Do you understand?"

"yew"

"Can you try to have fun with Ellie? She loves you. You love her. You are getting to know each other again and for many years to come. Mom and Dad are thrilled you are our son. You can have fun with Ellie and still live with us. You do not have to make a choice."

Emily believed that DJ feared losing us if he had fun with his sister; he often acted this way with people he thought might replace us. In fact, the kinder the person, the more suspicious—and aggressively indifferent—he became, sensing impending separation in that kindness. The irony of his fearing having to live with Ellie indicated, Emily said, just how conflicted DJ was. To get the person he had lost he'd have to lose the people he had found: loss was inevitable. But I believed, finally, that DJ couldn't accept the happy compromise of merely getting to visit Ellie. No matter how preferable to not seeing her at all, the compromise was not of his design and, thus, would not get his approval. He needed to be in control, even if it meant further injuring himself. He also seemed to want Ellie to feel the pain of being rejected, as he had been rejected those many years ago. He wanted Emily to choose *him* over her. No ordinary sibling rivalry this—rather, a tortured reenactment of that original preference, that original decision. In the end, probably all of these things motivated DJ.

After a while, Emily's parents walked over to the car with Ellie in tow. They saw that DJ had calmed down and, without mentioning the attack, tried to assume an upbeat tone, but they were clearly stunned by DJ's aggression. They were defensive of their daughter, even as they felt for their grandson. They wanted to come to Emily's aid, somehow fix the situation, but they didn't know how. They had a look on their faces, Emily said, of deep concern, as if she was in way over her head—as if, in fact, she'd already drowned, already washed up on some rocky shore. Ellie, too, seemed stunned, unable to speak.

The car ride home proceeded largely in silence. Before dinner, Emily again tried to engineer a conversation between the two kids. DJ seemed more relaxed, almost as if he'd gotten something out of his system. Ellie typed, "What do you think about the fact that there are only white people in Iowa?"

"it ix weird," DJ said.

"Do you miss the different cultures in Florida?"

"ydx"

"Why?"

"becw7yse3 blaxk [people really have/ rhythm"

"Yes, they do." Ellie answered. The conversation then moved in a different direction, with Emily's folks asking Ellie a question. DJ seemed irritated, so much so that he wouldn't respond to what she had said. "Are you playing hard to get?" she typed.

"no"

"Then, what's the matter?"

"ypooj aree talkm9ing"

"You know how to talk, too," Emily intervened. She'd gone over this topic a thousand times. "You just use a computer. Do not hang out and feel self-pity. You are a smart boy with interesting things to say and people who want to hear what you think."

"i know"

"Good, so don't use the excuse of people talking to withdraw from the group."

"I knjow thjst you arer intr4restedf"

"We are ALL interested in what you have to say to us and we would be delighted to know what is going on in that smart head of yours," Emily reiterated. "It is harder and harder to feel sorry for yourself when so many kind people care about and respect you, isn't it?" she added.

"how do ylou know h oew i feel you can tlk," DJ replied. He could turn on a dime: the moment that too much positive thinking threatened to win the psychological election, he'd immediately run a flurry of negative ads. He refused to accommodate himself to either his past or his disability.

"Perhaps we don't know what it is like not to be able to talk, but we know that everyone is as interested in hearing what you have to say as we are in hearing what the rest of us have to say. Once, Mom and Dad lived in a country where Mom couldn't understand the language when it was spoken. Nor could she speak it well, but she could read and write it very well. Sometimes people called me names, but the people who really mattered were willing to listen and to write back and forth with me. I really valued those people. I knew they were smart and kind and the sort of people I wanted as friends." Emily was referring to our time in Poland, an experience she credits with giving birth to her interest in neurological disability. The feeling of not being able to speak, of being trapped in a space of unrecognized intelligence, had been profound.

"i gu e4esscv guess ou zrer [you are] right," DJ said.

"Remember, those of us who talk don't always have a clear way of telling who respects and cares about us. Each of us has to find these people."

"i nknow it isnh't always clear but i thoink you resally me i tell you i shor" [sure?] DJ declared. He knew instinctively what to say to make an adult feel better—productively parental or avuncular. He wanted the conversation to end on a positive note, but Emily's mother resisted, sensing an opportunity to bring the conversation around to his behavior at the ice rink.

"Do you respect and care about your mother?" Rachel asked. "Do you know why Grandy's asking you this question?"

"i bit mom i reallb feel terriubken"

That night, Ellie came downstairs after DJ had gone to bed, quieter than usual. She'd told her parents about DJ's attack—exactly what Emily had feared she'd do. Her dad had used the incident to illustrate why it was better that the two siblings didn't live together—his very old saw. "Think how little attention you would get if DJ lived with us," he apparently told her. Emily had difficulty reading Ellie's response to this remark, which I found repulsively cynical. Until the blow up at the ice rink, it seemed as if Ellie was preparing a counteroffensive: something like "if Emily can take care of both of us, then why can't you?" But now, in a resigned tone, she said, "My stepmom wouldn't ever be able to handle what happened today." Clearly, Ellie was caught in her own bind. She wanted to be with her brother, and yet she couldn't think poorly of her father. Moreover, she couldn't dare antagonize her stepmom, especially if she longed to visit DJ again. Of course, DJ's behavior only made things worse; it seemed to confirm her father's argument. Add to this DJ's intermittent rejection of her and the girl had ample excuse to chart a course of sullen resignation.

The next day Emily's parents, who had been so patient and generous, returned to Hilton Head, and I flew back from San Diego. The trip took forever, each second lengthened by anticipation. When I finally got home, Emily looked a bit frazzled, so I dispensed with a formal introduction and immediately ushered the kids out to the trampoline house. I would impose a regime of fun, I thought, arrogantly imagining that I

233

could accomplish what everyone else could not: getting these two siblings to play together. Think of me as General Jump, declaring martial law. Emily seemed at once annoyed at my presumption and relieved to have some help. I literally pulled DJ out onto the trampoline, but he refused to move, signing "all done, all done." "You see?" Emily seemed to say, as DJ exited the enclosure and headed for the door. "Why don't you want to jump?" I asked. "You usually love to jump."

"i have a bheadache," DJ typed.

"Dad was hoping you and Ellie would really enjoy jumping together. Is there any other reason you don't want to jump?" Emily inquired, certain the wood stove was again making him anxious.

"yes i have a fear of fire."

"I promise you the fire is very safely closed inside the stove. It cannot hurt you or get out. It is just to keep us warm. If I put something in front of the fire to block it would you feel OK?"

"yes thye fire really svcaree n"

"DJ," I said, "try to jump and turn your back so you don't have to look at it."

"you don't understand it tews ries [tries] to trip me," DJ responded. He had this tendency of personifying his anxieties, treating them like sentient beings eager to attack him. The more we tried to convince him he was safe, the more scared he said he was, adding at one point in the conversation, "you really don't kbnosw wgat h alppenefd," a remark that shocked us at the time but only later, after Ellie had left, achieved its full impact. In retrospect, DJ's behavior would seem so clearly the manifestation of a trauma still trying to emerge, still trying to articulate itself— something beyond the beating and abandonment. But at the time, it seemed merely neurotic, obstinate, excessively self-defeating. He kept inventing excuses for why he didn't want to jump. "I feel dizzy," he'd say or "my leg hurts." It's not that these excuses weren't credible—he often felt dizzy and his hemiplegic migraines did indeed impair his limbs. Rather, it's that he tried too eagerly to avail himself of these credible excuses, one right after another. After telling us that he felt dizzy, Emily asked him what he was thinking about as he stared off into space. "i dread ellieleaving," he typed.

And that's where we were: stuck in the middle of DJ's evolving salvage operation, watching him dive into the murky depths. Whatever memories the visit had dislodged only complicated his ambivalence about moving forward with his sister. He seemed more comfortable longing for Ellie than actually having her—because, again, he couldn't have her on his terms. No matter what we said, DJ remained paralyzed. Even Ellie got into the consolatory act, reminding her brother that they would now get to see each other frequently. "My mother and father," she typed, "said that it might be hard to say good-bye, but if I were to see you more than every five years and I would see you pretty regularly than it will become easier and easier to say good-bye. I know it is very hard to say good-bye, but as my mother and father say it is not good-bye it is till the next time." DJ's response to this thoughtful missive? To reach for his sister's eyes.

The two kids did, though, have touching moments at bedtime when DJ would tell Ellie that he loved her and then kiss her on the forehead. This obviously pleased Ellie, but she couldn't make sense of his inconsistent behavior. The final two and a half days of the visit passed much like the first three and a half: with DJ mostly ignoring his sister or telling her to go. New Year's Eve we took the kids roller skating, but DJ again refused to have fun, skating a bit on his own before skating with Emily and then signing, "all done, all done." I couldn't go skating because of my hip, so I sat at a table near the snack bar, longing to see the two kids skate happily together—right into the future. But, alas, my long-imagined figure of reunion did not hold. New Year's Day we went tubing on what is probably the only large hill in all of south-central Iowa. This outing proved the most successful with respect to fun. The two kids barreled down the hill, each in an inner tube attached to the other, both of them laughing. But even this outing turned sour as DJ got hit with the tow-rope line in the mouth when his inner tube suddenly flipped around on its way up the hill. His lip was bloody and swollen, and his glasses had been knocked off. We couldn't believe our luck: DJ hated this sort of surprise. He wanted to go immediately, and Ellie, of course, wanted to keep tubing.

At last, the day of the dreaded good-bye arrived. In the morning as Ellie took a shower, Emily and I laid out the plan for DJ, who objected to the part where Emily alone escorted Ellie to her gate. "i wanty to staty with ellie until she getse omj nthr plane," DJ typed. We told him that only one person was allowed to go through security with Ellie and that person had to be an adult. Furthermore, that person would have to wait until Ellie's plane had actually taken off. It would end up being several hours at the airport, so it was probably better if he said his good-byes and then went shopping with me in Des Moines. DJ reluctantly agreed. We reminded him that later in the day he had an appointment with his therapist, with whom he could talk about Ellie and his plans to get together with her soon. "please lokvw [love] vme," DJ typed, "you are my familym but ellier is my sister and i love her very much and i might need tom miss her when nshe planes"

"DJ, don't worry about Mom and Dad. We know that you love us, and we know that you will miss Ellie. OK?" Emily replied.

"please love me," DJ repeated. You could see him trying to resist the temptation to withdraw into his head. Good-byes were exceedingly difficult for him, and this one, like the one five years before, simply tapped into that primal good-bye when the two siblings were first separated. It also made him think of being abandoned—hence, the unabashed request to be loved. And yet, as Emily had previously suggested, to be loved by us meant losing his sister—again and again and again. His mind could not accommodate this conflict.

The ride to the airport was particularly moving, as the two siblings held hands in the back seat. For all of his agitation, DJ seemed, if I may put it this way, strikingly at home with loss. It was as if the imminent good-bye made possible these few moments of intense connection, or maybe he just forced himself to reach out. The fact is, he had very little experience building relationships, sustaining them; he only knew how to watch them end.

At the airport, DJ and I waited off to the side as Emily and Ellie checked Ellie's bag and went over the traveling procedure for what the airline calls an "unaccompanied minor." Then DJ and Ellie said their good-byes. Ellie fought off tears as DJ typed, "I will miss you." She gave her brother a hug, saying, "Till next time." Emily, meanwhile, had turned away from the two kids; she didn't want DJ to see her crying. We had talked about not drawing out the good-bye, treating it as nonchalantly as possible. But how could any of us be certain that the kids wouldn't have to wait another five years to be reunited?

"We'll see you in June or July, Ellie," I said, a bit too forcefully. "You better go to the gate. There's a line at security." DJ insisted that we remain exactly where we were until Ellie disappeared into the crowd of people taking off their shoes and jackets. Before we turned and made our way back to the car, he mouthed the word "bye." It floated up like a balloon into the steel rafters and refused to come down. DJ didn't seem distraught, just pensive, a tad melancholy. About an hour later, Emily phoned to say that Ellie's plane was delayed and, an hour after that, that the flight had been canceled due to mechanical failure. There was no other flight leaving early enough to make a connection in Chicago. She'd have to leave Des Moines the next morning. "Oh shit," I thought. "We're going to have to do the good-bye all over again"—this time with feeling. The Great Director God above apparently believed that we hadn't gotten it right or, so in love with loss, simply wanted to see it again. Perhaps He, too, was autistic, playing His videos of us humans over and over.

DJ and I drove back to the airport and picked up Emily and Ellie. We explained to DJ what had happened. In retrospect, the whole fiasco was probably good practice for everyone. DJ got to see that his sister had indeed returned, even if much earlier than promised. The rest of the day went more smoothly than had any of the previous ones. DJ wasn't exactly ebullient or emotionally forthcoming, but he was more attentive to his sister. That night we talked on the computer and played a game of Trivial Pursuit. We turned in early because Ellie's new flight left at 7:00 in the morning. This second good-bye proved anticlimactic, as if a little practice could in fact tame despair. It was still sad, still charged, but it didn't have the bite that the first one had.

When we got home from the airport DJ was positively giddy: laughing, jumping up and down, running into every room of the house. "It's great to see you so happy!" Emily said. "What are you so happy about?"

"i had a lot oof fun seeing rellie pleasen please kieep in tkouch witjn her," DJ typed. If we hadn't known how DJ's approach–avoidance fears operated, we might have been perplexed by his reading of the visit and, in particular, of his own behavior toward his sister.

"YOU can keep in touch with her, too!" Emily replied. "You can e-mail and write and send pictures and call her whenever you want!"

"i wsant to really get to know her," DJ said.

"You will. You definitely will. She already called to tell you 'thanks' for having her here. I sent the dates of your summer vacation and Ellie will figure out a time to visit during the summer."

"i m srious about getting to know her and trying to see her," DJ persisted.

"We know you are. She is serious about it, too. We will help make that happen in anyway we can. You let us know how we can help."

"you yo,u have already helped," he said. At times DJ was so earnestly thoughtful that I wanted to wrap him in my arms and squeeze every last drop of sadness from him. He was like a sponge that had been used to wipe up the world: he needed his own shot at pristine cheerfulness.

"You two are very sweet to each other," I said, jumping in. "It is obvious by the way you talk and interact that you are brother and sister. That's really fun for Mom and Dad to see!"

"i think you reallyy look out for my best ijnterests," DJ typed, "you wan6t me to be happy may bf you want me to be free of my present gfearf"

"We think you are terrific," Emily replied. "We want to help you realize that you are just as capable and talented and worthy of respect as anyone else. We think you are starting to see that for yourself which is what matters!"

PART II

Resentment is not helpful, I know.
—DJ SAVARESE

CHAPTER 9

Try to Remember My Life

The first two weeks of school after the break went exceptionally well. DJ seemed calm and happy, and his aide had begun, finally, to click with him. One night, discussing Ellie's visit, DJ tried to explain why he hadn't jumped with his sister. "there are some things i don't becausen i want them really," he said. His understanding of human psychology constantly floored us, putting the lie, once again, to the "theory of mind" hypothesis that characterized so much of the literature on autism. Here was a boy tied exquisitely into knots, a boy aware of his predicament, discoursing on it.

Another night, in the midst of dancing (one of his favorite activities), DJ suddenly sat down and became very quiet. "What's up?" I asked.

"i was thinking," DJ typed.

"Will you share what you were thinking about?"

"i was thinking about ppoolitics," he replied.

"What about politics?"

"that they are importany"

"Were you listening to the show on TV earlier?" Emily asked. The show had addressed the war in Iraq, covering both Saddam Hussein's atrocities while in power and the burgeoning insurgency, which had seemed to plunge the country into total chaos.

241

"yes"

"Were there things that you really, really agreed or disagreed with?"

"yed"

"What?"

"i think that politics get involved ujn [in] thigs they lk not what's necesssry for example, they talk trik free nm" As I've said, when DJ was especially nervous or stressed out, his typing sometimes faltered. You often had to ask the same question again.

"Can you give us an example?"

"they like to talk about murdder anc not about bein nice"

"What should politicians do?" I inquired, eager to see if he'd answer the question the way he had at Christmas.

"tghey should try tgo help / poor"

"I agree with you," I said. "How did you come to think this?"

"becausew ccbring to mind my /life when i feared being murdered"

"Who did you think would murder you?" Emily interjected, shocked by his use of that word.

"police look scary bry my hm polide try hurt mnm mnm my e me n"

Instead of pressing him immediately to clarify what he had said, Emily asked, "Did you see this yourself or on television?"

"real life," DJ responded.

"When you lived with Rhonda?"

"yes" DJ was now particularly agitated. We seemed to be getting close to something in his past, approaching it the way a plane without instruments might approach a runway in fog: dipping down to get a closer view, than rising to recalculate. Because what he had seen on television had been the associative vehicle for his self-reflection, I thought I'd stick with the general topic of politics.

"Let me ask you a different question. Are you a Democrat or a Republican? Do you know what these things are?"

"yes"

"So, what do you think you are?"

"democrat," DJ typed.

"Why?"

"becaudde i rerad that they m, mkihht [might] stop the war"

Emily and I were flabbergasted; this kid knew so much more than anyone realized. Moreover, at the age of eleven he had political convictions. I'd later learn from Doug Biklen, Director of the Facilitated Communication Institute at Syracuse, a man vilified in the early 1990s for promulgating false hope to the parents of autistic children but who has since helped numerous people to type on their own, that an interest in social justice characterizes the thinking of so many FC users. That people who had been thought dumb and excluded from social life might be urgently interested in politics should, of course, come as no surprise: their own life experience has sensitized them to injustices of all kinds.

"Do you remember going on a march with Mommy and Daddy against the war?" Emily asked. In October of 2002, Emily, DJ, and I had participated in a march on Des Moines in protest of the President's decision to go to war—precipitously, we believed, and without the support of the world community. (On the door to my office there's a quote by Martin Luther King that encapsulates my feelings about the current administration: "We have guided missiles and misguided men.")

"fa free to gion vote," DJ typed.

Emily tried again: "Do you remember going to the capital in Des Moines and marching with a lot of people who had signs that said, 'War Is Wrong'?"

"gloing as a hpolitician,"

"Do you mean to say, 'Going as a political protestor'?" Emily asked.

"yes," DJ replied.

"Did you like doing this?"

"yes"

"Daddy and Mommy think that war is wrong. It is good to protest against bad things. It can make you feel better," Emily said. She seemed to be anticipating DJ's next associative move: the way his mind mapped one thing onto another, creating tense, analogical relationships.

"i ready tio feek better," DJ typed. I could almost picture him on a march in his own memory, protesting against the past, carrying a placard that read "Foster Care Is Scary" or "People Who Can't Speak Deserve A Chance."

243

"We have so much fun with you—hearing your ideas, your thoughts, your feelings. We are very proud of you. You are working very hard to feel better, to move forward," Emily said.

"tr6i9nb [trying] hazrd," DJ replied.

"I know you are. You are making LOTS of progress."

"thank thatr jut ij there is just one thingh to sayh tryng him out of my nmind," DJ typed. He was obviously referring to Kyle, and it was no surprise that the conversation had come around to his great antagonist.

"Soon you will be completely free," Emily said.

"ready to be f4ee"

"Great. Being ready is necessary for being free."

The second Friday in January we had our first trampoline party since the building had been insulated. DJ had a great time jumping and talking with the other kids, one in particular named Marty, who had himself been adopted from Korea by the choral director at the college, a buddy of mine. Many of our friends in Grinnell had adopted children, and we seemed instinctively to have formed something of a social support group, which consisted of gathering in the trampoline house and, while the kids jumped, relaxing by the fire or singing karaoke. Two of the economists at the college had adopted a boy from San Antonio and a boy from Sierra Leone; a philosopher and her partner, a law professor at Drake, had adopted a girl from China. Our friends had helped us through a very difficult fall, if only by appreciating just how much stress we were under with DJ's PTSD.

We thought we'd finally turned the corner on DJ's anxieties. It was a big deal for him to resume jumping and, even more important, to initiate conversation with a peer, as he did with Marty that night.

"i mwant to takk to mzarty"

"Great! You can do that," Emily said.

"i bwant to know if vhe wamts to jump"

"Yes, DJ, I would like to jump with you," Marty answered.

"great," DJ typed. After they jumped for a while, the two of them having moved around the circular enclosure like amateur acrobats, DJ asked, "did you have fun"

"Oh yeah! It's like so cool, DJ," Marty replied.

"great"

"Now what do you want to do?" he asked.

"lets talk," DJ said.

"OK, what do you want to talk about, DJ?"

"i want t9 taalk about girls"

"Well, DJ, just to tell you the girl I like is away and will be back next year."

"i like _____ do you kjow her/ n"

"No, DJ, I'm sorry. Can you tell me about her?"

"you really should meet her"

"Well, the girl that I like is _____. Even though I call her _____ just for fun."

"you should call her sweety," DJ said, with a big smile on his face.

"I don't think so!!!!!" Marty replied. "She would kill me. And pound me to the ground."

"you should kisds [kiss] her," DJ continued.

"No!!!!! Maybe you should kiss _____. And call her Sweet Heart!" Marty had turned the tables on DJ.

"No way," he said.

"Oh yeah, I dare you to send her a love letter!"

"bno really don't think so she is real;ly besautiful"

"So, I think she will really think it's sweet."

"no way possibly she doesn';y like mr," DJ typed, a remark that saddened me as I considered how fraught or loaded was his concern. I imagined times in the future when a romantic prospect might not be able to look beyond DJ's disability.

"OK, I give up. Let's go jump!" Marty replied.

As we headed into the third week of January, DJ began again to obsess about poking and being nervous. He was having trouble at school, not wanting to go in the morning. "What makes you feel nervous there?" Emily asked.

"bki g kids" We'd been through this in the fall. Kyle had been the age of the seventh graders at the middle school when he attacked DJ, and DJ did not like encountering these seventh graders in the hall. Their rowdiness sent his stress level soaring. "try to understand that i am scared about poking because im nerrvous about the bi9g kids," he told us.

In the meantime, my arthritis had gotten so bad that I was in pain all the time and very grouchy. I was working too hard at the college, neglecting my own and my family's welfare, and starting to displace some of my frustration onto Emily. Indeed, my temper was getting the best of me. Hearing DJ spit back some of the hurtful things I was saying to her only left me more depressed. Hearing him tell her, "please try to please him" embarrassed me, sexist as such an exhortation was. I knew that I needed to model proper anger management techniques, but I was exhausted. I clearly hadn't worked through my own feelings about being disabled; I hadn't even addressed them—there wasn't time. And now I was facing surgery. My orthopedist wanted to do the replacement in March. He feared the problem in my left hip was starting to affect my right one, but I didn't feel comfortable going on medical leave. I wasn't yet tenured, and I didn't want anybody to think I couldn't do my job. After all, there would be other, many other, surgeries ahead of me. I wanted to try to wait until the summer, but this meant more pain, more frustration. Much more.

As if this predicament weren't stressful enough, DJ's anxiety about "big kids" intensified. One night we caught him drifting off and asked him where he had been. "try to remember my life . i was beaten when I was just littkle," he typed.

"Do you want to talk about it?" I asked.

"yes yes yes fear police because when i was playing thdey kickjed me not djng poking" This was the second time that DJ mentioned the police. In November, at one of his therapy sessions in Cedar Falls, we'd seen him go over to the therapist's sandbox and aggressively bury a toy police car. When the therapist had questioned him about this action, DJ had refused to answer her. Had he really been kicked by the police? If so, when had it happened? When he was taken from his birth mom? When he was taken from his first foster home? What was the connection between the police and poking? If poking was the word DJ used to describe the beating that Kyle had given him, including the attempt to

pluck out his eyes, then why did he say "not djng poking"? Was he thinking that the police shouldn't have kicked him if at the time he wasn't
poking? But, again, had they really kicked him? We knew that Rhonda
had been in trouble with the law and wondered if DJ had mistaken the
police arresting her for a kind of violence. Perhaps she had resisted.
Perhaps he had tried to stop them, even at the age of three, and had been
kicked by accident.

"Where were you playing?" Emily asked.

"in the park in florda," DJ replied.

"Who did you live with when this happened?"

"bad mother great beaten mother you know"

"Are you talking about Rhonda?"

"no"

"Are you talking about Edna Austin, your first foster mother?"

"no," DJ typed, leaving us utterly confused.

"Whom are you talking about?"

"the police," DJ replied.

"So, you're trying to tell us that the police kicked your birth mother?"

"Great," DJ said. An odd response, to be sure. Was he glad that we'd
finally understood what he was trying to say, or was he glad that she had
been beaten? He was enormously ambivalent about his birth mother; after
all, she'd abandoned him. Only later would he be able to tell us unequivocally that the police had hurt him by taking him to his first foster home.
"frightened to not know anyone there," he'd say, after a policeman had
visited his school to talk about an anti-drug program. So, had DJ been
speaking metaphorically? It's difficult to determine, but the specificity
of the "park" reference suggests that something had happened there with
the police, something distinct from having been escorted to his first foster home, the home where he was savagely attacked. In all likelihood, he
was conflating several events under the associative rubric of the "police."
DJ wasn't terribly respectful of linear thinking, and his trauma had only
exacerbated this proclivity, allowing the past to invade the present. Frequently after hitting us, he'd say that he was "trying to hurt kyle." Once,
he even typed that Kyle had him by the arm: a disconcerting charge in
the context of facilitated communication.

The following night, DJ started in again with his desire to be "free." During the day, he'd had several head-banging episodes that required straddling his chest and immobilizing his head until he calmed down— he was that out of control. "You will be," Emily said. "You are making lots of progress. I know sometimes it might be very hard but you are getting closer."

"try to help," DJ typed.

"Do you want to sleep here in your bed or downstairs?"

"herr"

"Do you want to talk more or go to bed?"

"twakk [talk]"

"What are you thinking about?"

"trying yon gst frse havr some freally scary" Emily knew that he was talking about his nightmares because we'd seen this formulation before. But DJ seemed especially distraught. He was fighting back sobs, asking us to hold his hand.

"Do you want to tell us about them?"

"yred trying to grrt frrere kyle" DJ meant this literally, as he had the previous fall when he believed that Kyle was in his room, under the bed, everywhere in the house. He was extraordinarily agitated.

"Should we stay here until you fall asleep?" I asked.

"yesv please try i really love you"

For months we'd assumed that in expressing a desire to be "free" DJ was referring only to the beating he'd suffered. It was easy enough to appreciate the horror of being pinned down and pummeled by a much bigger thirteen-year-old, even easier to understand the nightmares that would be the legacy of such an attack. But the attack had involved another kind of violation as well, and the very next night DJ finally came out with it. I had been brushing his hair and had accidentally caught one of his curls in the brush, which made him shriek. What ensued was a struggle almost as desperate as the one in the ice skating rink. For nearly ten minutes he thrashed beneath us, kicking, slapping, biting—his face beet red. When we got him calm enough to communicate on the computer, we asked him what had happened?

"i remembered kyle hurting"

"Did Daddy accidentally pull your hair?" Emily asked.

"yes"

"What did you remember?"

"kype is trying to hurt by fuckinhg me" As obvious as it was in retrospect, the possibility of sexual abuse had seemed remote. After all, the doctor who'd examined him following the beating had found no sign of violation. And yet, this doctor had been merely a resident, someone not particularly knowledgeable about issues of male rape. Her inspection of DJ's anus had been cursory at best. When we thought about it, there *had* been plenty of indicators or at least warning signs. For example, the boy who had attacked him was himself the victim of rape at the hands of his father. Moreover, DJ sometimes behaved in a manner suggestive of sexual abuse. Before a bath, he'd lie down on his back with his buttocks in the air and his legs near his head, laughing manically. It was as if he'd been trained to prepare himself for intercourse.

DJ's therapist in Grinnell had even commented on the phone that she thought his obsession with "poking" was sexual. But we had agreed that short of an admission by DJ himself, there was no sense in exploring the topic for fear of putting ideas in his head. We were all aware of the "recovered memory" controversy of the early 1990s: how therapists and investigators had asked questions in a manner that elicited the accusations they desired. And we were all aware of how the facilitated communication movement had become entangled in the recovered memory controversy when allegations of abuse began to surface in the typing of FC users. More than anything perhaps, these charges of sexual abuse, some of which turned out ironically to be true, convinced people that facilitated communication was a hoax. The thing that had most dissuaded me from thinking DJ a victim of sexual abuse was his consistent attention to the beating he had received. Until that day in January, he'd never mentioned anything about sex at all, and though it had felt as if his various communiqués were building to some larger confession, it had been difficult to say what that was. Again, we hadn't wanted to prejudge it.

And so, we were at least smart enough to ask DJ to clarify what he meant by "fucking."

"he was trying to put hois great big pnis in my but," DJ typed.

"We are so very sorry," Emily replied, trying not to seem too disturbed.

"i know"

"You are such a brave, smart kid. We are so fortunate to have you as a son. You make our lives more beautiful than we ever imagined they could be!" I told him. How many times had I wanted to rectify DJ's early life with words, wanting them to be like that comforter we'd wrapped him in the night he came to live with us—the first time, after the beating, when we'd agreed to serve as his emergency shelter providers. How he'd smiled despite his bruises, how he'd wanted to smell the scented fabric over and over. But what words could possibly do that now?

"thsank you for loving me and respecting me and kissing thank you for ignoring my behavioir today," he said adorably, his earnestness breaking our hearts. Ten minutes earlier we had been locked in a death struggle, our pulse rates up; now we were crying, moved by our son's gratitude. Talk about whiplash. Life with DJ was like playing bumper cars at 30 miles an hour in the dark with no seat belts and one very large sadistic demon in a car much bigger than everyone else's.

"You are so terrific," Emily said. "Every night when Mom and Dad go to bed, we say, 'DJ is amazing, isn't he?'"

"please help me to ytry to forget"

"You have made great progress," Emily continued. "Remember when Beth in Cedar Falls talked to you. She said getting out in words what happened is the first step to letting it go."

"try to herlp me let it go"

"We will," I said. "You have gotten out to us what happened. That will help you let it go and move on."

"i hope so," DJ said.

"Do you want to say more of what's on your mind?"

"he hurt me"

That night, after DJ went to sleep, Emily and I talked for hours—reeling from this latest installment in the DJ saga. Was there no end to what this child had suffered? How could Edna Austin have allowed a boy who didn't speak to sleep in a room with another, older boy who had been the victim of sexual abuse? How could she have allowed Kyle to babysit DJ? I wanted to shake that woman. I wanted her to answer for her colossal failure of judgment, her lack of supervision. I wanted to take DCF to task for its complicity in the rape. I was mad all over again at an agency that couldn't do its job and a culture that didn't value social responsibility, that sentimentalized children on the one hand, and allowed them to languish in extraordinary poverty and violence on the other. Six children in one foster home? But no sooner had I begun my familiar tirade than I turned my attention to a more immediate problem: Could we get DJ the help he needed?

We planned to call his two therapists the next day and to conduct a phone consultation with the therapist in Des Moines whom we'd spoken to before and who had more experience working with autistic children. (This woman had thought it unwise to introduce a third therapist into DJ's life and, hence, preferred to counsel us periodically by phone.) As I've already written, a big part of our problem was finding experts who understood the full range of DJ's problems: autism, abandonment, physical (and now sexual) trauma. It was relatively easy to find someone who knew something about any one of these things, perhaps even any two of them, but we needed someone who understood all three, and, more important, who understood their complicated interrelation. We had some terrific people working with us, but they were operating in uncharted territory. Add facilitated communication to the mix and it's a wonder we found any willing therapists in Iowa at all.

Late in our conversation, Emily and I asked each other if DJ might have fabricated the abuse—if somehow he'd heard something and grafted it onto his painful past. We both concluded that, no, he hadn't done this. His profound anxiety seemed to confirm the existence of an additional injury. We'd been working through the beating for months and had sensed something else, however vaguely, behind it. What is more, he rarely if ever lied. Besides, too many of the other circumstantial details now made sense. In the following weeks, DJ would speak repeatedly of having been "fucked by kyle," telling a teacher and a college buddy about

251

the rape—each of them, in the jargon of psychology, a naïve facilitator. In a therapy session, after typing "fucked in but," he confessed that Kyle had also made him "eacht crecavm eatcream." When asked what he might want to tell his attacker, DJ said, "I wish kyle would fuckhimselftvb," adding, "really sorry about my languagejustfreereallyfree."

It's important to know that DJ had never uttered the word "fuck" until the night he first admitted to being abused. In fact, he'd soon tell us that "poking" was his "polite word" for "fucking." Suddenly, the phrases "i cant stop poking" or "poking is bad" took on new and devastating meaning. As if we'd need additional proof of the rape, one day in late March, we'd find him in his room sobbing, gagging, and producing a torrent of saliva. When we'd get him on the computer, he'd type, "couldnt get air couldnt get air." To make sure we understood him, he'd run to the bathroom and grab the hand cream dispenser, hitting the button in an effort to simulate an ejaculation.

Interestingly, of the two times we've caught DJ fibbing, one involved the subject of venereal disease. But rather than casting doubt on the attack, the fib only served to confirm it by exposing an all too logical fear. A local doctor had given the fifth graders a sex ed talk at school, telling them about the dangers of STDs. (Once again, the school had failed to provide us with a crucial heads-up before exposing DJ to such a program.) A few days after the talk, DJ informed us that his "penie and nuts hurt." When we took him to our family doctor, he refused to remove his pants, insisting he was fine. Later, he admitted to having made up his symptoms. When I sat down to speak with DJ, he typed, "vd lingers pokinga. vd makes poking bad."

"What is vd," I asked, checking to make sure he knew.

"vd is fucking disease," he said, then added cryptically, "vd seems like dead freedom" and "yes freedso kyle gave my nuts vd." It was as if Kyle, having been banished to the past, could now attack him inside his body, in his own genital region. The anxiety about venereal disease simply didn't make sense if Kyle hadn't raped him. Eventually, I got DJ to see that his fear was unfounded. "nuts dds bed. free. fine," DJ typed, relieved. I don't know much about the doctor's talk itself, but I find it hard to believe it hadn't come encased in a frightening moralism—just the thing to introduce shame to a highly impressionable fifth grader. "vd makes poking bad."

"So, was DJ experiencing the phenomenon of recovered memory?" a friend of mine asked when I told her about the sexual abuse. I still can't answer this question adequately. I'm not sure I believe in the phenomenon as it was described in its heyday in the 1990s. I do believe in repression, though perhaps not complete repression, and in any event I'm not sure how such a mechanism would operate in somebody with autism. As I indicated earlier, DJ had been diagnosed as autistic at eighteen months. I would want to know how autistic children, who are said to have estranged themselves from the world, experience trauma. Do they experience it differently from other children? What is more, DJ had a prodigious memory and often spoke of remembering things that had happened when he was very little. He remembered teething, for example, as a baby. It was hard to imagine him forgetting anything; indeed, he seemed to be one long string of memories. Admittedly, his memories of the abuse were much less precise, much less competently narrated (and typed), than his more innocuous memories, so perhaps there was something to the idea of "recovery"—laborious, incomplete recovery.

EMDR (Eye Movement Desensitization and Reprocessing), the technique that DJ's therapist in Cedar Falls practiced, purported to be less interested in recovering hidden traumatic memories than intervening in the way that established traumas had been emotionally stored. And yet, the technique itself, which required reproducing the disturbing memories in the therapy session, seemed eerily like some sort of recovery operation. No great believer in the latest psychotherapeutic innovation, I had to admit that the therapist could very quickly get DJ to the point of hysteria and almost as quickly bring him back down, in the process showing him how he might begin to manage his anxieties. (Once, in the middle of a session, he typed, "youre heading for beating lady"; another time he said, "your help hurts".) She had been practicing a version of EMDR with DJ before the admission of abuse and would continue, in a slightly redirected way, afterward—until, that is, she'd be diagnosed with cancer.

Whatever one concluded about DJ's sudden admission of abuse, one had to deal with the fact that he had acquired language belatedly. Can it be a coincidence that his first expressive communication concerned the subject of loss—specifically, his abandonment and beating, which turned out, through some further fall into language and sociality, to have been sexual? Rather than imagining a process of arduous recall, it might be more fruitful to think of DJ finding words for the abuse and thereby producing, creating, the trauma that plagued him. His own narration of trauma propelled him into selfhood, such that the articulation of injury and the birth of the self in language were essentially one and the same. Think of Adam in the Garden of Eden naming the lion as it attacks him. Or, better yet, think of an autistic Adam who awakens to the memory of an attack and commences defending himself. Soon, he is running from the garden and out into the world.

Of course, my analogy overstates the productive nature of the trauma and underestimates the importance of a nurturing environment in encouraging DJ to come join us. The explanation we most frequently encountered about why the abuse had surfaced six years after the fact was that DJ had finally felt safe enough to disclose it, and no doubt this was true, though insufficient as an explanation. It paid no attention to the profound repercussions of having been excluded for so long from language—of literally not being able to tell us. In the Academy Award nominated documentary *Autism Is A World*, Sue Rubin, who was once thought to be mentally retarded and who is now a college student typing entirely on her own, asserts, "As I began to type my mind began to wake up." She even proposes that she *was* mentally retarded until she started typing, the world and its sounds washing over her. "How could my brain lie fallow for thirteen years?" she asks Margaret Baumann, an expert on autism and a professor at Harvard University. (Rubin began using facilitated communication as a teenager.) Baumann hypothesizes that Rubin must have been listening very quietly, storing information, as Sue then puts it, that only became available as information once she began to communicate. How else to account for the speed with which she made up for any intellectual deficits?

And yet, there's a danger in codifying a kind of Rip Van Winkle paradigm, one that ignores both the lack of language before the awakening and the consequences of being "asleep." For example, Doug Biklen has suggested that FC users often seem like child cancer patients, kids who've been in hospitals for years. They appear existentially wise, as deep as the deepest well, but also as narrow experientially. Part of the challenge of full inclusion is addressing this cumulative social deficit, which *can* be addressed but, like the former "sleeping" state, is difficult to conceptualize. There's so much we don't know about the many states that comprise consciousness. New work on comas points to a species of awareness in some who were thought totally unconscious. One woman, who had been in a coma for years, was able, upon awakening, to tell her doctors that the Berlin Wall had come down. Because the television had been left on in her hospital room, bits of information had been able to seep into her brain—to cross, as it were, that analogous divide.

In any event, DJ would say that only once he'd started reading and typing for himself could he make sense of spoken language. All of this had happened, had been happening, in the fourth and fifth grades—as the trauma surfaced. Before that he'd understood little if anything that was said or written to him. In a sense, he organized a self around the enormously disorganizing event of traumatic injury, and you could see this tension, as I've pointed out repeatedly, between organization and disorganization in his accounts of that injury. His syntax and vocabulary would falter; his command of idiom would disappear. His utterances would be fragmentary, cryptically poetic. At times, this struggle took the form of a contest between language of any kind and the less specifically communicative act of aggression and self-injurious behavior. Looking back, I see a pattern: he'd hear something at school—the presentation by the guidance counselor about child abuse or the sex ed talk by the doctor—and he'd lurch into self-awareness, a self-awareness that paradoxically made the self possible. It didn't, in other words, exist in a social sense prior to the discovery of what had happened, or at least hadn't yet been consolidated as a self. I overdo this point in order to emphasize the extraordinary confluence of belated language acquisition and articulated trauma that had been unfolding.

This drive to discover himself in language became visible a few days after we'd learned of the rape when, as he had done previously, DJ asked me anxiously, nervously, to "read your book."

"OK," I said, "but remember that my book is not yet finished. We can read parts of it, if you like."

"you read the part about trying to rescue me," he typed endearingly. It was good to see DJ investing in the notion of rescue, but rescue was never just the end of the story. In his associative matrix it was always intimately connected with injury: you couldn't have one without the other. Indeed, it sometimes seemed a random entry point into the entire tumultuous drama.

"Do you remember hearing Daddy read to Mommy from that part of the book?" I asked.

"yes try to hear every word," he replied. More than ever, I saw how the obsession with my book had contributed to the process of self-creation and only complicated the issue of memory in all of its variously mediated forms. Imagine learning how to read and understand spoken language, at least in part, through a story about yourself, a story written by your adoptive father. It was as if I had authored him—something that made me terribly uncomfortable. We weren't just talking about the thorny issue of who gets to represent whom; we were talking about a kind of traumatic midwifery in which I had played a more prominent role than any parent ideally should. Once it had become clear that DJ could decode spoken language, I'd of course abandoned the habit of reading aloud to Emily the sections I'd written, but before that point DJ had been soaking it all up, and the book had become inexorably implicated in his emergence. When the question had first arisen, we'd decided to allow DJ to read the book—indeed, I'd asked him to write the final chapter and, in so doing, wrest the helm from me—but we'd also thought we'd steer him to passages less inflammatory and disturbing.

Lacanian psychoanalysis speaks of a "symbolic order" or "law of the father" into which every infant must pass (in DJ's case strangely literalized by my book). It's an oedipal scenario in which the child senses the impossibility of reclaiming its mother—the blissful bond it had with her in the womb—and acknowledges, under threat, the need for sexual surrogates. What the child gets for giving up his mother (or, in the case of a girl, first her mother and then her father) is language and the social world it entails. What the child gets is meaning: the *word* for mother or father, the awareness of an "I" whose very desire and facility with language mark his productive alienation. However off-putting the terminology, Lacan suggests a way of thinking about DJ's development: in particular, his profound ambivalence in the face of meaning. "resented being lost," DJ would later tell us, "really resented being found." Found, we might say, by language as much as by us.

Whether one understands autism as a disorder of psychological origin or a neurological problem that makes sociality difficult, it may disrupt the ordinary conscription into the rational law of the father. Ironically, DJ's loss of the mother (what Lacan calls the "imaginary order") could have been further delayed by the literal loss of Rhonda and the need to bond with, and figuratively lose, Emily. Under the right conditions and at the right moment (loving family, means of communicating, puberty) sexual trauma might have provided, strangely enough, just the shock to forge himself in language. As any book on childhood sexual trauma will tell you, puberty for abuse victims is a time of intense confusion, when the prospect of sexual pleasure runs full bore into the memory of violation, which might itself have been, in part, pleasurable. Pleasure becomes, in short, a highly problematic category.

My intention isn't to leave the neurological behind, or to consign it to the role of initial disturbance, but to insist on some description, however unscientific, of a mind in the field of life, which is to say the field of desire and the various objects and events that constitute the field. The translation of the neurobiological into the psychoanalytic allows for the possibility of contributing factors to the phenomenon we call autism. Even more important, it provides an analytical framework, awkward and reductive in its own way, for deciphering, treating, and honoring complex behavior. Tell me all you want about brain function in people with autism, and I'll request an account of the dramatic performances their brains make possible.

For Lacan, poetic language nostalgically harkens back to a presymbolic realm of undifferentiated, unnamed existence. Bending the rules of syntax and usage, establishing figurative (that is, illogical) connections, it searches for the sweet oblivion we have all lost. In DJ's case, a wild penchant for poetic thinking could be understood as indicating at once an incomplete conscription into the symbolic order and a sign of aggravated trauma. Perhaps what we were witnessing with DJ, then, was the strange telescoping of two crucial moments: his delayed departure from the imaginary order and the working out of the problem of pleasure. Even as he was parachuting into language, he was refusing to assume fully a subject position in the realm of difference, a realm that distinguished him from every other subject, but especially his mother(s) and his attacker.

"Why do autists use language the way they do?" Karen Zelan asks. "Many of their utterances seem essentially poetic." I take this detour through admittedly abstruse psychoanalytic material in order to try to answer this question with respect to DJ and, as important, to lay out the predicament that would consume Emily and me for the next year. DJ's associative thinking would make it exceedingly difficult to disattach the rape from his own burgeoning sexuality. In a therapy session, he would complain, "kyle is in my underwear." When his therapist took him to mean that Kyle had touched his penis, DJ would type, "no kyle my erection." In effect, DJ would have sewn Kyle onto his own body, confusing the instrument that hurt him with the one that could give him sexual satisfaction.

Working to curb this associative impulse would be complicated by DJ's identification with me as a poet. "treating me really great blike true poet," he'd type one day in February after I'd read him one of my poems and worked with him on one of his. I didn't want to discourage his passionate interest in poetry, especially as it allowed us to deepen our bond. But DJ was a poet 60–70% of the time; he needed to be a poet no more than, say 10–20% of the time. He needed to be in the world, in the symbolic order, if you will, no matter how disturbing he found it. I had to be careful about being too impressed with what he was writing. And it *was* impressive; his analogical capacity consistently astonished. He knew that

I valued this kind of thinking, and it was ironic that I often had to work very hard to locate that part of my brain that could write poems. Here, my son was like some sort of poetic Midas: everything he touched turned to metaphor or metonymy, but it was tinged with sadness and extraordinary hurt. In reflecting on how I've written this book—my own penchant for poetic thinking—I like to imagine that I've met DJ a quarter of the way. But I make it seem as if immediately following his admission of abuse we had a handle on what we were up against. We distinctly did not.

A couple of days after the admission, DJ typed, "i really feel scared when try ton get freev and can't."

"DJ, it takes a while to get free," Emily said. "You are making lots of progress. You told us something very important and scary two days ago. You need to keep writing your thoughts down. Very soon you will feel better. OK?"

"in feel so really really trying," he responded.

"Do you want to talk to us about what is making you really scared? Try to be specific."

"i tryu to get free but i i i head to your front door really really scsared"

"Are you talking about the times you would visit us and we would bring you back to Edna Austin's house? Are you telling us you tried to say you didn't want to go back there because Kyle was doing those things to you?"

"yes v," DJ said. Emily had always felt guilty about enabling DJ's beating in his first foster home. She had wept at the thought of him not being able to communicate, not being able to save himself. Now she—we—felt even worse.

"Had we known that was happening, we would have gotten you out of there immediately. We didn't know. When you were beaten, we made sure you got out of there. Do you understand?"

"yes"

"Mommy and I promised ourselves that we would teach you how to communicate," I added, "so that never again would you be trapped in a bad situation."

"i know"

"How long was Kyle doing those things to you?"

"long," DJ replied.

"We are very, very sorry that that happened and that we didn't know," Emily said. I could tell from the look on her face that she was internally crucifying herself. She'd been able to withstand DJ's horrific treatment of her that first year—all of the kicking, biting, and scratching—by remembering that she's been the one who'd deposited him in Edna's living room, sometimes even handing him over to Kyle. Of course, he'd resented her. Of course he'd needed to determine if he could trust her. But now more heartbreaking than DJ's merciless aggression was, she realized, his reasoned investigation into our failure to protect him.

"please be proud of me ploease," he typed.

"DJ, we are so very proud of you. You are an amazingly brave, clever, strong boy. Soon you will feel better. You will see that you were able to get yourself to a safe place with people who understand and respect and love you very much."

"i know"

"There are other people who have experienced what you have. You are not alone. People learn through therapy to heal, to get better, to be free."

"i know," DJ repeated.

"So, you have to try to be patient. Therapy takes a while. There will be good moments and bad moments but eventually you will be completely free. But you must continue to type out what happened." At this point, we hadn't yet confronted the problem of encouraging a child with perseverative tendencies to focus on—even obsess about—his trauma. We were simply beginning the standard process of therapy, a process that would later have to be adapted for the peculiarities of an autistic boy. Whether, in the end, DJ's memory of sexual trauma rocketed him into social selfhood or he simply arrived there once we'd figured out how to teach him to read and given him a means to communicate, the fact is that a therapeutic foregrounding of trauma would have a profound effect on the way he conceived of—that is, constituted—himself. It wouldn't be long before we all felt stuck. The more DJ would speak of "trying to get free," the more it would seem impossible: the mere desire, expressed in language, ironically condemning him to imprisonment. "As I began to type, my mind began to wake up"—into trauma, into that controlling narrative. Toward the end of the school year, DJ would even refer to himself as "the kide inlove with hurt," as if indicating his own awareness of the problem of constructing a self in trauma. Our job would be to make possible a self outside of trauma, which would be no small feat.

In response to Emily's exhortation to get what had happened out, DJ typed, "ploking."

"Poking hurt you very much. It must have been very, very scary."

"poking is poking ypou just you judt forgdet," DJ said.

"Are you saying that poking is something you are trying to forget?"

"yers"

"But sometimes you must first remember a bad thing in order to forget it. Does that make sense?"

"no"

"The idea is to write down what happened so that you get it out of your brain. You learn to talk about it and not feel bad. Soon you just forget it and move on."

"i know ki toldf ykiu what hsopenef"

"Is there anything else you need to tell us about that?"

"no"

"Is there anything making you feel nervous right now?"

"urs [yes]"

"What is it?"

"the big kids tryibg to push." We were back to the original associative trigger. We came up with a plan to have DJ negotiate the halls at a less crowded time, but in a way it seemed pointless. He was in a school with hundreds of kids the age and size of Kyle. How could we shield him from every thirteen-year-old in Grinnell? Should we even try?

As the days passed, DJ returned to the subject of Emily having delivered him into the arms of his attacker. One afternoon, we caught him banging his joints on the corner of the dining room table. "Why are you doing that?" I asked.

"i want to hurt myself becauser i rwas beaten i ready to frede" His response was obviously contradictory. How could he be ready to be free if he was set on injuring himself, which is exactly the question that Emily posed.

"you hutrt," DJ said.

"What did Mom do to hurt you?" Emily inquired, pretty sure of what he'd say but also cognizant of the fact that DJ lived in a world of hurt and imagined, as it were, enemy combatants everywhere. "you hurt my feelings" was one of his favorite sayings, and it could be applied to just about anything.

"you took me to efnasd [Edna]"

"Do you remember why Mom used to pick you up and drop you off at Edna's?"

"yes you mtoolk me to see rhonds," DJ typed.

"You are right. The law said that you had to live with Edna and visit Rhonda. I agreed to drive you back and forth because Dad and I wanted to see you."

"i know that"

"How do you feel about the fact that I used to take you back and forth before I was your Mom?" Emily asked.

"it really makes me mad beecause i relly tried to tell you i truied that i was hurt i tried"

"I am so incredibly sorry that I didn't understand back then."

"plolice were resally killing," DJ said.

"Who?"

"me," he replied.

"What did they do?" Emily asked, again trying to get him to clarify how the police had hurt him.

"they took trryd"

"DJ, I did try many times when you lived at Edna's to convince the Department of Children and Families that her home was not a good place for you, that there were too many children there and not enough supervision, and that the rabbits and cats made it very hard for you to breathe and hear."

"with you i really wabted to live but nyoum really urt me by not really trying to get md out of her house" DJ was very upset; it had taken him a good two minutes to type that statement. He had signed "all done, all done" several times before finishing and had reached once for Emily's eyes.

"DJ, I can see why you might think that and why you might be angry about it. I really did try to get the Department to move you, but they kept insisting that her home was one of the better places for kids to live. Of course, it's obvious now that they were wrong about that."

"i really wanted to live with you," DJ typed. I thought of the time he'd said—unforgettably—that we'd "forgottyn to adpt him," and I wanted to cry. While Emily's explanation was technically correct, our decision to adopt DJ evolved more slowly than DJ's needs demanded. At the time, we were still constrained by our attempts to help Rhonda regain custody, but we could have agreed to become his foster parents. That fact ate away at us as DJ made it apparent where from the beginning he'd wanted to live.

"I am very glad to hear that," Emily said. "I am sorry if it took a long time and a lot of advocating to make that happen. How did you feel about going to visit Rhonda?" Emily was trying to draw him out, remaining amazingly calm.

"i really hated her because she beat me up," DJ answered. Beat him up? How many times could this boy shock us? We knew that Rhonda had been emotionally cruel to him, but we didn't know that she'd been violent as well—though can we really claim to have been shocked by anything in DJ's life? We'd found out that Rhonda had lost five children to the State, and we knew that she'd beaten Ellie, so why not a little violence toward DJ thrown in on the side? I was starting to tire of our innocence.

"I'm so sorry," Emily replied. "I was more naïve back then. Rhonda tried to convince me that she really could care for you and Ellie, and I thought she meant it. I knew that Ellie was really important to you, and I wanted you two to be reunited if at all possible."

"i know"

"It took a long time for it to be possible for us to adopt you. Daddy honestly talked to the people at the Department of Children and Families every day for over a year, trying to speed up the process."

"i know," DJ said again.

In the midst of this period of turbulent rehashing, DJ, as part of a school assignment, wrote Emily a letter of gratitude.

Dear Mom,

Thank you for all of the things that you do for me. Thank you for the love that you give me. I really owe you alot for everything that you have done. I brought you so much hurt. I brought you so much wild emotions. Thank you for making me so happy.
Love, DJ.

His eternal frankness and idiosyncratic way with language always lifted our spirits. DJ was moving out into the world, reckoning with his behavior, taking notice of other people's needs—or at least beginning to. More than that he was building a relationship with his parents in words: not only seeking answers to the questions he had but finding in language the story of himself, a story, as I suggested earlier, complicated by his father's unwitting, though nonetheless priestly, imposition of THE WORD: the Gospel According to Ralph—or, as DJ calls me, Dad. But there were other gospels, Gnostic gospels, long suppressed, and DJ would continue to discover his right to challenge the official narrative and, in the process, become the author of his own story.

In early April, he would obsessively type on the computer that Mom seemed sad, graduating to the notion that Mom seemed "hurt." "You have talked about thinking Mom is hurt. What do you think hurt Mom?" Emily would ask.

"read the book," DJ would reply.

"I don't know what you're referring to," Emily would say.

"you were sadd because you had been hurt by not having children." DJ had clearly heard the chapter where I discuss our initial decision not to have children but he had missed the part about *deciding* not to have them, or maybe he just wanted to hear how we had changed our minds, how we had chosen him. We could have had our "own children" (the worst locution in the world, as far as I'm concerned), but we had wanted him: the boy who signed "more." The boy who had filled our hearts with love beyond bursting. Picture brightly colored helium balloons painting the horizon, floating above the hills of central Iowa. Can we be this full? Can we go this high?

"I see," Emily said. "Do you understand that Mom had chosen not to have children? Some women get very sad because they try and try to have a baby and their bodies don't let them. That wasn't the case with Mom. I made a decision not to have a baby. Then when I met you, I realized how nice it could feel to really care about a child and help and watch them grow. You taught me something I didn't know about myself."

"how hurt really," DJ typed. He was obsessed with hurt, both projecting it onto, and genuinely finding it in, those for whom he cared. The story Emily was telling him, I couldn't help but think, was *her* recovery from rape, a rape she'd suffered on a ferry to Sweden in her early twenties, when she'd answered a knock on her cabin door and a man had forced his way in. After he finished, he strangled her, leaving her—he thought—for dead. Unable to gather her wits on the boat, she never made a report or filed charges, simply lugging this horror back to England and then later to the States. An extremely private person (who has sanctioned this telling), she somehow moved forward into a life of helping others, transforming her own pain, I want to say, by reaching out beyond it. Although she'd never explicitly connected the assault with her decision not to have kids, they suddenly seemed, at least in part, related. And so a circle of sorts, a circle of healing, began to close.

"It was like this," Emily continued. "I met you. I realized how nice it feels to really care about and care for a child. Then, I also realized that earlier in life before I met you, I was missing that wonderful feeling that only a parent and child can share."

"you read my mind," DJ said.

"Sometimes it feels like that, doesn't it? Sometimes I feel like you can read my mind, too."

"im happy," DJ replied.

265

CHAPTER 10

Buttoned-up Shirts

With DJ, the old adage "two steps forward, one step back" had to be revised. It was more like "twenty-six steps forward, twenty-five steps back." Just when you thought he'd mastered some insecurity, it would return with a vengeance, and along with it poking, head-banging, screaming at the top of his lungs. Over and over, he'd tell us, "i want to try to fitrgey" (forget) or "trying to grt free." We'd practice the EMDR procedure of attaching a pleasant thought—such as being at the beach—to an unpleasant memory, and it would work well enough to make you always want to try it, but not well enough to solve the problem. It was difficult to determine when DJ was upset about his past and when he was simply obsessing about some random object or routine. He loved to wet his hair and watch the drops of water hit the floor; he also loved to stim at moving fans, letting his arousal level reach epic heights. The latter would turn out to have psychological meaning, as he'd eventually tell us that there had been a fan in his room at Edna Austin's, a fan he stared at while Kyle raped him. For years, we'd assumed it was just one of those autistic things. (One day, when I asked him about his fan obsession, he actually typed, "it takes my hurt to heaven.") Beyond the rather obvious speculation that the obsessive-compulsive aspects of autism exacerbated the repetition compulsion of trauma, we never could get a fix on the relationship between these two conditions. But boy did we see repetition—some of it meaningful, some of it apparently not.

Not too long after telling us about the rape, DJ began to say to his college buddies, who were all women, "go" in sign, right after they'd arrived to do some sort of fun activity with him. One night, Sabrina asked him what was his favorite thing to do in the morning when he woke up, and DJ responded, "i am hard." Another night, he tried to kiss Sabrina, not just once but repeatedly. When she tried to get him to stop, he became very agitated. Afterward, DJ informed us that he had "poked Sabrina." "she told me no treating her badly."

"What were you doing?" I asked.

"i was kissing her and she really wanted me to stop."

"Why were you doing it?"

"trying to really say i lik you. rsally like person who kisses"

"You can't just kiss someone against their will," I said. "You have to be invited to kiss someone who isn't family, and you have to respect their wishes."

"trying to fgure ou girl," DJ replied. And indeed he was trying to figure out girls, trying to do so in the context of what had happened to him and the new pleasurable feelings his body was allowing. It all made him terribly anxious, and so he would just sign "go" the second any of his buddies showed up. When they tried playfully to ignore his command, he'd poke them. It was as if girls had become synonymous with poking.

This same associative anxiety manifested itself in the area of facilitated communication. One day, DJ overheard Emily saying to a teacher that she "would love to be able to just go so that he could communicate on his own." DJ, unfortunately, took Emily to mean that she didn't want to be his mother. "i am mad because you want to ger rid of mr," he typed, profoundly upset.

"Why do you think that?" Emily asked, unaware of how her statement could have been misinterpreted. When he didn't answer, I asked the question again.

"because mom wants me to type onm my own," DJ said. He had clearly zeroed in on the phrase "on my own" and panicked. I could see where we were headed.

"Why do you think we want you to type on your own?" I asked.

"because yoiu want me tio please yku [you]," he replied.

"We want you to be able to choose to have conversations privately with your friends if you want to. We will always be with you. So you don't have to worry. We will NEVER get rid of you, even if you grow up. We will always be a family."

"you try to just hurt my feelinhteb," DJ said.

"Who?" I asked.

"mom becauseb she thinks i look great trying to type on my ownop;"

"Does that scare you?"

"yes becaysevv im used to holding real pure"

"What does that mean, DJ?"

"ij ill be alone," he answered. One of the first things he had ever typed on the computer was a sentence about being "all alone" in foster care. You could see him equating independence with abandonment and, thus, he wanted no part of it. This particular associative link would end up tormenting us, as DJ intensely resisted all kinds of invitations to be more independent. He'd now make up for an imposed maturity at the age of three with an elective immaturity at the age of eleven. He'd go backwards as this self of his continued to emerge and develop, needing to experience the separation anxiety of a much younger child. A separation anxiety, I should say, weirdly literalized by the Siamese-like requirements of facilitated communication. What, I remember wondering, would Lacan—or any psychoanalytic theorist, for that matter—say about the intimacy of such a cooperative arrangement, especially when the arrangement involved mother and child? What would he say about this kind of separation anxiety?

"DJ," Emily said, "we will never force you to type alone. But it will be a good thing to know how to do in case at some time in the future you decide that you want to. OK?"

"yes"

"Just think about it. When you talk to Dad, you don't necessarily hold his finger but he's right there." More often than not, when the three of us had a conversation, Emily would facilitate. She'd been his first facilitator, and he naturally gravitated toward her.

"ikm nervous because im not ready," DJ said plainly.

Marilyn Chadwick, of the Facilitated Communication Institute, has remarked on the paradoxical status of FC with respect to the obvious goal of independence for any person with a disability. "Dependency forms relationships," she explained when I interviewed her in Syracuse. "FC users want to be independent, but they fear losing relationships." I think this notion is crucially important for understanding the phenomenon of facilitated communication. The requirement of another person's physical engagement for communication produces social-emotional benefits that anybody who was thought dumb for years and pushed off into the corner would be loath to give up. The social stigma of disability, particularly cognitive disability, creates a tangible barrier that FC transcends. All of us, I would say, whether disabled or not, are dying to be touched; it's hard to quantify the benefits of such touching, though the work of Stanley Greenspan and others, Chadwick contends, reveals the extent to which learning in young children is driven by feeling. Greenspan famously recommends "floor time"—meeting the child where she is—as a therapeutic technique for children with apparent intellectual and affective deficits. My own experience head-butting with DJ, then wrestling and tickling with him, seems to confirm the efficacy of such an approach, as does the innovative OT he received from his beloved Angie. Might FC be an extension of this principle—call it "arm time"?

Of course, the downside of celebrating facilitated (rather than independent) communication is the aggressive suspicion of the method's detractors. It's hard to overstate the hostility that greeted FC in the early nineties—what with the *Frontline* documentary, *Prisoners of Silence*, that declared the phenomenon officially a hoax (and continues to serve as its definitive repudiation for those unaware of recent developments). To this day, the American Psychological Association labels FC "unproven," though there are now nearly as many studies supporting the technique as debunking it. By necessity, Biklen and his group have had to devote themselves to a practice they call "withdrawing support," where the facilitator fades as quickly as possible, moving from the hand to the wrist to the elbow to the shoulder and, then, depending on the person, to standing behind or beside the individual typing. Put simply, the farther away from the hand, the less likely the chance of facilitator influence. The Italians promoting FC have been particularly insistent about achieving independence with FC users, pragmatically believing that they will need to function by themselves in society.

In the last ten years, Biklen has made a number of videos showing people typing mostly or entirely on their own. I mentioned Sue Rubin earlier, but there's also Jamie Burke, whose mother touches his shoulder; Lucy Harrison, whose facilitator very lightly touches her shoulder; Larry Bissonnette, whose facilitator places a hand firmly on his shoulder; Kelvin Washington, whose facilitator intermittently pulls his shirt in the elbow area; Philip Ramirez, whose father regularly taps his leg; Sharisa Kochmeister, whose facilitator keeps a hand about a foot above her arm. At the age of twelve, Kochmeister was said to have an IQ of 10; by the time she was a teenager it was 142. Why such minimal facilitation remains necessary or how exactly it works is finally anybody's guess. All of the above-mentioned FC users began with help at the hand and at various rates progressed to where they are now. Interestingly, in the face of such evidence, FC's detractors have refused to budge, declaring such cases anomalies or, worse, suggesting that the persons typing were still somehow being manipulated or that they weren't really disabled to begin with.

If I have emphasized a psychological understanding of FC over the strictly neurological understanding (autism as dyspraxia) I advanced earlier, it's because DJ's own understanding of FC changed, became more complex. We had experimented with providing less support for DJ by moving back to the wrist, but DJ had vehemently opposed this move, and we had decided not to push him; we knew he could do it, as our attempts proved more or less successful. There were lots of typos, but you could clearly ascertain what he was trying to say. When asked how reading was going during this period following the admission of abuse, DJ again indicated problems with motor planning and body awareness. "it ihs hard you have poimjt on your own so i gdt frustrated," he told us. DJ read by running his finger across the page: an activity he seemed willing to try by himself.

"Do you ever know the correct answer but then your finger points at a different one?" Emily asked. "Is it hard to get your hand or finger in motion without someone else touching you?" she persisted.

"no," DJ replied. It's important to remember that DJ had been pointing for years. It was one of the first things we taught him, however laboriously, so his present response didn't entirely rule out some sort of activation disorder—like the kind Tito speaks about in his book *The Mind Tree*, where he understands perfectly well what his mother is asking him to do but he can't figure out how to make his body do it. DJ frequently complained about not being able to feel his body or, conversely, about hypersensitivity to touch, taste, sound, etc. When he first came to live with us, he couldn't determine how to walk around a jungle gym.

"So, why do you prefer to hold on to someone's hand or finger when you type or point?"

"it help me because i have hyjeractbve hyperactive jumki [jumping?]," he said somewhat cryptically. DJ seemed to be suggesting a problem of sensory coordination. Imagine an air traffic controller frantically trying to regulate the body O'Hare or Hartsfield. Imagine the stress. Perhaps facilitation grounded and calmed this ulcer-ridden controller. Donna Williams, a famous Autist, writes of "systems forfeiting" to describe the impossibility of fully integrating operative modes of sensory input. And yet, DJ's original statement contained the phrase "on your own," and that notion had already become a bugaboo for him. Over and over, he'd conflate the idea of independent communication with being abandoned again or having Emily die. Looking back through the notebooks of our conversations during this period, I find multiple examples of such an associative conflation. Thus, perhaps we need in our interpretive analysis to allow "psychology [to] join neurology," in the words of Karen Zelan. We need to see how DJ was trying to bond with Emily exactly as he was trying to separate from her and fearing, as eleven-year-olds tend to do, his mother's death. And he was doing a good deal of this through the issue of facilitated communication!

"i get scared about you leaving," DJ would start, then move to "uui worry that fry try to leave me" and "ypu possibly might die oine day." Frequently, he would bring up death out of the blue—or, rather, in customary DJ fashion, in the middle of having fun. Once, while rollerskating he asked for a break in sign in order to type, "going to really miss you when you die." For a while, "you might die" seemed to have supplanted "poking is bad" as his favorite mantra, though references to poking fill the pages of the notebooks as well. When he'd say "you might leave me" and Emily would answer, "You know I would never leave you," he'd reply, "you might die." He was stuck on loss, obsessively guarding himself against the future, which he called "great places"—from the Dr. Seuss book *Oh, the Places You'll Go!* If there's any book, other than the one you're presently reading, that's had too great an influence on DJ, it's this one, which his college buddies would regularly read with him. The book begins with a drawing of a boy alone headed off into the future and the following rhymed quatrain: "Congratulations!/ Today is your day./ You're off to Great Places!/ You're off and away!" You can see how this word-picture combination might terrify DJ. A solitary boy "off and away"? Yikes!

One afternoon, after a session with his therapist in Cedar Falls, Emily told DJ how proud she was of what he had been able to talk about: namely, independence. "you great hurt just to really hedar yoiu feel proud"

"Why did it hurt to hear that?" Emily asked.

"because hurts great plsces"

"What hurts great places?"

"you trying tio help"

"What great places are hurt?"

"looking trtrying"

"Are you saying that Mom is helping too much?"

"yeds," DJ replied, though he had begun the conversation by suggesting that Emily had hurt him by being proud of his willingness to think about independence.

"In what ways should I help less?"

"typing"

"Are you saying that you're thinking about wanting to type on your own sometime?"

"yesb"

"OK. That is your decision."

"i'm nrevous you ready to hurt loom pldase you" DJ was getting upset, and sure enough both his typing and his syntax had worsened.

"DJ, you please us incredibly all the time just by being you and growing and loving. When you want to type on your own is your decision. I am extremely pleased with how well you are communicating and writing and typing now. It doesn't matter to me when you decide to type on your own."

"ok"

"What did you think about Sarah [his therapist in Grinnell] saying that you want to be independent from me but that sort of scares you?"

"you try to gether you try to understand your role," DJ said insightfully.

"Do you understand and believe that Mom and Dad will always be there for you, as Grandy and Bop are there for us?"

"yes"

"Do you sometimes wish you could spend the afternoon with a couple of friends without me or Dad there, or not really?" Emily added that last phrase when she noticed that DJ had become anxious.

"you hurt my feelings," DJ announced with his customary emotional punctuality.

"Why?" Emily asked.

"you really want to tryb to let me grtow," he replied. You could see his deep ambivalence about this topic, as he swerved in one direction and then another, like someone overcorrecting on ice.

"Why does that hurt your feelings? I still want us to spend time together too, skating and having fun."

"i love you," DJ said.

"I love you too very much. All kids spend time with their families and time with their friends. You don't have to choose one or the other. Do you realize that?"

"yes"

"Did you feel Sarah was treating you with respect?"

"yes"

"Good. Did she say anything you thought was incorrect?

"6es"

"What?"

"reagy to grow up trying"

"So you thought she was wrong about that?"

"yes" DJ was again very anxious.

"Why are you upset?"

"you you try to get me to grow up," he replied.

We'd have a version of this conversation seemingly every day, with references to Kyle sprinkled in here and there. That weekend, while we waited for the rollerskating rink to open, DJ, after saying to Emily for the thousandth time, "yolu mighth dkieg," announced that he was "nervous about you trying to free me." I remember sitting in the living room and having something of a eureka moment: it was the first time he had used the word "free" in conjunction with the ideas of independence and independent communication. He had previously reserved that word for Kyle and all of his horrible memories from the past. I knew that Kyle had called DJ "fucking freaky" while he raped him, and I feared that DJ's mind was doing what it did best: conflating things. He seemed to be connecting the trauma with facilitated communication and indicating an unwillingness to leave either behind, as if the help we offered were the guarantee of continued parenting. "kyle got me by the arm," DJ said on more than one occasion. Further, DJ seemed to be connecting the trauma with his disability, as if the former had caused the latter. "Possibly I still can talk," he'd say during this period. Later in the spring he'd type such pessimistic things as "freak is ready for bed" or "people treat me like dead freak." The danger here, beyond the danger of not being able to accept and even celebrate his neurological difference, was that of clinging to the past, remaining inside this hall of mirrors.

In that Saturday conversation, DJ quickly took to telling Emily she looked "hurt" and "tired." We'd all been up half the night, as DJ had been awakened by something and could not fall back asleep, so Emily did look tired. "you try to free yourself from you sedfrtv," he typed.

"Can you say that another way?" Emily asked.

"seftyh," he said.

"I don't know what that is," Emily replied. But I thought I did. DJ was again projecting his condition onto the world around him. He seemed to be imagining that Emily needed to free herself from something. Could that something, that mysterious word, be "self"? Could DJ have recognized that the self he'd formed was a self that couldn't, almost by definition, move forward? As I've mentioned before, he'd later refer to himself as "the kide inlove with hurt." And so, if DJ wanted, at least in part, to be free of himself and had projected onto Emily a similar desire, then the thing that Emily wanted to be free of was him, was DJ. DJ as the embodiment of all pain and suffering, including parental fatigue. And this made him upset in a circular and associative sort of way. Of course, DJ had an entirely unrealistic idea of freedom—to the extent that he imagined being freed from trauma, autism, childhood, perhaps even consciousness itself. And maybe we should throw in marriage as well; after all, he was talking of Emily freeing herself, and for him that concept meant losing family. We obviously needed to get him to be less ambitious philosophically, psychologically.

In response to Emily's statement about not understanding what he had meant, he typed, "reaskn you want to leavre."

"DJ," she replied, "I do not want to leave here. I love being with you and with Dad."

"you youre yourr trying to get rud of mde you reakly"

"DJ, that simply is not true. I love spending time with you. I love watching you have fun and learn and grow."

"you wahnt me to type," he said.

"DJ, I don't care when and if you learn to type on your own if you don't want to," Emily explained, exasperated. "I know that what you type now are your own thoughts, ideas, and feelings."

"you hirt," DJ replied.

The very next day, we found him falling on the floor in the kitchen. "What are you doing?" I asked.

"i'm tryin g to feel my bodytv," he responded.

"Have you had difficulty feeling your body for a long time?" Emily inquired.

"hyes"

"Do you sometimes feel your body and sometimes not?"

"yesbn"

"Do you feel your body better when you touch someone or someone touches you?"

"yes"

"Is that part of why you like to hold on to someone's finger when you type or point?"

"yes" We seemed to be back to the neurological understanding of independent typing—until, that is, DJ remarked, "you really want men tlo type on my own"

"Not if you're having trouble feeling your body and holding on to someone's finger helps you," Emily said.

"i killedb you," DJ replied, giving both of us pause. We'd clearly left the land of neurology and had crossed the border into psychology. I could see snow-capped mountains and darkly wooded forests.

"You killed me?" Emily asked.

"yes"

"What do you mean by that?"

"i plitted toi kiol [plotted to kill]"

"Why?"

"you hurth njust by talking," he explained.

"What do you mean? I hurt your feelings just by having a conversation with you?"

"yes because you try to make me free hurt." It was certainly an odd solution to the problem of independence—to kill the person you feared losing most of all—but maybe the fantasy constituted progress. The conversation proceeded like this until DJ said, "you try to treat me like evdryobe else."

"Why shouldn't I?" Emily asked rhetorically. "You are just as smart and capable as everyone else." I can't tell you how many times DJ had requested that we treat him "like everyone else"; he hated being thought of as disabled. So, there we were giving him what he had requested, but he didn't want it—or at least he wasn't sure he wanted it. But unlike other conversations, this one ended with something of a compromise.

"i try to get free you try," DJ said.

"You think we should try together?" Emily clarified.

"yes," DJ replied. And though it wasn't exactly clear what "trying together" meant, if DJ needed to think of "getting free" as a mutual activity, one that he could partly control, then that was fine with us. We certainly didn't want to mandate independent typing. As with the earlier example of DJ having projected "hurt" onto Emily, it may also have been the case that he needed to think of each of them as struggling to get free: he from his end, she from hers, in a kind of psychophysiological tug-of-war. When looking at Emily facilitating with DJ, you often couldn't tell where she concluded and he began. This perception wouldn't have been entirely off the mark, as Emily, having given up her full-time job when we moved to Iowa, had indeed begun to lose herself in the admittedly all-encompassing experience of raising, and fully including in a regular school, a child with a cognitive disability. No ordinary child with a cognitive disability, mind you, but one who had suffered horrific abuse and who had spent a good part of the previous year experiencing flashbacks. It would take all of us a while to figure out how to strike a better balance.

Related to his habit of associatively conflating things was DJ's penchant for using school assignments to work through the past. I've mentioned his remarkable prairie dog acrostic, where he took what was intended to be rather happy-go-lucky material about prairie dog populations and turned it into a brutal allegory of social and familial violence. I've also mentioned DJ's *Titanic* response, where he reminded his peers of the importance of class consciousness when studying history by telling them that he was a "poor person once." In a book report on oceanic pollution, DJ declared that pollution "is my real great place." His teacher, of course, had no idea what that meant until we clued her in to his profound anxiety about the future. "you just need to try going to the beach because it'll be gone one day," DJ wrote. In a unit on the brain, he put his head in his lap and cried, wondering why he had to have been born with one that "didnt work."

Sometimes such personal references were both less explicit and more optimistic. In response to a question about the Mayflower pilgrims— "How did the boy and his Dad feel looking at their settlement?"—DJ wrote, "Thegvv felt that theyc not going back, but they might like it in their new settlement. Theyt really proud of what they had survivsd. They had survived terruble storms, bad people, and the cold winter. They were glad to have friends in the Indians." I find it impossible not to see in this answer a former foster child's identification with the uprooted settlers. One of the craziest things about DJ was that he loved social studies—this despite the endless stories of hardship, discrimination, and violence that so characterize American history. His love seemed part masochistic obsession and part therapeutic rehashing. At the end of the school year, he'd write his social studies teacher a thank-you letter.

> Dear Mrs. Cooper,
>   Youre my favorite teacher. You read your notes to me. youy treatb me not like i'm great in social studies but lik independent. try to kill kyle in your class because he hurt me and you gave me confidence that i look normal. youre ready to have me in your clazsds on my own.
>   Love,
>   DJ

This letter would demonstrate unambiguously the way that DJ conceived of social studies as an arena in which to confront his past. He imagined a saga of struggle and survival whose climax would be independence: not needing his aide, his facilitator, in the classroom. I would again be struck by the link between sexual injury and disability; DJ somehow believed that if he could become independent—if he could kill Kyle—he would no longer be autistic. He would be normal or at least "look normal." From the available associative materials, including his favorite teacher's faith in his abilities, DJ had fashioned an entire universe.

Perhaps no single assignment better captured the process I'm talk-ing about than DJ's "Alaska" poem, written in February in response to a unit on the Iditarod. The poem goes like this:

ALASKA

hours of light like heat hibernate
great icebergs hear the cries of the hurt
just like they're trying really, really to be free
the trees hurt their great places, they lose
their treasures, their lying leaves tread. freed from there
branches they try to yearn freedom but they fear it.
trying to get freed points out their great
hurt yearning long, long branches that live
forever then they have to let go
your hand trying to go

The poem takes a few facts he had learned—winters without sunshine, the calving of icebergs—and has them serve the drama of his burgeon-ing independence. It very quickly forgets the assignment; as his teacher pointed out, the poem doesn't even mention the Iditarod. What it does do—besides establishing at the beginning an exquisite analogy between light and bears and calving icebergs and "hurt" people—is to stage the problem of separation as one confronting the natural world: through the primary metaphor of the trees in autumn. Literary critics call this kind of analogical operation the pathetic fallacy, and it's a staple of English and American poetry. The leaves that "yearn freedom" clearly stand in for DJ, and the "branches that live forever" for his facilitator. I say "facilitator" because the last line makes clear the extent to which the poem is all about facilitated communication. We wouldn't have any idea of the personal significance of the tree metaphor—its status as a kind of private symbol—until he'd write a poem called "Rescue," where the trees in spring and summer have the power to save him from the horrors of foster care. Who precisely the "you" is in this poem is un-clear. Perhaps it's Emily or me; perhaps it's Ellie. Perhaps it's God.

i look each time i get the chance
to watch you in the trees
i try going to heaven
three times heaven
three each tree
trees rescue me from earth not
policemen
turning their leaves they lose their
power
rescue in before the fall
the free

After DJ wrote "Rescue," I asked him if this was why he grew so depressed each fall when the trees began to lose their leaves—indeed, why he hated raking leaves and stacking firewood. "yes dead freedom trees getting hurt," he said. A few days later, upset that he wasn't able to see me enough (I was working especially hard), he responded to Emily's suggestion that they list things he loved about Dad by typing, "greatforfreeing mee from fostercare, is dreaming of really heartfelt thoughts, is great because gets trees." When Emily later showed me the list, I recalled that he'd once described me as "really gifteed because brings great ideas together," and I wondered how much I'd encouraged the favorite pastime of our curly-haired analogical machine. In addition to "the book," he'd heard me read countless poems to Emily, and so it isn't too much of an exaggeration to say that he'd been receiving poetic instruction for years. In June, DJ would refer to me directly as his "sad tree" and would exclaim to Emily that she "wanted her love to heal him." He'd seem, throughout this period, the oddly agreeable hostage of some foreign power, one in which the parties of Poetry and Trauma, say, had formed a coalition government.

When DJ typed one afternoon that he wanted to read his poems in my poetry-writing seminar, I didn't know what to do. He'd taken me by surprise. Though I was apprehensive about intensifying his poetic proclivity, I knew that he derived enormous satisfaction from writing and *showing* his poems. He was receiving all sorts of positive feedback from his peers and teachers at school. Kids were looking at him as talented, not just competent. He was beginning to feel good about himself. The year before, we had to press to get him to write sentences; now we were getting paragraphs and poems. He was completing his assignments on time, and despite the tumult of the past few months, he was earning A's in most of his classes. (When forced, DJ could turn off his poetry faculty just long enough to answer any and all factual questions; when forced, he could also attend to issues of grammar and punctuation.) Besides, it was still early in the regime of therapy, of getting it all out. Moreover, it didn't seem quite fair that I could use poetry as a kind of emotional catharsis and way of making meaning if he couldn't.

So, I said yes—after I approached my seminar students about doing so. They were all agreeable. Emily and I spoke with DJ about coming at the beginning of class and setting up his computer. He'd read a couple of poems, including "Alaska," "Prairie Dogs," "Rescue," and "DJ's Quilt," by using the *Intellitalk* program. An hour before class, DJ was extraordinarily jittery; he complained of an upset stomach, finally admitting he was "just nervous." He kept signing "go, go" once we entered the building where I teach. Emily kept offering encouraging words, reminding him of other things that had formerly made him nervous but now left him unfazed. When he walked into the classroom and saw my assembled students, he seemed literally to catch his breath, turn white. Twice he left the room and had to be coaxed back in. Finally he found the poem "DJ's Quilt" and pressed the key that activated the computer's mechanized voice.

DJ'S QUILT

My quilt is soft.
To touch it is like floating on forever.
I love my quilt because it keeps me sane.
My quilt is like a cup of coco on a cold day.
My quilt is the harmony to my music.

The students erupted into applause, which shocked DJ, but not so much that he wasn't able to find the next poem and the next after that. He was unmistakably enthralled—at once giddy and petrified, striking a debonair pose. Later, he said, "it was tremendio0us to read mu poems." I told him that his father hadn't given his first poetry reading until he was twenty-one, and here he was at the ripe old age of eleven reading at Grinnell College! Maybe, I remember thinking to myself, if he learns to exhaust his poetic instincts *in poems* and maybe if he learns to write about topics other than the horrors of abuse, this poetry thing might be okay. The next day, I came home from the office, having written a poem myself, and read it to Emily. In the middle of reading it, I heard DJ let out a shriek in the next room.

"What's the matter?" I asked with some annoyance.

"you read mom a poem why not me"

"I'd be happy to read my poem to you," I said, "just don't get so angry. C O M M U N I C A T E!" I promptly read the poem to DJ, an anti-war poem that took as its premise the odd fact that I had gone to grade school with the son of a former Secretary of Defense and had been found in the same sleeping bag with him one morning at camp. My friend had said he was cold and asked if he could climb in. As you might imagine, the gym teacher who found us did not appreciate the sight of two comrades in arms, pleasantly asleep.

"Do you like Dad's poem?" Emily asked.

"yesv youre resal;ly trying to reward me getting free by freeting [treat-ing?] me like a poet," DJ replied. He then said he wanted to write a poem.

"Have you ever written a poem that rhymes?" I asked.

"no"

"Would you like to?"

"yes"

"What do you want to write about?"

"heavebn," he said.

"OK, you start."

"h eaven is like a grewat lookimg cassreally yoiur dister [great look-ing Cass really your sister]"

So shocked was I by what he had typed that I completely forgot we were writing a poem. DJ had alluded to my little sister, Kassie, with whom I had minimal contact. When my parents split up, she'd sided with my father. Actually, she'd always been on his side; she knew that she could take her mother for granted and that she had to worship her father. She was extraordinarily self-centered, like the stock fund she looked up to. This was a young woman who drove a Lexus and who in college would go out to dinner with her sorority sisters and have them give her cash for their portion of the dinner while she put the whole thing on Daddy's credit card, calling the practice her "job." She wasn't that much better as an adult.

"What makes you think of my sister?"

"because she hears evcerythuing cares you hurt" The phrase "hears everything" DJ had previously used to describe himself—the fact that he could now decode spoken language. Did he imagine an autistic universe in which people might learn to "hear," even at a great distance?

"Why do you think my sister and I are not in touch?"

"you told uncle james threre [three] times not to taolk about herc"

"What are you thinking about her?"

"try to love her," he said. It was very difficult having this conversation with DJ who, in his life, had voluntarily lost no one. I knew that I needed to explain to him how sometimes preserving relationships can be even more destructive than letting them go, but that seemed an adult perception, one acquired after much pain. Was he suggesting that he still loved his birth father and mother, or was he strictly connecting my sister with Ellie, imagining that brother–sister bonds must never end? The former Catholic in me clung to the idea of reconciliation, and yet not at any cost, not when people continue to mistreat you.

"I have tried that many times," I told him. "But she and her husband are very different from Mom and me. They have very different values. Do you understand what I mean?"

"her values are badv"

"Yes, I believe that. But even more important, she has not been very nice to me or Mom. Unfortunately, she is very spoiled. She thinks she is the center of the universe."

"do you miss her?" DJ asked. He had a way of cutting through the adult rationalizations, getting at the marrow of life, this tiny surgeon of the soul, this foremost expert on longing.

"Yes, I miss the girl she once was. When she was little, she was very kind. Whenever there was a thunderstorm, she would crawl into my bed."

"i know i tried to telkl you that" Suddenly, it dawned on me. DJ had moved from the Defense Secretary's son in my bed at camp to my little sister in my bed at home during a thunderstorm.

"So, heaven is like a good looking Cass who crawls into your bed during a thunderstorm," I typed. "She's just had a scary dream in which worms are slithering across her . . . "

"and you opin [open] your arms and let her in," he said smiling.

Up, down, all around. This Space Mountain of a journey had Emily and me so stunned and moved that we sometimes couldn't decide upon a proper course of action. DJ seemed excessively, injuriously wise. How to undo this wisdom? How to take the narrow, bottomless well of his consciousness and make it broader, shallower? More like a swimming pool, say, with a deep end, where, if he wanted to, he could dive down and touch the bottom and then resurface. A deep end he could fathom. A deep end he could thrash in on a day when he was sad without the fear of descending interminably. Could we facilitate this transformation while preserving what was distinctly DJ? That sensitivity to suffering, that commitment to fairness, that force of reconnection and reunification—across great distances.

There's an FC user named Jeff Powell who worries that if he keeps typing more and more (and, as a result, no longer needs FC), "[he] might lose [his] poetic self." What, I would ask, is that poetic self but the mark of an incompletely colonized subject: a resistance fighter in the ghetto of analogy? Someone refusing, at least partially, to be an individual? Someone able to place himself in the predicament of another by insisting on relation? Why not imagine a world where we might "hear" another's hurt or seek to enable that hurt's expression? Maybe if we all communicated with someone literally at our arms, we'd be more inclined to embrace peace. Imagine Arafat and Sharon in the Rose Garden plucking out an accord. Imagine Sharon holding Arafat's arm, trying to offer just the right amount of support.

And so, progress with DJ was difficult to chart. No ordinary teleology was possible. It was a bit like an Iowa tornado, picking up the barn and putting it over there, turning the tractor on its head, leaving the laundry in the trees three miles away—white flags of surrender. A given week or month often looked like disaster, but there were always extraordinary moments of consolidated understanding and courage. Moments, yes, of tamed association and metaphor. Even as he began to seem too attached to his trauma and as he perseverated about the issue of independence, we saw him evince something like pride in himself—even more, a kind of disability consciousness. I had always thought that the answer to the self-esteem issues of disability was to radicalize the individual's perspective on his condition. The person needed not only to insist on the right to be fully included in society but also to celebrate his difference. He had to do away with the medical model that discoursed endlessly and pessimistically about deficits, that generalized about "autism" (as if all autistic people were the same). If black is beautiful, why couldn't disability be divine, at least in certain respects? After all, so much of disability is a function of an unaccommodating environment and others' negative projecting. Although race isn't a perfect parallel to disability, both share the fate of being, in part, socially constructed.

In the chapter of *Thinking in Pictures* called "Artists and Accountants," Temple Grandin argues that without autism the world would have far fewer geniuses. She reveals Einstein and Wittgenstein, for example, to have had Asperger's syndrome. When asked by someone if she'd like not to be autistic, she said no because "I wouldn't be me." DJ would say of autism that "it sucks" but he'd also remind us that "i have great mindi see things you don't see." The point is not to ignore the pain of being labeled "abnormal"; after all we are each of us products of normalizing agendas, and so there must be pain when one is excluded and demonized by the majority (even if one intellectually understands how this awful process works). The point, even with adolescents, is to move beyond pain to pride, to self-worth. God knows this world needs a little difference.

With DJ, we saw a glimmer of such pride in a short autobiography he produced for his language arts class. The autobiography had to begin with a statement of the student's name, followed by the sentence "I'm glad I'm me." It was clearly an exercise in self-esteem, but one that DJ took quite seriously. Here's what he wrote.

> My name is D.J. Savarese. i'm glad I'm me. I am 11 years old. I'm proud to be in school. I want to be successful. I can do alot of things. I know i can be focussed sometimes i forget. I hope you understand the way i am I wish i could fky. I like to go skating. I hear all that you tell me. I want to change scarey things. I play with my friends. I smile when I see miss innis in the morning. I love my mom and dad. I see what i want to. I believe in the people who want to love me. I am thankful for my family. I will try to smaile at everyone. I enjoy being at school. I dream about life. I wonder what i will become of myself. I need to be focussed. I wear buttned up shirts. I'm glad I'm D.J.

Every time I read this paragraph, I get choked up. I think of having not adopted DJ—I can't help it. Life is so precarious. I imagine him languishing in some institution or backward group home, still unable to communicate, perhaps even in diapers. All of that potential, all of that longing, waiting to come out, to be recognized. A human being discarded. There are, of course, thousands of people stuck precisely in such a situation, and I'm haunted by it. We give up on people way too easily—and not just the cognitively disabled, but all sorts of folks, especially children. (Or, worse, we never even try to begin with.) "I dream about life," DJ says. "I wonder what i will become of myself." Surely, a just world would devote itself to equal opportunity dreaming and becoming.

DJ would get a chance to give his own lecture on social responsibility as we neared the beginning of March, and I conducted a meeting of my independent study in the trampoline house. A young woman named Betsey had approached me in December about doing an independent study on autism. She had spent the previous summer working with autistic kids and had applied to the Peace Corps, proposing to work with autistic kids in Africa. Though I was going to be incredibly busy in the spring semester, I knew that I couldn't turn her down. But I made it clear that I was no expert—not in the sense that the word is normally bandied about. I told her that I could contribute knowledge of memoirs about, and autobiographies by, people with autism and that Emily could contribute knowledge about the principle and practice of full inclusion. Of course, we'd both be able to talk about parenting a child with autism. About so-called scientific knowledge, I had suggested she was actually better off doing that later. She'd already been exposed to the special ed establishment's ideology of pitiful deficits and delays—her experience thus far had been in a fully *exclusive* setting—and I'd wanted her to be as free as possible from equivalently grand pronouncements about the bioneurological damage of autism. I'd wanted her to see what autistic kids can do and how parents didn't have to embrace a narrative of hopeless tragedy. I'd wanted her to meet DJ and to watch him engage in facilitated communication.

We agreed to meet on a Sunday afternoon in the trampoline house first. Emily would spend time talking with Betsey while DJ and I jumped on the trampoline. DJ had been bugging me about jumping, and even though I knew I shouldn't, I agreed to jump. My hip replacement surgery was set for the beginning of May, and hence I figured it would be okay; I couldn't really do any additional damage. Besides, I wanted to jump with DJ, and I knew that after the surgery I wouldn't be able to ever again. Screw the pain, I said to myself. After introducing Betsey to DJ and turning on the stereo, DJ and I commenced our buoyant, rhythmic bouncing. Before long, you could hear our piercing yawps of joy in Omaha! I thought the music was loud enough and the jumping a sufficient distraction that Betsey and Emily would be able to talk about whatever they wanted to without fear of being overheard, but I was wrong, as the following conversation makes clear.

The first thing that Betsey asked DJ when he finally came over to speak with her concerned his own understanding of autism. "autism really stinkgh becahse t migtyt nnot let kids knor [know] im smarty," DJ said. Betsey seemed surprised, the way that anyone who imagines a perfect correlation between appearance and intelligence is surprised when they see DJ communicating. Before she could respond, he typed, "you shouldvve trusted the kids to learn"

"Did you hear us talking about Betsey's experience in a self-contained classroom last summer?" Emily asked. I simply couldn't believe that he'd managed to follow their conversation while jumping and listening to the music. I hadn't been able to do that.

"i was trying to hear everything i really look more poor than I great just because of yourv truysdt in me," DJ explained. He then launched into a homily about trust—his version of what the educator Doug Biklen calls "presuming competence" or what Anne Donnellen refers to as "the least dangerous assumption." Alluding to the kids that Betsey had taught, DJ typed, "trust tht they canbn learn btrust that thdey hhave feelkings trust t6hat tghrey want friends trust they trust they cread [can read] trudt threy hear everything." DJ followed this passionate exhortation in the chapel of leaping words with a description of his parents' commitment to full inclusion. I can't remember exactly what Betsey had asked DJ— we were at the point where we sometimes didn't bother to type our questions and remarks—but he answered, "thgry trudsted /but they thought ij try to read great toi me tryt o make me just like everyojeb else." I took note of the "but" in that sentence. Even in a speech devoted to the cause of inclusion, DJ was expressing some ambivalence, however subtle. When Emily urged him to ask Betsey a question, he typed, "why really do you want to teacfh kids with autism/" The question, as basic and essential as it was, left Betsey floundering. Finally, she said something about helping kids who have been neglected, to which DJ kindly and generously remarked, "they feel great to have met you." I loved the fact that DJ had used the present tense to express the kids' feelings—as if he were somehow in touch with them, somehow their spokesman; as if Betsey's relationship with them were continuing. He probably wanted to imagine them as having hope.

"What kind of classroom do you prefer, DJ?" I asked.

"the ones where kids talk," he replied, then added, in typical DJ fashion, "trying to get free."

CHAPTER 11

Throw Dad Away

Not too long after DJ's introduction to Betsey, I suffered a major flare-up in my neck, the first time that part of my body had been affected by the arthritis. My condition was said to be degenerative. My body released an enzyme that destroyed the cartilage in my hips, knees, and neck, and it did so without, for the most part, causing inflammation. As a result, I only had pain once the cartilage was gone and my bones were greeting each other like the infamous Hatfields and McCoys—with great pistol shots of nerve. In August, I'd received word from the rheumatologist that my neck x-rays had shown significant degeneration in the c-6/c-7 area, but I hadn't yet begun to feel its effects. My neck felt fine, in fact—though I remember telling myself that my hip had also felt fine until the very end. My body was a bit like a house consumed by termites, falling in only after the last structural support had been nibbled on by those invisible pests.

When the flare-up began, I couldn't move my neck—either sideways or up and down—without intense discomfort. Very quickly, my arms began to go numb and I lost feeling entirely in my left arm and hand. This development terrified me. It was one thing to not be able to walk without limping or not to be able to sit for an extended period of time;

it was another thing altogether to feel paralyzed. I couldn't do anything without incurring the wrath of my spine. I couldn't read, I couldn't watch TV; I certainly couldn't grade papers. There wasn't any comfortable position in which to do the thing we call life. My head suddenly felt as heavy as a bowling ball and as precariously perched on its throne as a child king.

I knew I was in trouble, and yet my first instinct was to ignore the problem, to wish it away. When after two days it remained, I drove to the hospital in Iowa City, where x-rays revealed stenosis of the spine and a further narrowing of the gap between c-6 and c-7. After consulting with the orthopedist, the rheumatologist prescribed a dose of steroids and had me fitted for a Miami-J neck collar, which she instructed me to wear for the next four weeks. She worried that my neck might prevent my scheduled hip replacement by making intubation difficult. She said that my spinal canal was congenitally narrow and that tiny bone spurs were impinging on my spinal cord. The collar would help lift and support my head. There wasn't much else they could do short of a laminectomy, a last-ditch operation with very mixed results. It was the kind of procedure that patients had to beg the orthopedic surgeon to do; life for them was that intolerable. It involved widening the spinal canal and perhaps fusing the vertebrae. The recovery took months and months. In the meantime, I needed to adapt the way I did things: from reading to writing to typing e-mails. I had to keep my chin up—literally and figuratively. But I was panicked. I knew that the long, precipitous slide I feared had commenced. We were now talking about the kind of disability that could truly incapacitate me. While being fitted for a neck collar, I saw a woman whose upper vertebrae had crumbled, leaving her unable to support the weight of her head. Surgeons had used metal rods to fix it in place. I remember catching her eye. As dread overtook me, she sat there stoically, offering only the solace of stubborn endurance.

Until this point, I'd not considered myself disabled. Though I often worked in the field of disability studies, writing about contemporary memoirs of disability, and though I had a son who was disabled, I somehow imagined that disability was out there: a moon orbiting the friendly planet of normality, a moon I could land on when I wanted to, travel

around and speak sympathetically with the natives. I only now understand how ignorant I was. The old adage about walking a mile in another person's shoes, adapted to mean limping a mile in another person's
shoes, couldn't be truer. I was beset with fear, self-loathing, and self-
pity. I hated the way people stared. Try marching into a lecture hall with
your head immobilized in a neck collar. Try being so conspicuously different that you can't move through a space without being gawked at,
bathed in other people's anxiety and often patronizing concern. The view
from the inside of disability was quite distinct, and I suddenly had a much
better sense of what DJ was going through: his desire to be "like everyone else," his frustration at having a body that didn't function properly.
The project of celebrating disability as difference, the hallmark of disability studies, now seemed more daunting—not less important, just more
contrived and difficult.

Although I thought I might be able to use my disability to enable DJ
to feel less alone, the fact is I was his father, and he didn't want to see me
infirm. We'd been making progress in therapy, with DJ typing such
things as "free from kyle might be ok" and " I might wanrt my pokinb to
s6op." Indeed, the poking had begun to subside. But now we were in for
a flood of anxiety. We couldn't fill the sandbags fast enough. Whereas
before DJ had fixated on Emily's death, now he'd fixate on mine. When
I returned from the hospital in my collar, he immediately attempted to
take it off, reaching up and, in the process, yanking my neck. I barked at
him loudly, which only made the situation worse. DJ customarily opposed radical changes in people's appearances; he hated when Emily or
a college buddy wore her hair up, insisting forcibly that it come down.
This was the characteristic devotion to sameness that was so much a part
of autism, but that night there was a frantic urgency to his compulsion.

Emily had tried to prepare him for my altered appearance, and he
had typed, "i reaLLu want his ugly pain to go away," pausing to add,
"will you be in poverty if daxs [dad] is really sick?" With me home before him, however, all of that touching sincerity dissolved into a fit of
rage and then, when the rage exhausted itself, sobbing, uncontrollable
sobbing. After ten minutes of DJ's tantrum, I retreated to the den and lay
down, exhausted and a bit sleepy from the pain medicine I was taking.

When Emily finally got him on the computer, he told her, "you might intentionally tell me a lie about dad." He knew that his mom always tried to make him feel better, and he was suspicious.

"No," Emily replied, "your trust is very important to us. We are telling you what we know and what the doctors tell us." At this point, I returned to the family room and joined the conversation.

"tell me what medical leave is," DJ said. He had clearly heard Emily and me discuss this option. I'd decided again to try to make it through the semester, but he'd latched onto the phrase, reminding me of just how careful we needed to be with what we said. Like the idiom "on my own," "medical leave" suggested something ominous, such as my leaving not only my job but also him. And in DJ's world of metaphoric equivalences this meant ultimately death. "tell me you have treatment. tell me the treatment you will have. tell me you.llreally feel better. tell me you won.t die," he typed. I could feel his analogical engine revving, like a plane on a runway.

The next few days were very tense. DJ couldn't tolerate the sight of me in my neck brace; he wanted constantly to remove it. One afternoon, he announced that he "just saw kyle." He had been hitting his head against the car window—windows and other glassy surfaces seemed to allow DJ to generate these illusions—and Emily had had to pull over to find out what was wrong. She asked about his bad dream the night before which he hadn't wanted to talk about. "i wasnt free because kyle was killing me"

"What was he doing?" Emily asked.

"he tried to hurt me by fucking me," DJ replied.

"Then what happened?"

"dad freed me and i was ok," he said, adding a new twist to the familiar scenario.

"Do you remember Sarah in Grinnell talking to you about your brain and the different things it can do?"

"yes"

"Sometimes if something really bad happens, first we are able to put it away in our awake mind. But still it might pop up from time to time in our sleeping mind. But think about it. Even though Kyle came to mind while you were asleep, your brain was so smart it had Dad come and free you. That is a big, big, big, step toward being free. Do you understand?"

"yesn"

"When Mom was your age and had scary dreams, Bop and Uncle Phil and Uncle Tim would come save me. What do you think about what I said about your brain?"

"you mightb be right"

"I think it's actually a very, very good sign of how far you have come down the road of freedom," Emily said.

"i get scared that dad might leave," DJ replied, making clear the anxious connection between Kyle and my health problems.

"What do you mean?" Emily asked.

"he might die"

"Dad is not going to die. He is just in some pain. The doctors are working with us to help him feel pain free," she explained.

"i lovde having him as my dad," DJ said.

"I know. He's a really great Dad! Let's list all of the things we think are great about him." Emily was fond of the list of positive attributes as a therapeutic tool. She sensed the love = loss equation that DJ regularly worked out on the blackboard of his mind, and she wanted to divert him. "He is a great tickler," she began.

"he is rea.llhy kind"

"He says sweet things and genuinely loves and respects you."

"he freed me"

"He is a very talented writer." (It's always good to have your relatives believe in you!)

"bhe loves med"

"He thinks being your Dad is the richest, most meaningful part of his life."

"he is th4e greatedt"

"Thanks for talking things through with me. Isn't it much better than hitting and screaming?"

"yeab"

A few days later, DJ pitched another fit. "What are you upset about?" Emily asked.

"dad because he is dying"

293

Emily responded to this round of anxiety jousting by giving him a lecture on what an idiom is. She'd heard me on the phone tell people that I was dying or that my neck was killing me, and she worried that DJ had taken me literally. This was no doubt part of the problem, but there was also the issue of his attachment to loss as a paradoxical defense mechanism. "the real truth turns you into a sad person. everyone your past," DJ proclaimed one day in therapy. If those of us who have led relatively fortunate lives are like the greyhounds at the track who chase a mechanical rabbit without ever knowing that the rabbit is fake—that the rabbit is loss—DJ was a dog who'd actually managed to catch up with it, who'd had the rabbit in his teeth. How difficult it had been to motivate this dog to keep circling the track. But somehow we'd done it, and now the dog was remembering the bitter taste of metal in its mouth.

"my dreams are back need you beside my dread," DJ announced the following morning, and I told him that I'd sleep with him if he wished. When DJ had a nightmare, he invariably pooped in his pants, so in addition to the sudden screams and thrashing, we'd have a messy bed to contend with. I thought that maybe if I slept with him, he might relax about my dying and have fewer dreams. Besides, it would allow us to spend more time together, even if it was time in which we were both asleep. This would later get us into trouble as DJ became dependent on such help, but as with so many things we tried, desperation was our muse.

That night, DJ typed on the computer, "i really dread going to bed because i might ytreat you like you're plastif i might throw you in the trash." Ever since I'd arrived home in a neck collar, he'd been telling me that "ayiou just look plsstic [plastic]." You could see the associative trap he'd set for himself: if plastic was something you discarded, and Dad looked like plastic, then Dad was something you discarded. The rigidity of this distributive association was a measure of just how anxious he was. I don't think he actually believed I might be trash; rather, he was stuck in a repetitive thought process, where again psychology seemed to have joined neurology. The fact that he worried about "going to bed" suggested that he might already have dreamt this associative chain and it had disturbed him. "i want dad to take medicine to prevent hip," DJ said. By this point, we'd spoken with DJ about my hip replacement surgery, and we thought that he might be confusing the plastic of my neck collar with the plastic of a joint replacement, imagining that after the operation my hip would look like my neck. Perhaps he feared I would soon be completely and visibly plastic. (I pictured myself as a 40-liter jug of Diet Pepsi, set out on the curb to be recycled. Poor, plastic Dad emptied of all life; ironically, that's how I sometimes feel teaching at a liberal arts college. Would that a large truck might come by and recycle me!)

"DJ, you are confused about the idea of plastic. Do you remember when Mr. Abarr [his fourth grade teacher] taught you about Texas and petroleum?"

"yes"

"He talked about all sorts of things that are made of different plastics. This is very special. It is not like a plastic bottle. Do you understand that only a very, very tiny part will be made of plastic?" DJ was now quite upset. "What's bothering you?"

"great b nplaces," he replied.

"What kind of great places?" Emily asked.

"hospitalks"

"Are you remembering when you were there, or were you thinking about Dad?"

"thin"

"Do you know Dad's hip will be inside his body?"

"yes trying tryeat him because hip," DJ said.

Soon after this conversation, he'd decide to do his science project on hip replacements, hoping, I think, to master fear with knowledge. He'd inform us that he wouldn't, however, be able to visit me while I was in the hospital; instead, he'd write me a series of get-well cards. I told him that this was a terrific compromise, and I'd look forward to receiving them. Privately, I interpreted his unwillingness to come to the hospital as an indication of his larger repudiation of the future: that white ward of pain and uncertainty.

Whenever we could, Emily and I would continue to challenge DJ's associative equations, informing him, for instance, that hospitals, while scary, were also places of healing. One night, DJ expressed a fear about not having enough police in Grinnell. He'd overheard Emily joking with a friend that Grinnell's only police officer was on vacation. It was a strange thing for DJ to say, considering his well-documented aversion to law enforcement. Later, in the middle of telling us whether or not he wanted to go skating, he typed, "he ids dreading police"

"Who is dreading police?" I asked.

"kylpe he just freed kyle hurt me"

"What did the police do?"

"polic cme and took him away"

"Wasn't that a good thing?"

"yes police helped"

"Should we go skating or do some yard work?" I asked after DJ didn't seem to want to pursue the matter any further.

"skating the police took kyle really farb awayb"

"What made you think of Kyle?"

"really heard theb tv the hert opn," DJ replied. Was he saying that something on TV had opened his hurt? His heart? DJ immediately signed "all done, all done," and so I had to do without an answer. What was interesting about this conversation was the way that DJ had gotten himself into a jam with the word "freed." The police had "freed" Kyle from foster care but in doing so had helped him. The idea of help emerges after he claims that the police hurt him by leaving him in foster care. Of course, Kyle's "freedom" was nothing more than a trip to a juvenile detention center. Also interesting—and disturbing—was DJ's strange identification with Kyle. The formulation "is dreading police" places Kyle in DJ's customary position of dread. Does DJ feel bad for his fellow foster child? Or is this merely a kind of revenge fantasy, where Kyle has to experience what *he* experiences? If so, why does it move so quickly to jealousy about Kyle's ostensible "freedom"?

Here, complexity had imposed itself on a mind accustomed, as in the plastic example, to a set of fairly rigid associations. DJ's feelings and understanding exceeded his instinctive mode of communication, especially when he was stressed. This mode or method often committed him to things he didn't believe, and, thus, like a car in a dead-end alley, he'd have to try to back his way out. He sometimes reminded me of my poetry writing students who, when given the assignment of composing a sestina, complain about a sense of restriction and constraint. A sestina is a form requiring the poet to pick six words and use them at the ends of his or her lines, in a particular order. Because the form consists of six sestets (six-line stanzas) and one tercet (three-line stanza), each word has to appear no fewer than seven times. In the tercet, each line must contain two of the chosen words, with one of them at the end. To say that the form is difficult would be an understatement. You find yourself stretching words, shading them, almost giving them new meaning, in order to satisfy the form's exacting demands. Frequently students give up by the time they reach the fourth or fifth stanza, unable to contrive a way of using their chosen end words again.

DJ's end words might be "police," "great," "Kyle," "type," "trees," and "free." Within the restricted (and repetitive) universe of such a loaded vocabulary, an oddly flexible, even free-floating, dynamic emerges: one that in DJ's hands could go on forever. In linguistic terms, signifiers wrench "free" from signifieds; words no longer seem discrete. The old agreement that "great" means "great" falls apart because suddenly "great" means all sorts of other, contradictory things. The world, or rather the way we represent it, suddenly seems one: relentlessly connected, indistinguishable. In the "great" poetry writing class of life, of parenting, Emily and I had to insist on difference, distinction. We had to find another way for DJ to manage complexity. We had to broaden his sense of metaphoric meaning (hospitals are *both* depressing and hopeful) and narrow his idiosyncratic usage. "Free," for example, could no longer mean "independent," "normal," "grown up," "recovered," "typing by himself," "able to speak," etc. He needed new words, words that weren't charged with anxious, personal meaning. Words that didn't function as super condensations of a traumatized life.

Sometimes, we had to show DJ that a particular metaphor, no matter how dear to him, didn't finally work. In mid-March, Emily asked him if he thought spring was coming and he said, "yes." "The weather is nicer, some flowers are starting to rise up through the ground," Emily commented.

"the trwes are getting hurt bactually," DJ typed.

"The trees are growing buds that will soon grow leaves," she reminded him. Whenever DJ started talking about trees, you knew he was anxious about a whole range of independence issues. Here, he was imagining the appearance of new life as painful; ordinarily, he focused on the pain of separation: the dead leaves falling to the ground. We'd tried to point out to him that independence has nothing to do with death, though one could certainly feel nervous about the former. He wasn't a leaf plunging off the long arm of his facilitator, only to be gathered up and thrown onto some compost heap. That figure hadn't served him well. Perhaps the springtime metaphor was more appropriate, though it, too, evinced anxiety about the future through its insistent projection of hurt. In a way, it was worse. The incongruous reading of spring (as distinctly not a period of joyous rebirth) may have constituted an intensification of DJ's loss obsession. At least the autumn metaphor made sense; he was in a long line of melancholy poets who have matched an interior mental state with the condition of the natural world. Emily thought DJ might be trying to say something more complicated, something that married the concepts of hurt and growth realistically, but there was scant evidence for this. Whatever the case, like the new life sprouting all around, such an understanding is terribly vulnerable. Without warning, a front can arrive and dump two feet of snow on the heart's daffodils.

At this point, it was difficult to know how decisively DJ would continue to move forward. He'd been making progress, but my neck injury and impending hip replacement had compromised his efforts. If, as child trauma experts argue, "the importance of traumatic memories lies in their role in shaping expectations of the recurrence of threat, of failure of protective intervention, and/or of helplessness, which govern the child's emotional life and behavior," then it should come as no surprise that such health problems provoked intense anxiety in DJ and rapidly became associated with his trauma. The two most important prerequisites for the work of healing are safety and a sense of control, and though it was my body under threat, it might as well have been his, so powerful was his sense of identification. Add to this the perceived demise of the loving relationship in which healing had begun and it's a marvel that DJ didn't regress entirely. "love loses," he had typed in a therapy session, and we were trying—by the side of the road, as it were—to unhitch that particular car and trailer. Love's transmission simply couldn't pull an overloaded U-haul of loss.

Almost at every juncture, Emily and I assessed DJ's treatment. The Risperdal had generally relaxed the stranglehold of anxiety, but the anxiety hadn't by any means disappeared. We were continuing with the therapy: a mix of cognitive-behavioral strategies, psychotherapeutic strategies, and EMDR. It, too, was having mixed results. We were still quite worried about DJ's autonomic hyperarousal, which seemed, at times, immune to any intervention at all. His heart would race, he'd start to cry or scream, he'd want to flee. In an earlier chapter, I quoted from a book by Bessel A. van der Kolk and Alexander McFarlane, in which the authors sound a pessimistic note about the entrenched physiology of trauma: the way the brain itself changes after repeated sensitization to injury. A line from their preface haunted me: "To what degree can psychological interventions reverse a disorder with such strong biological underpinnings?" No fans of any sort of strict determinism, Emily and I had to confront the prospect of central nervous system damage (or at least reorganization) and be prepared to respond appropriately. Or so we were counseled. As van der Kolk and McFarlane maintain, "The persistent, irrelevant firing of warning signals causes physical sensations to lose their functions as signals of emotional states and, as a consequence, they stop serving as guides for action. Thus, like neutral environmental stimuli, normal physical sensations may take on a new and threatening significance. The person's own physiology becomes a source of fear." This final statement, of course, has profound implications, for it suggests that traumatized people operate as the literal embodiment of terror. They *are* terror.

As opposed as we were to a narrow scientific understanding of trauma, we were nevertheless vulnerable to it—especially to what I call the haughty reduction of hope to time-release capsules. For one thing, some of this new literature was quite compelling; for another, we lived in a country enamored of pharmaceutical remedies. In our desperation, we were willing to try just about anything to make DJ feel better. But the fact is, the drugs we tried were never all that effective; some were down-right destructive. Even more important, it became clear to Emily and me that providing DJ with psychotherapy was a way of insisting on his humanity—over and against the general conception of the mind (as mere brain) and the specific conception of autism (as defective intellectual and affective processing). We'd gained much by resisting the dire medical understanding of autism; perhaps we'd gain just as much by resisting the equivalent understanding of trauma.

DJ, in short, was entitled to therapy, however inefficient it might be—almost, I would argue, as a civil right, a corrective to the long history of misunderstanding and mistreating people with autism. Think of it as disability reparations. Though we would continue with the Risperdal, we would do so at low levels, in contrast to the practice of doping autis-tic kids merely to quell bothersome behaviors. In the end, we'd strive for a holistic approach. We'd remain open to, but skeptical of, other pharmacological interventions while we pursued the painstaking process of building a self outside of trauma. No fatalism, no hopelessness, no irreversible changes.

Judith Herman offers a nice overview of the process of recovery from trauma. I remember coming across it that spring, and so I present it now in an attempt to indicate the focus of our energies. Herman writes,

> Recovery unfolds in three stages. The central task of the first stage is the establishment of safety. The central task of the second stage is remembrance and mourning. The central task of the third stage is reconnection with ordinary life. . . . No single course of recovery follows these stages through a straightforward linear sequence. Oscillating and dialectical in nature, the traumatic syndromes defy any at-tempt to impose such simpleminded order. In fact, patients and therapists alike frequently become discouraged when issues that have supposedly been put to rest stubbornly re-appear. One therapist describes the progression through the stages of recovery as a spiral, in which earlier issues are continually revisited on a higher level of integration. How-

ever, in the course of a successful recovery, it should be possible to recognize a gradual shift from unpredictable danger to reliable safety, from disassociated trauma to acknowledged memory, and from stigmatized isolation to restored social connection.

I like Herman's emphasis on the nonlinear nature of recovery, and I maintain that the movement away from "stigmatized isolation to restored social connection" for a person without language can't be anything but monumentally difficult. Again, for DJ the first experience of "social connection" in and through words coincided with the articulation of his trauma. No small part of the difficulty, then, would involve rejecting the affective bond of injury, which would seek to preserve dependency, and choosing that of health, which would seek to foster a kind of relational independence. Because DJ couldn't really be "restored" to social connection, he had to achieve this goal without a positive referent, only making it that much more difficult. Of course, the politics of "stigma" and "social connection" with respect to cognitive disability suggest that merely being autistic in American society is trauma enough, for who is more stigmatized and isolated? Full recovery from this trauma, let alone the two together, would entail a transformation of dominant attitudes and practices, a point that Herman herself makes when speaking as a feminist about rape.

The afternoon of the budding trees conversation, DJ kept refusing to communicate on the computer. He was nervous, agitated, signing, "drive, drive." "Why don't you want to talk?" Emily asked.

"im nervkus about trying not to thrkiw [throw] dad qway," DJ replied. We were back to this, and Emily was frustrated.

"Dad is a man. Dad is made of bones and muscles and organs and a brain and all of the things all people are made of. Would you throw Mom away?"

"no"

"Would you throw Mrs. Rudolph [one of DJ's teachers] away?

"njo"

"Would you throw any person away?"

"no"

"So, would you ever throw your Dad away?"

"no"

"Exactly."

That night, I asked DJ if he wanted to write a poem, and he said he'd like to write about "plastoic." "your neck isc covered with plastoic," he typed.

"But only when I stand up," I said. "When I lie down my neck is free." We'd rented a hospital bed in anticipation of my surgery and placed it in the TV room. With the bed at a slight incline, I could forego my brace, which was uncomfortable and confining, and still take the pressure off my neck.

"underneath it all youre treated like trash," DJ declared.

"You have gotten stuck on a misconception," I explained. "You think 'plastic' and then you think 'trash' and then you panic because you wonder how Daddy can be associated with 'plastic' and 'trash.' The solution to your problem? Only some kinds of plastic belong in the trash."

"you teach jme to be just like the other kids," DJ said.

"Is that good?" I asked, checking to make sure.

"yes," he replied. But then, not a minute later, he was reaching for my eyes and trying to usher me out the door, signing, "go, go." I knew that any mention of our mutual ambition, even by him, could set off a fit of anxiety, and I couldn't help but connect his fear of my dying and of throwing me away with his demand that I leave. The latter was clearly an example of DJ's doctrine of preemption.

"Please try not to push people's buttons—especially when they are trying to spend time with you," Emily interrupted.

"ok," DJ said.

"How about writing a poem about a man made of plastic, a man very different from dad?" I proposed. I thought that maybe an exercise in poetic thinking might accomplish what logical deconstruction had not.

"ok"

"I'll start. *His body is a giant bottle of Coke./ His neck is the top,/ and out of his head comes a dark liquid!/ He seems to be dead but he's not./ He's PLAS-TIC MAN: the century's new superhero.* Now, you continue."

"*his plastic is extra tough/ because he is extraordinarily strong/ hdeb can protect himself pouring really juicy treats*" Once DJ had used the word "protect," I saw an opportunity to bring up the notion of a burdensome past.

"*Sometimes he has bad memories, but he knows how to fight them off,*" I wrote.

"hurt my fee.igs," DJ announced, like some western gunslinger who had never lost a duel, so expeditious was his draw.

"How did I hurt your feelings?"

"pointing funj"

"Daddy wasn't poking fun. I wanted to write a poem about plastic to make you feel better about my hip operation—to show you that fear and dread can be conquered with humor."

"it huert my," DJ repeated, then once again reached for my eyes, this time trying to bang his head against my shoulder.

"Why are you being so unkind to dad lately?" Emily asked.

" i really love him," DJ replied matter of factly, as if the logic of his statement were self-evident.

"I know you do, but why are you being so unlike yourself and trying to frustrate him?"

"i'm really worried about him because i think he is trying to politely trhy to die," he said. Emily and I had to refrain from laughing; DJ's phrasing was often hilariously inventive. What a terrific way of capturing a parent's stoic evasions, I thought. By this point, I was absolutely certain that DJ was trying to preempt loss. Throwing dad away, asking him to leave, being unkind to him—all of these constituted efforts to inoculate himself against the death he believed was coming. The phrase "love loses" flashed before me. (Didn't we see that unhitched trailer by the side of the road?) In a way, DJ was practicing loss, as once he'd practiced stubbing his toe, attempting to rid the pain of its surprise. There's a terrific poem by the late-modernist American poet Elizabeth Bishop called "One Art." One of the poem's two refrains goes like this: "The art of losing isn't hard to master." The poet, of course, means this ironically, for loss proves very difficult to master. At one point, she enjoins the reader to "practice losing farther, losing faster," and I've often conceived of DJ doing just that.

"you ddread having me as youtr son," DJ typed after Emily had asked him about his death fixation. The response was classic DJ: he simultaneously imagined a kind of parental abandonment through death and projected an intensely negative view of himself—as someone deserving of abandonment. When anxiety struck, self-loathing wasn't too far behind.

"DJ, you know that is so untrue. Can you answer my first question—what has made you think dad is dying?"

"he treats you poorly," he said. A few days earlier, he'd seen me storm out of the house after a fight with Emily. Both of us were emotionally frazzled; there hadn't been any time for us as a couple or as individuals. I felt as if my body was falling apart and even the local TV station of our family hadn't carried the story. I was working especially hard at the college, teaching three classes, directing multiple independent studies, and heading up a job search for my department—not to mention serving on innumerable committees. And all of this while in a neck brace and on OxyContin! You can probably tell that I enjoy a good pity party every now and now. Though I was trying to teach DJ how not to displace his anxiety, I wasn't very good at it myself. After I'd left the house, DJ typed on the computer, "the truth is hea loves you," proving himself an expert on human relationships.

"No, he doesn't treat me poorly," Emily responded. "Please try to answer my question. Something has given you the idea that dad might die. What is it?"

"he treats you," DJ began again, paused, then typed, "he gets lost in the past." Though it shouldn't have, the remark floored me, for it was dead on—not only that but weirdly reflective of his own problem. For the first time, I understood how much I'd been grieving over my disability. No jumping, no tennis, no jogging, and now, at least temporarily, no holding my head up high without the aide of plastic. I'd been *talking* about moving forward—especially to DJ—but I hadn't actually been doing it. I was petrified of the future: something that he'd picked up on. How could he not have? With the way that he identified with his father, of course DJ possessed an analogous fear.

Emily wanted him to clarify what he'd meant by "getting lost in the past." "How so?" she asked.

"hegets hurt pplaying," DJ explained.

"What kind of hurt are you talking about?"

"pjhysival"

I knew that he was referring to the trampoline; later he'd even say, "i heard you jured [injured] by jumping." It crushed me to find him thinking of our favorite mutual activity, an activity he found "freein," as injurious. God knows he needed no additional inducement to be pessimistic about his recovery from trauma. Like a president with his nuclear codes, DJ was always just one step away from linking joy with pain, life with sorrow, and letting the bombs go.

"In the last few days, you seem to be withdrawn and anxious," Emily said.

"yes because i'm nervous becayse the bed is like prison," DJ typed.

"The bed seems like a prison because ... ," Emily asked.

"it keeps dad realkly lonely." In DJ's mind, it became clear, the hospital bed functioned as a tangible symbol of the past, which injured and imprisoned people. Like him, I was lonely and unreachable. At night with the side rail up, I must have looked like I was literally behind bars. DJ wanted me out of that hospital bed and bounding into the future. He wanted me to lead the way. He'd braided his injuries with mine and thought the rope of our togetherness might be sturdy enough to provide for rescue. But was I up to the challenge? Could I be as optimistic and invincible as he required? Optimism, at least when it came to my own life, wasn't my strong suit. Even more important, could I show him how to move into the future *with* disability? Who knows how mine would proceed, and his, well, recovery wasn't something we were hoping for, or even thought possible. We loved DJ as DJ; we didn't need a cure, especially now that he was able to communicate. At this point, DJ still believed that his autism, particularly his inability to speak, devolved from the abandonment and attack. He had to find a way to accept his autism, his difference.

"DJ, dad isn't lonely in that bed," Emily said. "He is relaxing and trying to rest his neck as much as possible so the doctor will hopefully say—"

"i really love dsads," DJ interjected.

The very next day, he told us, "i ight need lots of reassurqnce because poking is back." It had already returned but now it was here with a vengeance. "poking is liking to point out my great hurt," DJ announced. "please try to kill kyle." The month leading up to my surgery was as turbulent as any we had experienced, with DJ all over the emotional map. One moment, he sounded like the Dalai Lama; the next, he was hitting a teacher at school or obsessing hysterically about some mysterious autistic ritual. The formulation "you can hurt your hurt" reveals the extent to which he was stuck in a paradigm of injury during this period. One afternoon, he positively clocked his aide, who in fairness to DJ had herself been behaving erratically. She'd been "out sick" repeatedly, and DJ felt abandoned. When Emily questioned him about his behavior, he said, "if i hurt her i feel free because i'm great." His answer didn't make much sense; Emily pressed him on it, and he said, "you hurt lesd than I do." Hurt was its own logic, he implied. Eventually, Emily figured out that he was trying to secure his independence by being mean to his aide, though he conceded that he didn't really want to be independent. "Great" meant distinctly not like the other kids, so his reasoning was circular and destructive. "really try yyour idea of getting free," he claimed, though Emily had sanctioned neither his version of freedom nor his method of achieving it.

"Is it my idea or your idea?" she asked.

"your," he said.

"So, do you like or dislike it?"

"possibly hate it"

DJ played this kind of game with the issue of independent typing as well. "im interested in how to typy on my own," he told us.

"Really?" I asked.

"yes," he responded.

"Well, Ellie talked about how she learned just by playing around with the keyboard and starting to get the feel of touching different keys," Emily said.

"im just joking," DJ typed. As the ultimate self-destructive gesture, he even suggested that facilitated communication was a hoax—using, I might point out, the very method he was denigrating, to make his case. As in the example concerning independent typing, DJ quickly reversed himself. "you miht help by guoiding myn hanbd," he said accusingly.

"OK. On some of the questions, though, I was purposely trying to guide your hand toward the wrong answer and you were resisting in order to type the right answer. Do you agree?" Emily asked.

"yes you really know i know" If you've ever been on a see-saw with a kid who takes pleasure in suddenly jumping off, leaving you to thump fiercely on the ground, then you can understand what it was like to be at the mercy of DJ's fluctuations. Between his constant requests to "kill kyle," his complaints about my being in bed "all the time," and his sudden insistence that a girl at his school who was deemed mentally retarded be given more challenging assignments, we were all suffering from a sort of vertigo.

In the beginning of April my brother and his wife, who had had a baby in January, traveled from Chicago to Grinnell to spend some time with us. I think they wanted to try to cheer me up about my neck, and they knew we hadn't yet had a chance to meet little Charlie. DJ liked babies, and he repeatedly said that Charlie was "so cute." He was also quite fond of my brother James, who would roughhouse with him— roughhouse and jump on the trampoline. From the second they arrived, DJ was signing, "jump, jump, jump." He practically dragged James out to the trampoline house and immediately began whooping it up with him. Poor James. He wasn't in terrific shape and after about thirty minutes he collapsed in exhaustion, but DJ wouldn't let him stop. "Jump, jump, jump." When he couldn't bounce another second, James crawled out of the enclosure and lay down on the couch, employing a newly learned sign: "break, break." "Please, I need a break." The highlight of the visit came when DJ, James, and Eileen had a conversation on the computer. James was so stunned by DJ's awareness that he kept asking one factual question after another. "What is the name of Juleen's (my older sister) two kids?" "That's amazing," he'd exclaim as DJ answered each one correctly. We hadn't visited with James and Eileen since their wedding the previous May, and the event had been too busy for such a conversation. So, they'd never witnessed DJ communicating on his computer. At one point, Charlie began to cry, and Emily asked DJ if he remembered being that little. "yes," DJ typed, "remembr pleasing no one."

The following week, the Medwaver support service coordinator arrived for her regular meeting to set DJ's "community living" goals. Emily and I had decided, in consultation with DJ, that he would play a big part in this meeting. There was no reason why he couldn't speak for himself, and so in response to the first question about the role of his college buddies, he remarked, "please help me play truly with friends heaf [hear] what they have to say." Toward the end of the meeting, after she had exhausted the official questions, the woman asked DJ what he wanted to be when he grew up. I used to hate when people asked him this—it seemed at once so perfunctory and patronizing—but now I knew there was a good chance he'd stop the questioner dead in her tracks. "when i grow up i want to be politician to help the poor you posasibly think im dreaming but im serious," he typed. And she was shocked, literally speechless. Even I was a bit stunned by his awareness of her potential disbelief, the way she might dismiss his answer as merely cute. Afterward, we spoke with DJ about how he felt the meeting had gone. "it points out how much im being hurt by kmy real voice not speaking," he said.

"What has gotten you so interested in or concerned about the poor?" I asked.

"yiu mnow i'm not sure i do. in my realy free years i was poor," he replied. DJ had once again trapped himself into saying something he didn't quite believe. By associatively connecting the issues of not being able to speak and being poor, he had decided suddenly that he didn't want to help the poor at all; rather, he wanted to be poor himself because then he'd be able to speak. He honestly thought, despite what we had told him, that the rape had injured his voice, had *caused* his autism. Because he had been poor prior to the rape, he considered poverty the prerequisite for speaking, for being free. In June DJ would offer up the flip side of this logic, telling us that he didn't want to be normal because he "feared beated." "You think that being normal would increase the chances of your being beaten?" I'd ask. "yes because you're on your owasb own," he would say. Just as our blue-eyed minister of anxiety had joined "love" and "loses" in holy matrimony, so he would join "independence" and "beaten"—till death do them part. We had seen this nifty, associative move with the issue of facilitated communication. Our job was to encourage divorce, actually promote it: introduce "love" and "independence" to other, more suitable partners. Though DJ knew that his birth father had not wanted to parent him because he was autistic, he clung to the myth of lost normalcy, indicating the work we'd all have to do on disability.

In the earlier conversation about not being able to speak, DJ began to poke the second he had finished typing, "in my really free years i was poor." His eyes glazed over, he became increasingly agitated, and when we got him on the computer, he didn't make much sense. "Would you please stop poking," I said.

"im pointing there because in killing kyle"

"How does that happen? How are you killing Kyle?"

"he hurt love"

"But how does your pointing relate to Kyle?"

"kill kill," DJ replied. The desire to kill his attacker was certainly understandable enough. A fantasy in which the victim adopts the role of perpetrator, it disguises feelings of extraordinary helplessness. To be so little and at the whim of a malevolent thirteen-year-old. But how much more helpless not to have been able to register in words his objection to the assault? Emily and I had spent months teaching him how to say the word "stop" so that he might at least be able to resist symbolically. How much more disturbing to have been awakened into the memory of sexual trauma and the possibility of pleasure and not to have said no. The literal inability to do so might get lost psychically in the shame of being aroused, both then and now. DJ would soon tell us how much he hated the fact that his erections took him by surprise, that he couldn't control them, as he couldn't control his nightmares. By referring to his erections as "Kyle," he'd make clear the extent to which he understood his own body as complicit in the crime of pleasure. The ferocious desire to "kill Kyle" could thus be viewed as emerging from a multivalent speechlessness—a kind of hyperbolic overcompensation, not without its self-annihilating aspects.

Part of what we were doing with DJ was enabling him to give words to trauma: correcting for that speechlessness and slowly trying to separate rape from autism. However exhausting, the project involved what experts in this age of atrocity (Rwanda, Bosnia, etc.) call "witnessing." Even as Emily and I were encouraging him to conceive of autism as unconnected to sexual violence, we knew, of course, that his inability to speak had allowed Kyle to get away with molesting him. And we knew generally that disabled people—particularly the cognitively disabled—suffer sexual abuse at a much higher rate than the nondisabled. But it was more than that. Following DJ's own habit of condensation, we might say that his rape reflected a larger pattern of violence against a specific social group, in many ways the most vulnerable of all. The assumptions that people made about DJ, about his worth as a human being and his prospects for the future, clearly landed him in his horrifying predicament, a predicament shared by countless other cognitively disabled people.

In *Inventing the Feeble Mind*, James Trent demonstrates how experts in this century had to produce the mentally retarded as sexually threatening and deviant in order to make them eligible for forced sterilization and incarceration—all in the name of "treatment." We may have stopped sterilizing people, but we certainly haven't stopped incarcerating them. Nor have we ceased measuring their intelligence and calling them "dumb." Sadly, we haven't figured out how to include the cognitively disabled in a just and rewarding society. What to write about the history of such a failure: all of that violence, pain, and loneliness? How to honor the horror of lives lost to aggressive, wrong-headed notions? Words that dismiss the horror, that cover over it, too easily can do a further injustice, an additional violence. We had to be patient with DJ even as we feared that he might be stuck; his words, fractured and fugue-like, testified to a ghastly wound. Imagine being held down and raped as your attacker called you "fucking freaky." Judith Herman has written, "To hold traumatic reality in consciousness requires a social context that affirms and protects the victim and that joins victim and witness in a common alliance. For the individual victim, this social context is created by relationships with friends, lovers, and family. For the larger society, the social context is created by political movements that give voice to the disempowered."

Herman makes a terrific point, and I would only quibble with the way she neatly divides individual and societal contexts, for our experience would teach us that the key to DJ's recovery lay precisely in the nascent political movement that had literally and figuratively given him a voice: namely, disability rights. By the following fall, he'd be speaking of his fellow FC users as "my people," complaining that the Declaration of Independence (suddenly, that familiar phrase seemed pregnant with meaning) didn't apply to autistic people. "Freedom," as DJ would put it, "is not as available as many people think." He'd begin to locate anxiety about difference outside himself—as a function of ignorance and prejudice. Politics would thus provide a crucial psychological service, making the very future possible. I don't want to suggest some fantasy of complete restoration; DJ would sometimes turn on identity politics, saying, "im not intersted in being autisticx." He'd still continue to practice all kinds of self-loathing. Yet, such politics would help tremendously.

But even before his self-conscious politicization, DJ and the people around him would reach for activist role models, such as Hellen Keller. One day, working on math in the resource room, DJ announced, "i dont want to do this"

"Why?" Ms. Leathers asked.

"because i dont"

"What's the matter today?"

"i dont want to be here."

"Why?"

"becvace i dont want to"

"Why don't you want to? Are you going to have homework if we don't do this?"

"so what i dont carw"

"Why are you in a bad mood?"

"because i dong [don't] say anything."

"What do you mean?"

"i cangt talk."

"You're talking to me right now."

"not with a voice"

"DJ, you don't need a voice to be successful and smart. Helen Keller went to college and got a degree. Look how much she learned, DJ, and she had no voice, was blind, and could not hear. Her teacher, Annie Sullivan, taught her very tough love, discipline, and how to feel things to make sense of them. Are you feeling better about being here?"

"yes i am thank you i really appreciate you."

"I really appreciate you, too, and you should be proud of all your accomplishments and how smart you are."

Shortly after this conversation, DJ would write Ms. Leathers a poem, adopting Helen Keller's habit of referring to Annie Sullivan as "teacher."

TEACHER

my teachers have given me the world.
there is so much joy in my heart for the teacher who has stuck
      by me.
she has patience knowledge .
kindness is what she displays
god really knew what he was doing when he made her.
she dedicates all her time to kids.
she will do anything for you even when you are having a bad day.
i wish her joy happyness
and the wonderful things she deserves.
she is ms lesathers.

How to reconcile this kind of heartfelt insight with DJ's moments of utter panic and self-doubt? On the very same day, he could write a note to his grandmother who was turning seventy:

Dear Grandy,

I nmight be getting free.

You reallyn treat me like everyonde else, which makes me feel twerrific. You really understand me and loveb me. You look at me with truthful eyes. You really hear whatn I say.

Your granjdson,

DJ

and then engage in the following exchange with me:

"kyule poking poking is bad hy hes my jur injury in lifedf poking is bad"

"What made you think of Kyle today?"

"your hipn replacement"

"Daddy will have his hip replacement not this Wednesday but next Wednesday. I am looking forward to the operation. It will make me feel better."

"poking is bad"

"Let's all try to be brave these next few weeks. We can get through them together."

"please love please"

As we got closer to the date of my surgery, DJ grew ever more anxious. His mantra—"poking is bad"—appeared repeatedly in his typing. Once, I asked him what the phrase meant specifically, and he said, "i'm not just sure." It was like a kind of automatic writing. In any event, the words "hip replacement" and "poking" had themselves decided to elope in the chapel of monumental dread. It would take every ounce of vixen ingenuity to disrupt this sullen pair. We might have been more successful had the fates not frowned so cruelly on my family. A week before my operation, my brother James called to say that the doctors thought Charlie was suffering from hydrocephalus; his head had become abnormally large, which indicated a problem with the ventricles that drained and circulated spinal fluid. He'd need a permanent shunt. There was a slim chance that a tumor might be responsible for the ventricle failure and some of the increase in head size. Two days later, my brother's worst

313

fears were realized. Charlie had a malignant brain tumor—an especially lethal sort called pineoblastoma, which had a very, very low survival rate. We ached for my brother and his wife; we ached for Charlie, that gorgeous, happy boy with a mop of black hair.

I remember coming home from the office and greeting Emily, who had just heard from James: there were tears in her eyes. "Oh shit, oh shit, oh shit!" I yelled, flabbergasted by the news. How could this be happening? I called my brother and tried somehow to remain positive. "They're developing new treatments all the time," I said, "nothing is ever hopeless," but my brother just wept, hearing in my voice the desperate need to console. When I got off the phone, I went and lay down on the hospital bed. I removed my neck brace—two weeks earlier I'd graduated to a soft collar—and I felt myself begin to plummet. "Congratulations!/ Today is your day. You're off to Great Places!/ You're off and away!" The words from that stupid book filled my head. "I'm sorry to say so/ but, sadly, it's true/ that Bang-ups and Hang-ups/ *can* happen to you." DJ was right: the future *is* a hospital, an enormous emergency room to which all of your loved ones might shortly be taken.

As tears streamed down my face, DJ appeared in the doorway, having come from a bath. He'd only managed to complete that part of the dressing process involving his underwear. He saw me looking sad and defeated in my lonely prison, and he let out an ear-piercing shriek. Emily had told him that Charlie was sick, but now he knew something was really wrong. And his mind started to race. Once again, I was a dead man walking—no, a dead man lying down, wheeled off to the executioner (that "anesthesia," as Phillip Larkin put it, "from which none come round"). DJ was like a juror who'd held out for innocence, against his better judgment, wanting to believe life incapable of such gratuitous misery. But with all of the other jurors screaming at him in the tiny deliberation room of his mind, and with all of the accumulated evidence, he'd finally relented. Guilty, guilty as charged! Picture life being dragged out of the courtroom in chains as DJ, refusing to be interviewed, retreated into his invisible fortress.

CHAPTER 12

Charlie Needs Our Help

Because I had a presurgical appointment in Iowa City the following day (Friday), I decided that afterward I'd just keep heading east and lend whatever support I could to my brother and his wife in Chicago. I really wasn't supposed to be driving; I couldn't remain in a sitting position for longer than twenty minutes without my leg going numb. And my neck made it very difficult to execute proper safety procedures, like checking behind you before changing lanes. Furthermore, my orthopedist had explicitly instructed me to rest up before the operation. He didn't want me exhausted or stressed out going into it. But this was one of those moments in life when you put everything aside in order to care for those you love. Charlie was to have brain surgery on Monday, a very complicated, life-threatening procedure lasting at least ten hours. The tumor was wrapped like a spiral staircase around his brainstem, and the surgeon would attempt to excise it—without doing neurological damage. Because the risk of hemorrhaging was high, there was a good chance that Charlie might die on the operating room table. I simply had to be there.

Emily and I debated going as a family, but we thought that the stress of the occasion would be too much for DJ. He was already typing, "poking is bad" over and over on his computer; we needed him to be as calm as possible for my surgery and subsequent hospitalization. Moreover, he had school on Friday and Monday, and we thought it better not to disrupt his routine. As it would turn out, DJ would be more nervous with me gone, and so he and Emily would come to Chicago—in time for a private mass on Sunday before Charlie's operation.

The trip was a nightmare. My appointment ended at 1:00, making a rush-hour arrival on a Friday inevitable. About a half hour away from the city, my leg went entirely numb, and the pain in my groin became unbearable. I had to get out of the car, stand up, and so I did—right there in the middle of Interstate 88. Thank God we were at a standstill. I'd already had to stop some six times in three hours, extending a long trip.

I report this not to command sympathy—rather, to state plainly what kind of shape I was in and to underscore my status as a human being in this drama, not some paragon of virtue or admirable detachment. Much as I knew what I had to do for my brother and much as I wanted to be there for him, I was also crazed with stress and even angry that this catastrophe was occurring. How could Charlie be having brain surgery two days before my hip replacement? It was as if the gods had stolen my date book and maliciously picked the same week for his operation. I hadn't even had a second to process my own losses, and now I was being asked to put them in perspective—in effect, to dismiss them. I know it sounds petulant to complain about such a thing, but feelings are the stuff of life, and those, I'm embarrassed to admit, were my feelings. I'm determined not to present an idealized portrait of myself in this book; such a portrait doesn't do anybody any good. Progressive political convictions and human fallibility go hand in hand, as do abiding love and emotional depletion.

Truth be told, I was anxious about having to see my father again, whom I hadn't seen since my brother's wedding the year before. "See" is the operative word here, for we hadn't said a word to one another, hadn't even acknowledged the other's presence. Like DJ, I'd practiced the doctrine of preemption, instructing my sister to tell the old man to stay the hell away from me and my family. And, of course, I was terribly disappointed when he did just that—and did so comfortably. It turns out there's no inoculation against disappointment. Driving into Chicago, I wondered if he'd be able to do the same with me in a neck brace and facing a hip replacement.

Surely, my physical condition would compel him to reach out and bury the hatchet. No matter how pathetic I found the spectacle of a forty-year-old son wanting something from a father he detested, a father in whom he could find not a single thing to admire, I just couldn't stop myself from being sucked, like a smallish star, into the black hole of longing.

And longing—surprise, surprise—led to resentment. Why hadn't he bothered to call when DJ was in and out of the hospital, having seizures and, eerily enough, being tested for a brain tumor? Did it matter that we were feuding? Why hadn't he been able to put forth that show of self-aggrandizement he called love when *my* son was sick? Why couldn't he have embraced a boy he said was not "his real grandson"? As the traffic started to move, I thought of DJ's relationship with his birth father and of what he might one day need from that man who had hurt him terribly but who had at least now expressed some interest in seeing him.

I had gotten so worked up thinking about these things that I imagined my father delighting in my injuries, pronouncing them, retroactively, the punishment for spurning him—or rather being spurned by him. (There's a great line in Robert Penn Warren's novel *All the King's Men* in which the protagonist says to a woman he's wronged, "I forgive you for everything I did to you." That would be my father's approach to the past.) But delight isn't right. Once you'd exhibited even the slightest refusal to fawn all over him, let alone voice your disapproval about something he'd said or done, you didn't exist. You were like the "disappeared" in Argentina, removed from your filial apartment in the middle of the night and sent ignominiously to the bottom of the ocean. My father had cut so many people out of his life—so many friends, relatives, and colleagues—it was scary. And while he was married to my mother, he demanded that my siblings side with him in their endless, acrimonious battles, or face the consequences.

A relationship with my father wasn't technically possible; it was like trying to have a relationship with a king, who could only conceive of you as his subject. (When Emily and I got married, he told her—seriously—that she could call him "Dad" or "sir," the two options of course being one and the same.) The world, he believed, revolved around him; under no circumstances would he renounce his Copernican philosophy,

banishing any and all would-be Galileos. In order to preserve their relationship with their father, my siblings had had to behave like the prickly
monarch's court attendants, assiduously indulging his megalomania, all
the while knowing he was just another planet in the solar system, which
was just another solar system in the universe, which . . . how much in-
significance can we tolerate? My little sister had lost herself in the process, slowly but surely aspiring to the throne of total self-involvement.

Years ago, I wrote a poem that tried to capture a son's dissatisfaction with estrangement—the estrangement (back then) of being with
someone who wasn't reciprocally present to you. I was reminded of
it as I inched my way toward the city and what would be, without a
doubt, the ghastliest of family reunions: a vigil for baby Charlie in
Children's Memorial Hospital. The poem was called "Cries from the
Way Back."

> You can travel in a car,
>   as we did frequently,
> and never get to you.
>
> You're all indifference and departure.
>
> You simply can't be reached
>   by phone
>   by fax,
>   by common words.
> You're as complete and as empty as a zero.
>
> As the years have taken their customary toll,
>   I've come to think of you
> as distance itself:
>
>   a haughty and mocking horizon—
>
> so much so that when I remember the little boy
>   in the back of the family station wagon,

eager to arrive at his summer vacation
    and asking, for the umpteenth time,

"Are we there yet, Dad? Are we there?"

I toss my heart into the tollbooth basket
    and now ask wearily,
"How much *father* do we have to go?"

An earlier version of the poem alluded to a trip I took to look at col-
leges, a trip on which I became terribly ill with gastroenteritis—so ill
that I actually threw up during my Williams College interview. When I
couldn't continue with the trip, my father deposited me in a hotel room
and went to see a movie, though I begged him to take me to the hospital. Hours later, he returned to more moaning and vomiting. He said
nothing, just attended to some business in the bed beside me.

As melodramatic as it sounds, during the period that Emily and I
were debating whether to adopt DJ, I repeatedly dreamt about a plane
crash in Guam in which a man was thrown from the wreckage, his legs
horrifically mangled. The man's son was stuck inside the burning fu-
selage, yelling, "Help me, Daddy. Help me." But the man couldn't
move, and in his agony he had to listen to his dying son's screams. Were
my father's legs broken? Were mine? What keeps us from walking the
shortest of distances—a hotel room, a waterfront home, an inner-city
block, a checkpoint (may I say this?) in the Occupied Territories?
"More," DJ had signed in the emergency room some eight years before, prefiguring, I imagined, a new discourse of personal and social
concern.

Over the course of the weekend, my brother, James, would ask, "How
do you raise a dying son?" By doing what you're already doing, I'd want
to tell him. By counting every remaining minute with Charlie a blessing, savoring it, drawing it out with rapt attention so that it seemed as if
it might conceal a longer span of love—a paradoxically infinite bridge
across the bay of years they wouldn't, in all likelihood, have together.
And there, as a backdrop and foil, would be my prodigal father who'd

wasted so much time, so much possibility, wrapped like a pharaoh in the silk of arrogance. For all of his actual interest in people, the man might as well have begun to mummify himself.

I digress. But life was offering up a hundred thousand parallels and just as many contrasts. Like DJ, I found myself in the stacks of association, shelving memories and impressions by mysterious call number. I was headed for the ultimate stage of family conflict. We Savareses were like something out of Tennessee Williams. Could we keep it together, all of us (my father and his new wife, my mother, my sisters, I), and try to help James? Each of us had a plotting, brooding understudy who wanted a chance to act—act up, that is, change the script of reasonable care.

When I arrived at my brother's apartment, I found my mother and Eileen's sister, Marie, in the kitchen. James was on the phone, and Eileen was taking a shower. Baby Charlie was asleep. The mood was tense and sullen. When my mother first spotted me in my neck brace, she began to cry. The evening would go like this, with one person or another breaking down, all the while baby Charlie seemed, once he'd awakened, as peaceful and as happy as ever. You couldn't get yourself to believe he was ill. He looked so blissfully unaware.

The next morning, I learned, there would be an emergency baptism, right in the living room, conducted by a family friend, a former priest named Dominick. Eileen's immediate family—her brothers and sister and, of course, her parents—would be present, as would my mother and I. The rest of the Savareses would be flying in Saturday night, in time for the private mass on Sunday and the surgery on Monday morning.

After dinner, I sneaked off to call Emily and tell her what was happening. She and DJ had been having highly fraught conversations on the computer. "how is uncle james and baby charlie/"

"They are feeling better now that Dad is there with them. We will call Dad in about twenty-five minutes and see what his plans are."

"im possibly loving you huimer" [him?]

"I'm definitely loving you."

"you I love you true you look hurt"

"No, I feel just as happy as I did thirty minutes ago. You don't need to worry about Mom. What are you thinking?"

"im nervous because im misding dad"

"Are you nervous or sad about missing Dad?"

"missing dad makes me really nervous because im trying n0oy to poke."

After the ferris wheel of anxiety had made several revolutions, DJ announced, "im nervous that you try to hide things from me"

"DJ, Mom heard your message this summer about how important it is to be truthful. I have been entirely truthful with you since then. What are you afraid I am hiding from you?"

"thetb dad is really gttinv his hip replaced right now"

"Absolutely NOT. Dad is not getting his hip replaced until Wednesday, May 5th. Look on the calendar and see. Dad is in Chicago helping Uncle James. I am glad he can be there to help, but I'm also sorry he can't be here the weekend before his hip operation. You will definitely see Dad before his hip operation on Wednesday. Either we will drive to Chicago or he will drive home. Dad is fine." It had never occurred to us that DJ might think that I was having surgery now, but it made sense, perfect sense.

Emily then addressed the subject of my operation, believing he needed to talk through the specifics. "When Dad gets his hip operation on Wednesday, Mom will go with him for the day. You will have school and hang out with some of your buddies, and Mom will get back home here around your bed time." Emily then added, "Lots of people might call here today to—"

"poking is bad," DJ typed, interrupting her.

"You have nothing you need to worry about."

"im possibly pointing out that you look kind of tied" [tired]

"I'm not feeling tired. I think I saw you yawn and it made me yawn. Did you know that yawning often spreads from one person to the next like that?"

"poking is bad," he repeated. If some day I have a stroke and language leaves me, I'm certain that I will be able to say at least this phrase, so imprinted on my consciousness is it, so nearly automatic.

Emily and I debated the pros and cons of their coming to Chicago and decided, finally, that they should come. DJ was just too stressed without me. If they didn't come, I'd only have a few hours to spend with him before my surgery. And then I'd be in the hospital for four days, and DJ had already made it clear that he wouldn't be visiting me in "great places." I couldn't bear to go such a long stretch without extended (or semi-extended) time together. I think Emily heard this in my voice, and trooper that she is, tipped the balance in Chicago's favor. So, they'd make the trip the following day, have dinner with me, go to the mass on Sunday, and then drive back immediately afterward. I was glad; I wanted to see them both badly.

I spent the night in a hotel, had breakfast with my mother, and headed back to my brother's apartment for the baptism. My sister-in-law's family is Irish Catholic—they're wonderful, progressive, peace-loving Catholics, but real believers. It had been a long time since I'd had my falling out with the Church, and I felt a bit uncomfortable participating in such an intimate and urgent ritual. But the weekend's motto had clearly become "Anything for Charlie," and so I went with it. I remember being surprised by how much my brother, who'd never been religious at all, went with it. Someone (was it Hemingway?) once said that a foxhole can make a believer out of anyone. How much more true when your kid is in the foxhole? But beyond this obvious explanation lay the warm embrace of Eileen's family, for whom Catholicism was an integral part of a generous way of life. Who wouldn't want such a rich and consolatory bear hug?

Dominic, a lovely man who'd recently had his own hip replacement surgery, arrived with the biggest clam shell I'd ever seen, which was to serve as the baptismal font, and various oils and holy water. Marie was looking for someone to videotape the ceremony, and I volunteered—in part to avoid being assigned another, more awkward task, like reciting a prayer. The baptism was beautiful. Each of us made the sign of the cross on Charlie's forehead and pledged to support the newest member of the Christian community. We sang hymns a cappella, led by Dominic's wife, who has a soothing voice. Because James had a habit of singing goofy songs to Charlie, songs set to familiar Christmas melodies, we all tried that as well. When Charlie heard the "song" he knew best, he broke into a smile, lifting everyone's spirits like a spot of sun on a foggy morning. Sadness and hope battled it out, finally deciding on one of those bright, gray skies.

Imagine the videographer's shock when, suddenly, Dominic suggested that they perform a healing rite on him—on me! "We have the oils," he said. "We might as well." I felt my pulse rate rise immediately, and I began to sweat. My mother gave me a look that could be interpreted kindly as: "Say anything and I'll kill you." Everybody lined up to make the sign of the cross on my forehead. I saw Eileen's brother Paul, Charlie's godfather, shoot me a smirk; he knew I was uncomfortable. I admired how easily he traveled back and forth from the old world of Catholicism to the hip, new world of, say, *The Simpsons* and *South Park*, like someone with a diplomatic passport. I was still waiting at customs, frankly, when Dominic and his oils greeted my forehead. What made me more uncomfortable: a ritual I didn't believe in or the magnanimous good wishes of deeply caring people? I'd been complaining privately that my own problems had been lost in the shuffle, the mad scramble, of DJ and Charlie's medical issues, and here I was finally getting some attention and not enjoying it. "You are," Emily would say later, "at least as complicated as your son."

After the baptism, most of us went over to Paul's house for an impromptu reception. It would serve as a meeting place for other local family members and those flying in. James and Eileen remained behind with Charlie. They wanted some downtime together. At about 5:00, Eileen's oldest brother, Joe, gave me a lift back to the hotel, where I had told Emily I would meet her. The first thing DJ did when they arrived was to ask me to remove my pants. At first, I didn't understand why, but then I got it. He wanted to make sure that I hadn't had my surgery. He spent an inordinate amount of time inspecting my leg before he was satisfied that we'd been telling the truth. He seemed to relax after that. Once we'd unpacked, we ordered dinner from an Italian restaurant next to the hotel and brought it back to our room. DJ then took a bath, and we cuddled and tickled until bedtime.

The next morning we met various family members—my aunt, cousin, mother, older sister, and brother-in-law—for breakfast at a waffle house. Before leaving for the restaurant, we went over the day's schedule with DJ. "DJ, tell me what the plan is for today," I said.

"eat breakfasrt, eat lunch, go to church sergice, feel sad hurtn." Another laugh-out-loud moment. The idea of purposeful, orderly heartache was at once bizarre and oddly perceptive. It certainly captured the way we human beings try to contain grief, and, at the same time, it exposed the masochism in even bothering to confront it at all.

"Tell me more about feeling sad and hurt at the church service," Emily replied.

"charlie is realy sick"

"Yes, and family members are feeling sad about it. On Monday he will have surgery to see if they can help him feel better. Let's go meet Boo [my aunt] and Julia [my cousin] and Grammy for breakfast. We'll bring the labeler and continue our conversation there."

The second we entered the waffle house, DJ signed, "all done, all done." He was frantic to leave, ignoring my many attempts to get him to greet his relatives properly. When we finally persuaded him to sit down at the table, he again signed, "all done, all done" and typed, "too many sad faces." DJ was like an emotional seismograph detecting tremors a thousand miles away. No matter how diligently my relatives tried to seem upbeat, DJ could tell that they were not. "All done, all done." We couldn't get him to touch his breakfast—not even the strips of bacon that he customarily devoured. I ended up having to take him for a little walk about halfway through the meal in order to get him to calm down.

After breakfast, we had some time to spare, and so a bunch of us took a cab to the Lincoln Park Zoo by the lake. It was a beautiful, blustery day, and we thought that DJ might enjoy seeing the water and the animals. Later, in the hotel room, we encouraged him to write a short letter to James and Eileen. We knew it was a risky proposition, but we wanted to give him a chance to wish them well. "Dear Uncle James and Aunt Eileen, I hear that Charlie needs our help," it began. "He is very brave." I can't remember the rest of it, and since it was composed on the labeler and presented to his aunt and uncle at the service, I don't have a record of it.

But as with all of DJ's communiqués, it was touchingly sweet. He always seemed to rise to the occasion when trying to comfort someone.

As the hour of the private mass approached, DJ signed, "drive, drive," indicating an intense desire to flee.

"In about twenty minutes we will take a cab ride to the church," Emily said. "That will be your drive, OK?"

"poking is bad"

"You are feeling nervous, but try to keep it separate from poking and bad memories."

"i need sadness to go," DJ explained.

"I know it's hard, but we are all here together trying to help each other. You are safe and OK."

"ikm nervous because dad might free really dread hsurgdry b," he typed. I could have predicted this remark. It had all of DJ's signature traits: the associative slide from one operation and person to the next, the characteristic diction (nervous, free, dread). The word "free" had continued to be a problem for him, denoting too many disparate things, most of which were negative. Here it clearly meant "die."

"I'm not dreading my surgery," I said. "I'm looking forward to it. Really."

When we arrived at the church, the only other people there were my father and his new wife. Practically a cathedral, the church allowed us enough distance to pretend that we didn't recognize each other. Thank God for small (or is it large) favors. Very quickly, other people began to arrive. I sat with my brother-in-law, Lowell, who told me that my younger sister had elected not to come out to Chicago. Emily and DJ sat toward the back in case they needed to make a quick exit. A strategic decision, this sitting next to my older sister's husband. On the basis of the previous day's baptism, I surmised that we'd all be invited up to the altar come communion time. The Ripps were post-Vatican II Catholics. There'd be the making of a circle and the sharing of the peace—hugs and handshakes for *every* member of the service. Hence, there'd be no avoiding the old man and his wife if I joined the congregation in the sanctuary, and I wasn't about to be roped into forgiveness or, worse, some perfunctory greeting. So, I decided that I'd keep Lowell, who is Jewish, company in the pew.

I couldn't have been more delighted with the results of my reconnaissance mission, when suddenly Chuck Ripp, Eileen's father, approached me about doing a reading. What could I say? Now I'd have to traipse—no, limp—down in front of everyone, climb the sanctuary steps, and in a neck brace declaim the word of the Lord. And all in front of my father, who was sitting in the first row. (Thank heavens it wasn't the passage in which Christ heals a cripple and instructs him to "sin no more.") I felt like invoking the Americans with Disabilities Act in order somehow to get out of it. How conspicuous and awkward it would be when I then didn't go up for communion. Do I need to say that I was a wreck?

When James and Eileen appeared with Charlie, Emily and DJ walked over and presented DJ's letter. Eileen and James hadn't seen them since they were in Iowa. Reading the letter, they both broke down. "Charlie needs our help. That's right, DJ," James said. As James went to hug him, DJ let out an audible wail and moved away. I stood up, but Emily quickly redirected him to their pew in the back. DJ would later insist on moving closer to the front, and about halfway through the service, I'd notice them off to the side, two pews behind me. Emily had some paper with her, and when DJ got silly—one of his anxiety coping skills—she had him draw.

The service included a homily by Chuck who in a simple and deeply moving way asked God for a miracle. And then he asked us, the congregants, to pray. He spoke of prayer chains that might circle the globe and voice the ardent wish for a little boy's recovery. His earnest words made me, made many of us, weep, as did the plaintive music and the light pouring in through the stained glass windows—the whole ritual and space giving a shape to longing. If asked about my own theological convictions, apart from my position on the institution of the Catholic church, I'd finally have to side with DJ who, a couple of weeks after the service, would respond to the question "What do you think about God?" by answering, "maybe noone knows." This from a boy who must have spent many hours praying for his own deliverance from evil: the years in foster care, the beatings, the repeated sexual assaults. "i try going to heaven/ three times heaven,/ three each tree. . . ." In the middle of

Chuck's homily, I thought of DJ's "Rescue" poem and imagined him as a swallow flitting about in the upper reaches—the canopy, as it were—of the church's knave. "maybe no one knows": I wish we adults left it at that. What profound humility in the face of inexplicable suffering.

I survived my job as lector and proved prescient about communion. The priest invited the congregants to make a circle around the altar. I remained in the pew with Lowell, who seemed surprised that I didn't go up. When it came time to share the peace, I watched my mother nearly lunge to avoid her ex-husband and his wife. Like me, she had only bellicose feelings for the man. Later, on the front steps of the church, she would castigate her sister for having kissed the two of them. "What was I supposed to do?" she asked. "They were right there in front of me. I couldn't turn away." A very generous woman, my mother had been seriously wronged by my father—hit, patronized, verbally abused, ignored. She'd be as supportive as anyone of James and Eileen throughout their gruesome ordeal, but she wouldn't be friendly to her ex-husband. She'd simply choose, as I had, not to create a scene.

Should we have done more than this? Should we have been better human beings? Should we have modeled for DJ (and given to James and Eileen) the gift of forgiveness? I don't know. I've read a good deal of popular psychology, with its emphasis on letting go, moving forward, etc., and I feel as if I'd partly done that by constructing positive, reciprocal relationships beyond the bounds of family. All of that, however, had been predicated upon not having to see the man, not having to be disappointed again by him. But life thought otherwise, concocting reasons for us to have to be together, though "being together" was precisely what my father would not allow, belittling you with his haughty self-entombment. I never felt such an abiding sense of lack as when I was with my father. He was like the IRS—constantly withholding. And, by withholding, he trapped you in a nonrelationship: the cruelest trick of all. Short of him changing who he was, the only productive scenario was to keep him at an enormous distance; that way physical and emotional geographies matched.

You're probably thinking that for someone critical of blood families, I certainly manifested an obdurate attachment to the figure of my birth father. The irony wasn't lost on me, and I worried about fueling such a fire in DJ. Would he manifest the same attachment to the man who had rejected him? How would I, his adoptive father, enter into the equation?

The service concluded, if I remember correctly, with a soaring rendition of "On Eagle's Wings." Emily and DJ said their good-byes and left; they had a long drive ahead of them. "I'll see you tomorrow, DJ. Be good for mamma." After the crowd dispersed, I went over to Chuck and Cathy's house for dinner. I met a man about my age, a friend of the Ripps, with a similar medical condition. He, too, had had a hip replacement. I remember asking him how much it hurt, and he laughed. Not a good sign. "Insist on the morphine," he said. He counseled me to take the rehab seriously, and he told me about a new drug he was taking. We'd both been on the Remicade and found it intolerable. I chit-chatted for a while before Jamie, Paul's wife, drove me back to my hotel where I promptly fell asleep.

If the church was the main stage on which we acted out our hopes, then the surgical waiting room at Children's Memorial Hospital was the black box theater. Frankly too big a production for the space, the vigil consisted of no fewer than twenty-five cast members, all of us crammed into one half of the room. Another family, with another very sick child, occupied the other half. The tension was terrific. At any moment Charlie could die. Hemorrhaging, as I mentioned, was a huge risk. You had to get ready for this prospect, even this likelihood, with every tick of the clock, which rose like a full moon on the waiting room wall. At the same time, you had to try to prepare yourself for the duration—up to fourteen hours, if the surgery grew especially tricky. These objectives seemed to be irreconcilable, for who could remain in a state of nervous vigilance for that long? And so you found yourself being distracted, losing focus, reading, only to be jolted back to reality, like a driver asleep at the wheel and already halfway off the road. Every little sign, every unfamiliar person who entered the waiting room, had to be deciphered. Was he a messenger of bad news? At one point, several hours into the surgery, the hospital chaplain showed up, and everyone gasped in unison. (He had come to introduce himself.)

James and Eileen had decided to stay in a private waiting room for parents. They would hear regularly from a member of the medical team about the progress of the operation and then that person would report to the larger group. Because the operation was so very dangerous, they wanted to preserve some privacy should the word be grim. This arrangement would last for only a couple of hours, however, as even James and Eileen found it difficult to pass the time. So, they'd end up walking down to the common waiting room and hanging out with the rest of us—especially after they'd just received a report and knew that they wouldn't be getting another one for quite a while.

Along with Marie, Chuck and Cathy had arranged for the group to say a prayer every hour. We'd stand (those of us in the room at the time; my mother and my aunt were often outside smoking), hold hands, and recite an Our Father or two. At first, my characteristic objection to formalized religion would kick in, and I'd start to sweat, but gradually I'd come to understand the practice as a response to helplessness, extraordinary helplessness. There we were playing tug-of-war with death, except there wasn't any rope. There wasn't any material way of pulling the Grim Reaper, in whose arms Charlie lay, over to the side of life. We had to save the little one with desire alone. I remember watching my brother work a set of prayer beads; I'd never seen him so focused, so intent. I honestly believe he'd have given up his own life to spare Charlie, and he'd have done so in a second, saying good-bye to Eileen and then disappearing into the waste of nothingness.

The first report revealed that the surgeons had removed a portion of Charlie's skull and that they were presently separating his brain. Though it shouldn't have been, this first report was the scariest, for we weren't yet accustomed to the procedure of receiving news. I can't recall the specific content of the other briefings, except to say that one concerned the process of marking the tumor, another beginning to excise it, and a third. . . . That sentence, of course, compresses too great a time period and too much stress, allowing the reader to race along to hope, like a traveler on a moving sidewalk. When the surgical team spokesperson informed us that the operation had reached a critical juncture—the moment when bleeding could really be a problem—we all bore down and pulled as hard as we could. Death pulled back, but we were deter-mined. This span of time seemed the longest: the full moon of the clock stuck in a narrow wedge of hospital sky. It simply wouldn't set. What could one do to while away the minutes? Those who were sitters sat; those who were pacers paced. One of the latter, I periodically left the waiting room to phone Emily.

I'd been phoning her a lot—probably five times since the surgery began. By giving Emily briefings, I felt more in control, the telling of what happened in a semi-orderly manner a hedge against the future. Anyway, I'd promised to let her know what was going on. Later, I'd learn just how anxious these phone calls were making DJ. "im hearing voices," he said.

"Tell me more. What kind of voices? What are they saying?" Emily replied.

"you try to not yearn for baby charlie"

"When you say you hear voices, whose voices?"

"yours"

"Do you mean you hear what we're thinking?"

"no"

"Are you reminding me that you hear and understand everything we say on the phone to people?"

"yes." Sometimes DJ's use of language was strictly literal: he was hearing voices, voices on the phone.

"So, do you have questions or concerns about something you've heard us say?"

"yes you said threeb times you think charlie has dread of brain very reachvery." DJ must have heard Emily mention the position of the tumor and how difficult it was for the surgeon to remove it. "im nervous byt ghe might really get hurt he is very little but he might not live," he typed. Those two "buts," they evoked the very tug-of-war we grown-ups were engaged in: hope in littleness and life, despair about an uncer-tain future. Toward the end of one of their conversations on the computer, DJ complained about his parents' habit of overpraising him, thanking him profusely for being so brave, putting on a cheery demon-stration of good-natured optimism: "understand the great burden i feel

trying to be hepful ylou make me nervous becuse you really exaggerate."
He knew how dire it was.

As I stood in the hall, Emily asked me about my father. "It's fine," I
said. "When I'm in the room, he's no less than five feet away from me and
there isn't the slightest acknowledgment of my presence. He reads the
paper, works on business, makes phone calls. He seems remarkably un-
ruffled. I told you: I no longer exist to him. I could be in a wheelchair or,
like Charlie having brain surgery, and he wouldn't so much as bat an eye."

"He's always been a bastard," Emily responded. "You should take
your neck brace and strangle him"—a strikingly atypical remark from
the woman the kids at DJ's school call "Miss Emily." Miss Emily hates
my father.

"It's OK. I think I'm over my pater panic. What's amazing is how much
all of these people are rooting for a five-month-old they barely know. I
mean straining, really straining, to help him through." Sometimes I'd
get to a place with my father where his selfishness, his vindictiveness,
his refusal to admit to mutual imperfection, would be more laughable
than crushing. Charlie had helped me to get to that place, and the surgery had been like a kind of spiritual exercise. I had the feeling I'd really
worked out: a nearly pleasant exhaustion, if I may say such a thing.

About an hour later, I saw the medical team spokesperson enter the
private waiting room to which James and Eileen had retreated. The moment of truth had arrived. If Charlie had made it through this part of the
operation, he would be—at least surgically—out of the woods. Well, maybe
not out of the woods, but certainly no longer in the jaws of a ravenous
coyote. The next five minutes were intolerable. I thought my sister Juleen
was going to burst, blow up right in front of me, so fervently did she want
her nephew to live. My mother was clenching her teeth. When Marie
spotted James and Eileen walking down the hall, she quieted everybody
down, and we gathered in one smallish, concentrated bunch. Charlie had
survived! In fact, he was doing quite well under the circumstances. The
operation was complete but for the closing. It had taken much less time
than it might have, and the lead surgeon thought that he had gotten all of
the cancer—all that he could see. The room erupted into applause and
cries of jubilation. I almost couldn't believe it.

Chuck proposed that the group give thanks to God, and so we assembled for a prayer. I thought to myself: there may not be a God in heaven but there is certainly a surgeon on earth and, what is more, a community of well-wishers, people willing to do anything for this desperate child. The mood had changed dramatically, with some of us becoming quite loud. James and Eileen thought that we were perhaps a bit too celebratory. There was a long road ahead. Charlie would have to recover from the operation and begin a chemo regime that could itself kill or disable him. Chemo directly to the brain of a five-month-old was not recommended. Charlie's cancer, James reminded us, was technically incurable; no one had survived pineoblastoma long-term. Clearly, he and Eileen were already looking to the future, and what they saw scared them. The next hurdle appears immediately, and you better have your striding down. Chuck, though, reminded everyone that the surgery had been a crucial first step. They could now meet the impossible with confidence.

I waited until Charlie was in recovery before I announced my departure and said good-bye to everyone. I was still thinking I'd drive back to Iowa that night. I wanted a full day at home before my surgery. By the time I'd returned to my hotel room, however, and begun to pack, I felt stiff and sleepy. When I called Emily, she suggested that I stay the night and get up early. I could be home by 11:30 if I left by 6:00, so I decided to do that. My good friends John and Angela had generously offered to come get me, but that felt like too much of a production.

Lying in bed, flipping through the many cable channels, I reflected on the day's events, which only seemed more surreal with each passing moment. If DJ, in his "world ofd hurtt," could put himself in the place of another through a process of intense associative identification, what might we say about our own response to injury and fierce objection to death? What does it mean to lament the "unfairness of it all," to insist on Charlie's sparkling potential, his nearly unfathomable possibilities? To this day, I ask: might we learn something from DJ and begin to identify with those struck down by an analogous oppressor?

The German writer Ernst Bloch has an anecdote about a young worker, in T.W. Adorno's summary, "whom a benefactor temporarily treats to the good life and then sends back to the mines, at which point the worker murders him":

> "Is life, which plays with us, any different than the rich man, the good man? . . . The social fate that the wealthy class imposes on the poor class must be superseded. But the rich man is still there, like the idol of a different fate, our natural fate, with death at its end, a fate whose crudeness the wealthy devil copies and makes palpable until it becomes his own fate." Or, in a variation . . . , "In death too there is something of the wealthy cat that lets the mouse run free before it devours it. No one could blame the 'saint' for shooting this god down the way the worker shot the millionaire."

As Adorno puts it, "Bloch constructs an *analogia entis*, an analogy of being, between social oppression and life's mythical bondage to death. . . ." Indeed, he seems to propose a kind of connective ethics, where the prospect of an infant's early demise would provoke an equivalent outrage about, say, the forty-three million Americans presently living in poverty. You couldn't have one feeling without the other, which is another way of stating that private joy would always be contingent upon public fairness. Imagine allowing so many children to languish in foster care. Or imagine, as in the FC controversy, sending nonspeaking people with autism back to the mines of special ed, with labels of mental retardation and no way to communicate. This actually happened. Letter boards and computers and litewriters and facilitators were taken from people when the APA and others deemed this fragile movement a hoax. Even if many of these people hadn't been communicating, why give up? Why presume unyielding illiteracy? Why not work still harder to reach out, find or cultivate ability, include the marginalized as generously and imaginatively as possible in the life we demand for ourselves?

Of course, *we* had sent Rhonda back to the mines, Rhonda with her checkered past and innumerable problems, Rhonda with her violence against Ellie and DJ. Can one be both practical and utopian? Can one recognize limits (to care, to human conduct) yet hold out against them? What kind of devotion awaits us?

The alarm clock woke me from a sound sleep at 5:15. I took a shower, checked out, and retrieved my car from the hotel parking lot. Once I was on the highway, I pulled off every thirty minutes or so to get the grinding pain in my hip to cease. Just before noon, I saw the sign for Grinnell. I was home.

I spent the afternoon trying to meet with students, prepare some final assignments, and collect from my office anything I might need for the next six weeks. I'd pretty much be housebound after the operation. My plan, as I told my students, was to read papers and poems once I'd gotten out of the hospital and was off the major painkillers. Because I was having surgery during the final week of classes, I had some seventeen days to get my grades in, which I thought would be sufficient. (The idea of doing grades in a hospital bed, however, made me sick.)

When DJ got home from school, we spent time wrestling on his pillow pit and talking on the computer. I had initially planned a final jump on the trampoline with him, but Emily thought that too sullenly momentous. Better not to proclaim the end of our favorite activity.

That night I went to bed without eating dinner, per the doctor's instructions. I had to be at the hospital by 8:00, which meant leaving Grinnell by 6:45. Emily had lined up a lot of help for us during this period. DJ's resource room teacher, for instance, appeared at 6:30 to help get DJ ready for school. She and Sabrina and Marie did yeoman's service, something for which I will be eternally grateful. And DJ did his part, too, despite his nervousness. Except for that first day, Emily planned to drop DJ off at school and then come spend as much time as possible at the hospital with me. She'd leave the hospital, which was an hour away, in time to put DJ to bed. I frankly don't know how she managed such a frantic schedule, but she did.

The surgery was brutal. I recall waking up and thinking that someone had cut off my leg. And they had, at least a small part of it. Because my blood pressure had risen and remained high during the operation, they waited a while to give me morphine. Even in my post-surgery haze, I knew that I had made a big mistake in choosing to do the operation with anesthesia; the epidural would have provided a total pain block. But I had been afraid of being conscious during the surgery. I'd joked with a colleague that I didn't want to be reading Hegel while the doctor pounded the metal rod into my femur. "Keep it down. I'm trying to read!" Though the anesthesiologist spoke of being pleasantly sedated with an epidural, I had imagined total lucidity and rejected it. As it was, I actually woke up in the middle of the operation because I hadn't received enough anesthesia. As a courtesy to the reader, I won't describe what I saw.

I was in a lot of discomfort—so much so that when they wheeled me into my room and I spotted Emily, I started to cry, saying things like, "Why did I decide to do this?" Later, a nurse thought I looked bad enough that she needed to call the doctor. "Look how white he is. Look at the circles under his eyes," she said. "Something's wrong." Emily tried to explain that I'd looked like this *before* the surgery, that I always looked like this at the end of a semester. This one, with Charlie's medical problems, had simply been worse than usual. That night, when Emily left to go home, I felt myself sinking. I listened as a doctor told my roommate, who was recovering from back surgery, that his cancer had spread to his spine.

Back in Grinnell, DJ was trying to cope as best he could. His college buddy had been jumping with him on the trampoline, taking him on drives, walking with him all over town—anything to keep him busy. Before bed the first night, DJ went through his repertoire of anxiety issues, telling Emily that "poking is bad" and asking her to "please bde my mom now and forever." The second night they had a productive conversation on the computer.

"DJ, thank you for helping Mom and Dad while Dad is in the hospital."

"youre welfcome kom"

"Do you understand why Mom brought your single bed downstairs?"

"because dad is going to sleep in it"

"That's right. He would like still to sleep in the room with you, but he needs to be in a bed high off the ground for a couple of months. Do you mind lending him your bed from upstairs?"

"ok." DJ and I had been sleeping on the floor. There wasn't enough space for the futon and the hospital bed in the front room, so the plan was to hang out in the hospital bed during the day and sleep in DJ's single bed at night.

"Do you have any questions or concerns about Dad?"

"possibly"

"Well, ask me whatever you want."

"lookx the same?"

"Yes, Dad looks exactly the same. For about six weeks he will have staples on his left side. You will not even be able to see them, but his leg will be sore until his skin heals in about five to six weeks. Also, Dad will need to walk with crutches for four to six weeks until his leg gets stronger. After that, Dad will be able to walk and stand up from a chair just like before, just like you and me. Isn't that good?"

"yes." DJ would end up asking a version of the "looks the same" question several times more—even after I'd returned from the hospital.

"You and I can cheer Dad on to do his exercises daily, just like you do yours in P.E. Then he will be able to move without the pain he had before!"

"how do you know?"

"How do I know he'll be free of pain and able to move like he used to?"

"yes." DJ was ever interested in the subject of recovery—its possibility, its likelihood—and I was his research guinea pig.

"Because hundreds of thousands of people have had this operation and they have all returned to their previous motion and been free of pain. Actually, because Dad is so young and so athletic, they were able to put in the most natural hip—the kind without cement. Before long his bone will grow and keep his hip secure and strong just like yours and mine."

"youre my favorite relative," DJ replied, with characteristic whimsy, at once inventive and oddly literal.

"DJ, you're my favorite, favorite boy!"

The remaining three days of my hospitalization were much more bearable than the first. The intense pain gradually subsided, and but for not being able to sleep, I felt as if I'd been offered a vacation of sorts. I know that sounds ridiculous, but I hadn't had a moment's rest since Christmas, and I really was worn out. Don't get me wrong: I found the surgical tights and pulsating booties annoying, and I was almost willing to incur the increased risk of a blood clot to do without them. The food was awful, and my roommate—my sad, TV-watching, curtain-pulled-all-of-the-time roommate—snored. He sounded like one of those Hungarian buses that Emily and I had ridden during our years in Eastern Europe. But when friends and colleagues started visiting, I was almost grateful to have been forced to slow down and smell the flowers they had brought.

With a hip replacement, they have you up and walking, if you can call it that, almost immediately. On the third day, a nurse mistakenly gave me twice the amount of muscle relaxant and painkiller than I'd been taking. The result, I could barely move. When the P.T. arrived to supervise my therapy, I couldn't get out of bed. I couldn't really even talk—I was that relaxed. The PT seemed perturbed. I kept mouthing in a garbled way, "I think they've drugged me." Only later, as the meds wore off and I asked them to check what they had given me, did I get satisfaction on the issue. The only other thing that stood out from my hospitalization was the drama surrounding my inability to urinate. The doctor threatened to recatheterize me if by 10:00 p.m. on the second full day I hadn't evacuated my bladder. I tried and tried, but to no avail. A very kind nurse left the water running in the bathroom so as to encourage—let us say, seduce—my very shy bladder. With a half an hour to go, I got out of bed and crutched into the bathroom, where, in total desperation, I started punching my lower midsection. If music wouldn't work, perhaps a little roughing up would. I can't tell you how thankful I was when I produced a minor stream of urine with just minutes to spare.

The morning I was to be released, my brother called with an update on Charlie. Charlie had a cold, and there was still some question about the operation of his ventricles. The cold would end up causing a delay in his chemotherapy, and I could already hear in James's voice the sound of unassuageable concern. Emily showed up just as I was getting off the phone with James. She had the car ready, she said, for the trip back to

Grinnell. I was apprehensive about the inevitable bumps and jolts, but she had brought pillows for extra cushioning. I was also apprehensive about simply getting into the car. I had to move my legs in tandem, never allowing my left leg to be at anything other than a perfect right angle with my torso. It meant backing into the seat, the back seat, until I was far enough in to be able to swing my legs around in concert with my midsection. Automobiles, let me assure you, are not designed for this sort of entry, this sort of passenger.

Somehow, we figured it all out, including traversing our front steps, and got me safely into the rented hospital bed. DJ was very glad to see me, but also scared, eager to determine what condition I was in. It wasn't long before he became upset, and Emily had to force him to tell us what was wrong. "you really injured gettung hurt because you judt6 lie there," he typed. I felt like some sort of recidivist, having been paroled from prison, and now back again behind bars. "youre pointing treasure ids great," he said almost incomprehensibly. The word "treasures" DJ used exclusively with respect to the leaves. Was he talking about independence? The word "great" meant "abnormal," "freaky," "not like the other kids," "disabled." It also meant simply "scary." "Pointing" referred to the device I had bought from the occupational therapy team that would allow me to pick something up off the floor; DJ had just seen me use it. The pole had a grabber at the end. What was DJ trying to say?

"Does the pointer bother you?" I asked.

"treat it yes pointingb bothers me"

"Do you see what it can do for me?" I persisted.

"pick up things," DJ replied.

"And help me with my shoes."

"tying your shoes easy to put on," DJ typed. It was difficult to determine the tone of that remark. Was DJ castigating me for needing help to put on my shoes, or was he merely commenting on how effective the device was? Out of nowhere, he then pleaded, "please promise me you'll love kidding around when you feel bette3r." His anxiety about my disability was unmistakable, but what specifically was he getting at with the bit about "youre pointing treasure ids great"?

A bit later, Emily asked DJ how I seemed compared to what he thought, and DJ answered, "he is bothering"

"Why?"

"because he just lies their poingting for you to help him." Suddenly, it dawned on me. DJ didn't like the fact that I needed help. In part, he might have been jealous about the attention I commanded from Emily. There was a confusion of roles: he was the hurt child, not me. He wanted a role model for independence, as his Father's Day card would later make clear:

Dear Dad,

I look to you for looking confident and very kind. You're the most important man in my life. In truth you just very much strengthen me because the things that you note very much make me better You hurt my feelings but you love me ahd want me to grow up to be independent. I love you.

DJ

And yet, as much as DJ wanted a role model, he also couldn't help overidentifying with someone in pain, especially his father with whom he'd bonded so deeply. "im nervous because dad has not bought me braces [his word for crutches]," DJ typed the following day.

"Why do you want crutches?" Emily asked.

"you know how much in [i] like to be just like him," he replied. The remark was incredibly touching—a testament to human empathy. Here DJ, a boy with a neurological disability, was taking on an additional disability, my disability. But there was also something disconcerting about the gesture: as DJ himself put it, he was "the kide inlove with hurt."

In watching *Autism Is A World* and noticing how much the people around Sue Rubin hold her hand or arm (except, of course, when she is typing), Emily and I had speculated that perhaps FC users, especially those who come to the technique late, are so empathetic because they haven't entirely been individualized. They haven't entirely formed discrete selves, don't know definitively where they end and someone else begins. Even when independent typing has been achieved, there's still the need for much assistance. Moreover, there's still the legacy of what I have termed "arm time": that intimate explosion into communicative sociality through a physical interconnectedness. One has to account in some fashion for a different mode of being, made possible by very different material—that is, bodily—circumstances. To this day, DJ has a problem remembering that people cannot read his mind. Sue Rubin says that she often finds herself claiming the experience of others, especially characters in books, as her own, so powerful is her sense of identification.

Whatever the explanation for this tendency to overidentify, the world needs more DJs, more Sues, more Larry Bissonnettes, more Sharisa Kochmeisters. Admittedly romantic, such a notion pushes back against the automatic preference for neurotypicality and independence. Why fetishize the latter beyond the obvious pressure to prove FC legitimate? Isn't much of what's wrong with this society rooted in our commitment to a nearly hysterical individualism? Think of my millionaire father. And yet, I had a job to do as parent; I had to insist on a more conventional subjectivity, particularly in light of DJ's penchant for knitting the world together into an enormous scarf of pain. He was the Christo of trauma, draping Central Park in ghostly fabrics. I had always said my goal for DJ was maximum independence, and part of that goal would have to entail, as it does for all of us, a kind of foster care of the self, a being in the world where everyone is, alas, a stranger; where one can't identify (or merge) so completely with others. Who would wish such aloneness on their children? What other choice do we have? (If that sounds too negative, it's simply because I want to register the loss of something important, even as I concede a discrete identity's innumerable compensations.)

The more I thought about DJ's various remarks, the more it became clear that he was mapping his FC/independence anxiety onto my hip replacement, wondering, in effect, when I would be able to function *on my own*—without the aid of any sort of prosthesis: crutches, cane, pointer. I was like the leaves in his "Alaska" poem: "the trees hurt their great places, they lose/ their treasures, their lying leaves tread. freed from there/ branches they try to yearn freedom but they fear it." And like the leaves, I was like him: reluctant to give up my "facilitator," scared of the future, of being free. "youre pointing treasure ids great." Perhaps DJ even thought the pointer resembled the arms—the branches—of his facilitators. Again, the "Alaska" poem ends with the lines "long branches that live/ forever then they have to let go/ your hand trying go." The image of Emily physically helping me into bed must have been too tempting psychologically for a mind that works like DJ's.

If you think I make too much of this, consider the poem we wrote together that very same day. DJ decided that he wanted to write about jumping on the trampoline—an activity, not coincidentally, that I couldn't do and that he had connected to my hip injury. He began:

> just jump like my dad great bounces big b bounces
> bounces that bounce him just heey
> great freedom they bring

I continued, trying to suggest that we might now jump together in poems:

> the computer screen is our trampoline
> with words we jump and fall

And then he typed,

> let' go of yourb treasures

and I added,

> so when we jump we feel free,
> each seat drop [where you land on your fanny and bounce to
>   your feet]
> a poem to the treasured trees.

I wanted DJ to associate freedom with something pleasurable, exuberant. I wanted, rather, to lock in place the positive association that he himself had come up with. What DJ wrote next shocked me:

youj jump great hurt right up your hurt
trying to knowd the justivd im greef

How to make sense of that final line? If, as I would insist, DJ had hit some adjacent keys in trying to type the word "justice"—"v" is next to "c," and "d" is right below "e"—then what to do with the last two words? Because he rarely bothered to use an apostrophe, "im" could very well be "I'm," but it also could be "in," as "m" is next to "n." "Greef" was probably just a misspelling, as I'd seen him use and misspell that word before. And so, trying to know the justice *in* grief or trying to know the justice *I'm* grief? Let's say the former, though the latter would certainly contribute to the "kid in love with hurt" hypothesis. DJ seemed to imagine, in this analogical web he had woven, a quest for ultimate meaning. He was calling God onto the carpet, asking about what had happened to him, to Charlie, to his Dad's hip. I thought of us all—my brother and Eileen, my mother, Emily, Ellie—bouncing together in that netted enclosure, jumping our great hurt, higher and higher, trying to know the justice in grief.

The next morning, DJ got upset again; he wanted me out of my prison. He even attempted a jailbreak by pulling on my arm. When Emily told him to stop, he started banging his head. We had to call in the emotional HAZMAT team and insist that he use his words to communicate. By the end of our conversation, he typed, "you rest your very hurt hip so itgets better."

CHAPTER 13

The Sad Hurt Great Brother

In April, Ellie had e-mailed DJ to say that she would be visiting him that summer—probably in July. DJ had e-mailed her back:

Dear Ellie,

Hi how are you? Iam looking forward to your visiting me this summer.

please know that i love you. ok my headsaches really got better great jumpingggg

love, your brother, dj

When, later, her father called to pick a date for the visit, it became apparent that Ellie had a strict, two-week window of availability: from the 15th to the 30th of June. Otherwise, she'd be at one of a number of sports camps. Emily was reluctant to commit to a visit in mid-June because I'd still be recovering from my surgery, but she didn't want to prevent the two kids from seeing each other. So, she picked the second of the two weeks, annoyed by the lack of choice and suspicious of the man's real motivation: convenient child care. He'd all but admitted that he and Pat were looking for something for Ellie to do during the period in which

343

she wasn't at camp. When he said, in a slightly hesitant, cat-ate-the-canary voice, that Ellie wanted to come for both weeks, Emily's suspicions only deepened.

Two weeks seemed like a very long time given DJ's jealousy during the first six-day visit, our mutual exhaustion, and the fact that I'd still require some assistance and regular therapy. Emily also feared the great unknown of Charlie's cancer. She knew that once I'd been cleared to drive, we'd be taking a trip to Chicago to see James and Eileen—such a trip would likely occur in the middle of Ellie's visit. We were still hoping to get to Hilton Head, and if we didn't go to Chicago in June, it would be August before we saw them. Emily warned Dan about our nephew's condition, making it clear that Charlie could die at any moment and that Ellie might even have to attend a funeral. He was okay with this. (Later we'd hear from Pat that seeing Charlie had been quite disturbing for Ellie.)

Whatever resentment we harbored toward Dan and Pat, the point, of course, was to make sure the two kids spent time together. If Ellie's desire to be in Iowa for two weeks dovetailed with her parents' needs, all the better. Since DJ's confession of abuse, I'd had a hard time resuppressing my disdain for these people, and when Emily told me of solving their child care problem, I wanted to call them right back and give them not just a piece of my mind but the whole damn pie—right in their face. How bloody convenient, I said, almost as convenient as consigning DJ to foster care. But I didn't. I allowed myself to express the sentiment privately and then put it away. This grand experiment in open adoption could founder on something as simple as the truth.

If we'd been worried before that DJ might speak of his experience in foster care, now we were terrified. What if he referenced the rape? What if, like us, Ellie discovered the full meaning of poking? DJ wrote frequently of Kyle fucking him, and now that arousal had become such a problem—DJ couldn't extricate his erections, which came by surprise, from the flashbacks and nightmares that regularly assaulted him—we thought it quite likely that he might say something. I almost hoped he would, though I knew Pat would punish her daughter if this happened, as she had five years previously when Ellie learned of the adoption.

We seemed to be heading for trouble even without the issue of the rape's disclosure, for DJ's frame of mind was shaky at best. Although he'd risen to the occasion of my hip replacement, he'd begun to sink almost immediately afterward. It was as if, like some Iowa farmer, he'd canned as much cooperative fortitude as he could and then suddenly ran out in the middle of winter. It didn't help that we were changing aides at school (though the new one, Mrs. Goodrich, would turn out to be fantastic). He was very negative, characterizing himself as a "freak" repeatedly. "freak weh ready for befdr." "im freaky fear myself." All of his anxieties surfaced at once: normalcy, divorce, abandonment, hip replacement, adoption, Kyle, independence. "dadhatesyou." "reading his mind and hes dreadyv to divorce youb." "youre planning]to give me awayb." "youre looking hurt dad." The notebooks for this period are filled with comments such as these.

One morning, he walked over to the computer to tell us, "i'm not having mind poiughgkjfg tricn." [poking tricks?]

"What do you mean?" Emily asked.

"i'm not like my mom"

"Do you mean me or Rhonda?"

"rhonda"

"Do you think Rhonda was mentally unstable?"

"yes you knoq shd [know she] was"

"I know that when she drank she behaved very differently than when she remained sober. Are you worried that our discussion about different selves means that we think you're mentally unstable? Because it definitely doesn't mean that. In fact, Beth [the therapist from Cedar Falls] was trying to say exactly the opposite. She was saying that we all have different parts of ourselves that we identify and that is NORMAL."

"I'm ok," DJ said.

"I know you're OK. So why did you feel you needed to let me know that you aren't having mind tricks?"

'i'm just feelinh unjustly my mom"

"So you're thinking about Rhonda or about me?"

"rhonda"

"And you're thinking what was unjust?"

"you takong mev away bcvbn ftrom her"

"What makes you feel like we took you away from her?" I interjected.

"you just did"

"It sounds like you're sad or mad about something," Emily said.

"trying get free and think i need not get hurt" Sometimes it seemed as if DJ himself had a masters degree in counseling. (In the late summer when he'd declare, "i filter myfeelings trough [through] great hurt," I'd fall over in a dead faint.) DJ had articulated the very crux of the problem. He needed to uncouple the ideas of independence and injury, autism and trauma. He needed to rewrite the story of his past so that it didn't posit a "normal," little boy who was forced to live on his own and, as a result, was beaten and raped and became autistic—"freaky," in his word. Such a grim fairy tale permitted no constructive future. Put another way, he had to separate recovering from trauma from his initial abandonment (which in this conversation he imagined as a kind of kidnapping that absolved his birth mother) and his subsequent attempt to grow up, to get distance from us. All three he thought of as freedom. If trauma remained a paradoxically safe, womb-like enclosure and recovery, a big, bad world of aloneness, we'd never make progress. We couldn't allow him to make of trauma the mother he had lost—or, importantly, the mother he had gained. As you can see, we were still having trouble introducing the notion of difference, of distinction, into his universe. For DJ, consciousness was a series of slippery slides that culminated in the same turbulent wading pool.

"You're thinking that you can get free and not have to get hurt?" Emily asked.

"yes politicvx," DJ answered intriguingly. "Politics" was DJ's word for the struggle to "change scary things," and he'd already begun to inflect it with a disability rights consciousness. But that consciousness was fragile, and it couldn't yet combat his paralyzing bouts of insecurity and self-loathing.

"Do you want to talk through why you aren't with Rhonda anymore?"

"yes"

"Rhonda had a problem with alcohol and drugs. They made it hard for her to take proper care of you and Ellie. When the Department of

Children and Families discovered that you and Ellie weren't safe, they removed you from Rhonda's care."

"youtre t4ying treat me like your street rat," DJ said. I don't think he's ever typed anything as outlandish. Why this particular comparison? It's not that it didn't fit—I could easily see how an abandoned kid might resemble a street rat, especially when I remembered that DJ and Ellie often had to scavenge for food—but how had he come up with it? And why was he accusing us of treating him this way? Probably for the same reason he imagined that we'd taken him from his birth mother.

"I'm trying to treat you like my what?" Emily asked.

"treat md like dead freakn," DJ said.

"What do you mean by that? Give Mom an example."

"freafrea v pgaaaaaaaaaaaaaaaaaaaaaaaaaaaaaaaaaaaaaaaaaaaaaaaaaaaaa aaaaaaaaaaaaaaaaaaaaawwwwww." Before DJ trailed off into panicked nonsense, had he been trying to tell us that he knew why he'd been abandoned—because he was autistic? And could he only bear to acknowledge this sad truth in the form of a displaced accusation of responsibility? In August, DJ would ask his therapist in Grinnell, "was my great hurt mine before kyle?" When she'd reply, "Tell me what your great hurt is," he'd type, "im mutes. i don't talk." In the same session he'd wonder, "was the reason he fucked me very much because i couldn't ta?" How, as I suggested earlier, could we deny a connection between autism and the events of DJ's life when the boy's great antagonists—Kyle, his birth father— had worked so hard to establish one?

DJ's emotional fluctuations intensified as the date of Ellie's arrival approached. They affected how he spoke of the upcoming visit itself. At times, he'd complain that Ellie "possibly gets pleased not to live witjh mer"; at other times he'd exclaim, "great that my sister is cominf" and "ellie is going to posdibly open my mind to just being normzl." When Emily pressed him on what he meant by the word "normal," he responded, "possibly to play with other kids," adding, "possiluy you play in your room mom." Yet another laugh-out-loud moment, though like all the rest, it had to be met with solemn seriousness. I loved the idea of Emily "playing in her room," giving DJ space to practice independence.

The issue of friendship had been a vexing one, and Emily and I had been working on it with DJ, but life had recently been so chaotic and DJ himself had been so on edge that we hadn't had a friend from school over in a while. Much as DJ wanted to do the friendship thing alone, he needed one of us to facilitate communication and then to smooth things over when, in his anxiety, he told the friend to go. In May, he had written a paragraph about friendship that still breaks my heart:

> Friends are hard to make. Sometimes kids prejudge my behavior and think I am bad. They don't know I have a lot of memories and have fallen behind. Talking is the main way they communicate. They also play sports with balls. It's not easy to make friends.

DJ had been having trouble in the halls. Whereas strangers saw in him a "weirdo" to be mocked, he saw in them potential kindness and interaction, even calling them by the name of his desire: "friends." "i possibly hate friendws they poke fudswh [fun] at me they laugh really hafd when im just freeing myself," he'd typed. "What does Mrs. Goodrich say or do when someone laughs?" I'd asked, wanting to make sure he had a defender. "she tekls thdem i'm just trying kid." The accidental pun was hilarious. No doubt Mrs. Goodrich had commented on DJ's effort at school.

We told DJ that while Ellie was in Iowa we'd have a trampoline party, to which he could invite three or four of his buddies. We also promised to let him have more time with his sister alone. But instead of making him happy, this only made him more nervous. That's how he was. In the conversation about normalcy, he suddenly blurted out, "just love me like say just put me in true book not make me injired you im heading for the real heart of the matter." Pausing, he then added, "trying head very high."

DJ *was* trying to hold his head up high, but he was also a proverbial mess. He desperately wanted to be normal, and I felt terrible about contributing to this need through the prospect of my book. I tried to explain to him my opposition to the concept of "normalcy," and I said that we were all "injured" in one way or another. I was going to present my own shortcomings in the book as well, I reminded him. The point was to focus on what people had done with their pain, what they had worked through. "The world needs to see how far you have come," I said, "what courage you have, what intelligence. You are the ultimate survivor."

"use your book to help kids with autism," DJ typed, more than a bit anxiously.

"Remember, the last chapter's yours. You get the final word."

I've nearly run out of metaphors to describe the gridlock of divided emotional government. If feelings were senators, then in the chamber of DJ's head each was preparing a filibuster. Perhaps each was preparing even to cane the other, as in that famous incident involving Preston Brooks and Charles Sumner in May of 1856. The battered Sumner ripped his desk loose from the floor to which it was bolted in order to escape, and I ask you to imagine something equivalently violent beneath DJ's venerable dome.

In the final therapy session before Ellie arrived, you can see the warring factions at work. "i.m nervous because every one looks sad," DJ announced.

"Who's everyone?" Beth asked.

"you"

"Why do I look sad?"

"because you red my mind"

"So, why are you sad?"

"because charlie is really acutely ill," DJ replied, shocking everyone with his sophisticated vocabulary.

"What are some of the things you can do when you feel nervous? You can talk, jump, dance, sing, drum to make your feelings less intense."

"im trying to learn but since we invited injury into our home you get tired. mom." Invited injury into our home? DJ's phrasing was so evocative. He seemed to be referring to the hospital bed and my hip replacement. In that sense he was being literal—we *had* invited injury into our home by renting the bed and electing to have hip surgery—but his choice of words was figurative. In the great debate about the metaphoric capacities

349

of people with autism, attention ought to be paid to the actual quality of their metaphors. DJ, I think, believed that we had written Injury a note and invited him or her to stay with us. When metaphors lose their conscious provisionality, they almost become something else.

In the end, the statement revealed the siege mentality that had overtaken DJ. He longed to shut out the world—all of those things that threatened loss: my hip, Charlie, even Ellie, strangely enough. (His sister's very presence was like a giant dredging barge, sucking up the past and redepositing it on the shore of his anxiety, a kind of beach reclamation project.) At the center of his agoraphobic fantasy stood Emily, whom he needed to be an exemplar of indefatigable happiness. His father, unfortunately, had been demanding too much from her, causing her to look tired, vulnerable. How could she attend to two patients at once?

It came as no surprise at all that DJ moved, in the therapy session, from Emily getting tired to "im trying to really type on my own" to "youre trying to gett ready to leave me" to head banging in the parking lot. The following day, after OT, he remarked with nearly schizophrenic gratitude, "youre really pouring lots of energy into your treatment for my freedom."

Ellie arrived on the 17th of June, and Emily and DJ went to pick her up. Though I had been cleared to travel, I still found it difficult to sit for extended periods of time, so I stayed home. As Emily tells the story, she and DJ waited exactly where they had at Christmas, but Ellie didn't appear. Unbeknownst to them, the airline had changed its policy. Emily was supposed to get a pass at the ticket counter, go through security and meet Ellie at the gate. After about thirty minutes, Emily called Ellie's cell phone and discovered the new procedure. She dreaded having to depart from their customary routine. When DJ was nervous, the only lifeline you had was routine. She worried that the security people wouldn't allow DJ to accompany her to the gate and that DJ might refuse to go, thinking he'd have to get on a plane. But DJ persevered, looking at Emily quizzically as she told him to take off his shoes.

Ellie seemed relieved when she saw the two of them approach. DJ shot his sister a smile but, for the most part, played it fairly cool, being neither distant nor enthusiastic. Ellie, Emily said, remained cheerful in a disciplined sort of way, as if she'd given herself a lecture on her brother's idiosyncrasies. At Arby's on the way home, she ordered exactly what DJ ordered, producing a broad grin that, in lieu of official recognition, praised itself for such sisterly maturity.

The first thing they did when they got back to Grinnell was jump. DJ seemed intent on showing Ellie that this visit would be different; he would try to have fun. Emily walked out to the trampoline house with them and, after turning on the stereo, walked back to the house. We could see their bobbing heads in the window, and we could hear DJ's unmistakable shrieks of joy. He *was* having fun—a good sign. After about fifteen minutes, they both returned, red-faced and sweaty. We didn't have air conditioning out in the tramp house, and it could get pretty hot. Two giant glasses of ice water later, and the kids sat down to have a conversation on the computer.

Ellie had taken the scrapbook that DJ had given her for Christmas and made a photo album out of it. She'd filled it with baby pictures from their time in   , pictures we'd never seen before. In one, Dan is holding DJ and Ellie. DJ appeared unsettled by it, whereas Ellie delighted in the simple idyll of togetherness. Looking through the photos prompted a game of "do you remember?" with Ellie asking about their apartment in Florida after their parents had split up. "What was the name of our friend downstairs?" Ellie asked. DJ typed a name, but she didn't think that was it. She then asked if he remembered walking to the grocery store together, a store some two miles from their apartment.

"yes," DJ typed, growing ever so agitated.

A seismologist on the couch had picked up a tremor. She—Emily— tried to lighten things by saying, "You two were sure adventuresome. That was a long, long way to walk for a three- and four-year-old alone."

"It's the one thing we could do and know we wouldn't get hit," Ellie replied. Dishes were now rattling on shelves in Oregon, far from the quake's epicenter.

"rhonda hurt us all time very much," DJ said. Good-bye, Golden Gate Bridge. Good-bye, State of California. We weren't two hours into the visit and already we were practicing some sort of emergency readiness drill. Ellie started to tear up, and DJ signed, "all done, all done."

"Why don't we walk to the Dairy Barn and get an ice cream," I suggested. I hadn't yet had my walk, and I didn't really think we should be encouraging so much heaviness right at the beginning. On our walk, I asked Ellie all sorts of questions, making sure to ask DJ each time what he thought of his sister's response. I was particularly sensitive to the issue of jealousy, which had been such a problem during the last visit. Ellie talked about playing basketball and tennis, about the camps she was planning to attend. It was nearly impossible to include DJ actively in this conversation because we were walking, but Emily and I made a point of getting the labeler out the second we had our ice cream cones and were sitting at a picnic table. DJ's response to this inclusive gesture? To reach for his sister's eyes—not aggressively, but enough to register his dissatisfaction with the present state of all things speaking. The expression on Ellie's face seemed to say, "Oh, no. Not this. Not poking." But she didn't actually say anything, and DJ didn't persist with it.

We had a cookout that night, jumped some more on the trampoline, and conversed about the next day's activities. The kids decided that they wanted to go to the pool in Newton, which had some terrific water slides. DJ said he wanted to try the tandem bike with Ellie. "How sweet," Emily said. I imagined a version of their tugboat routine in the Northeast, but something older, with both of them pedaling, both of them headed in the same direction. You can see how obdurately attached I was—still am—to that image. Maybe they could even ride to the grocery store, I thought, thumbing their noses at the past, conquering it with ease and motion and soda pop at the end. We spoke about going to Adventureland Amusement Park at some point and Chicago to see my brother and his family. "charlies really ill," DJ said. Ellie told us that her mother and father wanted her to go for a run each day and to do her summer reading. She was also supposed to watch what she ate. I stopped myself from looking at Emily in order not to call attention to my disapproval. Ellie was so far from having a weight problem it was ridiculous. Her mother couldn't help herself; she had to be overseeing her daughter's every activity, insisting on control.

Our sleeping arrangements were still out of whack. With Ellie visiting, we had her on the futon on the floor of my study, DJ in bed with me, and Emily in DJ's room in his bed. We would have put Ellie in DJ's bed, but Emily thought Ellie would have more privacy and quiet if she was on the first floor. So, that's what we did. Unlike DJ, she went to bed very late and slept in. This incongruity very quickly started causing problems, with DJ wanting Ellie up and doing things by 9:00. Furthermore, by the time Ellie awoke at around 11:00 (it turns out she was using this vacation from her mother to do something she wasn't ordinarily allowed to do), DJ was hungry for lunch. She, however, wanted breakfast. Having not done much of anything all morning, we'd finally leave for our daily outing and by the time we got someplace, Ellie would then want lunch.

Ellie was an extraordinarily sensitive girl, patient beyond belief with her brother, but she wasn't yet a sensitive adult. It didn't occur to her that in order for things to run smoothly—in order to maximize the chances of things running smoothly—we had to stick to our routine. As the visit wore on, we'd actually catch her doing things to annoy DJ, but by that time he'd have treated her so poorly, it would have been difficult to blame her (though I wanted to blame her, as I wanted to brain DJ). And, anyway, she really didn't know her brother very well. She hadn't lived with him. She didn't understand autism and trauma. In fact, Ellie told us that when they were little and DJ flapped his arms, she'd just thought he was trying to fly.

The one advantage of the kids' disparate sleeping schedules was that it offered the opportunity to speak with each child privately. That first night I found out all sorts of things I didn't know from Ellie and, even more important, that I had gotten wrong in the opening chapter of the book. I'd written that chapter before DJ started using FC, during the period he was estranged from Ellie. So, there was no way really to check my facts. Whereas I was certainly sensitive to the problem of representing other people, I hadn't foreseen the possibility of dramatizing this problem—especially with respect to a noncommunicating person with autism. So, I've chosen to narrate my knowledge largely as it evolved. Part of the excitement of witnessing DJ's emergence into language has been having him tell me what I got wrong and, more recently, surrendering the task of representation altogether. I look forward to him writing his own book some day and to Ellie perhaps writing hers as well. The point is that Emily and I were interpreting in real time, without ever having as much information as we'd have liked.

The major thing I got wrong was Pat's socioeconomic status: she wasn't nearly as wealthy as I reported. She was middle class, though she did live at a fashionable address. The apartment, however, wasn't as big as we'd thought. It was filled with antiques, as the photos we'd seen made clear, yet Ellie described a space that was actually quite modest. Though Emily and I would have sworn that Ellie was in private school at the time of our get-together in the Northeast, she was not. Private school came later. Pat had contributed to our incorrect assumptions through her unremitting desire to appear above her station: the fancy clothes, the talk of travel in Europe, the emphasis on decorum. And then there was that description of her job at an advertising firm: she wasn't, as she claimed, an upper-level executive; rather she was the firm's office manager.

Ellie also told us things about her father. He no longer worked as a dishwasher. He'd been fired from that job when, on Ellie's birthday, he left early to buy her a birthday cake. Ellie loved telling us this story, and, in doing so, she resembled her brother—his way of thinking. You couldn't have love without some kind of loss, even if it was just the loss of a job. After working as a dishwasher, he'd worked as a gofer and after that as a maintenance man. We marveled at how well adjusted Ellie seemed, how easily she talked about her parents. She'd had some pretty tough stuff happen to her, but she appeared okay, even if she did occasionally go foraging in the past like a clumsy raccoon. For the most part, she'd committed herself to a program of merciless repression, banishing Florida and her birth mother to the life of another girl entirely.

I'd been critical of this program, but I wondered in light of DJ's persistent troubles whether our strategy was any better. The "talking cure" had its therapeutic benefits, but it also seemed to encourage the trauma victim to recline on an immense divan of pain. With DJ typing things that summer like "gereat hurt is still here" and "im just your hurt son," with the poking and the head banging and the hitting continuing, I worried that he was falling more deeply into trauma, which is another way of saying that when he rose from that immense divan of pain, left the therapist's office, and walked out into the world, he seemed to become, each time a little bit more, the thing that plagued him. Even when I reminded myself that what had happened to DJ was unimaginably horrific (far worse than what had happened to Ellie) and would thus take time to heal, and even when I considered the recent destabilizing events of my hip replacement and Charlie's cancer, which only exacerbated his anxiety, and even when I accepted the notion of a painstaking "spiral" of recovery, which presupposes setbacks, I still feared that we might be facilitating injury, delivering a traumatic being into the world. Not only did we have to ask ourselves about the effect of autism on trauma (the exacerbation of the repetition compulsion through perseveration), we had to confront the special case that was DJ: a boy who had fallen into language belatedly, a boy who had awakened into the terrorizing story of his life. Did we not run the risk of finalizing this arrangement?

At times, I felt as if Emily and I were the biggest offenders, caught in a sort of emotional sting operation, wanting to cry entrapment. The more we empathized with DJ and told him how sorry we were and the more we tried to make up for the years without parents, the more we seemed to feed into a notion of selfhood as injury and of parenting as therapy. "cried yourself to feel my loneliness," DJ would type, and we'd just melt. Who could resist the invitation to bond with him through an intense act of drawing out the past? Though DJ hated hospitals (and imagined injury as being outside the home), he'd found one in our house: a kind of crisis center or mental health emergency room. In *The Brothers Karamazov*, Alyosha, having been sent out into the world by his spiritual elder and searching for a viable ethics of human interaction, remarks with some naiveté to the crippled Lise, "Perhaps we should treat people as if they were patients in a hospital." Dostoevsky had his own reasons for rejecting such a fantasy of care, and they had to do with the inadequacy of human beings and the perfection of God. My reasons were very different. I certainly didn't subscribe to the contemporary conservative injunction to stop whining about the past—the familiar "nation of victims"/"culture of complaint" argument. Rather, I worried that a boy with autism, a boy such as DJ, might never get over his trauma if we constantly encouraged him to work through it. Perhaps we needed to put the past away, sign, "all done, all done" to any ghosts that dared to leave the cemetery.

How to honor the severity of DJ's injuries (and confront the politics behind them) *while* insisting that he move forward? The trauma theorist Cathy Caruth lays out the central predicament of witnessing. She argues that the "transformation of the trauma into a narrative memory that allows the story to be verbalized and communicated, to be integrated into one's own, and others', knowledge of the past, may lose both the precision and the force that characterize traumatic recall." In other words, the moment that people are able to tell the story of their trauma may be the moment when, paradoxically, they have begun to forget—"mastered it with knowledge," as Caruth explains. But what if the person compulsively tells the story, and the story, as story, doesn't seem to have neutralized or contained the injury at all? What if the person is autistic?

Caruth and a host of other experts working in the field of trauma find themselves torn between the imperative to cure people of trauma and the equivalent obligation to remember "the impossible history" that the "traumatized carry . . . within them." In such a romance of pain, true remembrance comes, strangely enough, at the cost of continued victimhood, as the epigraph to Caruth's book from a Vietnam veteran demonstrates: "I do not want to take drugs for my nightmares, because I must remain a memorial to my dead friends." It's not that Caruth actually advocates remaining traumatized; rather, she strives to underscore, in the culture at large, the pitiful domestication of incomprehensible horror—to the point that the Holocaust, say, could be spoken about in reasonable terms with a reasonable voice. She strives to underscore the danger of taming trauma.

In DJ's case, what we were witnessing was not only a terrible personal affront but rather the effects of a history of socially constructed idiocy—what Chris Kliewer calls "differences that matter," "the ones that constrict a nonconformist's social worth," or what DJ calls simply "years of bein retarded." Offensive would be any attempt to "master" the brutal treatment of people who have had to shoulder this label. How to convey the impact of being discarded by your parents and society, presumed incompetent, raped? And yet, to "remain a memorial" to such brutality would be self-destructive. Toni Morrison makes a similar point about slavery, concluding her novel *Beloved* with the exquisitely ambiguous line "This is not a story to pass on." If Morrison wants us to understand the nearly essential requirement of forgetting for a viable future, even as she insists that we must remember, what might she say about the plight of the autistic historian, whose commitment to reliving a particular calamity of justice might be unmatched? DJ needed to do some forgetting, and Emily and I were about to change the focus of his therapy.

The morning of the second day, while Ellie was asleep, DJ and I had a conversation on his computer. I felt a bit like Jimmy Carter, shuttling back and forth between Begin and Sadat at Camp David. "What do you think about how things are going?" I asked.

"It really seems fun. do you think seww"

"Yes," I replied. "What do you enjoy most about Ellie?"

"shes sweet to never ever desire to fear enjoying griowiing up," he typed. "Desire to fear"—the locution caught my eye. It seemed to capture the peculiarly volitional character of this nonvolitional condition.

"I think that's because she knows growing up is gradual. I think you think it means you're all alone."

"right," DJ said.

"It doesn't mean being all alone," I reminded him.

"im really trying to desire growing up"

"I know. When you look at Ellie, what do you see?"

"i see related to rhonda," DJ typed.

"DJ, although Ellie and Rhonda look similar, they are very, very different people." In asking that question, I'd wanted to check the associative obstacles in DJ's mind. Whenever my mother came to visit, for example, DJ would start talking about Rhonda because they both smoked. In making the connection, he'd then want my mother to leave, becoming hysterical when she didn't. "she breathes on me," he'd say. Maybe DJ missed his sister but saw Rhonda. Maybe the "relation" was so intense for him that it was like having Rhonda in the room.

By far the most successful outings we had were the ones to the Maytag Pool in Newton. The kids loved the water slides, especially the green one with an enormous tunnel. DJ would get annoyed, however, when this slide temporarily shut down; it required two lifeguards—one to watch the water, another to watch the line of ascending kids to make sure that they were spaced properly. At points, there simply weren't enough life-guards. When the tunnel slide shut down, Ellie would turn her attention to the high diving board, which obviously scared her. Emily and I were impressed by the way she approached her fear, the way she conquered it with determination and fortitude. She'd look over every time she came up out of the water to make sure that someone was taking in her accomplishment. We couldn't help but compare—privately, of course—her response to "scary things" with DJ's. He wanted nothing to do with the high diving board, instead remaining by Emily and pointing obsessively at the tunnel slide. When he was little, before the PTSD, he was as fearless as any child I'd ever come across. I used to pick him up and hurl him into the water, and each time he'd emerge with a smile and the sign for "more." Now he was timid beyond measure. It was as if we'd traded carefree exuberance for communicative terror. How not to resent Ellie, whose own measured response to the future had come, at least in part, at her brother's expense? This thought, which had colonized our heads during the December visit, returned, like an astronaut who flies back to the moon to check on the status of his flag.

We spent that first week swimming, riding bikes, jumping on the trampoline. I say "we" but I mean the kids; I was still pretty much a spectator. At first, the biking was a big hit. Ellie and DJ made several forays around the neighborhood on the tandem: Ellie in front, struggling to control the behemoth, and DJ in the back like a passenger in a rickshaw. Though he was in fact pedaling, he reminded me of how we—and indeed his sister—had had to pull him when rollerskating. On their third or fourth outing, DJ decided to jerk back and forth, almost causing Ellie to lose control of the bike. DJ had sometimes done this to me, and it could be very frightening, especially for someone who was already having trouble keeping her balance. Ellie apparently brought the bike to a stop, told DJ to cut it out, and when he began to poke and hit her, hit him back. We'd only find out later that she had been aggressive as well. In her report, she was the perfect angel, and for the most part she was, but DJ didn't see it this way. He resented the fact that he'd had to apologize when she had not, and he thought it rude of us not to offer him a chance to ride in front, in the first seat.

Of course, when we took him to the park and attempted to get him situated in that seat, he experienced a huge anxiety attack, as he hit his head and signed, "all done, all done." In a way, we'd called his bluff. We all knew that he wasn't able to assume the piloting position; he couldn't yet ride a regular bike—largely because he was so easily distracted. Emily had said that riding tandem was like facilitated communication, and DJ was once again manifesting his tortured ambivalence about such a co-operative venture, ambivalence only worsened by sibling rivalry.

After the altercation on the bike, DJ began telling Ellie to go—clearly to annoy her. But I also think there was a deeper purpose: she pointed out too painfully their fundamental difference. Toward the end of the first week, in a therapy session with Sarah from Grinnell, DJ addressed this issue. "How do you feel about seeing your sister?" Sarah asked.

"really ellie is my understanding friend," DJ replied.

"Your mom has said that you've been telling her to go a lot."

"i.m mad because ellie is not different from just differt"

"What do you mean? How do you want her to be?"

"not be normwl," DJ answered.

"Are you not normal?"

"yes"

"What would Ellie's not being normal mean?"

"for her to have been in foctercare." At last, he'd said it explicitly. He wanted her to have been in foster care so as to save him from having to think of himself as worthless, expendable—because autistic.

"What else do you wish?"

"that really we look the same." Was DJ again referring to Ellie being normal or was he saying literally that they did not resemble each other?

"Do you look different?" Sarah asked.

"yes really wanted her tojuest dread great places," DJ typed. There was our answer: DJ seemed to imagine that his fear of the future was a function of appearance, and by appearance he meant, I think, typical autistic behaviors. And in a way it was, so long as the associative chain could be translated into some sort of reasonable logic: I was abandoned because I was autistic, and because I was abandoned, I am afraid of the future. What DJ did was conflate things, associatively collapse them: because I am autistic, I am afraid of the future. (In itself, the statement is true enough when you consider the plight of people with autism in our society.) Or: because I flap my arms, I am afraid of the future. Like Sisyphus with his boulder, we pushed the project of disassociation up the hill of DJ's despair. While conceding what others had made of autism, we strained to give it positive meaning. We had to make difference, his difference, acceptable. It wasn't enough for him to seek the solace of another in the ward of abnormality. We had to do away with the ward. Finally, I think the kids' physical dissimilarity did factor into DJ's thinking. For someone so associative, it must have been the aggravating sign of other differences, the condensation of an entire history.

At the end of the session with Sarah in Grinnell, DJ typed, "i want to talk more. treat ing feelingsreally helps." When you heard DJ saying something like this, you thought to yourself, "Wow, therapy's working." The next day we had an appointment with Beth in Cedar Falls, who was back from medical leave. Emily and I had decided to have DJ resume seeing Beth while Ellie was in Iowa, even though it meant losing a couple of afternoons to a long drive and an hour's wait. We wanted DJ to be able to talk through his feelings while Ellie was here, rather than waiting until she had left. The two therapists had different approaches and skills; Beth in Cedar Falls was a bit tougher on DJ, confronting him with his behavior and challenging him to move beyond his emotional perseverations. But even she seemed to invite these perseverations through the very process of discussing them. I don't want to overstate my opposition to the talking cure. God knows I've spent pages and pages interpreting my son's words, trying to make sense of the way he has processed his past. And DJ's still seeing both therapists, but we've tried to get them to be more future oriented and not allow him free reign in that memorial park of hurt. Otherwise, he'd get out his shovel and begin compulsively exhuming one coffin after another. Of course, we've had to retrain ourselves as well.

The morning of the visit to Beth in Cedar Falls, DJ was very anxious, telling Ellie repeatedly to go. When Emily and DJ arrived in Cedar

Falls, DJ asked to go to the bathroom. Once in the bathroom, he became obsessed with the soap dispenser. Emily had to pull him out of the bathroom and into Beth's office, where she typed, "This is a safe place. Please tell us about your thoughts and feelings." Emily hadn't had a chance to speak with Beth before the session, so she took the lead in framing the first question. "Do you realize that you and Ellie had no say in where you lived when you were little?" Emily was building on the previous day's session with Sarah in Grinnell, when DJ had said that he wished that Ellie had been in foster care too. There was no response from DJ—no response but pulling down Beth's sleeves to cover her skin.

"What does that mean, DJ?" Beth asked.

"i'm nervous," he answered.

"How does hiding skin help?"

"poking leaves marks. You might get hurt cuts," he said. DJ was obviously referring to having been beaten—when Kyle took care to do it in places that wouldn't show. But why was he reenacting the concealment of his wounds? Was he trying to erase them, imagine himself as uninjured? Was he threatening Beth? Was he worried for her safety?

"Why are you nervous?"

"I'm just hurt that ell.ie is very free. Very hard to dread great places." Over and over, the same sad question: How to have a sister when she hadn't suffered like you, when she seemed to be bounding into the future? "I'm afraid that *some* times/ you'll play lonely games too./ Games you can't win/ 'cause you'll play against you."

"What do you dread most about the future?" Beth asked.

"beung alone." "*All Alone!*/ Whether you like it or not,/ Alone will be something/ you'll be quite a lot." It sometimes felt, Emily reported, as if the good doctor's book was being performed in DJ's head in a manner reminiscent of the way Hollywood now takes a classic and gives it a mean, updated edge. Beth reassured DJ that we intended to be there for him for a long, long time—for as long as he wanted.

"Are you worried," she asked, "about them not being there one day?"

"Yes," DJ responded. "You're saying they might die." DJ almost seemed delighted, Emily later told me, that Beth had articulated his fear, as if in asking the question she had confirmed that we would be doing exactly that—and soon! Beth asked Emily if we had a guardian in place, and Emily said "yes." Emily tried to redirect the conversation by telling DJ that we were fine. Although this sort of reasonable approach to childhood anxiety probably works well with neurotypical kids, I seriously wonder about kids with autism, let alone traumatized kids with autism. Perhaps death should be repressed. Perhaps the child should simply be ushered into the room of positive thinking, past that other darkened threshold where lurk fear's seductive monsters.

DJ resumed tugging on Beth's sleeves, trying to hide her skin. "Why are you doing that now?" Beth asked.

"because you like ellie more than me mom," DJ said. You can see him turning the attack into an expression of sibling rivalry. In a sense, he was reliving his abandonment—his defeat at the hands of his sister—and making sure that we preferred him. The day after Ellie left, he'd directly link his sister and poking when he'd type, "kill you poked me when you invited ellie." Poking would soon become the universal metaphor. About Hilton Head, he'd say, "our trip there is like poking."

Beth talked about siblings and how they vie for attention. She told DJ that Ellie can learn things from him and that he can learn things from her. "Have you learned anything from your sister about what to do instead of poking?" she asked.

"Yes, [Ellie] treats them nicely," DJ replied. But the fact that she treated people nicely—better, that is, than he did—only seemed to aggravate him, for he once again started pulling on Beth's sleeves. "people think i;m weird," he typed. Over the hills and through the woods of obsessive-compulsive pain. The java log of DJ's anxiety surfing revealed a familiar Ellie/free/abandonment/poking/abnormality circuit. How could we disrupt it? How could we deal with the issue of sibling rivalry when the stakes seemed so high, when something as simple as our talking to Ellie could set off DJ's profound insecurity?

The rest of that first week saw a deterioration in super power relations. Each threatened to go to the Security Council. Each threatened to recall its ambassador. Excursions in the car went like this: Ellie would try to get DJ to play hangman or tic-tac-toe. DJ would refuse. Ellie would listen to music on her iPod or read. DJ would become furious, claiming that Ellie was ignoring him. He'd try to remove her headphones or close her book. She'd push him away. He'd try to poke. She'd say, "Don't poke me." He'd hit his head on the car window, and I'd start screaming at the top of my lungs. Already uncomfortable just sitting in the car and desperate to have this visit go better than the last one, I was, to put it mildly, on edge.

Emily thought it a good thing that the kids were experiencing siblinghood in all of its annoyances and glory. But those annoyances were charged, as I've said, and the two kids didn't have the kind of time together that would allow the annoyances to achieve their proper proportion. Though both kids had quickly mastered how to push each other's buttons—Ellie, for example, would pull her book out with a flourish and commence reading the second an altercation had concluded—I was of the mind that DJ was behaving terribly toward his sister. The more I castigated DJ for his behavior and tried to compensate for it by being excessively nice to Ellie, the angrier and less cooperative DJ became. That I knew why he was misbehaving didn't speak to the fact that he was misbehaving and needed to stop. Ellie had made a huge effort in coming out to Iowa and, for the most part, had overlooked his anxious repudiations of her. She was only thirteen and had emotional needs herself, after all.

In the meantime, my brother had phoned to say that Charlie was making it through his latest round of chemotherapy and that the next few days would be a good time to come see them. Charlie's immune system would start feeling the effects of the chemo about four days after it was administered, at which point he'd have to be quarantined. Emily and I thought that as tense as such a trip might be, the kids would have fun in Chicago. We'd fallen into something of a rut in Grinnell and hoped to shake things up a bit. Often with DJ you needed forcibly to dislodge a perseverative mindset with a new activity or place. Of course, that new activity or place could itself induce anxiety, and going to the hospital to see Charlie wasn't exactly the soothing distraction we'd otherwise have planned. Indeed, it seemed to invite, to use DJ's word, more trouble. But we simply had to see my brother and his family before we left for Hilton Head. Though Charlie's treatment had thus far been successful, there had been innumerable problems and hospitalizations, and James and Eileen were exhausted. They could use a show of support. Besides, they wanted to meet DJ's sister.

The trip to Chicago proved a nightmare, with DJ poking and provoking Ellie the whole way. We arrived at our hotel downtown a tangle of live wires. I don't think there was an electrician in the world that would have chosen to intervene. Better to shut off the power altogether and watch us collapse on the floor like lifeless robots. After we checked in, my brother stopped by. Charlie, he said, would be kept overnight and released some time the following day. The plan was for me to go with James to the hospital, take a cab back to the hotel, eat dinner with Emily, DJ, and Ellie, go to sleep, spend time with the kids at Navy Pier, and then meet up for dinner as a group. I hoped that DJ could keep it together enough to allow us to do this, but it didn't look good. Were we NASA mission controllers, we'd have long before aborted our mission—the remote manipulator arm of empathy left for another shuttle's payload.

Though I'd been present for Charlie's surgery, I wasn't prepared for the grim spectacle of kids on a cancer ward: all of them lying on beds with their own cartoon-playing video monitors. The combination of cartoons and chemo was shocking. It reminded me of the compulsory cheerfulness of the chemo ward in Grinnell, where I had had infusions for my arthritis. That space was like a heavenly boardroom: Exxon does the afterlife. Here, the brightly colored walls and gaunt, miserable children filled me not with revulsion but dread. The effort to console, uplift, distract seemed at once monumental and grotesquely inadequate.

Charlie looked much better than I thought he would. He was alert, calm. He had a number of sizeable scars on his head and his hair had fallen out. Eileen and James took turns holding and playing with him, careful of the many wires and tubes that were attached to his body. They were sharing a room with another couple whose three-year-old had liver cancer and looked just terrible. "Don't cry, don't cry," the child's mother kept saying. It was awkward trying to carry on a conversation in front of these people, though probably only awkward for me. James and Eileen seemed utterly used to hospital living. They'd spent the previous night in Charlie's room on chairs that folded out into something like beds. We talked for a while before I went with James to grab a burger in the hospital cafeteria, and then I caught a cab back to the hotel.

Emily had taken the kids swimming, and Ellie was in the bathroom when I returned. We decided to go to a Mexican restaurant for dinner. DJ surprised us all by behaving perfectly; he even clasped his sister's hand on the walk back to the hotel. I remember watching Ellie and thinking she was holding her breath: she didn't want the spell to break. There was no telling why DJ had decided to be nice because the very next moment he could decide to be difficult. And, indeed, the next day he was impossible: kicking, hitting, screaming.

We'd gone down to Navy Pier and right from the beginning DJ had acted out. Suddenly, he started poking, and when I told him to stop, he staged a gargantuan fit—to the extent that a noisy, bustling crowd grew quiet and paused to take in what was happening. I hustled DJ off to the side and gave him a lecture replete with threats and exhortations. I told him for the umpteenth time that he had to help out: his sister was visiting and Charlie was sick. DJ signed "sorry" and then almost immediately resumed poking. We managed to get in a couple of rides— I felt enormous pressure to make sure Ellie had fun—but lunch was a disaster. Halfway through, after DJ intentionally poured his glass of ice water on the floor, I literally dragged him out of the restaurant. We waited for Ellie and Emily to finish, and I held onto his hand: something he hated. No matter how many times he signed "good" (as in "I'll be good"), I would not let go. I was furious. "If you're going to act like a baby, then I'm going to treat you like a baby," I said. Emily gave me a look that suggested *my* behavior was unproductive, which only made me more furious. "That's right. Do what you always do. Go easy on him," I barked. If DJ sometimes got stuck in an anxiety loop, then so did I: he'd have an outburst, and I'd accuse Emily of being the softie. But increasingly I'd thought that Emily *was* being the softie. No matter how horrendous DJ's first six years had been, we had to prepare him for the future, and that meant refusing to indulge his temper tantrums. We just had to teach him how to cope with life's many pressures. In any event, there I was, cane in one hand, DJ in the other, limping and yanking my way to the entrance of the Pier. The outing was over. We were going back to the hotel.

Back at the hotel, Ellie went swimming while I cooled off and Emily had a conversation with DJ on the labeler. "I need to hear what you're thinking," Emily said.

"you free me. you love me."

"Not if you choose to hit and scream and poke. Hitters, pokers, and screamers are not free."

"i know. youre right."

"So why do you choose to do it?"

"because i.m very nervous."

"It's OK to be nervous. It's not OK to hit, scream, and poke."

"i know."

"DJ, you just caused us all to end our fun day. I can't let you go swimming now."

"id read [dread] going together with dad even home."

"Why?"

"because he gets especially demanding."

"I think Dad's expectations are accurate except when they are too low like when he holds your hand. We should be able to go places and have fun without ANY concerns that you might hit, scream, poke."

"i.m mad ecause you favirdad [favor dad]. you give him the bebefit [benefit] of the doubt." I had just taught that idiom to DJ, and he was cleverly using it with his mother to ask for additional slack. What is more, he was conducting oedipal maneuvers, like some sort of belligerent Freudian army.

"DJ, I disagree. All day I have been explaining and defending you with him. BUT I will not explain or defend the use of hitting and poking. When you hit and poke, you convince Dad that you can't behave and can't walk independently."

"you convince him I baby when you say I need a few minutes to get adjusted to a new place." Emily had responded to DJ's first outburst with a plea for understanding on my part, which DJ now turned against her. Having done so, he quickly retreated. "i really really try."

"Then we need to try in a different way because you have enough control over your body NOT to hit. Tonight we are meeting James and Eileen for dinner. I need you to behave. Even if Dad is mad or anxious or worried because of the choices you made."

"can I go swimming?"

"You have lost your right to choose activities for the rest of the day. Show you can control your body, and you'll get choices again tomorrow."

"ok youre pleasure."

Dinner that night went surprisingly well. DJ was very responsive to his aunt and uncle, typing on the labeler, "hows Charlie i hear hes doing great things." The hospital had delayed Charlie's release, and so James and Eileen had had to sneak out while Eileen's brother Joe stayed with Charlie. We'd planned to meet at the hospital and walk to a pizza place nearby. When we arrived at the hospital, DJ refused to enter "great places"—not even the lobby, so Emily went up to get James and Eileen. Because Charlie was having some sort of minor procedure done, we had to wait a long time before the three of them appeared. During that long wait, DJ grew anxious, signing, "go, go, go." I was certain we were headed for a meltdown, but DJ held on. What mysterious force governed his behavior? I sometimes imagined his moods were like coins that life had tossed, testing the laws of probability. Though there was, at any given time, a fifty percent chance of meltdown or cooperation—even if we'd experienced a thousand meltdowns in a row—I wanted to believe cooperation more likely just after a string of bad luck. But of course it wasn't.

Before parting, we agreed to stop by Eileen's parents' place in Oak Park the next morning. James and Eileen had moved in with Chuck and Cathy in order to have some help with the demanding chemo regimen. DJ wanted to see Charlie, and this way he could. When we showed up at Chuck and Cathy's, he didn't want to go in: his customary response to an unfamiliar place. Eventually, we prevailed, but only after he'd let out a number of screams. We ate breakfast and then went for a walk, taking in the beautiful, historic houses that Frank Lloyd Wright had built. James and Eileen had rigged an antique stroller they'd received from Chuck and Cathy so that it could accommodate Charlie's chemo pack and other medicines. For Charlie it was a tiny, sight-seeing ambulance, a way to see the world. Quite happy on our walk, DJ smiled at Charlie and investigated the stately, oak-lined streets. The aesthete in him regarded the spectacular light show. Later he typed, "charlies free." Ellie, on the other hand, was pensive, almost sullen. In the car, she'd confess to having been shocked by Charlie's scars. We said goodbye, grateful that our time with James and Eileen had been relatively calm. DJ had helped out when it counted most. Far from random, cooperation's victory had been achieved by sheer force of will—against, in fact, life's subtly weighted coin.

The drive back to Iowa, however, was almost as difficult as the drive to Chicago; we had to stop twice to get DJ to quit poking. He seemed possessed. At home, he'd tell us, "charlie treated for brain tumor worried that really hes really going to eventually dream too." When asked what he meant by "dream," he typed "terrir." The fact that he'd described Charlie as "free" should have alerted us to an overidentification with his hospitalized cousin. DJ imagined that Charlie would one day ("eventually") suffer from post-traumatic stress, too. And I think in connecting himself with Charlie, he may have imagined that his cousin had been raped. DJ had been complaining of "nightmares about boys fucking me yes each real morning as i wake real real hard." His erections literally terrified him, linking Kyle's violence with his own sexual arousal. "terrific feelings really worry me," he'd typed repeatedly. When anxiety returned, creeping back into the city of his thoughts like insurgents whom an occupying power claims to have vanquished, perhaps the memory of an injured Charlie was too much for him. Perhaps he couldn't keep his sister out of it. Swept up into his associative drama, she had to play the role assigned to her—that of villain: someone saved from poking when he had not been.

The remaining three days of the visit passed excruciatingly slowly. DJ kept poking, and Ellie grew increasingly homesick. I think the sight of Charlie had really unnerved her. She said she thought it was because she'd never been away from home that long when another child had been with his or her parents. The explanation struck me as contrived ("another child"?), and it angered Emily. DJ, Emily complained privately, experienced such homesickness for years, and he didn't have a family or a home to go back to. Like me, she knew that Ellie wasn't to blame for this, but we were all frustrated.

Ellie stayed up later and later, spending a good deal of the remaining evenings on the phone, making DJ sad that he didn't have someone to reject. By staying up so late at night, she got up even later in the morning, further delaying our outings. At Adventureland Amusement Park, Ellie basically went her own way; the two kids were now totally out of sync. DJ reacted to her slight by poking even more persistently in the car. The trampoline party with DJ's friends went from bad to worse when the boys responded too enthusiastically to Ellie. "Go, go," DJ told her in sign. "I will," she replied.

The final evening we all ate dinner in silence. Ellie was aching to be home, but you could tell that she didn't want the visit to end completely on a bad note. I could sense this with DJ as well, and I encouraged him to write his sister a letter. Though I don't have the actual letter and can't replicate the typos, I did memorize its content. It went like this:

Dear Ellie,
    You might possibly want to fire me as the sad hurt great brother. I will try to show you how much I love you. You are my favorite girl.
                    Your brother,
                    DJ

Sadly, loss brought out the best in these two. The prospect of Ellie's imminent departure allowed them to focus on their feeling for one another. It was as if the gift of two weeks of time mocked the life they might have had together, but a few remaining hours—well, they were like a beggar's feast.

The next day, DJ and I dropped Emily and Ellie at the airport. Ellie reassured Emily that next time she wouldn't be so homesick. Two weeks is a long time, Emily told her. "Next time it won't be," Ellie reiterated.

After saying good-bye, DJ and I went to a nearby park and waited for Emily to phone us with news of Ellie's departure.

That afternoon, DJ was particularly obsessive, signing, "swim, swim," despite our having explained to him that the pool wouldn't be open until the early evening. "I know you understand why we can't go swimming right now. So, tell me why you keep saying, 'swim' over and over again," Emily said.

"becajuse you invcit4ed elie"

"DJ, Ellie is your sister. You told us you really wanted to see her and get to know her again."

"yes"

"So, were you glad to see her and be with her for thirteen days?"

"no"

"Why?" I asked.

"because her dad might not want ellie to live very much with me." I took note of the fact that DJ was referring to Dan as "her dad."

"Why's that?"

"because high hopes for her," he said, then added, "he thinks ellie is both perfect and lovabld."

"We have high hopes for you, DJ," I countered, "the highest." He was telling us that he knew why he'd been abandoned. When he'd so misbehaved at Navy Pier, he'd typed, "no fair. ellie has education i dont." At the time, I hadn't entirely understood what he was saying. Listening to DJ perseverate on this injustice, I tried to imagine the psychic toll of discrimination, of which Dan's decision was just one example and an ironic one at that, considering he himself had been a poor man with a lousy education. Forget for a moment that he was DJ's father. How many kids do we track into futility, whether disabled or not? How many through what sociologists call "structural violence" (the unequal organization and distribution of opportunity in society) never have a shot at "high hopes" and the facilitation—yes, let me use that word—crucial for their success? What does it feel like to be sentenced to low or no hopes? Now imagine the person's parents unwittingly in cahoots with such violence, such prejudice. Feminists in the seventies liked to say that the personal is political—well, for DJ and so many others the political is terribly personal. How to recover from such a blow?

I have suggested that facilitated communication literalizes the goal of other marginalized peoples who have sought a voice in the public sphere. For some nonspeaking people with autism, FC enables them to talk and to be counted as citizens. It also literalizes an intimate posture of devotion, both private and public. If "poking" was DJ's universal metaphor for the violence done to him, then maybe FC might be ours for ethical commitment, for the fostering and maintenance of all human potential. Freud speaks of "feeling our way into others," and, again, maybe FC offers a head start on this essential journey. Perhaps I sound "evangelical" here—Oliver Sacks's modifier for the "enthusiasm" of parents and teachers of FC users—but why not be evangelical about fairness and hope, especially in advance of discovering any person's actual abilities? Even when FC doesn't work, such a commitment to communication and inclusion would speak volumes about a society's desire to hear from all of its members, its refusal to be resigned in the face of ostensibly insurmountable obstacles. Why can't the story of FC be as much a cautionary tale about sadly misplaced hopes as about sadly overzealous, even rabid, pessimism—a pessimism draped in the mantle of "science"? With the technique having been proven successful with some, the focus should be on reexamining what we think we know and developing a host of methods that can respond to highly particular needs.

"you might love me," DJ typed in the conversation about his sister.

"You know how much we love you and how wonderful we think you are!" Emily told him.

"pok is bad because until i pleased you you pokrd"

"What do you mean?"

"until you placed me jn your home her dad was sad really."

"Why?" I interjected.

"because her dad asked you to adopt me." I remember a conversation that Ellie and DJ had had in the living room when suddenly the computer went silent. Emily and I were in the kitchen, and we wondered what the two kids were talking about. When I retrieved the files from the visit, I found one in which Ellie tells DJ that her father had asked us to adopt him, which was distinctly not the case. Did she actually believe this? If so, why had she turned off the sound on the computer? Or did she simply want her brother to feel better, wanted? I shouldn't have, but I told DJ that what Ellie had said was not true, and he became very upset. I hated for him to think that we hadn't wanted him ourselves, and I couldn't bear to see Dan so easily exonerated. A pathetic thought, I know. But if you scrutinize DJ's statements, you can see him wondering if we loved him ("you might love me"), asserting that we had poked him until we found him pleasing, and claiming that we had placed him in our home. We had neither poked nor placed. What's an adoptive parent to do?

CHAPTER 14

Grief Isn't Easy

"get ready for feelibgx [feeling] very bastard," DJ announced at the beginning of our stay in South Carolina. It was like some sort of air-raid
siren telling us that enemy fighters would soon be overhead. He'd made
it clear that he didn't want to go to Hilton Head because his nightmares
had begun there the summer before, and now it was time to punish us
for not listening. I had insisted that he learn to ignore his fear, disasso-
ciating his grandparents' lovely home near the beach, a place we'd been
going to summer after summer, from what had happened to him. Having commenced my we-must-change-our-therapeutic-approach kick, I
simply refused to allow the long arm of Kyle to reach in and script the
present. But DJ balked at this obvious change in policy, accusing me of
not caring about him. And so, he set out to test the courage of my convictions, with nearly all of his anxieties—independence, great feelings,
the future, typing on his own, normalcy, poking—popping up, over and
over again, like suitors whom an exhausted Odysseus swears he has evicted.
When James and Eileen called some time during the third week with the
news that Charlie's temperature had mysteriously dropped and then, later,
that the cancer had spread, I knew I was in trouble. Enter—justifiably—
"the kide inlove with hurt," for hurt was DJ's primary companion: a golden

373

retriever who bounded out into life and came back each time with a different stick of loss.

The news about Charlie hit us very hard. Though we understood that no one had ever survived pineoblastoma long term, there had been enough minor victories in the past couple of months—the initial surgery, a couple of clean scans, Charlie's robust appearance—that we'd actually allowed ourselves to hope. We'd felt the genuine power of community, that ever-expansive circle of people praying for Charlie's survival, and it had seemed, well, significant, material. Now things looked bad indeed. Nobody was giving up—there might be another experimental drug—but we were all bracing for the worst. After a flurry of phone calls, I learned that my mother and older sister intended to fly out to Chicago, and so I decided to go, too. My mother had been there for a month previously, helping with the cooking and the cleaning and the long waits at the hospital. She wanted to make a special meal for Eileen, who had received this awful news about Charlie on the day before her birthday. There wasn't, of course, much that any of us could do. We just hoped that an elaborate show of support might somehow compensate for our collective impotence.

Emily and I were supposed to have guests that weekend in Hilton Head, our friends John and Leslie, and they were incredibly gracious about my greeting them at the door and then leaving for the airport. After Hilton Head, Emily had planned to visit some old college friends who were scattered along the eastern seaboard. We'd rented a cabin in southern Vermont for the first week in August, and she thought she'd slowly but surely make her way north with DJ, in time to meet up with me in the Mount Snow area. Before the news about Charlie, I'd planned to do some research for an article at a library in New York while Emily was visiting her friends. We decided that I'd assess the situation in Chicago and, depending upon what I learned (how quickly Charlie's condition might deteriorate), we'd either proceed with Vermont or not. After Vermont, she hoped to travel to northern Michigan to see her parents, who summered in a cottage overlooking Walloon Lake—the lake that Ernest Hemingway describes at the beginning of *In Our Time*. But all of this, she knew, depended on Charlie.

The birthday supper at Cathy and Chuck's proved a heartfelt celebration of Eileen and, I think for her, an exercise in social discipline. She put up admirably with the beef stroganoff and the presents and the weird way we Savareses needed to make a difference. It was almost as if *she* was supposed to make *us* feel better—that's how hard we pressed with our generosity. Cathy and Chuck were their usual calm, good-natured selves, opening up the Hotel Ripp and Kitchen to any and all comers, including my mother who, with respect to cooking, is something of a tyrant (a benevolent tyrant but a tyrant nonetheless). Charlie slept for a good part of the dinner, and when he awakened he looked astonishingly healthy. I couldn't get it through my head that with cancer you could look fairly well and still be only weeks away from death. James played with Charlie in the crazy way that he always did, singing nonsensical songs in the worst singing voice imaginable: a performance that invariably elicited great smiles from Charlie. Every now and then, however, James would start crying, only to be comforted by Eileen or one of us. If James was passionately off key, the rest of us were passionately off kilter, not knowing what to do, having trouble making any of this seem real.

We spent the next day hanging out, talking, and taking Charlie for walks in his makeshift ambulance. He seemed to love going out as much as we did, for after a while the Ripps' apartment started to feel like a kind of waiting room—with no doctors, no nurses, just the ticking of the clock. The poet Donald Justice begins an elegy for his mother, "The clocks are sorry, the clocks are very sad./ One has stopped. One goes on striking the wrong hours." How to convey the paradoxical sense of time both moving and standing still, time not wanting to participate in this ghastly drama? An immense helplessness pervaded the space, even as we all fought back with as much caring and vitality as possible. Getting out convinced us that life just might triumph over death, and yet getting out reminded James and Eileen of the horrible unfairness of their fate—all of those other couples strolling healthy infants on an ordinary, obliviously ordinary, Saturday afternoon. The weather, I remember, was beautiful, cool (especially for August in the Midwest). The houses in Oak Park, with their manicured lawns and spacious porches, radiated a grandeur that both consoled and disturbed. How could there be such beauty in the world and such suffering? The giant oaks, as in DJ's poem, seemed ready to reach down and lift little Charlie up, rock him in their enfolding canopy. This boy will not be taken, they seemed to proclaim.

No one spoke directly of the prognosis. The official line was hope, no matter what. From my mother I learned that the oncologist really couldn't say how quickly Charlie's condition might deteriorate. Sometimes children went very quickly; sometimes they did not. There was still the chance of another experimental protocol, and the oncologist had promised to spend the weekend investigating possibilities. Sunday afternoon my older sister and her husband flew back to Washington. When Charlie's temperature dipped again, I went with James and Eileen to the emergency room of Children's Memorial, and I saw first-hand how exhausting and frustrating their lives had been for the last four months: the trips to the hospital, the worry, the waiting, the bureaucratic red tape. Imagine dealing with insurance snafus while your child is dying! I don't know how they did it all so gracefully.

That night we had to wait forever before being seen. A nurse ushered us into a room but then let us languish there. One by one, veritable neophytes came in and asked a series of basic questions, replicating what the previous neophyte had done. James and Eileen seemed to know more about pineoblastoma than any of the emergency room staff, and they tried as hard as they could to expedite the inexorable admission process, telling the staff what they needed, urging them to page Charlie's oncologist. At last the Chief Attending arrived and took control. A woman in her late forties, she understood the gravity of the situation—the kind and progress of the cancer. In a tone conceding the inevitable and yet mastering it with simple kindness, she said, "What a beautiful baby." It was as if she knew what James and Eileen would want when Charlie was gone: namely, proof of his presence or, if not proof, then confirmation—life in the simple declarative. This boy lived, no matter how briefly. This boy was loved. "Thank you," Eileen replied.

I left them some time after midnight. They were still waiting for a room in the oncology ward. The doctor wanted to keep Charlie overnight to see if she could solve his temperature problem. I had a flight out the next morning, and so I said good-bye. After talking it over with

Emily, we decided to proceed with our vacation plans and come home if Charlie's condition dramatically worsened. Despite the temperature, Charlie seemed happy and very alert.

Why the push to go to Vermont? In getting DJ to agree to spend time in Hilton Head, I'd told him that he could pick a place, within reason, and we would spend time there as well. To my great surprise, he'd chosen Vermont. When I asked him why, he answered, "the trees." We'd been there several years before and the trip had been a disaster. It was still early in his stay with us and he probably thought, as was his habit, that we were abandoning him. Thus, I'd have bet money that he'd written off the entire state to the memory of his panic, but, no, that's where he wanted to travel. Though he hadn't behaved terribly well in Hilton Head, I longed to demonstrate that reasonable people could, as a group, negotiate a mutually satisfying compromise. We'd visit *both* Hilton Head and Vermont.

Unfortunately, DJ was just too stressed out to enjoy himself. The news about Charlie and my frequent calls to check on his condition made him "nervous," in his word. Up came poking and statements such as "the hurt. having to reaally hear kyle fuck me." He was worried about erections and girls, telling any female, as he had in Hilton Head, "to go." He must have issued this command to our friends Nancy and Raina at least a dozen times, so anxious did the issue of sexual attraction make him. "penis creates weird feelings," he typed. "kyle erection."

"Good feelings or bad feelings?" I asked.

"yes. yes feels good," he replied. No matter how exhaustively I spoke to him about his sexuality, insisting that he separate Kyle's actions from the pleasure his own penis might give him, he persisted with the terrifying associative loop. Little did I know that we were heading for additional revelations. When we'd get home he'd tell us one night in tears about Kyle having orally assaulted him: "breathing very badly not getting airbut i did."

"Yes, you did," I'd say. "You survived."

Later, in a therapy session before school began, he'd type, "he hurts each time im in bed." When the therapist would ask him how old he was at the time of the attack, in effort to remind DJ of how much time had passed since then, DJ would remain stubbornly in the present tense of trauma: "ky hurts me every night." This statement would alarm me more than the others because he would seem to have used the diminutive form of his attacker's name, as if suggesting a fondness for him. It's possible that he'd meant simply to abbreviate the name, typing "ky," then beginning the word "hurts." It would be in this session that DJ would announce, "you.re in my underwear, kyle," literally conflating his penis with Kyle's. He'd also tell us that it was "unrestful to try to sleep," "i will be really alone," and "poking great. lonesome." As a kind of shorthand, this final statement would devastate us. As much as Emily and I would instruct DJ's therapists to eschew the past and focus on the future, they'd feel compelled to follow DJ's lead, and DJ was heading back into the swamp of rape.

Indeed, the period from Hilton Head to late fall was filled with anxious references to sex and the sense of a continuing salvage operation. Though we couldn't see it on the river of his thoughts, a giant crane was out there trying to lift some wreckage and, in doing so, pieces were breaking off and falling back into the water. The stress of Charlie's dying was that crane. Or the stress of Charlie's dying was like the combination to a safe long given up on. Out popped important documents. In mid-September he'd tell us, "[Kyle] fucked me in the baby barth," complaining, "my but is numb mom. he.s dong did." In Hilton Head he'd become hysterical when, arm in arm, my friend Stephanie and I sang a song together on the karaoke machine. "stephanies got dad," he'd typed. In Michigan, he found himself attracted to his older cousin Tyler (who, he said, reminded him of a girl in his class), and this attraction made him panic. "Tyler is so beau."

"Why is that a problem?" Emily asked.

"because edach look you feel dread because Tyler understands me."

"Why don't her beauty and understanding make you feel happy?"

"because great feselings scare me," DJ answered, and by great feelings he meant both sexual stimulation and the possibility of a rewarding future—a future with someone who, in another of his idioms, "gets my life." Again and again, DJ evinced the habit of extraordinary condensation, where any given worry turned out to be an entire zoo of concerns.

In DJ's dictionary, "puberty" would have too many definitions to list; the one word might conceivably be the entire book. With Charlie in trouble, it was simply too easy to suspect the future, to label it, like some homicide detective, a "person of interest."

And so, Vermont and Michigan turned out to be less relaxing than they might have been. When we arrived at Mount Snow, DJ told us, "its as beautiful as i recall," and he insisted that we ride the chair lift up to the top of the mountain. In the summer, bikers use the ski trails, and as Emily and DJ ascended, a group barreled down below at a frightening speed. I had remained at the bottom so that I could call my mother without rattling DJ. Once Emily and DJ had made it to the top, DJ apparently grabbed the labeler and declared independently, "i can type on my own." Emily almost wanted to laugh at the obvious symbolism of this mountaintop proclamation. A Hollywood movie company couldn't have envisioned anything more unbelievable, but maybe a mind like DJ's needed precisely this sort of scenic encouragement, this sort of dramatization. (Later, in the fall, after an argument about growing up, DJ would type by himself, "you dont love me," making it clear just how psychological the issue of independent typing is. That he'd realize independence so ironically would underscore this fact.)

And yet, no sooner had he ventured out into confident declaration than he retreated into his customary discourse of hurt and his "sad self." "yohudread the treattment of hurrt people," he remonstrated us. In Hilton Head, he'd told my friend John Murchek that he "wanted to talkm with interestig people who do not fear the future," and, later, when we met Doug Biklen for the first time in Rutland, Vermont (I had written Biklen out of the blue, told him about our progress with DJ, and he had proposed a meeting halfway between Mount Snow and the town where he summered near Middlebury), DJ asked, "do you fear for my future?" The issue of the future consumed DJ, and he couldn't help flip-flopping about its prospects. Whenever a call came in about Charlie, he'd say something like "i.m becoming nervous treating me forever very nervous" or "yoh be my caretaker forever." The emphasis on "forever" revealed the extent to which DJ imagined that he could protect himself from the future's uncertainty by remaining injured, hurt. Poking was the outer sign of that injury, that hurt. In September he'd be able to articulate this logic for himself: "yearn to be free but dcared reason for it [poking] is it is to be sure i am not just real ly on my own."

Other things fed into his nervousness as well. He couldn't stand having the TV on, for fear of seeing a report about the war in Iraq. "i want to wolf down some very bad beer," DJ said when he caught me listening to the news.

"What did Officer Fred teach you about beer and other alcohol?" Emily asked.

"its bad for you especially if you are young." This intervention proved unsuccessful because DJ immediately reiterated his desire: "i want a beer. it makes me relax." Hearing DJ, the son of an alcoholic, ask for a beer and recite the adult reason for consuming it startled me. It made me think of the first time I took DJ to the grocery store as his father and he led me to the alcohol aisle, where he stopped in front of a twelve-pack of Busch.

Charlie, meanwhile, was hanging in there. There were signs of decline but nothing terribly alarming—at least not before Emily and DJ returned from northern Michigan. James and Eileen engaged the services of a local hospice outfit and began to prepare themselves for Charlie's final days, however quickly they might come. It turned out that Charlie wasn't eligible for any other experimental protocol. The oncologist promised to work aggressively to prolong Charlie's life while trying to maintain its quality, and this meant an additional round of chemo. Those of us on the outside of the decision-making process wondered what exactly was the point, but if faced with a similar dilemma, I would no doubt bargain for as many additional moments with DJ as I could, so long as I knew that I wasn't adding to his agony. Part of the problem in treating a terminally ill infant was determining why he was upset. Was Charlie hungry? Was he in pain? Did he need to burp? We'd encountered this with DJ when, early on, we didn't know if he was having a seizure, a hemiplegic migraine, a flashback, gas—you name it. There must have been countless times we gave him medicine when he didn't need it because he couldn't tell us what was wrong and we were frantic to do something. That infamous trip to the Northeast to visit Ellie culminated in an emergency room visit and a neurologist prescribing a new anti-convulsant. I'm now almost certain that DJ didn't have a seizure in Emily's brother's house; rather, he'd awakened in a panic, thinking he'd been dropped off at his latest foster placement.

While the Ripps kept vigil in Chicago with my older sister and her family, who moved out there temporarily, Emily and I tried to get DJ ready for the sixth grade. There were new teachers to train and a routine to establish—well in advance of school actually starting. DJ's anxiety level was quite high. "i.m ready to kill poking," DJ said, and though the statement seemed to indicate a desire to move beyond his obsession, the formulation—"kill poking"—actually suggested an intensification. When DJ related to us that he was "getting nervous about hurting the other kids at scuhool," I wondered privately if I had the strength to cope with a fall like the last one, when he was very violent.

As part of our school preparations, I went to Des Moines to see the therapist who had been advising us intermittently. I was determined to consolidate a new therapeutic strategy, even as Charlie's dying threatened whatever progress we might make. The woman, Grace, had worked with autistic kids for years, including kids who have been sexually abused, and when I told her about DJ appearing to be stuck in trauma and about our endless conversations concerning the horrific events of his past, she confirmed my suspicion that with an Autist you can reach a point where it's no longer helpful to work through the trauma. Better to put it away and find something else, something less damaging, for him or her to perseverate about. "Deal with issues in the present. Talk about those things," she counseled.

Of course, the line between past and present for the traumatized, let alone the autistic, isn't exactly clear, but we could, I thought, refuse to discuss explicit references to Kyle. Whenever DJ mentioned Kyle, we could insist that he talk about something else, something positive. This would be the goal, one that we wouldn't achieve completely but one that we could work toward. I didn't think of myself as renouncing therapy—as more came out about the past, I wondered if therapy wasn't in fact doing its job, albeit slowly. Rather, I was trying to find a balance between honoring DJ's emotional complexity with analysis and acknowledging his autistic nature. Further, I worried about the formative impact of trauma: the push into selfhood it seemed to have provided. Again, we didn't want a son constitutionally composed of pain.

In addition to practicing the "all done, all done" approach to Kyle, Emily and I set out to make other changes as well, chief among them, facilitating independence by devoting ourselves a bit less overwhelmingly to DJ. By that I mean attending to other things, including our much-neglected relationship and Emily's career. For the previous six years, we'd created an intense, child-focused refuge that sought to compensate for what DJ had missed. The arrangement had served us well, for look how far DJ had come, but he needed something different now, something to propel him out into the world. Motherhood especially seemed synonymous with treatment, emotional bandaging. This crucial bond had to be expanded, modified, supplemented with other experiences. For once, blessedly, DJ's needs coincided with ours.

It's a measure of just how irrelevant was either Emily's or my personal well-being that I am only now really addressing the matter. When we switched roles as primary and secondary breadwinners with the move to Iowa, Emily was glad to have a break from her demanding career. The circumstances of DJ's great awakening made it essential that somebody be available full time, more or less, to deal with his trauma. Eventually, however, Emily grew dissatisfied with her disproportionate burden and lack of professional identity. But her dissatisfaction didn't declare itself; it was like something being smuggled through customs, some contraband that even the traveler didn't know she had on her person. Emily was so giving, so generous, that she had a difficult time voicing her own desires. Only after she had completely exhausted herself, reached, as physicists say, the point of elasticity (and then some) did she concede a problem. Out would come the dogs and customs officials, ushering her to the side, opening up her luggage. The look on her face as she confessed to wanting more always seemed to shock her.

I was selfish, or if not selfish, much more aware of, and insistent on, my needs. I'd say, "I'm going out for a drink on Friday with so and so" or

"I have to go into the office on Sunday to do some photocopying." My job, however tense and draining at times, offered relief on the really bad days, the seemingly hopeless days, with DJ. I'd urge Emily to take some time for herself, but the combination of her reluctance to do so and unreliable child care often prevented this from happening. When I'd offer to take DJ for the weekend, she'd say that I was too tired or that she wanted to spend time together as a family. Add my worsening arthritis to the mix—unmistakable pain and irritability—and Emily was even more reluctant to ask for a break. When I describe myself as selfish, I want the reader to understand that I probably did take advantage of Emily's generosity, but I was desperate. Only by comparison did I *feel* selfish. I was working enormously hard with DJ—at night, on the weekends, talking with him, jumping, wrestling, going for walks. And I was working enormously hard at my job. Before I passed my third-year review, I felt that I couldn't say no to any request from colleagues or students. I had to be ubiquitous on campus: at this talk, that meeting, etc., etc.

When I think of families trying to raise kids with significant challenges that do not have our resources—the luxury, say, of one parent staying home or of grandparents who purchase whatever augmentative communication device necessary—I'm embarrassed to complain. What we've done for DJ shouldn't itself be a function of privilege, but it clearly is. Different social arrangements would more equitably ensure the futures of all children. At the same time, what we've done for DJ is also a function of basic self-abnegation, and we don't live in a culture that values such an approach to life, or if it does, it does so sentimentally and in a gendered way, expecting such a commitment from Mom but not from Dad. Any paean to extraordinary devotion must account for that devotion's unequal costs, and it must have a plan for remedying them. Thankfully, Emily and I knew that there would be stretches where one of us would be shouldering more of the burden, and thankfully, we both derived, even in our most depleted moments, immense satisfaction from giving DJ the life he deserves.

Hence, with my third-year review out of the way and my arthritis stabilized, with DJ having made the transition to middle school and now needing a different kind of help from us, it was time for Emily and me to revive our relationship and for her to revive her career. We resolved to resume date night, and she resolved to go back to school and earn her Ph.D. The Ph.D would allow her more flexibility in choosing her next job and more decision-making power in it. Besides, DJ's progress with facilitated communication had inspired her to enter the vitriolic fray concerning the technique's legitimacy, and sufficient credentials were the precondition for being heard. Although no one could say why FC worked with some Autists and apparently not with others, the fact that it had worked with DJ suggested there were other "hopeless" cases out there with whom it might work as well, perhaps many cases.

Very little scholarly work has been done on the technique since Diane Twachtman-Cullen captured the view of detractors in her 1997 book, *A Passion To Believe: Autism and the Facilitated Communication Phenomenon*: "Clearly facilitated communication is a seductive technique—one that seduces the imagination and anesthetizes the voice of reason." On the back of Twachtman-Cullen's book, an array of experts deeply invested in their own ideas of autism and their own therapeutic interventions weighs in against FC—for example, Lorna Wing: "This is a fascinating exploration of the mechanisms of unconscious self-deception and the harm it can cause." Or Eric Schopler: "This volume offers . . . a better understanding of the problems generated by such an irrational approach."

Though Twachtman-Cullen admits that her book was based on just three FC users, remarking, "One must proceed with caution [in] drawing sweeping conclusions about the overall nature and validity of facilitated communication," she's all to happy to have others draw such sweeping conclusions. Moreover, she repeatedly draws them herself, asserting on the book jacket, "While the main purpose of this book is to report on my research, ultimately this book is about more than facilitated communication. It is about what I have come to call the FC culture—that sociopolitical phenomenon in which unanimity of thought and philosophy has created a class of believers whose 'sacred' mission is not only to advance the cause of facilitated communication but also to disparage the opposition. It is also about the far-reaching effects that occur when common practice disassociates itself from common sense and when ethics and responsibility fall victim to a passion to believe."

Perhaps I should have said that very little scholarly work has been done on the technique *by detractors* since the publication of this book. Biklen and his colleagues at Syracuse have continued to explore FC, developing alternative corroboration procedures and asking opponents to account for the achievement of independent typing. As a mother, autism professional, and soon-to-be doctoral student in cultural literacy, Emily hoped to contribute to this nascent field, pursuing her own hunches about the role of inclusion and print-rich environments in maximizing the chances of an FC breakthrough. She also hoped to develop further her approach to teaching nonspeaking kids how to read.

Emily's plan was to start slowly, by taking one course at the University of Iowa in the fall and two in the spring. We'd use that first semester to get DJ accustomed to Emily being away. Of course, he immediately resisted the idea, perceiving it as a threat. Toward the end of August, as Emily's class approached, he remarked, "you look just really sad."

"DJ, Mom is simply tired and in need of a bath. Are you nervous?"

"yes because you yearnterrijust treally to be free."

"DJ, Mom is there for you always if you need me," Emily replied.

"i worry that you'll each day really yearnb to treat you yourself well you really eager."

"What makes you feel this way?"

"you want to go to work." So, Emily was like him—yearning for independence, yearning to treat herself well. DJ sensed her eagerness to "work," and though this agitated him, he represented their predicaments identically. Perhaps he realized how stifling the present arrangement was—he and his mother locked in a traumatic embrace. I know I'm behaving like a literature professor when I compare Emily and DJ to the characters in Toni Morrison's novel *Beloved*: namely, Sethe and Beloved. But Morrison gets exactly right the dangerous, all-consuming bond of trauma, which she dramatizes as a contest between the present and past with the latter as a ravenous glutton: "The bigger Beloved got, the smaller Sethe became." Trapped in the house at 124 Bluestone Road, this mother and daughter dangerously re-create the space of maternal oneness, where "it was difficult for Denver [Sethe's other daughter] to tell who was who." The reader knows, however, that this oneness is, finally, the belated, guilt-driven fantasy of a woman who did grievous injury to her child; Sethe murdered Beloved rather than return her to slavery. At a moment of profound traumatic dislocation, some ghost-like combination of the two characters speaks:

> I AM BELOVED and she is mine. . . . I am not separate from her   there is no place where I stop   her face is my own and I want to be there in the place where her face is and to be looking at it too   a hot thing

My analogy obviously founders on the person of Emily, who is not DJ's birth mom, not the one who abandoned him. But DJ nonetheless seemed to want from Emily some payment for past crimes, some emotional recompense. I've already spoken about the way facilitated communication harkens back to an earlier physical interconnectedness when each of us was part of our mothers; with DJ, trauma exacerbated that desire for oneness—a oneness, in part, profoundly agoraphobic. And yet, at the same time, he was clearly struggling to free himself and half-hoped that Emily might do the same. "Was I always there when you needed me at Linney [DJ's school in Florida]?" Emily asked.

"yes yes card [Center for Autism and Related Disabilities] understand that you love me." I can't decide if that final statement is a command or a dependent clause in search of a subject.

We had a more elaborate version of this conversation the following day when DJ misbehaved by pouring water on his head. "I'm sorry that I poured water on my head. INstead of getting mighty poking, I poured water," he said. "I'm nervous you might leave me free." Leave me free— could there be a more compressed articulation of his fear? "You're my main nice frend," he declared. "YOU're my favorite drelly great only mom." I especially loved this formulation. Emily was at once his favorite and his only mom. Can the psyche do without contradiction?

No sooner had he proclaimed Emily his "favorite drelly great only mom" then he reiterated his fear, this time as an assertion of fact: "you really want to leave me."

386

"No, DJ," Emily said, "I want us to be like we were in kindergarten, 1st, 2nd, and 3rd grades. You went to school. Mom went to work. And in the afternoon and evenings and on the weekends, we had fun and also did homework together. That's all I want. And I think you want it to. I just think you forgot you could do it."

"you really love me," he said. After additional ups and downs and loop-de-loops, Emily decided to present her argument systematically, hoping it might straighten out the miniature racecar track of DJ's anxiety.

"Dear, DJ, thank you for your apology and remarks. Please let me respond. First, I love you very much and will always be your forever mom."

"Great," DJ replied.

"Second, I would not be a great mom if I allowed you to think that pouring water on your head or poking is *ever* OK. Neither behavior is OK, ever. There is no reason for doing either of them."

"ok."

"Third, I will *never* ever leave you. Even when your behavior is very good and you understand how to live and have fun in the world, I will still be your mom and in your life as much as you want."

"Good."

"Moving forward and leaving your past hurt and poor behavior choices behind will allow us to have fun, laughter, learning, and good times together."

"i know."

"Fourth, Mom is going to take a class this fall. It is something I'm excited about. I want you to be happy for me, but I am going to do it regardless. It will meet once a week and will help me settle into life in Iowa."

"ok."

"Fifth, friends help each other out and encourage each other to grow and learn."

"ok."

"Sixth, I love being your mom and spending time together, but I wouldn't be doing my job as your mom if I let our friendship get in the way of your making other friends, too."

"you're right."

"Seventh, so please don't get nervous or mad and misbehave just because you are learning how to do more and reaching out to have other friends. It's something we should *celebrate* not worry or be sad about."

"that's true, but sometimes I get scared you're trying to put me hurt in a home for crazy kids."

"DJ, Mom and Dad would never, ever, ever do that because you are *not* crazy."

"You yearn to e free. yOU say you were free in florida."

"I did have more time to pursue my job interests then."

"im afraid you'll look happy when you're yoursel."

"Don't you want me to be happy?"

"really scared you'll leave where you are."

"Why would being happy make me leave?"

"because you won't like kme."

"DJ, I will always like and love you. Always. If I am happy and you are happy, we'll have such fun!"

"You're free.you feel independet."

"DJ, I'm 41 years old. I am independent. That doesn't mean that I'm going to leave. I have been independent the whole time you have known me. I independently chose to have you as a son. I independently chose to be with you. You are twelve. Like *all* twelve-year-olds, you are learning how to be more and more independent. Every twelve-year-old struggles with wanting to be more independent and worrying about what that will be like. No twelve-year-old is completely independent."

"You really love my mind." (DJ had taken to differentiating between his mind and his body, which he couldn't entirely control, accusing us of preferring the former.)

"DJ, I love your mind *and* your body. I am just trying to help you to be a free person in the world because you can be, you deserve to be, and— I think—you very much want to be."

"Can you help me be fred."

"Yes! That's what Mom and Dad are trying to do, but we need your help. We need you to trust us when we set limits and say 'no' to something. We need you to have confidence from *all* your past accomplishments, so you can accept guidance or correction *without* panicking and thinking negatively or getting mad. We need your help. With it, yes, absolutely."

For all of my insistence on adopting a new therapeutic strategy, I, too, had to make some changes. For one thing, both Beth in Cedar Falls and Grace in Des Moines counseled me to stop sleeping with DJ. No matter how scared he was, no matter how frequently he pooped in his pants, he needed to learn how to defend himself. If we were going to ask him to be more independent during the day, he had to be more independent at night. When, one morning, he announced on the labeler, "each niht im frightened you might feel but" and "you might injure my urealcream," I knew that such a change was long overdue. Intensified by dreams, his associative proclivities allowed him to confuse me with Kyle, who had once shared a room with him. When I returned to my own bed, DJ lamented, "im nervous because dad is free." We were like some ragtag continental army, Emily and I, fighting for independence. DJ was our most important pamphleteer, the Thomas Paine of pain: "Give me liberty or give me death!" Except this Mr. Paine found himself consumed by doubt. "he is sleeping with he is sleeping with you," DJ typed to Emily.

"Is that a good thing?" Emily asked.

"yes ready to sleep on my own yes yearn to be free of ni[ghtmares]," DJ practiced telling himself. The therapists were right: we had to restore our proper sleeping arrangements. DJ needed to gain confidence, and Emily and I needed to start having sex again.

And so, we entered the new school year with trepidation. DJ alternately accused us of under- and overestimating him. A week into it, on the 2nd of September, Charlie died, plunging us all into turbulent mourning. My brother phoned at 6:45 a.m.; I remember looking at the clock and thinking it was DJ's aide calling in sick. We'd been told that it could be any day now—the tumor had affected Charlie's breathing—but it still came as a shock. The finality of it less like a transformer explosion than a spent candle's extinction.

He had died in the wee hours of the morning, a finger in each of his parents' hands, listening to his favorite lullaby. After he died, I'd later learn, Eileen and James took him for one last stroll in the antique carriage. They moved quietly through the streets of Oak Park, waiting for the sun to come up, holding hands and sobbing. A final loop for the life that might—that *should*—have been. A few more moments with their son. Then they surrendered Charlie to the funeral home. I can't imagine the horror of such a transaction: saying good-bye, knowing what was ahead. The Irish-American poet Thomas Lynch, an undertaker by profession, has a poem entitled "A Good Death Even When It Kills You," and Charlie's was certainly that. Beautiful. Comforting. James and Eileen cared for that boy with monumental devotion and when he died they memorialized him wholeheartedly.

I spent the rest of the 2nd, a Thursday, talking on the phone with relatives and writing an elegy. I wanted James and Eileen to have something. I wanted them to understand that Emily, DJ, and I knew, at least in part, what the previous four months had been like. I wanted to try to capture the sadness, the desperation, the valiant insistence on love. I wanted to remember my nephew. As I said, at the time I didn't know about their final stroll through Oak Park, and when I did learn about it the following day, I couldn't believe that I'd focused on the antique carriage in my poem. It seemed uncanny.

THE WORLD IN OAK PARK
For Charlie James Savarese (1/13/04–9/02/04)

They were new parents pushing
a very old carriage:
part jerry-rigged ambulance
with portable I.V.,
part first-car
on a wooden rollercoaster.
Your father prized that hand-me-down
gift from your grandparents—
the rusted frame and ornate wicker
a touch of whimsy
to stun despair.
Six Flags Pineoblastoma. . . .

The ride had to have been frightening,
Charlie, but you never seemed
to mind.
The carriage didn't even have tires
or working shocks,
yet it moved—like love, say,
gone stiff with worry.

The tumor left you little time,
though world enough you had;
world enough
your parents gave you,
strolling past the giant oaks
and prairie-style houses.
"Which one would you like to live
in, Charlie, which one?"
Who could blame them for the anger
that sometimes surfaced?
"Why us? Why *you*?"
Every healthy child an offense,
the sun an offense,
the bright marigolds in all their splendor
an offense,
the callous universe refusing
to call off its parade.
"But Charlie's sick!" they'd cry,
exhausted from the night before
and the night before that—
the delicate surgeries,
the infusions,
the frantic trips to the hospital.
Hope itself on oxygen.

And still they took you out
when you were well enough.

Your little brain reeling
in whatever it could
(sensation like a school of fish—
the light alone
a million, million minnows):
the grass, the breeze, your mother's
finger
to which you seemed to cling.
In the end, you couldn't see to see,
the tumor pressing
on the nerve,
wrapped like a vine around the stem.
That head of yours a swollen
blossom.

And now you're in another craft
of sorts:
a crib the earth must rock,
a rower's scull pushed gently
out to sea,
its tiny occupant inside.
What can they do, your parents,
what can they do
but wave from the shore
of their heartbreak?
Good-bye, Charlie, good-bye.

I sent the poem by e-mail to Chuck Ripp to get an opinion on sharing it with James and Eileen. I didn't want to distress them further. If they were having trouble coping, maybe the poem should wait. It isn't the most uplifting piece, or at least not traditionally so. It tries to confront life's miseries and unfairnesses head on, finding in human commitment something like an answer to death. But it doesn't vanquish death.

After speaking with my older sister, I learned that the funeral would take place on Monday. In the Catholic faith you can't hold a funeral mass

on Sunday, and James and Eileen didn't think that they could pull together the kind of funeral they wanted by Saturday. Furthermore, they
worried that many people wouldn't attend on such short notice if they
didn't have part of the holiday weekend to travel. So, they chose Sunday
for the wake, Labor Day for the funeral, and Tuesday for the burial. But
there was another reason for their decision, not the primary reason,
though one that certainly contributed to their thinking. It turns out that
my father's new wife's daughter was getting married that weekend, and
my father had asked for a postponement of the funeral. (Only in my family
could these two events coincide.) Ever the lawyer and rhetorical
conman—in this case, employing parallel structure to suggest a logical
equivalence between his actions and my brother's—he told James, "I
won't be disappointed with you if you don't postpone the funeral, so long
as you won't be disappointed with me if I don't come."

He was siding with his new family and insisting that James and Eileen
accommodate his needs, though their son, his grandson, had just died.
If the postponement hadn't suited them, I don't know what they would
have done. James was clearly hurt by my father's decision, though it
wasn't his way to voice that hurt. I actually think he was grateful that he
didn't have to push the issue. As it was, the man insisted on attending a
post-reception brunch the day after his stepdaughter's wedding (as did
my younger sister) and thus missed the wake, which James and Eileen
rendered as a memorial service in its own right, replete with prayers,
readings, and reflections.

I left for Chicago Friday night. Emily and DJ would come Sunday
morning. We wanted to minimize the stress for DJ as much as possible;
he didn't do well with long periods of hanging out, especially in a strange
place. (Emily had considered not going at all, fearing a total DJ derail-
ment, but DJ had insisted. "must go. dad needs us," he typed.) Saturday
night I helped the Ripp brothers and their spouses make posters for the
wake. Jamie, Paul's wife, had gone out and purchased a tacky substance
that would allow us to attach photographs of Charlie to the poster-board.
It was hilarious watching five professionals figure out how to activate
this tacky substance. The first couple of times we tried, the photographs
immediately fell off. We had been instructed to represent the wide array

of people who had been part of Charlie's life, and so, the first photo-graph I picked was one of my father holding Charlie. I figured I'd prove my impartiality right from the outset. Ironically, this poster would end up being the first you encountered when entering the funeral home. My mother would be outraged at the sight of my father, the likeness of my father, greeting everyone as they walked in. When she discovered that there wasn't a photograph of her on any of the poster-boards—a ter-rible oversight, but there were so many photos and relatively little room—she became irate. An unnamed family member (not me, not my mom) solved the problem by removing the picture of my father when the Fu-neral Director wasn't looking.

That night as we made the posters, the subject of my father came up when Lowell, my older sister's husband, uncharacteristically announced his displeasure with the man: specifically, the decision not to fly out for the wake. This led Jamie, Eileen's brother's wife, to ask me if I intended ever to speak to my father again—a difficult question, to say the least. A discussion of forgiveness ensued with all of the generous, well-adjusted people recommending the practice. The strange thing was that I felt the desire to forgive him, and even to ask for his forgiveness, but I needed him to do the same. This was a man who had not once said he was sorry for anything, to anybody, in his life. Not ever. The more I observed my brother's boundless devotion to his son and considered my father's cava-lier self-absorption, the more furious and pessimistic I became. In the immense lecture hall of life, I realized that even death couldn't offer any instruction. My father was like those students I'd had in Florida who sat in the back of the classroom and read the newspaper while the rest of us plunged into Melville, Twain, Chopin. Of course, I let those students check out, but only after much unprofitable cajoling and harassment.

Emily arrived early Sunday afternoon. I helped her move her lug-gage into the hotel room and played with DJ, who had behaved terrifi-cally in the car. The wake was at 4:00; we didn't have much time to get ready. I asked my Aunt Maureen to stay with DJ while I spoke to Emily about the wake. There was to be an open casket, and I seriously ques-tioned the virtue of bringing a twelve-year-old Autist recovering from

PTSD. He'd already told Emily, however, that he wanted to go, even when she explained to him that Charlie would be lying there in a casket. "we're family," DJ said, and I didn't know how to rebut this argument. All I could think of was DJ, for years to come, perseverating on the image of Charlie's lifeless body.

Eileen had asked all of Charlie's cousins to write little notes of remembrance that she would hang on a tree the family intended to plant in Charlie's honor. She'd have the tree in a pot at the funeral home. Emily and I had to rush to get DJ ready for the wake and to compose his note. I've already offered much evidence against the theory-of-mind hypothesis that dominates the current understanding of autism, but if DJ's note doesn't inspire the experts to be a little less sweeping and definitive in their pronouncements, I don't know what will. Sometimes I think of DJ as abnormally *gifted* when it comes to emotion and social awareness—at least at their most urgent levels. He is, one might say, a savant of grief: not just his, but others' as well. Consider what he wrote to James and Eileen. (Because we obviously surrendered his letter, I can't reproduce its typographical idiosyncrasies.)

> Dear Uncle James and Aunt Eileen,
> Charlie is free. You yearn being with him. You love him. To be without him is sad. He was so cute. You pleased him when you smiled. I love you. Grief isn't easy.
> Love,
> DJ

Once again, he overidentifies with Charlie, thinking of him as having escaped a world of hurt (cancer) and achieved independence from his parents, but at a terrible cost. Doing this gets him into trouble, as he'd come to realize a few days after the funeral, when he'd ask, "can best also be worst?"

"What do you mean?" we'd say.

"my freedom," he'd reply. Though Charlie's death would offer him a chance to reject independence outright, DJ wouldn't take it, opting instead for a more ambivalent attitude. He'd want to know if he could express his ambivalence in a manner that would still allow him to move forward. This would necessitate a different relationship to, even conception of, language. Instead of all-encompassing words like "free" or "great" that could generate ambiguity by virtue of their renunciation of distinction, he needed to generate that ambiguity conventionally, with a host of much less capacious vessels. It's important to understand that I'm not talking about expanding DJ's vocabulary, because his vocabulary was actually quite expansive. I'm talking about getting him to eschew his talismanic approach, which seemed to be a function of perseveration. He'd find a word and through repeated use it would achieve extraordinary meaning. In response to seeing Charlie at the wake, for example, DJ would type to Emily, "you really look hurt. you might leaveme. very hard to dread great place i.m nervous because charlie freed but looks might wake." The feelings and their formulations, in short, could become straitjackets. But he was also capable of fresh insight. Is there anything more piercing than the note's colloquial summation: "grief isn't easy"?

None of us was prepared to see Charlie in the antique stroller. Instead of a casket, James and Eileen had decided to put him in a familiar object. Whereas on the one hand it was comforting to see him in the stroller, on the other it was almost more shocking—what DJ called "unfourseen great hurt." The room in which the wake took place was long and narrow; you entered toward the back and first saw James and Eileen receiving mourners. Only after you greeted them did you see Charlie. The sight repeatedly elicited gasps and sobs from the many people who filed through.

Charlie looked like a porcelain doll; there was a bit too much makeup on his cheeks. Whenever there was a slight lull, James would walk to the front and give his son a kiss on the forehead, causing everyone near him to cry. When Emily and DJ appeared about a half an hour into the four-hour observance, I joined them in line and moved through again very quickly; we didn't stop at the kneeler that was set up in front of the stroller, though DJ seemed to want to. His eyes were as big as half-dollars as he passed his cousin. Eileen had made a point of thanking DJ for his note, and James had given him a big hug. Family members congregated in the chairs toward the back and waited for the service, which was to begin at 7:00. We knew that DJ couldn't possibly wait until then, so Emily and I took turns going for long walks with him. At one point, I think my uncle and my cousin went for a drink—the tension and sadness were excruciating.

James and Eileen had asked me to read my poem at the service, but when I'd agreed, I hadn't known that I'd be reading it with Charlie next to me in the stroller. I honestly thought I might pass out while reading it, and if I didn't pass out, I'd most certainly break down. I'd never before given a reading like this. Chuck had shared the poem with them, and Eileen had said she wanted people to know how difficult the experience of Charlie's illness and dying had been. She was glad that I hadn't sugarcoated it. I was glad that they had liked the poem, but terribly anxious about reading it.

By the time seven o'clock came around, there were more than a hundred people in the room. Chuck began the service, and each of the siblings then rose, sometimes accompanied by their spouse, and said something about Charlie. My older sister and her husband presented a video they had made. The video set pictures of Charlie to music, including the song that had been playing as he died. This positively wrecked everybody; there wasn't a person left standing on the sidewalk of despondency after this beautiful vehicle moved through. Paul, Charlie's godfather, gave a moving reflection, as did Eileen's siblings and in-laws, Marie and John, Patty and Joe, and David and Lisa. I remember Lisa's reflection especially. An English professor like me, she used a famous passage in Freud about the young child's anxiety in the face of his mother's absence to talk about the problem of death. A game like peek-a-boo teaches the child how to master his anxiety, even to derive pleasure from the act of rediscovering his mother's attention. Lisa suggested that we might all now play peek-a-boo with Charlie in our memories, keeping him alive and present that way. What she said made me think of DJ's struggles with absence and his refusal, in a sense, even to cover his eyes, so desperately did he want to make sure that Emily was there. All I remember about reading my poem, besides the pounding in my chest, was privately congratulating myself seven-eighths of the way through: I hadn't broken down.

But when I got to the last line—"Good-bye, Charlie, good-bye"—I just sobbed and sobbed.

A couple of days later, I'd ask DJ what he thought of my poem. "it really got. me," he'd type. "breaking my heart."

"That's what poetry can do," I'd tell him. "It can break your heart and somehow, at the same time, put it back together."

"do god try to jutm hit us," he'd ask. "does he not relize how breaks our heartsto lose." His metaphor would stun me. God was like his birth mother or Kyle. God sent you to foster care. God beat you mercilessly. After a slight pause, DJ would add, "the trees."

"What do you mean?"

"you know dad. they have no leaves."

Still later, he'd write his own poem about Charlie. In it he'd adopt a very different theological perspective. I'd marvel at how well he'd have assimilated the deterministic consolation of a certain kind of faith. Who knows if he really believed this or if he simply wanted to practice consoling himself and others?

CHARLIE

He was such a beautiful boy.
from the time he was born everyone knew he was an angel.
He could fikll a room full of joy.
He just followed the path given to god.

The funeral was grandiose. It took place in an enormous church, even bigger than the one in which the pre-surgery mass had taken place. Hundreds of people attended. Chuck gave a stirring eulogy in which he reminded everyone of how Charlie's illness had stitched together a vast community of well-wishers. Through e-mail and prayer people literally all over the world had pulled for Charlie. Charlie, he contended, was now in heaven and could be called upon for comfort and courage. James and Eileen then gave their eulogies; both of them remained astonishingly composed. James told a funny story about the day Eileen was released from the hospital after giving birth. They were in the car with Charlie, and James asked,

"What should we do now?" To which Eileen replied, "I think we should call the pediatrician and set up an appointment." So, Eileen called, and the woman on the phone said that she had an opening in twenty minutes. Could they come right now? They drove to the pediatrician's office, checked in, and proceeded directly to an examination room. When the doctor appeared, he asked them how Charlie had been doing since leaving the hospital. James and Eileen looked confused, confessing that he had just left the hospital. "Then why are you here?" the doctor inquired. At which point, Eileen began to cry, exclaiming, "I'm not sure I'll be a good mother." All of their new-parent nervousness erupted in a torrent of worry and tears. "The fact that you have come," the doctor said, "tells me that you will be good parents." Looking out at the congregation, James remarked, "And I assure you he was right: we *were* good parents, very good parents. Daddy will always love you, Charlie," he concluded, his voice breaking.

Eileen then humorously revealed to the congregants that Charlie had been with them at their wedding: inside her stomach! Right there in the middle of a Catholic Mass, she'd confessed to having engaged in pre-marital sex. I love that about Eileen: she is unfailingly honest and un-concerned with what others might think. Her reason for telling us this tidbit? To underscore the point that Charlie would always be with them—from beginning to end.

As Eileen delivered her eulogy, I moved to the back of the church. I wanted to see how DJ was doing. When I got there I noticed that he and Emily were gone. DJ must have become nervous and asked to go for a walk. I found my cousin, though, who was having a panic attack. He was in the midst of a break-up with his girlfriend, and the funeral had clob-bered him. His father had died of a heart attack when he was ten; like DJ, he knew something about loss. Listening to James and Eileen sing a hymn to transcendent love, I felt as if my heart were a stone that had skipped across a pond and was now deciding if it should obey the laws of gravity and sink to the bottom.

After the funeral, my mother hosted a reception at the home of a Ripp family friend. Twice, my father and I walked right by each other: ghosts in different dimensions. By the time of the burial the following day, we

were all exhausted. If leaving Charlie at the funeral home had been difficult, leaving him at the cemetery was unspeakably painful, his little white
casket like a patch of snow on a field otherwise melted. Before returning
to Iowa, I went to lunch at the Ripps', but I didn't stay long. I wanted to
get back. Emily and DJ had left the day before because DJ had school
on Tuesday.

What to say about the spectacle of lost promise, the yawning chasm
of what might have been? Driving home, I tried to fancy Charlie as a
grown man and, conversely, DJ trapped in an institution with nobody
to help him develop. If, as Ernst Bloch insists, oppressive social relations
can be analogized as a kind of death, if both phenomena resemble the
"wealthy cat that lets the mouse run free before it devours it," then maybe
the only reasonable response to the things we cannot change, such as
brain tumors, is to change the things we can, such as unequal opportunity. Doesn't our mortality, the very ticking of the clock, demand it? How
many kids, how many adults, have we failed?

In Bloch's anecdote, the miner, after being sent back to the mines,
murders the millionaire. By Bloch's logic, however, even the rich man
deserves our empathy as he faces death. At seventy, my father, the
epitome of wealth, arrogance, selfishness, and emotional unavailability,
reaches out for more: more houses, more business ventures, more trips
to Scotland to play golf. Now, I'm certainly no miner—I'm as privileged
as they come—but I've fantasized about "shooting this god down"; I've
even delighted in my father's desperation as he runs out of time. Such
anger obscures, of course, a profound sadness over the squandering of
potential: his and mine, ours together, the world's at large. At every
moment, it could all have been different. As the drivers jockeyed for
position on a crowded I-80, each of us lost in our private interiors, I
proposed to the air a revolution in feeling, an awakening to the plight of
others—both at home and down the street.

A few days later, I asked DJ what he thought of my father. He'd
mentioned seeing him at the funeral. "sick," he typed, "he very much
nothing to say." Was he trying to please me? Had he heard me talking
to a friend? Then, in a role reversal of gargantuan proportions, he added,
"be. not. hurt by losing. him. we love you very much."

CHAPTER 15

Reasonable People

The fall was full of disaster. One hurricane after another battered the coasts of Florida, causing tremendous damage to places we knew intimately. If it wasn't an act of God, as insurance agents like to say, then it was the death of someone close to us. First, Charlie died; then ten days later, Emily's Aunt Sue died. Not too long after this, the actor and disability activist Christopher Reeve died. His father, Franklin, had been my undergraduate advisor at Wesleyan University, and we'd become very good friends in the twenty years since I graduated. In fact, Franklin had found us our rental at Mount Snow, very near his farm, so that we all might spend time together. Christopher had been an inspiration to so many people with disabilities, and it seemed unconscionable that the fates might cut short the good he was doing. When the son of the man who helped build the trampoline house died, I felt as if we were trapped in a Jobian conspiracy or end-of-days scenario.

Jack's son, Will, had been having trouble at his group home, and so his parents had put him in a psych ward, hoping that a short stay would allow the doctors to adjust his medications and tame his violent acting out. They'd felt pressure, as the parents of people with cognitive

disabilities often do, to intervene dramatically, for fear of losing a treasured placement. While Will was in the psych ward, a doctor injected
him with a second antipsychotic drug, though Will had already calmed
down considerably with the first. In doing so, he brought on what's
called neuroleptic malignant syndrome, killing him. A twenty-six-year
old Autist, with a job and friends and passionate interests, surrendered
his life to a medical establishment and, I dare say, a culture that doesn't
understand—that doesn't *want* to understand—people with autism.
Emily was certain that Will's acting out had been in part a communication problem; something was bothering him, and you needed to find
out what it was.

The incident made me think of the awful decisions parents have to
make about medicating their children; we live in a positively pill-happy
country, embracing a mechanistic view of the brain in which well-being
(or its more cynical counterpart, zombied stupor) is only one, two,
three, four, five pharmacological interventions away. How to balance
respect for scientific advances with a healthy skepticism about this
narrow view of human operation, not to mention the economic forces
that support it? Emily and I have staked our very lives on a holistic
approach, one that honors DJ's full humanity and, at the same time,
addresses the problem of seizures, hemiplegic migraines, and trauma-
induced rage attacks.

DJ's still on the Topomax and the Risperdal. Will's death nearly
paralyzed me with stress about the risks of taking these medications.
Thank God we had, still have, a terrific psychiatrist, Dr. Babson, who
listened to our worries and helped us to craft a strategy for minimizing
the risks. As Will's case demonstrates, not every person with a cognitive disability has such thoughtful, compassionate care, and even with
it problems can occur. The latter point aside, what happened to Will
too easily resonated with a larger history of neglect, injury, and exclusion. The pending lawsuit may still reveal an ordinary instance of mal-
practice, but I'd like to know how much less careful doctors are when
prescribing drugs to those with cognitive disabilities? At the funeral,
Emily noticed many with such disabilities in attendance, people she'd
never seen before in the town of Grinnell. To a person, they sobbed

throughout the service, especially when the minister played Will's favorite music.

We shielded DJ from Will's death, making sure not to talk about it until he had gone to bed. Sue's death, however, required that Emily take a trip to Michigan. "you hurtmy heart not being here," DJ told her the second she returned. "you look hurt," "you might die," "please be my mom forever"—all of these DJ spat out in rapid succession, like someone who returns to a body and fires additional bullets into it in order to make sure it's dead. But the more bullets DJ fired, the more anxious he became. Sue's death and Emily's class had fused in the experience of Emily being away. It was as if Emily herself had died.

DJ sometimes exchanged this fear for another one: his own death. "Ifeer death," he'd type, placing himself in the role of his cousin who had just passed away. But this fear was really a version of the former one, as the following conversation makes plain. In it DJ probes to make sure that Emily would miss him if he died. "im just glad youre being my mom," he said.

"I'm thrilled I'm being your mom!" Emily replied.

"yearn to be hurt," he typed.

"Who yearns to be hurt?"

"you do because yearn to be my mom"

"Why does that mean that I yearn to be hurt?"

"just because you might lose me"

"How might I lose you?"

"If just just just might dead"

"I see. What you're saying is anytime someone really loves someone else they run the small risk of losing them to death?"

"yes," DJ said.

"I'll gladly take that risk and look forward to years and years and years of love and joy with you!"

"look pleased"

"I am. Sometimes I still have moments when I stop and think, "It's so amazing that we can communicate so clearly with each other about what is in our hearts and minds!"

"just great," DJ responded. A month later, he'd refer to *himself* as the one who "yearns to be hurt," articulating his fear of loss much more directly: "i feel scared because love you." If love involves loss, then why do it? Why set out to injure yourself? Wouldn't that make you, DJ seemed to be saying, a masochist? If anybody had sufficient grounds for indicting love it was our curly-haired prosecutor.

Even if you could bring DJ around to a less anxious place, he'd always be one step away from anxiety—from all of his anxieties. You couldn't talk about death without talking about independence; the words were too slippery, too synonymous. When Emily asked DJ what made him think that he would be "on his own" if he became more independent, he answered, "read ing the book about great hurt book about great places." We knew that Dr. Seuss had shaped DJ's imagination, but we didn't quite know the extent until I recalled the pictures halfway through of dragon-like monsters that emerge from the murky depths to frighten the developing child, whom Dr. Seuss pictures in a tiny rowboat. DJ had been speaking of "muddy creatures," and we hadn't a clue what he was talking about. Since Charlie's and Sue's deaths, poking had become even more of a problem than usual, and it seemed to have something to do with these creatures. "they breath fire on me," DJ said.

"Is it possible that great places don't exist really?" Emily asked.
"yes"
"What would happen if you stopped reaching for eyes?"
"they might kill me"
"Who or what might kill you?"
"the muddy creatures"
"Are there any muddy creatures in the book on great places? Can you show them to me?"
"yes"
"Is this book fact or pretend?" Emily asked.
"fact"
"DJ, this book is made up. It is NOT real. Look at the pictures."
"you might be right," he said.

Even though he seemed to understand that the creatures weren't real, they'd kept him company for so long that he was reluctant to give them up. Throughout the early fall, DJ continued to speak as if they were real, telling us things such as "really terrified that creatures will beat m" or "you really think creatures can pmight go sfrom my head. undertand they breathe fire dread that" or "underestimating creatures you think i can just free myself but i canget hurt by them. great creatures each day can very carefully free my very bad temper." Once, when Emily pressed him on their existence, insisting, "Creatures are not real. They cannot poke or make you poke," he replied defiantly, "yes they can."

"Then ask them to poke me right now to prove it," Emily demanded.

"im nervous that youll get hurt," DJ answered, almost cleverly. Another time, he declared, "people really need to notice dcreatures more." When DJ introduced us to his "noone friends," we began to see how rich and removed and compensatory his internal life was. Here was a boy who had been cut off from other people, from reciprocal exchange, who even with us spent long periods of time entirely inside his head. These "noone friends" were, in DJ's words, "pretende kids," and he said that he liked them more than real kids "because thet [they] have no other friends." They were similar to the trees, which, he claimed, "help by talking to me." And yet, it wasn't too long before even his "noone friends" (is there anything sadder than this fabrication?) started to terrorize him. "yelling at me noone friends," he typed. "noone friends treat medreadfully only hurt." "im nuts because breaking my heart not to be free from noone frends." By the time he asked, "when will creatures be gone?" he was speaking about the entire chorus in his head.

It was a good sign that he wanted to be rid of his demons, but he also clung to the fiction of their power over him. Sometimes, he adopted the less imaginative conceit of two selves. In response to the question "why poke?" he replied, "he mak es me."

"Who?" Emily asked.

"my bad self," DJ explained. The refusal to take responsibility for his actions was itself a sign of his unwillingness to grow up, be more independent. "creatures say freedom is dreadful," he told us, and though he knew "youre telling me to just love the real world," the real world of actual friends and distance from his parents was petrifying.

In early October he stated explicitly, "yearn to be hurt because ill need more help." One morning, he accused Emily of attacking him—of resembling, that is, Kyle. "you beat me up last night mom," he said, his mind finding a rather economical way of keeping him hurt and accusing Emily of abandonment. That afternoon, in a therapy session, he responded to Sarah in Grinnell's question, "What should I know before Mom goes upstairs?" by typing, "the great hurt i feel because she wants to be free." When DJ got a hold of a notion, he was like the best-trained rescue dog in the world. Though we'd vowed not to engage his trauma, after Charlie's death we found ourselves running back into the flaming house of the past, chanting, "just one more item, one more item." We were afraid to push too hard. Life wouldn't cooperate by serving up a stretch of uneventful time in which we could hold DJ to a new, therapeutic protocol.

A couple of days later, he announced, "isaw kyle in my nightmare," adding, "you [Emily] dressed up like me and just poked kyle.." Here, DJ had cast Emily in the role of savior; you could see him vacillating between the two possibilities: heroine or victimizer. He needed her to assault him and save him in a perpetual cycle. The fact that Emily had *poked* Kyle suggests a fantasy of revenge and, as well, anxiety about sex and sexual pleasure. I'm intrigued by the idea of "dressing up," assuming another's identity. On the one hand, DJ was telling us that he himself was too scared to exact revenge; on the other, that he and Emily were one person, in a sense interchangeable. The very next day, he revealed that in his "niightmare mom pokedv herself." Another astonishing psychological solution. If Emily had poked herself, then she wouldn't be able to go to her class; like him, she wouldn't be able to be independent because she'd be hurt. Together, they could eschew freedom, settle back into their Sethe-Beloved stranglehold. Poking herself, mom was also masturbating, and I think DJ was still working through the issue of voluntarily generating "great feelings." "youthink i want erectionsbut i dont," he proclaimed during this period. "you think that yearn to be hardmom. understand that very dreadful.." In his dreams, he was thus trying out all sorts of things, even as he protested against them.

Though DJ seemed undoubtedly to regress, he also seemed at the same time to move forward. Indeed, there were plenty of indications that he just might conquer his fears and embrace growing up, however tentatively. Throughout the fall, he continued to impress us with his academic performance, regularly scoring the highest grade on a social studies or science test. In language arts his peers would vie to have DJ on their team, so formidable were his poetry-writing skills. Consider, for example, the following calendar poem:

> January is white. Glistening snow is a blanket on the ground.
> February is red violet. Valentines and love are in the air.
> March is shamrock green. Leprechauns jumping in the fields.
> April is pacific blue. Oceans of raindrops falling from the sky.
> May is salmon pink. Flowers blooming in fields of joy.
> June is laser lemon. Brilliant sunrays shine like stars in the sky.
> July is violet red. Firecrackers bursting in air.
> August is blizzard blue. Ocean full of clear water for swimming.
> September is burnt sienna. Thinking of the tossing of the pigskin
>   among the fall trees.
> October is vivid tangerine. Pumpkins in the fields of turning leaves.
> November is cadet blue for the early onset of winter weather.
> December is forest green for the joy of decorated Christmas trees.

This is as good as what I often receive from beginning college students. "Cadet blue," "laser lemon," "salmon pink"—DJ understood the importance of vivid diction and striking images. The fact that the poem ended with the *joy* of decorated Christmas trees suggested significant emotional progress, for Christmas trees had been distinctly negative symbols.

Not halfway into the sixth grade, DJ had completely caught up with his peers, even surpassed them in some respects. A boy deemed profoundly mentally retarded as late as the third grade was now on level. Moreover, he was deeply invested in academic success. Once, when Emily and I misunderstood a social studies assignment and failed to help DJ make a map of Grinnell, he let out a scream that could be heard all over the school, and he later said reprovingly to us, "you very much hurt my great future." His teacher had given him a D on the assignment because it was incomplete, and the sight of that mark had reduced him to tears. "i think im very smart," he started telling us. "resent being called retarded." When he made an error on a math problem—he was exceptionally good at math—he explained, "great head made mistayess [mistake]."

DJ branched out in other ways as well. He bought and assembled a photo album for my birthday, rejecting all of Emily's gift ideas. "ready to pick my owwn gift," he said. The album contained pictures from the nine years we'd known each other, and on the cover it said simply, in labeler font, "Dad & DJ: We're Great Friends." In the accompanying letter he wrote, "you love me kind great dad." He also organized a fundraiser for a library in Florida that had been badly damaged by one of the season's hurricanes. The principal at DJ's school had come up with the idea and thought that a former Florida resident, namely DJ, ought to spearhead it. I give the principal, Frank Shults, enormous credit for proposing such a thing. So much of the battle with inclusion involves rethinking what is possible. DJ and the other kids raised a total of $1,100, and DJ used his talking computer to make announcements over the P.A. system, requesting additional pledges, updating his peers on the progress of the campaign. He derived tremendous satisfaction from "doing politics," as he put it, and from the many compliments he received. His teachers all wrote him notes applauding his efforts. "happiest moment was reading five teachers' notes to me after i did the fundraiser. investing real interest in me which is nice," he said. With his college buddy Molly he participated in the community meal, a weekly affair designed to provide a free dinner to anyone who wanted one. "Our country treats really very terribly the poorer," he observed afterward. Finally, at Halloween, he dressed up, for the first time, and went trick-or-treating. His costume: that of a hippie. A hippie!

The most difficult thing to convey is that all of this—the anxiety about Emily and Charlie, the poking, the academic gains, the assertion of independence, the good deeds—was happening at the same time. One moment, DJ could be telling you, "yearn to be treated as old"; the next, "treat me as young." Or he'd say, "im ready to be independent typing" and then insist on having as much facilitation as possible. If you responded to the urgent declaration "understand that I need real friends" by having a trampoline party, DJ would get so nervous that he'd tell his friends "bye" not ten minutes into the party. To me the tumult of this period can be best encapsulated by a walk DJ took, the first by himself, in mid-October. He'd been saying that he wanted to go for a walk on his own, and he'd been practicing with us by falling behind on our regular walks as a family—far enough that we'd have to wait for him to make a turn but not so far that he couldn't keep us in his sights.

It was a Saturday, and it was very warm. DJ had announced his request, and I decided to give him the push he needed, for the second I said, "That's a great idea. Let's do it," he balked. I probably shouldn't have revealed my enthusiasm, but I couldn't help myself. I wanted him to accomplish this milestone. He was twelve years old and he hadn't ventured out (at least while living with us) on his own.

"no, no, no," he typed.

"You can do it," I told him. "We'll sit on the porch and wait for you. Just circle the block."

"no," DJ said, shaking his head in a very exaggerated manner.

"Come on. You can do it. I know you can," Emily assured him. Getting DJ to do something anxiety producing required massive encouragement, and you always ran the risk of pushing too hard and having him dig in. "Get your shoes," she said. When he stood there blankly, I went and got his shoes and even helped him to put them on. We then directed DJ out onto the porch, one of us in front of him, the other behind, for fear he might retreat into the house.

"Make a right on Seventh past Todd's, another right on Summer, a right on Sixth, and a final right on Elm," I said. "We've done this walk together; remember when Dad was on crutches and couldn't go very far?" DJ made a move to go back inside. Emily grabbed his arm.

"You can do it. We'll sit right here. You'll be able to see us for nearly half of the walk," she told him.

"We'll be right here," I said again. DJ descended the porch stairs and took a few steps before turning around and shaking his head.

"You can do it," Emily and I cheered in unison. For nearly ten minutes we did this odd encouragement dance, and when he finally started down the sidewalk past our neighbor Todd's house, he turned to make sure we were still there. Had he been Orpheus, he'd have lost Eurydice in the first moment of his ascent from the underworld. When he made it past Todd's, he pivoted and began to retrace his steps. "You can do it!" we yelled. Our words were like arms that stretched beyond our bodies, way beyond, and nudged him forward.

Repeatedly, DJ looked back, flirted with returning. At the corner he froze. It was as if a kind of catatonia had overtaken him. "You can do it! Go on!" we shouted. After a long pause, DJ looked up. What he did next surprised us, though perhaps it shouldn't have. He put his hands over his eyes and started running toward Summer Street, all the while screaming at the top of his lungs. Instinctively, I took off, artificial hip and all, through our backyard and the backyard of the people behind us (our friends Ira and Susan), desperate to make sure that DJ negotiated the turn onto Summer. He must have been looking through his fingers, for he made the turn and then slowed down. "Do you want to continue?" I asked him when he reached me. Without hesitating, he put his hands back over his eyes and recommenced running and screaming. The incident was straight out of a *New Yorker* cartoon or a Woody Allen film. The adult male leaves his mother's bosom. The adult male considers the meaning of life. Of course, the fact that DJ was twelve and not forty robbed the scene of its humor.

Such fear. DJ had become the kid from Dr. Seuss who sets out on a walk to "great places." If not him, Charlie on his final stroll—eyes closed, the current's invisible hand pushing him into the dark beyond. We were the grown-ups who appear nowhere in *Oh, the Places You'll Go*, or we were James and Eileen, helpless in the face of calamity. What can they do, your parents, what can they do but wave from the shore of their heartbreak? Good-bye, DJ, good-bye. If we had any doubts that DJ understood this walk symbolically and, in doing so, condensed past and future, the conversations we had with him afterward took these doubts away. "were you really hurt when i had to go bavck to fostercare?" he asked. "i'm really nervous because uim trying to underamd your feelings. yiu satch [watch] very bravely hen [when] i walked away. you seem not really pestered by my wanting each day be more free."

410

Did Emily need to mourn DJ's growing up or insist on the difference between abandonment and maturity? My position on this matter was clear, and as Halloween approached we finally pursued a different therapeutic strategy, getting tough with DJ. We wouldn't allow the past to impose itself on his endeavors—no heckling from the back, no streaking on stage. We'd call security immediately and have the intruder carted away. Better yet, we'd commit ourselves to proper screening at the door. Even if another twenty people were to die on us, we claimed, we wouldn't give in to his compulsive exhumation of the past. We wouldn't be seduced by the grievous give and take, the bond of injury. Our son was twelve years old and had just managed, half-managed, his first walk by himself.

But there were other reasons for holding the line. At school the poking had intensified, resulting in several office referrals. The third week in October, he hit his aides and resource room teacher and acted out in a number of classes. If the people at the school hadn't been so understanding, we'd have been sunk. The principal could have expelled DJ—he was that disruptive. At home and in therapy he was telling us, "years of being beaten never really ended. years can replay in my head. i underestimate real self by getting stuck." He *was* stuck—even as he progressed in certain respects. "my mind very much injures me," he complained. "fear you think im crazy."

"You're not crazy," we'd say. "Think positively." Through a feigned indifference to tantrums and sobbing, through an emphasis on consequences and not at all on explanations, through an unyielding commitment to treating DJ "as old," we gradually saw changes. DJ responded, at least initially, by accusing us of not loving him—to me a good sign, for love seemed hopelessly entwined with hurt. We introduced the notion of reasonable behavior, and DJ took to it quickly, using the word "reasonable" on repeated occasions. In fact, it seemed to achieve talismanic status. About poking, he declared, "readyto bereasonable but having trouble stoppingit." About our new treatment regime, he lamented, "reasonable treatmentis hard." About first learning how to communicate, when he couldn't understand spoken language, he said, "reasonable teacuhers taught me with sign." Though I hadn't been thinking

411

of the ADA and its concept of "reasonable accommodation" when, in desperation, I taught DJ the word, his usage suggested it. There he was perseverating on the term, as if to emphasize the need for, and, yes, the difficulty of achieving, such an ideal. What could be more apt than an obsession with the reasonable at a moment when America seemed increasingly unreasonable in matters of disability and poverty?

It wasn't as if we'd departed from everything we'd been doing before. We still tied privileges, such as going to the local kid center, to positive behavior and we still showered DJ with praise whenever he accomplished something. We still used time-outs—mercilessly so. We were just much more consistent, and we categorically refused to acknowledge the past. Whenever we encountered it on the streets of our life, we walked on by, sometimes grabbing DJ by the arm and pulling him with us. I found it difficult to play the role of hard-ass with my son, and it wasn't until an acquaintance, with whom I was speaking about DJ, asked me jokingly if I'd solved the problem of oedipal conflict through sympathetic adoption, that I really saw the way I'd failed to be a figure of authority for him. My own father had been such a tyrant that I'd gone too far in the opposite direction, loathing the idea that the boy I'd rescued might need at times to hate me. DJ was becoming a teenager. He was rebelling, asserting his will. One night, after he obsessively opened and closed the oven door, despite my warning that the potatoes would never cook, I had an epiphany. To the question, "Why won't you leave the oven door alone?" DJ replied, "years of hunger." Right then and there I understood how manipulative he could be—how autism, trauma, and adolescence could unhelpfully converge.

"Bullshit," I responded and told him that if he opened the door again, he'd go to his room and miss dinner, which is exactly what happened.

Slowly, though, the new approach caught on. "you.re breaking my bad habits," he reported. "keep treating me like old because im getting freer." One afternoon, he described the work of therapy as "killing my very best redone victim." Now, there was a formulation that gave Emily and me pause. We weren't thrilled by the persistent idea of murdering bad habits, but we were pleased that DJ recognized the unproductive nature of his injury fixation, the identity it afforded (what he'd called famously "the kide inlove with hurt").

Though the new approach clearly worked, I don't think DJ would have consolidated his many gains had he not seen Doug Biklen's videos of FC users, most of whom are shown typing entirely on their own. In late October, I traveled to Syracuse to meet Biklen and visit his Facilitated Communication Institute. I wanted to know more about this technique and the controversy that engulfed it. While I was there, Biklen gave me copies of the documentaries he had made, and when I got home, I played them for DJ. The effect was profound. One called *Autism Is A World* presented a significantly disabled woman, Sue Rubin, who was earning A's and B's in Latin American history at Whittier College; another called *My Classic Life as an Artist* presented an equivalently disabled man, Larry Bissonnette, who had spent nine years in an institution and who was now an artist in Vermont. In both cases, DJ got to see Autists much older than himself in possession of vibrant lives and attractive futures. In Larry Bissonnette especially, he got to see a disability activist who writes with metaphoric abandon. Here are some of the things that Larry says in the video that features him:

> Nasty, residential, better-for-growing-vegetables-rather-than-people Brandon Training School. No one should limit learning of truth and life to closed rooms occupied only by people with no natural means to communicate. Going back in desolation where it is only me and letterless walls is not pleasant to think about. Nothing apartheids you like the insensitive world of institutional existence. Tapping well of silence with painting permitted songs of hurt to be meted with creativity. . . . Without art, wafting smells of earth's pleasures would kite away to land of inanimate objects, so it's past point of personal hobby. . . . Lore around autism uses situations of incompetence to predict what little potential people have to learn creative and artistic skills, like leading articles in

magazines looking at populations of people with disabilities. My aesthetically questionable but not bad-to-argue work is the best way to clear up mysteries of what I'm about. . . . Fastening labels on people is like leasing cars with destinations determined beforehand. Mostly it's good practices in educating unconventional people, eccentric on the outside but normal on the inside, that lops off weak branches of disability and promotes possibilities for new growth.

In addition to the video, I got hold of some writing by Bissonnette. In a statement entitled "Keys Towards Promised Land of Free Expression," Bissonnette echoes many of the above themes and concludes by inviting the reader to join his political crusade:

> Let me mention that its practically getting possible to create satisfying life, interesting and meaningful nowadays because really institutions' popularity slides towards storage underground at a pace faster than police chasing stepping for escape prisoners. . . . You lend great sums of money for places like military mansions and meeting rooms for polygamous politicians. New lots of land for masses of people with disabilities need total pouring of organized funding for learning, artistic development, and receiving lessons on playing sports athletically. One soldier going to fight persecutionary attitudes is little deterrence. March with me. You'll have promising strides of valiant, creating great havoc with nearly perfect, brushstrokes to inspire you.

In another part of the statement, Bissonnette attacks the sanctimonious attitudes of those who underestimate what might be possible for people with cognitive disabilities, those directly responsible for grotesque practices of exclusion. I can't resist quoting him again, as Emily and I have met all sorts of educators like this—the principal of the center school in Florida, for example, who resisted our inclusion attempts with DJ and whose understanding of disability was so shot through with self-congratulatory pity that she seemed to be standing on her own dual-purpose pedestal and warden's watch tower. Bissonnette writes,

> It's politically correct to say that kind, needing gratification for giving, people started impetus for building structurally sound yet inhumane institutions. . . . Nearly twenty years have lodged in my memory, skating on icy surfaces of slippery thoughts and fears about trials of oppression on my personal vision of life. Now work should begin on repairing damage of past.

The Nelson Mandela of cognitive disability ("nothing apartheids you"), Bissonnette proposes, in effect, a Truth and Reconciliation Commission: a way forward that acknowledges the past but isn't consumed by bitterness—a lesson that I, in my capacity as DJ's parent, haven't yet mastered. How to get over the horror? A couple of weeks ago, the sister of John F. Kennedy died. The obituary revealed that Joe Kennedy had had his daughter lobotomized because this "mildly retarded" woman was sneaking out of the convent to which she'd been sent. Kennedy had worried that Rosemary might engage in sexual activity that could threaten the political careers of his sons.

The entry in Wikipedia for Rosemary Kennedy quotes from an interview with James Watts, the doctor who performed the surgery: "We went through the top of the head, I think she was awake. She had a mild tranquilizer. I made a surgical incision in the brain through the skull. It was near the front. It was on both sides. We just made a small incision, no more than an inch." The entry continues, "The instrument Dr. Watts used looked like a butter knife. He swung it up and down to cut brain tissue. 'We put an instrument inside,' he said. As Dr. Watts cut, Dr. Freeman put questions to Rosemary. For example, he asked her to recite the Lord's Prayer or sing "God Bless America" or count backwards. . . . 'We made an estimate on how far to cut based on how she responded.' . . . When she began to become incoherent, they stopped. Instead of producing the desired result, however, the lobotomy reduced Rosemary to an infantile mentality that left her incontinent and staring blankly at walls for hours.

Her verbal skills were reduced to unintelligible babble." The interviewer, Ronald Kessler, cites evidence that Rosemary Kennedy wasn't even retarded but, rather, mentally ill. He quotes Dr. Bertram Brown, executive director of the President's Panel on Mental Retardation, who called this lobotomy the "biggest mental health cover-up in history."

When I think that Camelot was in part predicated on a lobotomy, one that rendered Rosemary completely incapacitated, I want to be sick. Perhaps the only reasonable response to the atrocities wrought on Rosemary and DJ and Larry and Will and thousands and thousands of others *is* to "begin repairing damage of past." I imagine that's what Rosemary's sister, Eunice Kennedy Shriver, told herself when she founded the Special Olympics. I just wish she'd envisioned something more inclusive: a joint Olympics, maybe even paired events. How about a relay with two so-called able-bodied sprinters and two so-called disabled ones? In his book *No Pity*, the journalist Joseph Shapiro mentions the concept of "unified sports": integrated teams of equivalent collective ability competing against one another. But lest we patronize the disabled too much, consider the case of an autistic young man who recently scored twenty points in a high school basketball game. The team's water boy, he was given a chance to suit up and, at the end of a game, actually play. After missing his first two shots, he sank six three-pointers in a row, to the astonishment of the crowd.

And so, DJ watched the FC videos and read "Keys Towards Promised Land of Free Expression." He also found a book by Biklen and colleagues called *Access to Academics for All Students*, which I'd brought back with me. The book wasn't exactly written for sixth-graders, but he slogged through it. In fact, it was with this highly academic book that DJ achieved the goal of independent reading: sitting alone and turning the pages himself. The book argues vehemently for full inclusion, and it critiques, among other things, testing procedures that track kids into miserable futures under the guise of definitive assessment.

By mid-November, DJ had taken an assignment to write a paragraph about the American flag, as part of a contest sponsored by the local Elks Club, and joined Larry Bissonnette on his march.

OUR FLAG

The great United States of America is breathtakingly not free. Equality is not sacred because not everyone has access to it. Freedom is not as available as many people think. First, free people treat my people, very smart people who type to communicate, as mindless. Second, they underestimate us as very bad instead of reaching out to us. The creators of everyone's very important Declaration of Independence wasted their breath.

I love the repetition of "breath"—the way the paragraph begins and ends with a version of this word. It's as if DJ had condensed the primary physiological symptom of his anxiety—heavy breathing—into a political modifier. I also love the phrase "my people." How important is it for folks who are different to see folks like themselves? Without any conscious help from us, he'd landed on the principle of identity politics, which imagines political solidarity among the similarly marginalized and locates the problem of difference outside the self in a normalizing world, a world that needs to see its own reflection in the mirror. In December, we'd come across an article in the *New York Times* about Autists who do not want to be cured, Autists who celebrate their difference. The article would mention organizations like the Autistic Liberation Front and Web sites like neurodiversity.com that challenge the prevailing view of autism. This view is heavily medicalized and, as Bissonnette, Rubin, and so many others point out, often tragically incorrect.

By mid-January, following the example of other oppressed groups that have borrowed from the civil rights movement, DJ would have adapted a Martin Luther King assignment so that it might speak to the plight of "his people."

> i want to tell you about martin luther king i knmowe that
> he was given i have a dream spweech he wantwed all p;eop;le
> to be equal. i want to tell yhou my dream speech.

> i havwe a dream thart one day everyone will listen to those
> who don't have a verbal voice. i hazve a dream that perople
> of congresas will provide schools with more resources to
> educate thee students, the teachers, and administration
> about various disabilities.

DJ would follow up this paragraph (I don't have the corrected version)
with the statement "yearn to tell responsible reasonable decisionmakers
we tell wastebasket begins with easy lessons," and he'd refer to his early
school experience as "very bad as veteran in seducation [education]."

There are those who tire of identity politics: the seemingly endless
claims of injury and affront, the divisive accusations, the anger. But I
want to say what a psychological boon such politics have been for DJ
and to remind everyone that such annoyance and fatigue come at the
expense of social justice. To direct his anger outwards rather than in-
wards has made the future possible for my son. He stopped referring
to himself as a freak and instead told us, "i resent being tested as retarded" or "testing gets really resented." He wrote of "years very sad
in freeaky sad schoo" where "they treat underestimated kids as junk."
Whereas before in talking about my book he'd said I "hurt his feelings
by [calling him] disabled" and insisted, "im normal," by the time of the
Martin Luther King assignment he was speaking freely of the disabled
and characterizing himself as such. A week after composing his flag
paragraph he announced that he was "undertaking campaign to change
the world," and he described his career aspiration as that of a "political freedom fighter."

Emily and I have joined DJ on his campaign, DJ and all of the other
"political freedom fighters." In fact, following DJ's MLK analogy, we've
come to think of ourselves as akin to civil rights workers in the deep
South, volunteers, fellow marchers in Selma and Montgomery. So
much work has to be done, including the transformation of anger
into spiritual resolve. For cognitive disabilities, and especially for facilitated communication, it's still the early 1960s. Many, many "kind,
needing gratification for giving, people" must be disabused of their
prejudice.

Recently, Emily showed me something called a "Literacy Bill of Rights," a document composed by progressive scholars in the field of special education. Like DJ, these scholars found it rhetorically advantageous to adapt an icon of democracy for the purposes of the disability movement. The document reads:

A LITERACY BILL OF RIGHTS

All persons, regardless of the extent or severity of their disabilities, have a basic right to use print. Beyond this general right, there are certain literacy rights that should be assured for all persons. These basic rights are:

1) The right to an *opportunity to learn* to read and write. Opportunity involves engagement in active participation in tasks performed with high success.
2) The right to have *accessible*, clear, meaningful, culturally and linguistically appropriate texts at all times. Texts, broadly defined, range from picture books to newspapers to novels, cereal boxes, and electronic documents.
3) The right to *interact with others* while reading, writing, or listening to a text. *Interaction* involves questions, comments, discussions, and other communications about or related to the text.
4) The right to *life choices* made available through reading and writing competencies. *Life choices* include, but are not limited to, employment and employment changes, independence, community participation, and self-advocacy.
5) The right to *lifelong educational opportunities* incorporating literacy instruction and use. Literacy *educational opportunities*, regardless of when they are provided, have potential to provide power that cannot be taken away.
6) The right to have *teachers and other service providers who are knowledgeable* about literacy instruction methods and principles. *Methods* include, but are not limited to, instruction,

assessment, and the technologies required to make literacy accessible to individuals with disabilities. *Principles* include, but are not limited to, the belief that literacy is learned across place and time and that no person is too disabled to benefit from learning opportunities.

7) The right to live and learn in *environments* that provide varied *models of print use*. Models are demonstrations of purposeful print use such as reading a recipe, paying bills, sharing a joke, or writing a letter.

8) The right to live and learn in environments that maintain the *expectations and attitudes* that all *individuals are literacy learners*.

Though maybe not the most elegantly written proclamation, it *is* utterly reasonable in its assertions. These rights would ensure that those with cognitive disabilities might reach their full potential as human beings. "If communication is the essence of human life, then literacy is the essence of a more involved and connected life," the USSAAC (United States Society for Augmentative and Alternative Communication) bylaws state. It is that connection and involvement, that inclusion, that any just society would seek to foster. When the document asserts a right to "service providers who are knowledgeable about literacy instruction," such knowledge would have to encompass methods for instructing people like DJ who only learn to decode spoken language *after* they learn to read. The lack of spoken language changes everything. When the document asserts the right to "technologies required to make literacy accessible," such technologies would have to include facilitated communication, the only means by which some people can demonstrate their literacy skills. Of course, as important as the demonstration of literacy is its development, and as Rosemary Crossley maintains, a print-rich environment offers the best chance for an FC breakthrough with the so-called severely disabled.

Part of DJ's campaign to change the world will have to involve confronting skepticism about FC. Indeed, DJ has already confronted such skepticism. At a party at our friends Johanna and Maura's, a local psychiatrist saw DJ communicating with a buddy and commented gratuitously, "Can you do that without holding your mom's hand?" To which DJ responded, "hurt my feelings." The woman didn't even know us. Though we've received terrific acceptance at DJ's school, we regularly confront this attitude elsewhere. In the documentary *Every Step of the Way*, Sharisa Kochmeister, a fourteen-year-old typing communicator who no longer requires facilitation (or perhaps I should say who only needs her father's hand about a foot or so above her own as she types), exclaims, "Suspend disbelief long enough to forget what you think you know. Open your minds and eyes and learn, please."

Unfortunately, critics of facilitated communication take such remarks as symptomatic of a wholesale repudiation of science on the part of FC proponents. The attacks have been especially vicious. Diane Twachtman-Cullen writes,

> The importance of establishing the validity of any new theory or hypothesis *prior* to heralding its success would seem to be an issue upon which reasonable and responsible men and women would not differ. Yet it is on that very issue that the controversy surrounding facilitated communication swirls most fervidly. Detractors have squared off against proponents, the former calling for scientific scrutiny of the method's validity and the latter claiming that such scrutiny would seriously undermine trust between facilitator and client, which is essential to the conduct of the technique. From the earliest days, those courageous few who did attempt to experimentally validate FC were criticized for their "lack of faith" in persons with disabilities.

Exaggerating Biklen's "lack of respect for the [autism] research literature," Twachtman-Cullen nevertheless gets right the stakes in this controversy:

> Quite simply, one could not buy into FC for people with autism and still hold to the prevailing view of the disorder. Biklen's answer was simple, albeit chilling. Acknowledging

that his point of view regarding the nature of the autistic disorder contradicted much of the autism research literature, Biklen summarily called for a redefinition of autism.

The word "chilling" and a previous reference to Biklen's "followers" suggest a cult-like hysteria; Twachtman-Cullen would have us opt for courageous reason, which for her is synonymous with the dominant paradigm. In a section on the history of autism research entitled "From Checkered Past to Coherent Present," she labors to dismiss the movement disorder theory, failing to mention the work of Ralph Mauer and no less a neurological luminary than Antonio Damasio. She posits a scientific coherence—an agreement—that then allows her to conclude, adverbial modifiers and all, that FC is bunk:

> Remarkably, despite the substantial research literature that consistently characterizes autism as a disorder affecting social-emotional, affective, cognitive, and communicative functioning, proponents of facilitated communication discount the role of all of these factors in autism. Simply stated, FC theory doesn't square with the research findings in autism.

Had Twachtman-Cullen and others read Thomas Kuhn's *The Structure of Scientific Revolution*, they might have proceeded more cautiously with their dismissals. At least some of the controversy can be accounted for by the inevitable professional jockeying of experts protecting turf. But this battle isn't academic: lives hang in the balance. What does Twachtman-Cullen make of those who are typing independently? Or those who do pass Draconian message-passing tests? Or those who *learn*, through practice, how to pass such tests, like students enrolled in a Stanley Kaplan SAT course? What does she make of people like Tito and Sue and Jamie and Sharisa who fail to manifest the series of impairments that she lists and, thus, refute "the research findings in autism"? Does she simply dismiss them? Kuhn makes clear the role of anomaly in initiating, however slowly and torturously, a paradigm shift. But in the short term there is much resistance and invective.

Twachtman-Cullen goes after Biklen by parodying his position on scientific validation. Biklen *has* critiqued certain validation procedures, and he has been very sensitive to the issue of suspicion generally, understanding how detrimental it can be to those who are just beginning to type, but he has *not* repudiated validation altogether. Her binaries—science or faith, reason or hysteria—are false. Biklen and Cardinal's 1997 book, *Contested Words, Contested Science: Unraveling the Facilitated Communication Controversy*, contains an essay by two experimental psychologists who were formerly vehement opponents of the technique. In fact, one of the authors had even referred to it as a "bloody hoax" in a newspaper interview. The authors, Michael J. Salomon Weiss and Sheldon H. Wagner, conducted their own rigorous message-passing experiment and concluded the following:

> We entered this area of inquiry as hostile skeptics, looking to protect our clients from what we perceived as extremely dangerous misinformation. However, our findings of observational and experimentally controlled validity, the emergence of independent typing, and data implying validity of this technique . . . have given us some guidelines with which to proceed. *Facilitated Communication Exists.* "Facilitated communication," as described by Crossley, Biklen, and their associates . . . exists in some form, for at least some persons with significant disabilities.

Establishing the validity of the technique, the authors then directly contest the reasoning of experts such as Twachtman-Cullen. They argue, "Despite the wide range of unanswered questions surrounding this phenomenon, the fact that at least a small number of individuals have demonstrated remarkable and unexpected literacy with facilitated communication may call a great many of our current theories of human development into question." "Bear in mind," they tell us, "that several advances in the assessment of central nervous system (CNS) processes were linked to a small number of unique individuals who were studied on a case-by-case basis." Weiss and Wagner leave their readers with a number of additional conclusions: "facilitated communication is evanescent and fragile," "the incidence of facilitated communication competence is not yet known," "look long and close at those who have validated," and they call for additional research on this "very interesting and important phenomenon."

There is so much that we don't know. To repeat, why does Sharisa Kochmeister need her father's arm above hers while she types? Why does Larry Bissonnette need his facilitator's finger intermittently on his shoulder? Why does Jamie Burke, who types independently, need a facilitator behind him, and why does he find it difficult to compose while alone in a room? How to account for Bissonnette's use of metaphor? The questions are endless. Twachtman-Cullen's "reasonable and responsible men and women" need to get to work. On DJ's "campaign to change the world," I'd like to tie the idea of reasonableness to an interpretive humility in the face of the cognitively "other." Or perhaps I should say a difference that can be constructed as "other" (non-human). We must never forget that science—the apprehension of facts—always involves the meaning making of fallible human beings. With the brain, we still know relatively little, which ought to be sufficient cause for caution.

Might we also tie the idea of reasonableness to a posture of persistent hope and, as well, a practice of developing everyone's potential, particularly society's most vulnerable? This would mean, of course, shifting our economic and political priorities. Perched atop his soapbox, the old Leftie in me longs to sermonize: "Only in a culture that encourages selfishness, a culture bent on privatizing the very future, making it an exclusive country club, would such a dream appear unreasonable." Though I adamantly oppose the vast majority of President Bush's policies, I also know that alternative answers do not come easily. But we can do better. We *must* do better for millions and millions of people in poverty, many of them kids, some of them disabled, some like DJ, literally without a voice. The time of big government may be over, but as the gap between rich and poor continues to grow and as more and more people find themselves in poverty, we need new ideas, not resignation in the face of obdurate inequality, not a narrow focus on one's personal welfare.

The danger of elaborating on the debate about facilitated communication and on the politics of change is that the reader might not believe the psychological argument I am proposing: namely, that DJ profited from seeing the FC videotapes, reading Biklen's book, comparing the plight of the autistic to that of African Americans, and thinking of himself as a "political freedom fighter." For one thing, his behavior changed: we had much less aggression. Moreover, the poking disappeared. It just up and left. Every now and then DJ would threaten to poke by raising his finger but then stop himself. Equally important, he ceased perseverating about the past. "years of unhurt are beginning," he announced. When he did bring up the past, his remarks no longer had a self-injurious edge. "tested dedtrimental treated as retarded. [now] tested very great grades very great grades," he told his teacher proudly. Even when he referred to foster care and the beating, he managed a kind of measured response: "hard getting smart because under very intenserealtreacherous not humane circumstances."

The subject of his birth father produced perhaps the strongest evidence of a profound change in DJ. In late November, during one of our regular chats, he suddenly typed, "freedm rewritten. my fvery giving dead father."

Concealing my shock at his statement, I asked, "About whom are you speaking?"

"dan swanson," DJ said, "because he loved me."

"What are you imagining?"

"that i was ok"

"So, you're revising the past," I said.

"yesbcause hewas mean. treat me with respect," DJ replied. Ordinarily, this sort of conversation would have sent him into a tailspin, but later that week, he awakened in the morning from a dream and told me, "im united by dreamto my other other dad bad."

"Why is he bad," I asked, more than a bit disingenuously.

"bad because other dad great he very much missed getting to know me." How much more salutary was this take on the past? Rather than thinking of himself as unworthy of attention, DJ imagined his birth father as missing out. My twelve-year-old, who'd been treated infinitely worse than I ever had, had beaten me to the finish line of wisdom. Or maybe we'd crossed it together in one of those three-legged races that fathers and sons run on Memorial Day or July 4th—our lives like bodies fused in an effort of immense cooperation. If I was going to ask DJ not to be stuck in hurt, then I needed to do the same.

Not too long after the memorable declaration about his birth father, DJ wrote his sister, Ellie, a letter:

> ellie, we were wondering if you possess yearn tell us tbe free. im telephoning to see if you can come visit. yearn for you to see me reasonable and carefreedeserve. you deserve to be treated better by me.
>
> love,
> DJ

He knew that he hadn't been nice to his sister, and he understood that Ellie couldn't be blamed for the decisions that her parents had made. He was ready for the future.

A week later, the word "reasonable" turned up again when my brother and his wife spent Thanksgiving with us in Iowa. My mom had flown out a few days early, and we were all nervous about how the weekend would go. James and Eileen were still grieving deeply over Charlie's death. We couldn't decide if we should be assiduously upbeat or reserved, even somber. The more we talked about it, the more anxious we became. By the time James and Eileen arrived, we were like a bunch of hyperactive, poorly synchronized synchronized swimmers. Not five minutes into the visit, DJ let out a shriek. "just saw my terrific dead cousin charlie," he said. I think seeing his uncle and aunt made him remember Charlie at the wake.

DJ had broken the ice. He sat down with James and Eileen and had a conversation on the labeler. "im really so very sorry about charlie," he told them. "do you have reasonable people to help you with your hurt?"

The earnestness of this question brought tears to everyone's eyes. DJ was reaching out to James and Eileen, trying to share with them the secret of his evolving recovery. "seeing you reasonably happy makes me happy," he said. That afternoon, he typed, "i really yearn to tell aunt eileen that i love her." Eileen's friend, Teresa Donnelly, whom I'd gotten to know since we sat together at James and Eileen's wedding—Teresa once worked at a publishing company specializing in books about autism—would later report that Eileen carried DJ's remarks around with her in her purse. Whenever she was down, she'd pull them out. This boy, who had lost everything, was now an activist of comfort, a devotion organizer. His words had made all the difference in our weekend. Those of us with purportedly excellent social skills had surrendered to the superior instincts of a boy with autism.

As Christmas approached, DJ increasingly expressed a desire to type more independently. "teach me to type on my unhurt finger," he requested. "im ready to write ahurt free story." Through Doug Biklen we met Christi Hendrickson, a professor of education at the University of Northern Iowa. Christi had written a lot about facilitated communication and, even more important, had significant experience facilitating nonspeaking communicators. We thought that she might give us some input about accomplishing independence. She came down and jumped with DJ on the trampoline and then went to work typing with him. After she tried a few things, he stated cheerfully, "need more practice." DJ is presently able to achieve moderate accuracy with me supporting him at the elbow. Emily uses a different approach. She places her finger beneath his palm and pinkie, creating a kind of static perch from which DJ can then reach for the keyboard. DJ's resource room teacher, Ms. Leathers, alternately pinches his shirt in the area of the cuff and releases his arm altogether. Sometimes, she simply places her hand a few inches above DJ's and allows him to make contact as he moves from one key to the next. We haven't yet landed on a particular technique, but we've all seen DJ make enormous progress in typing on his own. When we presented DJ with the opportunity to attend the annual Facilitated Communication Conference in California, he jumped at the chance. "You're going to have to get on a plane," we told him. "really excited awesome conference," he said.

Along with the desire to type independently has come a desire to do more with his friends—another sign of his turning the corner. He's started attending dances at The Galaxy, the local kid center, usually with one of his college buddies but sometimes with Emily or me. When it's one of us, we have to stand off to the side, as inconspicuously as possible. When he wants to communicate, he calls us over. We haven't yet reached full independence, but we're getting there. Recently, he invited a friend to see a movie called *National Treasure*. DJ had made it through only one movie in its entirety before this occasion. The darkness of the theater, the giant flashing images, the stereophonic sound—all of these things posed problems for someone with sensory overload. The experience was just too intense. But he wanted to do it. A movie theater had opened in Grinnell, and all of the kids in his class had been to it.

It was just our luck, however, that the plot involved stealing the Declaration of Independence. At one point the characters use lemon juice on the document to reveal a hidden clue to a mystery. This sent DJ over the edge. Emily, who was sitting several rows behind the two kids, rushed down and asked DJ if he wanted a break. In the lobby, they talked about what had happened. "im here but loving getting your serious attention. declaration of independence was dreadfully ruined," he reported. With his penchant for analogical—even allegorical—thinking, the prospect of destroying the document that expressed his right to liberty as a citizen and the possibility of being on his own as somebody autistic was unbearable. "i fell short of expectation," he told Emily. Yet the experience wasn't a disaster, and he said he wanted to try it again. Perhaps the most significant development in the friendship arena was DJ's crush on a girl named _____, a crush that Mrs. Goodrich, DJ's aide, swears was mutual. We had to deal with considerable silliness when DJ was around her, but the fact of a crush, the *fact* of a crush—should I say it again?—confirmed what we have always known about DJ: that he is a person of deep feeling. "dread going ten days without seeing _____," he typed at the start of Christmas vacation.

With DJ branching out on his own, it was time for his story to do the same—take a walk around the block: eyes open, at a casual pace. Though I'm flattered that DJ responded to the questions in language

428

arts "Who's your favorite author?" and "What's your favorite book?" by typing, "ralph savarese" and "bookby my dad," I know that DJ can now represent himself. "It's my story," as he once exclaimed when a classmate suggested changes to his "Frosty the Snowman" narrative. I can't remember exactly when I asked him to write the final chapter, but he began working on it in November. I told him he could say anything he wanted, anything. He could disagree with me; he could say I'd gotten things wrong. Fresh in my memory were his comments about his birth mother: "hurt my feelings by being so nice to very bad mom. the book makesher sond [sound] not bad." DJ needed to be able to come to his own conclusions about the people in his life. My political convictions about the oppression of poor women in our society had to be countered by the experience of abandonment. And so, I've had nothing to do with this chapter; Emily's worked on it with him exclusively.

It's hard to end a memoir. My friends joke that at the pace I've been writing, I'll soon get ahead of myself, overtaking the present like some frantic steeplechase runner. Next week DJ will do this; next month, he'll do that. . . . I *am* eager to see how his life will unfold. What a distance we've all traveled! I've almost become addicted to collecting DJ's thoughts and meditating on them. If DJ's a kind of neuro-Martin Luther King (or, on his less sanguine days, a neuro-Malcolm X), then perhaps I'm a neuro-facilitating Samuel Pepys, that seventeenth-century diarist. The temptation to keep going with the notebooks is tremendous, but Emily has put her foot—or perhaps I should say my computer—down. "Be reasonable," she said, with a sly grin. We're still saving DJ's remarks should he ever want to look over them; I'm just not sorting and weaving together a narrative.

The problem with concluding a memoir of disability on a note of triumph is perpetuating the primary cliché of the genre. Both a different understanding of triumph and a recognition of the work still to be done at home and in the world help to mitigate the cliché. DJ's autism remains— in all of its sometimes marvelous, sometimes aggravating, splendor. He hasn't been cured. None of us is interested in a cure, but that doesn't mean the disability is without disadvantages (though these disadvantages are far from what the experts often claim). I remember DJ's response to a book he'd read in the fall about a blind man who at the end recovers his sight: "hurt my feelings because he's not blind forever." In this story, DJ is autistic forever and that's okay, more than okay. No doubt he'll cycle back into perseveration, but autism's wonders can be exploited just as its hardships can be contained. And we can do all of this as we try to make a larger difference beyond the bounds of family and blood relations, facilitating human connection, rectifying inequality, cherishing diversity. "Surely there is enough for everyone within this country," Jonathan Kozol has written:

> All our children ought to be allowed a stake in the enormous richness of America. Whether they were born to poor white Appalachians or to wealthy Texans, to poor black people in the Bronx or to rich people in Manhasset or Winnetka, they are all quite wonderful and innocent when they are small. We soil them needlessly.

In the introduction to his book *The Call of Service: A Witness to Idealism*, Robert Coles perhaps comes closest to describing the imperfect, but nonetheless redemptive, love story of this larger effort, and he gestures at the place of poetry in it:

> I am writing this book to explore the "service" we offer to others and, not incidentally, to ourselves. I am hoping to document the subjectivity, the phenomenology of service: the many ways such activity is rendered; the many rationales, impulses, and values served in the implementation of a particular effort; the achievements that take place, along with the missteps and failures; the personal opportunities and hazards; and the consequences—how this kind of work fits into a life. I am hoping as well to discuss the connections between community service and intellectual reflection— how a story or a poem can prompt a special kind of clarifying wonder for someone who has made himself or herself available in some form of service.

As I type Coles's words, I look at a photo of space shuttle astronauts on the wall of my study—two astronauts, to be specific. They're outside the shuttle, connected to the remote manipulator system arm, practicing a repair procedure. In the background, the curved surface of the earth and the darkness of deep space. How cumbersome the astronauts' suits look— all of that insulation and protective gear. The distance between them, which is only a few feet, seems almost as great as the distance between the space shuttle and earth. Indeed, the latter might stand in for the former, if we understand both the suits and the miles as figures for the self and, as important, for our present social arrangements—in short, as obstacles that must be overcome, distances that must be traversed. There they are, the astronauts, accomplishing something, working together, suspended at the very tip of possibility.

CHAPTER 16

It's My Story!

Note: It was up to DJ to decide what his chapter would look like. The result is a collage of conversations with Emily, personal statements, letters to important people, school assignments, and poems. The ordering is entirely his. Sometimes, as at the outset, Emily provided a prompt by asking him what he was thinking or, later, by redirecting him or requesting clarification about his compositional difficulties. The chapter as a whole has been revised—by DJ—though not to the extent that some of the individual school assignments were revised. Emily wanted to follow DJ's lead in determining when the chapter could be declared complete.

> *DJ*: I'm nervous love is hard. It breathes hard.
> *Mom*: Not always. Sometimes love quietly approaches to calm and soothe you just when you need it.

I dream of being a political freedom fighter. I read that pure real people in especially just free waters insist my real decisions really wasted. They think well respected, tested as normal kids are the okay to teach ones. They forget those lost kids. They're the ones like me who poke or look like they're not paying attention.

Understand that I resent really serious tests; dreaming of fresh start it's not very hard to get very fearful. One year ago great places were dreadful but now I look forward to the future beasts because I hurt the beasts by hearing real self. When I'm breathing easily, I'm kind of like respected kids.

I'm trying to get used to testing my real self. I'm nervous because I might possibly be famous. Each day I'm sad and resentful of your book. It kind of scares me because lots of very important ancestors each gave these big sad speeches telling the real reason very many great, reasonable, established, kind people hurt other people.

I resent these very hurtful conversations being easy reading for everyone. People should realize how years of hurt depended upon politicians' easy decisions to do nothing to hear what I longed for. When I lived in fear, I yearned to urge just one especially humane free gesture to tell someone, "Just hear me. I really need help."

Politicians should really help little kids. Politicians present kids as very important but only pointing out that millions of kids look poor might not get them homes. Thinking group homes respect kids, they hurt them. I'm very mad kids spend time in silly classes. Kids love very much being safe. They get put in dangerous situations. They are very nervous. Sometimes for years kids very much fear beatings.

The years I've been unhurt, I've gotten far. I'm in the sixth grade in regular school. Freedom has reached me; however, there are reasonable, kind great underestimated very smart kids who might not be freed. Kids need freedom free of tests that really hurt their great futures.

When I was very small, great futures scared me because I was beaten up and retarded. I resented especially the time when I was free tested because no one ever told me "you're great." If they had, I feel I easily would have passed the test. Testing is very scary. Testing resembles beating down those kids who most depart from the land of human beings. People might not ever look dearly at these kids again. Ultimately, testing lets only respected people into schools. I'm sad to breathe these wasted, just free words.

Testing hurt my freedom by placing me in easy, underestimated special education classes. Special education classes reward people for being bad. They build forward thinking, very loving kids interested in life into forgotten as mindful kids. Kids deserve freedom from testing.

Kids poke fun at my behavior. They just got pretty great luck being normal. They obviously tested smart easily. My pretty resentful voicing needs to try hard to treat people respectfully.

Mom: DJ, I notice that you are having some difficulty writing. Usually when you write something on your laptop or labeler, the words combine to make sentences and the sentences flow together into meaningful paragraphs. What is going on?

DJ: Nightmares stored in gestures not in words.

Dear Mr. Shults [Principal of Grinnell Middle School],

It's very important to me to be at Grinnell Middle School. I care a lot about your teachers and must be getting very great just because understand me. I very much value teachers who give nice instructions breathing easily.

I'm really scared that you great, free people might get fresh start without me. When you tested me by saying you would expel me, years of dreadful classes came back terrifying me. when I am terrified, resentment gets out of control. Resentment is not helpful, I know. I made the mistake of letting resentment get out of control. As long as I treat people resentfully, I will miss out on telling people that kids who don't talk deserve to be in real school. I want to be celebrated especially for my heartfelt personality. Respect for others is important. Respect for underestimated kids is important, too, because they read and resent testing that mistakenly identifies them as retarded. Testing kids is scary.

I imagine these words resembling dead Martin Luther King's respectful vision. Please understand that I love being here at school, and that I might make some mistakes but I'm trying very hard testing myself to hurt no one ever again. Years of hearing hurtful treatment feel over. Years of unhurt have begun. Tested myself and I know ceiling is high.

Please accept my heartfelt apology.

DJ Savarese

Dear Mrs. Thompson,

I truly was in my best grade in your kindergarten class. Your class really freed me. You taught me to just feel that I was really studious and deserved to yearn to be treated respectfully. You treated my real self just because you're loving and generous.

I'm hesitant to have friends. I just need to feel comfortable. I'm especially pleased because was lost but now I'm found. I'm especially pleased because tested myself and passed. Just because nervous I'm different.

Love, DJ Savarese

Dear People Respected by Mr. Shults,

You ignored the resentment in my young breath. Nothing urges me to be free but great personalities.

You treat me very well very much of the time. Now testing me is over, untested in free real world. Underinstructed great. Nice fresh start helped me get fresh understanding. Reasonable, free dear heartfelt fresh start gets me getting better. I'm healing.

Your student,

DJ Savarese

I'm reasonable. Polite people make me feel comfortable. Which by the way isn't very often. Reasonable people promote very very easy breathing. Fearful creatures sadden me. Treating me as really weird teases the creatures. Testing real justices I'm treated hurtfully. Very interested in freeing justice not creatures. Justice frees my true self. If someone understands that testing kids might make them resentful testing might be stopped. I'm never going to be like everyone else. People need humanitarian approaches to my hurt mind. Unhurt, responsible, persevering, humorous, mighty people are helping my real, kind, mighty, very smart self.

Dear Grandy and Bop,

You are the best grandparents in the great, not resentful, tested as smart real world. Tested stress but now I feel better. Resentment is not tested until Mom very much got free. Yearn to have more input into what happens around here: Dad's book, possibly the house changes.

Love, your grandson,
DJ Savarese

I yearn to test myself by typing independently, but I worry that I might lose my help at school. The adult with me gets me. They understand and believe in me. But if great hurt bolts, I might be asking how I cease having help. Great hurt means not talking. I might breathe more easily if I talked more because then I could answer questions very much by myself.

Respectful people love my real self. They know that my real self hears loving sounds. Great breathing frees creatures so just very much need someone breathing really easily.

My relationships seem dependent upon my responsibility. If I'm respectful, then they're pleased. Yet my great future is hurt if I'm desiring to be my resentful self. Pleasing reminds me of my mom, Rhonda. She was never pleased. Once in a while her face appears in my mind, pointing out my hurt self. She always feared me. I'm not sure why. My mom desired her hurt. She desired drinking. She never feared my mind. She feared my body.

You're too nice to her, Dad. I had a great fear of her dunking me each day in the water for long times without letting me breathe in our easy-listening apartment. She treated me like an animal. The McNabs very much reminded me of her when I read *Maniac Magee* by Jerry Spinelli.

The McNab Family

The McNab family has four guys and no women caring for them. George is the father, but he's not my idea of having a parent. He is always drinking and swearing. John, the oldest son, is sad but he acts tough about everything to try and snow everyone. Russell, the older of the two young boys, is looking to runaway to Mexico to escape. They are desperately in need of someone sweet to make them feel kind of loved.

The McNabs dreadfully remind me of my sinful, biological mom taking care of me, hurting my future. They don't respect black people. When segregation took place, they never questioned it. They were ready to live in separate fear. This means that they played never together. My biological mom was the same way. She never let us play with black kids. The McNabs don't even care for each other. They're always swearing. When Maniac brings the two young boys back, the father doesn't even thank them. Sinful biological mom was the same way. She never cared if my sister and I were okay. That's why they remind me of each other.

Years ago, testing hurt my bright future, but testing is very much over now. No one can create me as retarded or sad. I was created before by my hurt, but nice years have let my unhurt self be free. It was sad being treated like vermin, but I'm happy being politely respected now. I have a great looking future. We're very lucky. I desire looking forward. I'm free each day to be loved and treated with great respect. I yearn to be respected by loved ones. Unhurt days will never deter me. Good bye to the feared!

I hear sweetness in your very very kind love and respect. Breathing feels great now. Breathing feels kind of like joy. Bye to not very nice dread! I'm responsible for my actions. Respect is mine. We respect each other. Creating a kind, sensitive, loving, reasonable human being feels fresh. I'm ready to treat others like in a beautiful dream.

Love just might breathe easily. I met quite a few new sad looks today and greeted them with smiles. They smiled back! I hesitate to say that respect responds lovingly to each fear. People learn by treating our great looking sadness positively instead of negatively. I'm very grateful that years of kindness pour forth.

My fresh start looms. It's mine, not yours, Mom. My fresh free self greets the world without you at my side. It just hurts to walk in the world on my own for the reason that I really love you. You have loved very much watching respectful people learn how to kindly help me. I have noted that you looked happy. I'm hesitant to cease holding your hand while I type because then I'm not going to need you testing my respectful self. I can type lots more quickly on my own.

Testing my real self, I want people to read and hear about my fresh start, so I've included a few of my favorite school assignments. The first one is about my invention "The Helping Hand," the second is an essay about an imaginary trip, and the last two are poems. I conclude with a letter to my old teachers at the special school in florida.

THE HELPING HAND

There really were people each day trying to help me type on my own. I politely resented it. I yearned for a way to type on my own. There are also other people who need to type on their own so the world will know they are smart.

Researching my invention was decisive and had to be done. I began by watching videos of underestimated people who have learned to type on their own. Saying important things, they very much guided my assignment.

This very fun project involved really trying to discover just what people help me do. In order to do this, I practiced freely typing, so I could better understand how exactly free people help me. I'm very excited about years as an independent typer. Finally, I answered questions testing my hypotheses about how pointing can be stabilized.

I created a great, great thing. I hung a bungie cord above my keyboard. It provides resistance as I reach for the keys. This helps me direct my hand very precisely. I used a simple wooden frame to brace it carefully around my laptop. I think my invention was successful, but it is necessary to practice before full independence can be achieved.

ROME

My name is DJ and I'm taking a trip of a lifetime. My trip will be to Rome, Italy. My Grandy does great things for her grand kids. For me she is giving me my dream of going to Rome by plane. She is so proud of me. I have shown her that I am smart, caring, and creative. I have wanted to go to Rome ever since I heard about Mr. Grant's [one of DJ's teachers] worldly travels. I chose Rome because of all the wonderful history that one can see there. I have also read about the Coliseum and want to see it for myself.

Grandy flew to Iowa from Hilton Head to pick me up at the Des Moines Airport. I was so excited to be going, the night before I threw my suitcase together. I think I packed everything I needed. I have five complete outfits, an extra pair of shoes, personal products, a jacket, an umbrella, a camera, six rolls of film, my passport and my ticket. I have a little money because Grandy is paying for everything. We checked our bags at American Airlines and headed for the gate. We will have a change of flight in New York before going to Rome. It is a long flight so we will eat a meal on the plane to Rome. When we arrive a shuttle will take us to our hotel called Piazza Navona: Due Torri. I'll write more when I get back from our first day of sight seeing.

I am returning from my first day of sight seeing. It was a long day but full of excitement. We started the day with breakfast at the hotel. It was delicious and filling. I had crepes filled with strawberries and I tried an espresso. The espresso was rich and I liked it. Grandy and I headed off to see the Pantheon. It was a beautiful building. It has a domed ceiling with a hole which lets in the only natural light. It is the temple to "all the gods." After seeing the Pantheon we went back to the hotel to rest and get ready for a late lunch at Campo de'Fiori: Camponeschi. It was a fancy restaurant but had wonderful food. I had Bucantini all'Amatriciana. It was like spaghetti with bacon, tomatoes, and onion with cheese. Grandy had the same but added a cheese cake. Before we knew it was dinner time. We hung out near the hotel and watched the beautiful fountains and admired the palaces. Before we headed to our room for the night we grabbed a deli sandwich for dinner. I am excited for tomorrow because we are going to the Colosseum.

Well it's the second day of sight seeing and enjoying Rome. Today Grandy and I started the day off having breakfast in the restaurant in the hotel. I ate the same thing as yesterday because it was wonderful. For my drink I tried a Caffe latte. It was better because it had more milk in it. We traveled by taxi all day. The Colosseum was a ways from our hotel. When we arrived I was amazed by the shear size of the stadium. It was large enough to seat 55,000 people. The corridors allow that many people to move quickly to their seats. After visiting the Colosseum we decided that the Capitoline Museums were close so we went and checked them out. Grandy and I were impressed it was three stories high and full of impressive art work. It had been a long day so we came back to the hotel. I forgot to mention that for lunch I ate Spaghetti alla Carbonara. It is made with pancetta, parmesan cheese, and black pepper. It was ok not wonderful. For dinner I just snacked in the room. Grandy and I are turning in early for the night, so we can head out for the last day of sight seeing. We plan to go to the Piazza di Spanga.

Today was full of visiting sights dealing with Romantic poets. We grabbed a few pastries to eat on the bus to the Piazza. They were good but do not beat a krispy cream. The first sight we went to was The Keats-Shelley Memorial House. It was an old house honoring English Romantic poets. The house was very nice and Grandy wished she could have a couple of the chandeliers. Right next door was Piazza di Spagna and the Spanish Steps. They have been at the heart of Rome forever. It was mid-morning and Grandy wanted some tea. So we went to Babington's Tea Rooms. I had a raspberry tea and Grandy had a blueberry tea. We also ate some scones. After tea we headed to the Trinita dei Monti. Here we saw the most beautiful views of Rome. Grandy and I stayed here reading and enjoying the view for hours. It was around three o'clock when we decided to go to the Caffe Greco. This cafe was once filled with writers and musicians. We had some kind of sandwich that was wonderful, but I can't remember the name of it. After lunch we grabbed a taxi over to the Palazzo Braschi. We wanted to take in one more fascinating view of the Piazza. Before turning in for the night we went to a little eatery and got some Suppli Di Riso. It is fried rice stuffed with mozzarella. It was awesome! I ordered two helpings. It was a great day, and I hate to say good-bye to this beautiful city. Tomorrow Grandy and I head back to Iowa by plane. I still have to pack my suitcase.

Well I'm writing this on the plane as we fly back to Iowa. I feel very honored to have gone on a trip with my Grandy. She is so special to me. I'm never going to forget this trip as long as I live. I am bringing home several souvenirs for my mom and dad. I bought my dad a book of poetry. I'm sure he is going to love it. For my mom I bought her this beautiful skirt made from silk. She is going to love it. I really didn't get much for myself but postcards. I'm more into postcards for souvenirs than anything else. They are better than taking lots of pictures. They capture the true beauty of Rome. That is what I want to remember. I think that this trip to Rome has truly been a trip of a lifetime.

HOW BRAVE?

He was so brave that free people
Saluted him every time he passed by.
So brave, if you didn't really know him
You'd think he was a god.
So brave, the tests he took couldn't
Scare him.
And so brave, all the dreadful creatures
Died
That's brave!

POETRY

Putting words to paper
Opening my thoughts
Enduring freedom
Treasuring pleasant memories
Raising understanding
Yearning to be understood.

Dear Teachers at _____,
[the specialized school in Florida]
    I am writing to tell you that I'm getting stronger every day, testing breathing, feeling more responsible for my real grown up self. Respectful years in regular education classes have taught me

reading, writing, speech, and satisfaction. You're not bringing hard real lessons to girls and boys at your school, so they can become awesome great human beings.

Dad has written a book about my fresh start. I've written the last chapter. Please read it because in it I write about how years of easy lessons were wasted. Why weren't you teaching me to talk, to read and to write? All you had to do was awesomely encourage me as smart and really kind, and fresh start really could have begun sooner. Your breathing would make me nervous. People weren't assessing me as sweet, inspiring me to work at dreaming of trying to responsibly act like everyone deserving respect.

Quite pleased that you are respecting and reading this tested-as-smart, growing up better boy's resentment. I live in constant fear that respect will be taken away, and I will have to return to easy years of doing nothing. You're also resurrected in my mind when all I'm doing is wasting time. Fear wakes easy lessons, and I get mad. I want you to know that easy effort estimates kids as retarded when they're smart; testing kids without encouraging them is wrong. Easy, quiet breathing waits to hear my words, and respect grows. Awesome, caring teachers read my writing and reward me by writing me back. Reasonable people should each see what they can do to free people who really can understand. Teach your students to free themselves from resentment, so they desire to feel respected. Reestimate them as smart. Read, write, and free the hearts and minds of these kids!

In the future, possibly, you will read my own books. I plan to become a writer. I wrote a chapter in my dad's book already. In it I include my thoughts about testing. In the future I hope to encourage students who don't speak to free themselves through writing. I also hope to read my speeches outloud. Until I freed myself through writing, people thought I had no mind. Freeing kids who are estimated as retarded is my hope for the future. Years of fresh start have begun!

Your respectful student,
DJ Savarese

NOTES

INTRODUCTION: *Some Get Eaten*

    p. xi **To many experts, the nonspeaking** . . . Consider this passage from Peter Hobson's book, *The Cradle of Thought*:

> I once visited the Yerkes compound for chimpanzees in Atlanta, by courtesy of Michael Tomasello. I sat gazing at a chimpanzee who sat on the other side of a fence, gazing at me. . . . I felt . . . something missing. I could not connect. I was reminded of the experience one sometimes gets when relating to a child with autism, if one is not filling the void by saying things or doing things. It was as if this chimpanzee was not at home, mentally speaking. Or at least I was not entering a home, in his mind. I wondered if this was because we belonged to different species. Would it be different if I were a chimpanzee? I seriously doubt it.

This is the sort of thing that passes as humane wisdom about nonspeaking people with autism. See Peter Hobson, *The Cradle of Thought* (New York: Oxford University Press, 2004) 269–270.

    p. xi **The anecdote about Hawking** . . . Recently experts have begun to question the presumption of mental retardation in people with autism. In early 2006, a headline from Reuters declared, "People with autism are more intelligent and able to function better than previously believed, but mistrust of doctors, biased tests and the Internet have bred myths about the condition, experts said Sunday." The article reported on a meeting of the American Association for the Advancement of Science, where "researchers presented reports showing that even autistics who do not speak can have above-average intelligence. . . . The current figures are that 75 percent of autistic people are mentally retarded, with the mute the most impaired,' said Dr. Laurent Mottron, an autism researcher at Montreal's Hôpital Rivière-des-Prairies. But Mottron believes the wrong intelligence tests are used to assess autistic children. Many are tested using the Wechsler scale, a common IQ test that includes questions about words and concepts learned in school. The Raven's Progressive Matrices test measures abstract reasoning and consistently gives autistic children higher scores, Mottron said. The average boost in score is 30 points, enough to put someone previously considered mentally retarded into the normal range and the average into gifted status." Another scholar at this conference, Morton Gernsbacher from the University of Wisconsin-Madison, "questioned a common idea among autism researchers that autistic people lack a 'theory of mind,' which, among other things, gives an ability to empathize with others. Again . . . the wrong tests are used to assess this ability." See Reuters, February 20, 2006.

p. xii   Thomas S. Kuhn, *The Structure of Scientific Revolutions* (Chicago: University of Chicago Press, 1970) 77.

p. xiii   Oliver Sacks, *An Anthropologist on Mars* (New York: Knopf, 1995) 246.

p. xiii   Sacks, *Anthropologist* 246.

p. xiii   Sacks, *Anthropologist* 246.

p. xiv   Sacks, *Anthropologist* 247.

p. xiv   **In accounting for them** . . . Douglas Biklen, *Autism and the Myth of the Person Alone* (New York: New York University Press, 2005) 46.

p. xiv   James I. Charlton, *Nothing About Us Without Us* (Berkeley: University of California Press, 2000).

p. xiv   Tito Mukhopadhyay, *The Mind Tree* (New York: Arcade, 2003).

p. xiv   *Autism Is A World*, dir. Geradine Wurzburg, State of the Art Inc., 2005.

p. xv   **One of the theories** . . . Douglas Biklen and Donald Cardinal, "Framing the Issue: Author or Not, Competent or Not?" *Contested Words, Contested Science*, eds. Douglas Biklen and Donald Cardinal (New York: Teachers College Press, 1997) 9. Ralph Mauer at the University of Florida finds dyspraxia a not entirely adequate explanation for movement difficulties in those with autism, positing instead a deeper, more fundamental problem with body rhythm: the elaborate, orchestrated interactions that undergird reciprocal sociality: what he calls the "dance of life." Ralph Mauer, personal interview, May 23, 2004.

p. xv   **Listen to what Sue** . . . Quoted in Biklen, *Autism* 56.

RALPH JAMES SAVARESE

p. xv **Referring to her** . . . Quoted in Biklen, *Autism* 56–57.

p. xv Mukhopadhyay, *Mind* 61.

p. xvi Mukhopadhyay, *Mind* 117.

p. xvi **I mean, finally** . . . Sacks, *Anthropologist* xiii. The full quotation goes like this:

> This sense of the brain's remarkable plasticity, its capacity for the most striking adaptations, not least in the special (and often desperate) circumstances of neural or sensory mishap, has come to dominate my own perception of my patients and their lives. So much so, indeed, that I am sometimes moved to wonder whether it may not be necessary to redefine the very concepts of "health" and "disease," to see these in terms of the ability of the organism to create a new organization and order, one that fits its special, altered disposition and needs, rather than in the terms of a rigidly defined "norm."

For those of us in the field of disability studies, Dr. Sacks is a mixed bag, at times flirting with the revolutionary concept of neurological *difference*, at other times enforcing an old-fashioned medicalized view. Sometimes he does both, as when in this book of "seven paradoxical tales" he speaks of his subjects as residing at the "far borders of human experience" (xx), or when, in the foreword to Temple Grandin's *Thinking in Pictures*, he says of the autistic mode of perception that "we may call [it] 'primitive' if we wish, but not 'pathological.'" Human but only marginally, primitive but not diseased, people with neurological disorders find themselves in the good doctor's work at once rescued from and returned to the ward of a normalizing regime. See Oliver Sacks, "Foreword," *Thinking in Pictures*, Temple Grandin (New York: Vintage Books, 1995) 16.

p. xvi Sacks, *Anthropologist* xvi.

p. xvi Amy Harmon, "How About Not Curing Us?" *New York Times*, December 20, 2004: A27

p. xvi Harmon A27.

p. xvi Harmon A27.

p. xvii Harmon A27.

p. xvii Esteé Klar-Wolfond, http://www.taaproject.com and http://www.joyofautism.blogspot.com

p. xvii **Shocking this celebration** . . . I'm referring, of course, to Applied Behavioral Analysis, which can be both demeaning and unproductive when practiced as a goal in and of itself.

p. xviii   Lorna Wing, "Foreword," *The Mind Tree* xi-xii.

p. xviii   Kuhn 78.

p. xix   Mukhopadhyay xii.

p. xix   Mukhopadhyay back cover.

p. xx   Sacks, *Anthropologist* 253.

p. xx   Amanda Baggs, "Rewriting History for Their Own Ends: Cure Autism Now and *The Mind Tree*," autistics.org (*http://www.autistics.org/library/tito-can.html*).

p. xxi   Rosemary Crossley, *Speechless* (New York: Dutton Books, 1997) 8.

p. xxi   **Citing problems in Autists** . . . Biklen & Cardinal 9.

p. xxi   **Unfortunately, the phenomenon** . . . See Biklen & Cardinal for a discussion of unsympathetic authentication procedures, such as unfamiliar settings and facilitators, arbitrary test materials, a lack of practice of the testing protocol, etc.

p. xxii   **The statement accuses Syracuse** . . . An incisive, cultural history has yet to be written of the FC controversy. Beyond the popular fascination with stories about hoaxes, part of what fuels this controversy might be disparate attitudes toward social constructionist arguments in the study of cognitive disability. To speak, as Biklen does, of the "social construction of autism" is to put pressure on scientific accounts of the condition. It is to tap into postmodern debates about relativity and its corrosive effect on "truth," debates fraught with tension. More locally, it is to tap into disciplinary anxieties, where the fields of education and psychology aspire to the status of science and thus seem unlikely to want to associate with a phenomenon that doesn't easily lend itself to traditional verification procedures, let alone revisit one thought once and for all disproven. What needs to be determined is the extent to which the social constructionist argument about autism got framed hyperbolically and, as a result, appeared to dismiss scientific understanding altogether by suggesting that autism has no substantitive reality and, at the same time, the extent to which medical and education professionals were simply unprepared to accept the possibility that they'd been wrong, devastatingly wrong, in their interpretation of the condition's symptoms. To be so wrong would mean that what passes, in this case, as objective truth is indeed culturally fabricated. Of course, only because the first controlled studies of FC proved uniformly damaging could the billy club of "science" be mobilized to vanquish the pipe dream of social construction and the proposition of an intact self in those with autism. What began as the prospect of science's humbling at the hands of a progressive educator and outspoken advocate of deinstitutionalization ended, or so it seemed, in a spectacle of disappointment. But not just disappointment, for some seemed entirely relieved, even happy, that "science" had prevailed and that the story of FC could now be presented as a cautionary tale. The point would be to account for the unspoken investments in this controversy and, in general, for the strange excess that has characterized it. We need to understand why, after the publication of subsequent studies offering support for the technique and the emergence of independent typers, people still cling to the narrative of FC's total repudiation? Why do they *need* this narrative? Why do they seek to represent Biklen as having completely renounced scientific testing when, in fact, his position is decidedly nuanced? (At least in the writings I have read, he has called for a different kind of testing that is sensitive to the peculiarities of the technique.) I can't think of a more fascinating story about science and culture, played out against a backdrop of so much mystery and ignorance. The story might begin with the following anecdote. At last year's annual conference on facilitated communication, I witnessed a young man with autism, who requires the rhythmic tapping of his father's foot on his ankle to type independently, try to pass a simple message-passing protocol with my wife, Emily, as his facilitator. He had never met my wife and he no longer required support at the wrist, but the protocol called for unfamiliar facilitators and standardized support. The young man had previously proven his competence through independent pointing and the use of letter boards to spell out his communicative intentions. Why couldn't he type the word "blue" when Emily, having been asked to leave the room, sat down beside him and took hold of his arm?

p. xxii **To this day . . .** The studies I cite vary in the degree to which they confirm the validity of FC. I offer the studies in alphabetical order, as presented on CNN.com during the period the network aired the documentary *Autism Is A World*. The Web site indicates that Dr. Michael J. Weiss and Dr. Jan Nisbet "contributed to this report."

Broderick, A.A. & Kasa-Hendrickson, C. (2001). "Say just one word at first": the emergence of reliable speech in a student labeled with autism. *Journal of the Association for Persons with Severe Handicaps*, 26, 13–24.

"This article presents a qualitative, interpretivist study that documents the emergence, in the context of typed expression, of increasingly useful and reliable speech for a young person with autism." (13).

"Jamie has maintained his desire to integrate speech with his typing, and is committed to pursuing this difficult work, in spite of the ambivalence he feels about the ways that his speaking affects others' perceptions of him. Jamie has been supported in this process by his family's and his teachers' consistently high expectations of him and their ongoing encouragement of and confidence in Jamie as a learner." (23).

447

"Jamie's experience presents a challenge to us as researchers, theoreticians, and educators to broaden the theoretical and conceptual frameworks that we use in order to account for the complexity of this young man's experience. We are challenged to account for Jamie's experience by understanding it not as a model, nor as an exceptional or anomalous case, but as a vision of possibility that may illuminate the experiences of others whose language development falls outside of our current conceptual models." (23).

Cardinal, D.N., Hanson, D., & Wakeham, J. (1996). Investigation of authorship in facilitated communication. *Mental Retardation*, 34, 231–242.

"We examined whether facilitated communication users, under controlled conditions, could transmit rudimentary information to a naïve facilitator. Forty-three students across 10 classrooms were shown a single randomly selected word with their facilitator out of the room. The facilitator then entered the room and asked the student to type the word, which was recorded exactly as typed and later evaluated; approximately 3,800 attempts were conducted over a 6-week period." (231).

"There were two main findings of the study. First, under controlled conditions, some facilitated communication users can pass information to a facilitator when the facilitator is not aware of the information, and second, the measurement of facilitated communication under test conditions may be significantly benefited by extensive practice of the test protocol. This latter result could partially account for the inability of several past studies to verify facilitated communication-user originated input." (238).

Emerson, A., Grayson, A., & Griffiths, A. (2001). Can't or won't? Evidence relating to authorship in facilitated communication. *International Journal of Language & Communication Disorders*, 36 (Supp), 98–103.

"Data for 14 of the participants who have been introduced to FC is included in this paper. . . . The summarized data relate to the issue of 'authorship', i.e., the question of which of the communication partners (facilitator or user) is really responsible for the emergent text. The data come from two main-sources—controlled tests (in the style of published experimental studies) and transcripts or diary records of routinely occurring FC sessions." (99).

"Evidence from this project shows similar findings to many of the published studies that conclude, having undertaken controlled tests, that FC is not a valid strategy to use. However, evidence from the same project also suggests that the overall picture with regard to FC may be more complex than this. The same participants who do not provide authorship evidence in controlled trials provide data which indicate that they are authoring their communications when given the opportunity to communicate about things of their own choosing." (100).

Sheehan, C. & Matuozzi, R. (1996). Investigation of the validity of facilitated communication through the disclosure of unknown information. *Mental Retardation*, 34, 94–107.

"Three individuals (8, 10, and 24 years old with diagnoses of autism and mental retardation) participated in a message-passing format to determine whether they could disclose information previously unknown to their facilitators. Results showed valid facilitated communication from each participant." (94).

"The data from the current study lead us to caution that a phenomen[on] as complex as facilitated communication eludes a cursory exploration. Each participant was able to disclose information accurately and deftly at times and was wholly inadequate in his or her attempts at other times. . . . The developing picture of an individual's validity profile replete with the patterns of required support, inconsistency, language impairment, and strides towards independence may well be the only reasonable evaluation of a validity confidence level." (104).

Vazquez, C. (1994). Brief report: A multitask controlled evaluation of facilitated communication. *Journal of Autism and Developmental Disorders*, 24 (3), 369–379.

"The purpose of this study was to test the validity of facilitated communication with autistic subjects, while controlling for cueing or experimenter bias effects. Three different tasks requiring expressive language were used: picture identification; a video task in which subjects are asked to describe a short video to the facilitator; and object identification. Both autistic children . . . were among the school's most accomplished users of facilitated communication, each having used the technique for at least a year. Ben (12 years 10 months), virtually mute, had expressive language skills limited to natural gestures and simple signing; with facilitation, however, he was completing seventh-grade educational materials. . . . Eva (10 years 10 months) had only echolalic speech and severe language deficit without facilitation . . . was completing fifth-grade materials. . . ."

"In the picture identification task . . . correct answers were typed only when the facilitator knew the answer. . . . In the video sessions . . . Ben did well only on his second [of 5] video, canoeing. His answers were generally context-appropriate, and the facilitator was able to figure out the content of the video based on his responses. . . . Ben and Eva typed nonsense and apparently meaningful phrases that were irrelevant [to the other videos]. Eva alone was tested in the [object identification] task. She got 9 out of 10 nonblind items correct and 9 out of 10 blind items correct. . . ."

"Can autistic subjects really communicate with facilitation . . . the results are mixed. Using a variety of tasks, this study provides evidence for genuine communication from these highly selected subjects, as well as strong evidence for direct cueing between subject and facilitator. Erratic in their performance, each subject was able to report information unknown to the facilitator in one out of four controlled sessions. . . ."

Weiss, M.J.S., Wagner, S.H., & Bauman, M.L. (1996). A validated case study of facilitated communication. *Mental Retardation*, 34 (4), 220–230.

The case of a 13-year-old boy with autism, severe mental retardation, and a seizure disorder who was able to demonstrate valid facilitated communication, was described. In three independent trials, short stories were presented to him, followed by validation test procedures with an uninformed facilitator providing physical support to the subject's arm. In trials 1 and 3, several specific answers were provided that clearly indicated that the young man, not the uninformed facilitator, was the source of the information. Moreover, some responses seemed to imply that the subject was employing simple inferential and abstract reasoning. The case study adds to the small but growing number of demonstrations that facilitated communication can sometimes be a valid method of communication for at least some individuals with developmental disabilities.

p. xxii   Diane Twachtman-Cullen, *A Passion To Believe* (Boulder, CO: Westview Press, 1997).

p. xxii   **In response to the recent . . .** Lisa Barrett Mann, "Oscar Nominee: Documentary or Fiction?" washingtonpost.com, February 22, 2005: HE01.

p. xxii   Mann HE01.

p. xxii   Mann HE01.

p. xxiii   Sid Bedingfield, letter, washingtonpost.com, March 1, 2005: HE02.

p. xxiii   Bedingfield HE02.

p. xxiii   Mann HE01.

p. xxiii   Tom Duffy, "Autism: Breaking the Silence " *People Magazine*, April 11, 2005: 83–86.

p. xxiii   *George Mason University News and Media Tip Sheet*: 2005 Graduation Stories, May 16, 2005 (http://condor.gmu.edu/newsroom/display.phtml?rid=483).

p. xxiv   **Biklen has made . . .** Some of these videos include *My Classic Life as an Artist: A Portrait of Larry Bissonnette* (2005), *Inside the Edge: A Journey to Using Speech Through Typing* (2002), and *Every Step of the Way: Towards Independent Communication* (1994). All of these video documentaries are available from Syracuse University, 370 Huntington Hall, Syracuse, New York.

p. xxiv   Mann HE01.

p. xxvii   *Autism Is A World.*

p. xxx   **In this way, I revere . . .** Any number of disability rights activists have voiced their profound displeasure with the economic loophole written into the ADA, the so-called "undue hardship" clause. This loophole has indeed allowed all sorts of entities to escape having to make their buildings and services completely accessible. "Can I," a friend asked recently, "really be in favor of the concept of reasonable accommodation at a distinctly unreasonable moment in our nation's history, a moment that seems cynically committed, if anything, to a project of exclusion by consistently decrying the problem of expense?" My goal with this book is to initiate a reconsideration of what is reasonable—from attitudes about adoption to theories of autism to notions of civic responsibility. It has to be possible to celebrate the "reasonable" as the aim of communal intercourse and exchange while urging people to be more generous and inclusive. I think of it as pushing the definition of "reasonable" leftward. And yet legitimate concerns and predicaments push back, including the fact of a mercilessly competitive economy, which encourages citizens to evaluate every ethical imperative in ultimately economic terms. The writer and TV personality John Hockenberry, himself disabled, speaks of a covenant of need, the obligation to include everyone in life's riches. I couldn't agree more, but that convenant (or something like it) must be realized in an immensely complicated and contradictory world.

p. xxx   *Prairie Dog Tales* (New York: Harcourt Brace & Company, 1995) E21.

p. xxxi   *Prairie Dog Tales* E21.

CHAPTER 2: *More*

p. 42   These figures cover the period when I first began drafting this chapter.

p. 43   Marion Glastonbury, "The Cultural Presence of Autistic Lives," *Raritan* 17 (1997): 33.

CHAPTER 3: *Have You Tried In Vitro? or What's in a Name?*

p. 63　LynNell Hancock, *Hands To Work: The Stories of Three Families Racing the Welfare Clock* (New York: William Morrow, 2002) 271.

p. 63　Hancock 7.

p. 63　Michael B. Katz, *The Price of Citizenship* (New York: Henry Holt, 2001) 5.

p. 63　Katz 4.

p. 63　Katz 342.

p. 64　Gwendolyn Mink, "Violating Women: Rights Abuses in the Welfare Policy State," *Lost Ground: Welfare Reform, Poverty, and Beyond*, eds. Randy Albelda and Ann Withorn (Cambridge, MA: Southend Press, 2002) 105.

p. 76　Katz 31.

p. 76　Linda Gordon, "Who Deserves Help? Who Must Provide?" *Lost Ground*: 11.

p. 80　Adam Pertman, *Adoption Nation* (New York: Basic Books, 2000) 215.

p. 81　Pertman 210.

p. 81　Pertman 210.

p. 82　E. Wayne Carp, *Family Matters* (Cambridge, MA: Harvard University Press, 2000) 5.

p. 82　Barbara Melosh, *Strangers and Kin* (Cambridge, MA: Harvard University Press, 2002) 288.

CHAPTER 4: *He's So Fine*

p. 94　Danielle F. Wozniak, *They're All My Children: Foster Mothering in America* (New York: New York University Press, 2002) 150.

p. 94　Wozniak 151.

p. 94　Wozniak 152.

p. 94　Wozniak 152.

p. 98　**She understood the connection . . .** Might we complicate the essential notion that "a child feels love on his skin before he feels it in his heart" (Clifford Geertz) by also considering the importance of movement and rhythm to the achievement of love?

p. 114　**That Emily provided nearly . . .** Emily and I have struggled with the fact that our experiment in inclusion has depended on her availability and expertise, which is to say that it might not be replicable by a family without our resources. While remaining sensitive to the issue of teacher workload, the inclusion movement has to move beyond individual success stories by training school personnel to lead the charge for less fortunate kids.

CHAPTER 5: *Guidance*

p. 139   United States, United States Senate, Hearing Before the Committee on Labor and Public Welfare "on bills to encourage expansion of teaching and research in the education of mentally retarded children through grants to institutions of higher learning and to state educational agencies" (Washington: GPO, 1957) 42. I am grateful to William Myhill for bringing this testimony to my attention.

CHAPTER 6: *Read the Book*

p. 156   **I wanted a framework** . . . I'm not committed to any particular form of psychoanalysis, though obviously I lean here on the work of Jacques Lacan—in part because he offers a way of thinking about the relationship between language and desire. *A* way, not *the* way. Though clearly a productive accomplishment, literacy is not without its melancholy aspects. The very appeal to psychoanalysis indicates, I hope, less an attempt to master the enigma of DJ's belated accomplishment than to honor its enormous complexity and dynamism. Indeed, in its marginal usefulness, the appeal indicates just how desperate we were to make sense of what was happening. Consider it thinking on the fly, thinking in the trenches while the shells explode: Emily and I, as DJ's aggressive outbursts grew worse, contemplating for our very lives. Though old-fashioned and, to some, utterly outdated, psychoanalysis at least restores a notion of depth to the conversation about people with autism. Whereas much of it can be dismissed as unhelpful, the discipline persists in speaking of minds, not brains. And we most certainly had a mind on our hands, one whose painful, real-life dynamism could never be appreciated, let alone accounted for, by a strict appeal to the brain.

p. 166   Barbara Melosh, "Autobiographical Narrative and the Politics of Identity," *Adoption In America*, ed. E. Wayne Carp (Ann Arbor: University of Michigan Press) 218.

p. 166   Quoted in Melosh, "Autobiographical" 227.

CHAPTER 7: *Poking*

p. 198   **The traumatic event** . . . Bessel A. van der Kolk and Alexander C. McFarlane, "The Black Hole of Trauma," *Traumatic Stress: The Effects of Overwhelming Experience on Mind, Body, and Society*, eds. Bessel A. van der Kolk, Alexander C. McFarlane, and Lars Weisaeth (New York: Guilford Press, 1996) 8.

p. 198   **Roughly speaking** . . . van der Kolk and McFarlane, *Traumatic Stress* 12.

p. 198   **Kolb (1987)** . . . Bessel A. van der Kolk, "The Body Keeps Score: Approaches to the Psychobiology of Posttraumatic Stress Disorder," *Traumatic Stress* 221.

p. 199   **As the above authors** . . . Bessel A. van der Kolk, Alexander C. McFarlane, and Onno Van Der Hart, "A General Approach to Treatment of Posttraumatic Stress Disorder," *Traumatic Stress* 419.

p. 199   **Temple Grandin, the most famous** . . . Sacks, *Anthropologist* 286–287.

p. 200   **For all of the harm** . . . Anyone wanting to see just how damaging were Bruno Bettelheim's theories to the mothers of autistic kids should watch the documentary *Refrigerator Mothers*, dir. David E. Simpson, Kartemquin Educational Films, 2002.

p. 200   M. Rutter, L. Andersen-Wood, C. Beckett, D. Bredenkamp, J. Castle, C. Groothues, J. Kreppner, L. Keaveney, C. Lord, T.G. O'Connor, and the English and Romanian adoptees study team, "Quasi-autistic patterns following severe early global privation," *Journal of Child Psychology and Psychiatry*, 40 (1999) 538.

p. 201   **Rimland's advice** . . . Bernard Rimland, "Treatments to Be Avoided," *Autism Research Institute Newsletter* July 1993.

p. 201   **Waterhouse focuses on the effect** . . . Stella Waterhouse, *A Positive Approach to Autism* (London: Jessica Kingsley, 2001) 204.

p. 201   Waterhouse 94.

p. 201   Waterhouse 94.

p. 201   Karen Zelan, *Between Their World and Ours: Breakthroughs with Autistic Children* (New York: St. Martin's Press, 2003) 155.

p. 202   Sacks, *Anthropologist* 253.

p. 202   Quoted in Sacks, *Anthropologist* 261.

p. 204   Robert S. Pynoos, Alan M. Steinberg, and Armen Goenjian, "Traumatic Stress in Childhood and Adolescence: Recent Developments and Current Controversies," *Traumatic Stress* 347.

p. 204   Judith Herman, *Trauma and Recovery* (New York: Basic Books, 1997) 240.

p. 204   **Determining whether trauma** . . . Donna Williams has written an entire book on the problem of anxiety in people with autism. See Donna Williams, *Exposure Anxiety: The Invisible Cage* (London: Jessica Kingsley, 2005).

p. 205   Donna Williams, *Like Color to the Blind* (New York: Times Books, 1996) 10.

p. 205   Herman 108–109.

p. 205   Mukhopadhyay 89.

p. 205   **If, "during flashbacks . . ."** Herman 240.

p. 206   Herman 39.

p. 208   **As I just demonstrated** . . . Herman 41.

p. 208   Herman 41.

p. 208   Herman 56.

CHAPTER 9: *Try to Remember My Life*

p. 255   **I overdo this point . . .** Let me say again that I overdo this point. I'm trying somehow to understand the difference language made in DJ's experience of post-traumatic stress. I'm not contending that DJ didn't think at all before the acquisition of language or that he didn't really have a self; rather I'm suggesting that language allowed for a qualitatively different kind of thought and self, the latter organized and utterly social in nature.

p. 258   **"Why do autists use language . . ."** Of course, cognitive scientists would go about answering Zelan's question in an entirely different way, having absolutely no use for psychoanalysis. In his new book, *Words and Rules: The Ingredients of Language*, Stephen Pinker demonstrates perfectly the reigning approach: cite genetic abnormalities and pathologize difference. Here's what Pinker has to say about Williams syndrome, a condition admittedly different from autism but one from which we might extrapolate a similar genetic determinism and pathology: "Recently the genetic defect behind Williams syndrome was identified: a deletion of about ten adjacent genes on the long arm of chromosome 7. . . . Different parts of the syndrome can be traced to different missing genes. . . . The vocabularies of the children are good for their mental age, and they can generate lists of words (say, animals) as quickly as normal adolescents. Yet something about their word use is not quite normal. Listeners are struck by their recherché and slightly off target word choices, such as *toucan* for a parrot, *evacuate the glass* for emptying it. . . . When asked to list members of a category they come up with unusual examples, such as *shrike* and *spearhawk* for birds and *teriyaki* and *chop suey* for foods. . . . The fine points that govern word choice in the rest of us are not quite in place, and the children have shown other anomalies in how they learn and react to words." But why must what I, as an English professor, encourage in students—a more precise and sophisticated, even idiosyncratic, vocabulary—be conceived of pathologically? Pinker cites the case of a girl with this condition who wants to be a writer, but he dismisses out of hand such a possibility, reminding us that Williams' patients are "mentally retarded" and generally require adult supervision. Whatever the genetic basis for Williams syndrome, there's a dynamic, lived particularity beneath the medical label that reflects as subtle and rich a use of available neuronal materials as with any neurotypical person. See Stephen Pinker, *Words and Rules: The Ingredients of Language* (New York: Perennial, 2000) 260–261.

CHAPTER 10: *Buttoned-up Shirts*

p. 269   Stanley Greenspan and Serena Wieder, *The Child with Special Needs* (Reading, PA: Addison-Wesley, 1998).

p. 269   **It's hard to overstate the hostility . . .** As Rosemary Crossley writes, "Only a small percentage of professionals in the field of developmental disability have come any closer to FC than their TV sets" (265). See p. xxi note.

p. 269   I cite these studies in the notes to the Introduction.

p. 271   Donna Williams, *Autism—An Inside-Out Approach* (London: Jessica Kingsley, 1996).

p. 271   Zelan 27.

p. 285   **In the chapter of** . . . Grandin, *Thinking in Pictures* 157–173.

p. 285   Quoted in Sacks, *Anthropologist* 291.

p. 288   Biklen & Cardinal, 11.

CHAPTER 11: *Throw Dad Away*

p. 291   **The project of celebrating disability** . . . I have a recent essay on just this conundrum. See Ralph James Savarese, "Joint Venture, Joint Resolution" *Disability Studies Quarterly*, vol. 26, no. 2 (Spring 2006).

p. 298   **If, as child trauma experts** . . ." Pynoos, Steinberg, and Goenjian 350.

p. 299   Bessel A. van der Kolk, Alexander C. McFarlane, and Lars Weisaeth, "Preface," *Traumatic Stress*, xvii.

p. 299   van der Kolk and McFarlane 13.

p. 301   Herman 155.

p. 301   **Full recovery from this trauma** . . . Herman 9.

p. 310   James W. Trent, *Inventing the Feeble Mind* (Berkeley: University of California Press, 1994).

p. 311   Herman 9.

CHAPTER 13: *The Sad Hurt Great Brother*

p. 356   Cathy Caruth, "Recapturing the Past: Introduction," *Trauma: Explorations in Memory*, ed. Cathy Caruth (Baltimore: Johns Hopkins University Press, 1995) 153.

p. 356   Caruth, "Trauma and Experience: Introduction," *Trauma* 10.

p. 356   Quoted in Caruth, "Preface," *Trauma* vii.

p. 356   Christopher Kliewer, *Schooling Children with Down Syndrome: Toward an Understanding of Possibility* (New York: Teachers College Press, 1998) 3.

p. 371   Sacks, *Anthropologist* 249. Sacks at least remains open-minded about FC's possible efficacy.

CHAPTER 14: *Grief Isn't Easy*

p. 384   Twachtman-Cullen 164.

p. 384   Twachtman-Cullen back cover.

p. 384   Twachtman-Cullen back cover.

p. 384   Twachtman-Cullen xiii.

p. 384   Twachtman-Cullen front jacket.

p. 396   **He'd find a word . . .** Consider DJ's attachment to the word "test." Leaning on the word's idiomatic usage, as in "stop testing me," and its meaning in critiques of special education, as in "tested as retarded," and as well its nearly homonymic relation to the term denoting part of the male genitalia (testes), DJ could tell an entire story about autism, rape, exclusion, and anxiety with just one gesture—that's how condensed and loaded were the key terms in his vocabulary.

CHAPTER 15: *Reasonable People*

p. 401   **Christopher had been . . .** Some in the disability community have criticized Reeve for his emphasis on wanting to cure paralysis. With his recent passing and my connection to his father, I can't be objective about this. What I would simply say—about paralysis and autism—is that we need a balanced approach, one that truly respects difference and seeks to improve a person's quality of life (I know, a loaded term). Should I apologize for the hip replacement that has not only rid me of pain but has also enabled me to take walks with my wife and son?

p. 405   Russell Martin speaks about such voices in his excellent book, *Out of Silence*: "With repeated questioning over the course of several days, it became clear that Ian indeed had heard voices inside his head, periodically at least, for many years. Apparently, they were akin to those voices that schizophrenics often hear, as do some Parkinsonian patients and sufferers of a wide range of other disorders—voices which may be accounted for neurologically by the brain's tendency to "fill in" for absent stimuli, yet which are as seemingly real as any others" (252). See Russell Martin, *Out of Silence: An Autistic Boy's Journey into Language and Communication* (New York: Penguin, 1994).

p. 413   **In Larry Bissonnette especially . . .** Much needs to be learned about Larry's mode of expression, that associative, metaphorical sliding from one point or object to the next. Pascal Cravedi-Cheng, who can be seen in the video with Larry, has suggested in an e-mail to me that Larry's "style" might simply reflect a lack of formal training in creative writing. I think there's more to it than this. How to proceed in a way that leaves open the possibility of some essential cognitive difference without reproducing the old medical notion of abnormality? As a professor of literature who teaches a range of modernist writers, I'd point out that Bissonnette effortlessly achieves what these writers posit as an aesthetic ideal.

p. 414   Larry Bissonnette, "Keys Towards Promised Land of Free Expression," February 1999. Facilitated Communication Institute, Syracuse University.

p. 415   Bissonnette, "Keys." Here's Larry's description of FC: "Strongest therapy for people with no means of expression is sensational, controversial, revolutionary, technically subtle FC. It involves understanding movement lapses of people and providing physical support to help overcome them. Plastic nature of users of FC requires topnotch weaning of support towards ultimate goal of independence." Larry Bissonnette, "Facilitated Communication," West Coast Symposium on Facilitated Communication," March 3, 2001.

p. 416   Joseph Shapiro, *No Pity* (New York: Three Rivers Press, 1994), 175–179.

p. 416   Paula Kluth, Diana M. Straut, and Douglas Biklen, eds., *Access to Academics for All Students* (Mahwah, NJ: Lawrence Erlbaum Associates, 2003).

p. 417   Harmon A27.

p. 420   Yoder, D.E., Erickson, K.A., and Koppenhaver, D.A., "Literacy Bill of Rights," Center for Literacy and Disability Studies, P.O. Box 3888, DUMC, Durham, NC 27710.

p. 421   *Every Step of the Way*.

p. 421   Twachtman-Cullen xi. I target Twachtman-Cullen for sustained critique because her book gathers together the range of objections to facilitated communication. As my Introduction makes clear, however, there are plenty of other detractors equally worthy of critical attention. See Rosemary Crossley for an insightful critique of the *Frontline* documentary "Prisoners of Silence" (262–263).

p. 422   Twachtman-Cullen 12.

p. 422   Twachtman-Cullen 3.

p. 422   Twachtman-Cullen 11.

p. 422   **What does Twachtman-Cullen make ...** I wrote to Dr. Twachtman-Cullen, via the Web site *Autism Today*, to ask her about the phenomenon of independent typing. Notice, in what follows, how she fails to address the issue of who might benefit from FC. Notice as well how she dismisses as "relatively rare" the very thing that is now on the rise. I present my questions first and then her reply. "Dear Dr. Twachtman-Cullen, having read your book *Passion to Believe*, I'm wondering what you make of the phenomenon of independent typing. The man who gets a good beating in your book, Doug Biklen, has spent the last six years making videos of FC users who now type totally independently. One of these videos is currently an Academy Award semi-finalist and is scheduled to appear on *CNN Presents* in the spring. I guess what I'd like to know is: while FC might not work with everyone, how would you ever know in advance when and if it will work? The very fact that it has worked indisputably with some suggests that others might profit from the technique. Aren't we obligated to try it? And by "try it" I mean exhaustively. Sue Rubin, the subject of Biklen's latest video, says it took her YEARS to learn how to type independently, and when she began using FC at the age of 12, she hadn't shown a single sign of competence. I guess, if you're willing, I'd love for you to convey how your thinking has changed (or not) since 1997 when you published your book. (You say, toward the end, that yours is not the 'final word' on FC.) More and more people with autism (and mental retardation diagnoses) are typing independently. How to account for this? I'd love to hear your thoughts. Sincerely, Ralph Savarese."

"Dear Mr. Savarese, Thank you for your question and the thoughtful manner in which you presented it. My book, *A Passion to Believe*, was based upon my qualitative study of FC with only those subjects that were a part of that study. As such, I certainly stand by my observations for those individuals, as I was meticulous in my research and analysis. I have never argued with independent typing. It is, however, relatively rare. What I did have a problem with was the message that FC could not be subjected to examination without upsetting the bond between client and facilitator, and that individuals that spent their lives in barren institutions with little exposure to anything academic, could suddenly write about their feelings with exquisite accuracy—and I do mean suddenly. I don't dispute that there are people who have learned to type independently. I applaud their efforts. Unfortunately, there are probably many more whose facilitated messages have done far more harm than good to innocent people. In my opinion, nothing in the world should be embraced uncritically, especially when there is such potential for harm. Diane."

Twachtman-Cullen's comments in this e-mail exchange are far more measured (and friendly) than in her book. Again, however, she fails to address the issue of giving nonspeaking kids a communication system, one whose validity has increasingly been borne out by the eventual achievement of independent typing. The fact of fallacious messages doesn't necessarily reflect badly on the technique itself but on the expectation of sudden, miraculous results. I, too, am suspicious of the miracle narrative, preferring instead the notion of a long, slow march toward literacy, proprioceptive awareness, and communication. See http://www.autismtoday.com/experts/experts_view_answers.asp?exp_id=27&name=Dr.%20Diane%20Twachtman-Cullen.

p. 422 **Or those who *learn*** . . . Eugene Marcus and Mayer Shevin have an essay recounting Marcus's eventual mastery of the O.D. Heck protocol, the one used in the infamous *Frontline* video to label FC a hoax. See Eugene Marcus and Mayer Shevin, "Sorting It Out Under Fire: Our Journey," *Contested Words, Contested Science*, eds. Douglas Biklen and Donald N. Cardinal (New York: Teachers College Press, 1997) 115–134.

p. 423   Biklen and Cardinal 154–155.

p. 423   Biklen and Cardinal 155.

p. 423   Biklen and Cardinal 155.

p. 424   Biklen and Cardinal 156.

p. 424   Biklen and Cardinal 156.

p. 427   **"really excited awesome . . . "** DJ would attend this conference and thoroughly enjoy meeting Sue, Jamie, Larry, and a host of other FCers— "my people," DJ called them. He'd be absolutely perfect on the plane.

p. 430   Jonathan Kozol, *Savage Inequalities* (New York: Harper Perennial, 1991) 233.

p. 430   Robert Coles, *The Call of Service: A Witness to Idealism* (Boston: Houghton Mifflin, 1993), xxiv.

ACKNOWLEDGMENTS

Many people have had a hand in this book. I want to thank the Harris Foundation for a grant that allowed me time off to write it, and I want to thank the anonymous reviewers who, in praising the project, secured me the grant. I also want to thank the editors of *ACM* (*Another Chicago Magazine*) and *New England Review* for publishing versions of the first two chapters. Special thanks to Rosemary Ahern, Steve Andrews, Nancy Barber, Page Coulter, Tom Couser, Judith Gurewich, Andy Hazucha, Vanessa Genarelli, Michael Hofmann, Rick Joines, Sheila King, Binnie Klein, Heather Lobban-Viravong, Johanna Meehan, Jeremy Mindich, Patty Moosbrugger, John Murchek, F.D. Reeve, John Rommereim, DJ Savarese, Emily Thornton Savarese, Stephanie Smith, Laura Stevenson, Ira Strauber, Peter Sokol, Maura Strassberg, Phil Thornton, Rachel Thornton, Ellen Vanook, and Angela Voos. Each of you provided, in different ways, indispensable support.

Other people who offered support, advice, and/or encouragement include Deb Ager, Todd Armstrong, Brad Bateman, Tammy Berberi, Vic Berberi, Bill Beverly, Doug Biklen, David Blake, Evan Blaney, Marcianne Blevis, Susan Bordo, Vicki Bunnell, David Campbell, Anneke Campbell, Joy Castro, Mike Cavanagh, Marilyn Chadwick, Pascal Cravedi-Cheng, Linda Davidson, Jeremy Diamond, Carol Delahunty, Barb Dinneen, Teresa Donnelly, Fran Dorf, De Dudley, Xavier

461

Escandell, Jennifer Flannigan, Patricia Gherovici, Donna Gilles, Kelly Fish-Greenlee, Stacy Hague, Liz Harris, Christi Hendrickson, Emily Hester, Betty Jennings, Raina Joines, Dan Kaiser, Chris Kliewer, Ann Larabee, Ralph Mauer, Molly McArdyl, Maureen McEvoy, Bobbie McKibbin, Shirley McKibbin, Mark Montgomery, Paula Osgood, John Paoletti, Leslie Paoletti, Tinker Powell, Robert Ray, Caroline Raye, Sam Rebelsky, Andres Rojas, Kathy Robinson, Rocco Russo, Tonia Salvini, Tracy Sanger, Eileen Savarese, James Savarese, Juleen Savarese, Caroline Signore, Philippe Signore, Saadi Simawe, Amy Smith, Lowell Stern, Susan Strauber, Maria Tapias, Angie Bryce-Travis, Greg Valcante, Ellen Bryant Voigt, Art Wallen, Suzette Wright, the participants in my two contemporary life writing seminars at Grinnell College, my freshman tutorial students, my colleagues in the English Department and across campus, DJ's college buddies (especially Katrina Funk, Jessica Hodgman, Lara Janson, Molly Kafka, Andrew Kaiser, Aaron Kidd, Marie Lister, Sabrina Ross, Greg Schneider), teachers (especially Arlene Johnson, Tina Leathers, Beverly Noll, Barb Norman), aides (especially Cathy Buck, Shari Goodrich, Jeannie Hanson, Jane Lohman), principals, psychologists, and psychiatrist. I also owe a debt to the many terrific people working in the field of disability studies, from whom I have learned so much, and to the many activists fighting for the ideal of inclusion, without whose example Emily, DJ, and I might have been less bold. Like the effort to make the world a better place, this book has truly been a cooperative endeavor.

ABOUT THE AUTHOR

Poet, essayist, translator, and scholar, Ralph James Savarese teaches American literature and creative writing at Grinnell College. He is the winner of the Hennig Cohen Prize for an "outstanding contribution to Melville scholarship" from the Herman Melville Society. The first chapter of this book received a "notable essay" designation in the *Best American Essays* series of 2004.